POETRY AND POLITICS IN THE COCKNEY SCHOOL

Keats, Shelley, Hunt and their Circle

Jeffrey N. Cox refines our conception of "second-generation" romanticism by placing it within the circle of writers around Leigh Hunt that came to be known as the Cockney School. Offering a theory of the group as a key site for cultural production, Cox challenges the traditional image of the romantic poet as an isolated figure by recreating the social nature of the work of Shelley, Keats, Hunt, Hazlitt, Byron, and others as they engaged in literary contests, wrote poems celebrating one another, and worked collaboratively on journals and other projects. Cox also recovers the work of neglected writers such as John Hamilton Reynolds, Horace Smith, and Cornelius Webb as part of the rich social and cultural context of Hunt's circle. This book not only demonstrates convincingly that a Cockney School existed, but shows that it was committed to putting literature in the service of social, cultural, and political reform.

JEFFREY N. COX is Professor of Comparative Literature at the University of Colorado, Boulder, where he is also Director of the Center for Humanities and the Arts. His *In the Shadows of Romance: Romantic Tragic Drama in Germany, England, and France* (1987) was followed up by an edition of *Seven Gothic Dramas 1789–1825* (1992); with Larry J. Reynolds he coedited *New Historical Literary Studies: Essays on Reproducing Texts, Representing History* (1993).

CAMBRIDGE STUDIES IN ROMANTICISM

General editors

Professor Marilyn Butler
University of Oxford

Professor James Chandler
University of Chicago

Editorial board
John Barrell, *University of York*
Paul Hamilton, *University of London*
Mary Jacobus, *Cornell University*
Kenneth Johnston, *Indiana University*
Alan Liu, *University of California, Santa Barbara*
Jerome McGann, *University of Virginia*
David Simpson, *University of California, Davis*

This series aims to foster the best new work in one of the most challenging fields within English literary studies. From the early 1780s to the early 1830s a formidable array of talented men and women took to literary composition, not just in poetry, which some of them famously transformed, but in many modes of writing. The expansion of publishing created new opportunities for writers, and the political stakes of what they wrote were raised again by what Wordsworth called those 'great national events' that were 'almost daily taking place': the French Revolution, the Napoleonic and American wars, urbanization, industrialization, religious revival, an expanded empire abroad and the reform movement at home. This was an enormous ambition, even when it pretended otherwise. The relations between science, philosophy, religion and literature were reworked in texts such as *Frankenstein* and *Biographia Literaria*; gender relations in *A Vindication of the Rights of Woman* and *Don Juan*; journalism by Cobbett and Hazlitt; poetic form, content and style by the Lake School and the Cockney School. Outside Shakespeare studies, probably no body of writing has produced such a wealth of response or done so much to shape the responses of modern criticism. This indeed is the period that saw the emergence of those notions of 'literature' and of literary history, especially national literary history, on which modern scholarship in English has been founded.

The categories produced by Romanticism have also been challenged by recent historicist arguments. The task of the series is to engage both with a challenging corpus of Romantic writings and with the changing field of criticism they have helped to shape. As with other literary series published by Cambridge, this one will represent the work of both younger and more established scholars, on either side of the Atlantic and elsewhere.

For a complete list of titles published see end of book

POETRY AND POLITICS IN THE COCKNEY SCHOOL

Keats, Shelley, Hunt and their Circle

JEFFREY N. COX

CAMBRIDGE
UNIVERSITY PRESS

PUBLISHED BY THE PRESS SYNDICATE OF THE UNIVERSITY OF CAMBRIDGE
The Pitt Building, Trumpington Street, Cambridge CB2 1RP, United Kingdom

CAMBRIDGE UNIVERSITY PRESS
The Edinburgh Building, Cambridge, CB2 2RU, United Kingdom   http://www.cup.cam.ac.uk
40 West 20th Street, New York, NY 10011-4211, USA   http://www.cup.org
10 Stamford Road, Oakleigh, Melbourne 3166, Australia

First published 1998

Printed in the United Kingdom at the University Press, Cambridge

Typeset in Baskerville 11/12.5 pt   [VN]

A catalogue record for this book is available from the British Library

Library of Congress cataloguing in publication data
Cox, Jeffrey N.
Poetry and Politics in the Cockney School: Keats, Shelley, Hunt, and their Circle / by
Jeffrey N. Cox.
p.   cm. – (Cambridge studies in Romanticism: 31)
Includes bibliographical references and index.
ISBN 0 521 63100 9 (hardback)
1. English poetry – England – London – History and criticism. 2. Politics and literature –
England – London – History – 19th century. 3. Shelley, Percy Bysshe, 1792–1822 – Political and
social views. 4. Hunt, Leigh, 1784–1859 – Political and social views. 5. Keats, John, 1795–1821 –
Political and social views. 6. English poetry – 19th century – History and criticism. 7. London
(England) – Intellectual life – 19th century. 8. Political poetry, English – History and criticism. 9.
Hunt, Leigh, 1784–1859 – Friends and associates. 10. Romanticism – England – London. 11.
Authorship – Collaboration. I. Title. II. Series.
PR8477.C69   1998
821'.709358 – dc21   98-12838   CIP

ISBN 0 521 63100 9 hardback

#38430401

To IGHLS

Contents

Illustrations

xi

Acknowledgments

The production of this book, like that of all cultural artifacts, is over-determined, and thus it is difficult, perhaps particularly for its author, to identify the various sites – ideological, cultural, institutional, personal, and social – from which it arises. It is now clear to me that this project on a group of early-nineteenth-century writers would not have taken the shape it did if it were not for the presence of a group of late-twentieth-century scholars as its context: the Interdisciplinary Group for Historical Literary Study at Texas A&M University. It now seems almost inevitable that I, as a member of the group and as a firm believer in its communal goals, would write a book arguing that we can best understand the work of a Shelley or a Keats in the context of an intellectual circle. It is certainly the case that I have learned firsthand how much one's work is shaped by the day-to-day exchanges and interactions with the members of one's group, in my case from living life with such fine scholars and friends as David Anderson, Donald Dickson, Mary Ann O'Farrell, James Rosenheim, Howard Marchitello, Steve Daniel, Dennis Berthold, Paul Parrish, J. Lawrence Mitchell, Pamela Matthews, Lynne Vallone, Susan Egenolf, David McWhirter, Melanie Hawthorne, Mark Lussier, Kenneth Price, Samuel Gladden, Robert Newman, John O'Brien, Charles Snodgrass, and Terence Allan Hoagwood.

Three members of the group who are in their own right important voices in contemporary scholarship's larger turn to history have had a particularly strong impact on my work: Katherine O'Brien O'Keeffe – whose important work on the material basis of Anglo-Saxon culture and its transmission has influenced my thinking in many ways – helped to create the Interdisciplinary Group and continues to inspire those she left behind at Texas A&M University; Margaret J. M. Ezell – who has influenced this book from its first conception to its final revisions – has led the way in her work to an understanding of collective and communal literary production and has through her everyday exercise of her intelli-

xiii

gence, wit, and simple kindness demonstrated what it means to collaborate; and Larry J. Reynolds, first intellectual and administrative leader of the group, whose own work is an example of brilliant historicist scholarship and committed professionalism and whose now decade-long discussion with me has shown me what the shared vision and simple talk of a group can mean. It is also true that the Interdisciplinary Group is, as Sartre says of all group affiliations, both a clearly defined group and an undefined group, both a circle at Texas A&M and part of a broad movement towards historicizing. We have had many opportunities to catch sight of that larger movement as we have invited distinguished guests to visit with us; and if routine interchanges within the Interdisciplinary Group shaped the intellectual life of this book, so did the extraordinary visits and work of scholars such as Jerome McGann, Stephen Greenblatt, Marilyn Butler, Marjorie Levinson, Hayden White, Lawrence Buell, Ralph Cohen, Terry Castle, J. Paul Hunter, Robert Darnton, Seyla Benhabib, Michael Rogin – the list is much longer and just as illustrious. It is simply the case that this book would not have existed without the support and inspiration of the Interdisciplinary Group, both its A&M Fellows and its many friends from other institutions.

As I complete this book, the Interdisciplinary Group for Historical Literary Study is undergoing its own historical transformation into the Interdisciplinary Group for Humanities Studies, on its way to becoming the Texas A&M Center for Humanities. Soon there may be no official Interdisciplinary Group, and thus I dedicate this book to the Group, to the lives and work of its members.

It hardly needs to be said that this project would never even have occurred to me were it not for the brilliant historicist work that has been taking place in romantic studies. I have received important help and encouragement from many contributors to this work, including (beyond those already named) Catherine Burroughs, Stuart Curran, William Galperin, Michael Gamer, Gary Harrison, John Kandl, Greg Kucich, Thomas McFarland, Anne Mellor, David Pirie, and Nicholas Roe; in particular, I thank Paul Hamilton and Kevin Gilmartin for their insightful and generous readings of this book and Marilyn Butler for supporting my efforts. At Texas A&M University, I have benefited from the support of two department heads, Hamlin Hill and J. Lawrence Mitchell, and two deans, Daniel Fallon and Woodrow Jones, Jr.; I have received research support for this project from the Department of English, the Interdisciplinary Group for Historical Literary Study, and the Office of the Dean. I offer my thanks to all these friends at A&M and also to the staffs of the following libraries and collections: Sterling Evans Library, Texas A&M University; Humanities Resource Center, University of Texas; Special Collections, University of Iowa, particularly Robert McCown; the Huntington Library; the Beinecke Rare Book and Manuscript Library at Yale University: the Wallace Collection; the Victoria and Albert Museum; The Royal Collection of Her Majesty Queen Elizabeth II at Windsor Castle; the New York Public Library; the Library of Congress; the British Library; the British Museum: the Bristol Central Library; and Keats House, Hampstead, particularly the curator Christina Gee and Roberta Davis. Jane Van Tassel, my copy editor, has been wonderfully helpful. Josie Dixon at Cambridge University Press has offered invaluable support and guidance as this book has developed.

Several pieces of this book have appeared in earlier versions elsewhere: a version of chapter 4 appeared in *Texas Studies in Literature and Language* 38 (Fall–Winter 1996), 245–64, and is reprinted here with permission; a shorter version of chapter 6 appeared in *Studies in Romanticism* 34 (Fall 1995), 365–400, and appears with the permission of the Trustees of Boston University; and portions of the argument in chapters 1 and 3 appeared in *Romanticism* 2.1 (1996), 27–39, and this material is used here by permission.

My final thanks are to Amy, Julia, Emma, and Claire, the circle closest to my work and heart.

Abbreviations

While I have usually worked from texts as they first appeared in the work of the Cockney School, I have for the reader's convenience cited modern editions where available. Unless otherwise indicated, I have used:

Lord Byron: The Complete Poetical Works. Ed. Jerome J. McGann and Barry Weller. 7 vols. Oxford: Clarendon Press, 1980–93.

The Poetry of Leigh Hunt. Ed. H. S. Milford. London: Oxford University Press, 1923.

Complete Poems of John Keats. Ed. Jack Stillinger. Cambridge: Harvard University Press, 1978.

Shelley's Poetry and Prose. Ed. Donald H. Reiman and Sharon B. Powers. New York: Norton, 1977.

Wordsworth: Poetical Works. Ed. Thomas Hutchinson, rev. Ernest de Selincourt. Oxford University Press, 1936.

Allot	*The Poems of John Keats.* Ed. Miriam Allot. London: Longman, 1970.
Autobiography	*The Autobiography of Leigh Hunt.* Ed. Edmund Blunden. Oxford University Press, 1928.
Correspondence	*The Correspondence of Leigh Hunt.* Ed. Thorton Hunt. 2 vols. London: Smith, Elder, 1862.
CWH	*The Complete Works of William Hazlitt.* Ed. P. P. Howe. 21 vols. London: Dent, 1933.
Diary	*The Diary of Benjamin Robert Haydon.* Ed. Willard Bissell Pope. 5 vols. Cambridge: Harvard University Press, 1960–63.
Journals	*The Journals of Mary Shelley.* Ed. Paula R. Feldman and Diana Scott-Kilvert. 1987, rpt. Baltimore: Johns Hopkins University Press, 1995.
KC	*The Keats Circle: Letters and Papers 1816–1878.* Ed. Hyder

	Edward Rollins. 2 vols. Cambridge: Harvard University Press, 1948.
KH	*Keats and History*. Ed. Nicholas Roe. Cambridge University Press, 1995.
KL	*The Letters of John Keats 1814–1821*. Ed. Hyder Edward Rollins. 2 vols. Cambridge: Harvard University Press, 1958.
KR	Lewis M. Schwartz. *Keats Reviewed by His Contemporaries*. Metuchen, N.J.: Scarecrow Press, 1973.
KSJ	*Keats–Shelley Journal*
KSR	*Keats–Shelley Review*
LB	Leigh Hunt. *Lord Byron and Some of His Contemporaries; With Recollections of the Author's Life, and of His Visit to Italy*. London: Henry Colburn, 1828.
LBL/KH	Leigh Browne-Lockyer Collection at Keats House, Hampstead
L&J	*Byron's Letters and Journals*. Ed. Leslie A. Marchand. 12 vols. Cambridge: Harvard University Press, 1973–82.
LT	*The Life and Times of Leigh Hunt: Papers Delivered at a Symposium at the University of Iowa, April 13, 1984*. Ed. Robert A. McCown. Iowa City: Friends of the University of Iowa Libraries, 1987.
Recollections	Charles Cowden Clarke and Mary Novello Clarke, *Recollections of Writers*. London: Sampson, Low, Marston, Searle, & Rivington, 1878.
SC	*Shelley and His Circle 1772–1822*. Ed. Kenneth Neill Cameron and Donald H. Reiman for Carl H. Pforzheimer Library. 6 vols. Cambridge: Harvard University Press, 1961–73.
SiR	*Studies in Romanticism*
SL	*The Letters of Percy Bysshe Shelley*. Ed. Frederick L. Jones. 2 vols. Oxford: Clarendon Press, 1964.
SR	*Shelley Revalued: Essays from the Gregynog Conference*. Ed. Kelvin Everest. Totowa, N.J.: Barnes & Noble, 1983.
TLS	*Times Literary Supplement*

Introduction: or, The Visionary Company, Inc.

I

A few years ago, when I was attending a conference in Florida, I decided to take an afternoon off to visit a local state park which featured a "restored" section of a swamp – I was intrigued by the notion of repairing a swamp. Upon arriving at the park, I entered a stylish administration building which featured, as its back wall, a two-story plate-glass window overlooking the swamp. From this vantage point, I was told by the park's information, I could look out at a piece of Florida restored to look the way it had appeared to the first European visitors to this part of the state; the guidebook went on to talk about the work necessary to this restoration, such as the removal of several centuries of accumulated human junk on the site and the nurturing and sometimes the reintroduction of animal populations. I was to be privy here to "natural" Florida.

What interested me about these pronouncements was less the clearly Eurocentric desire behind this project or even its unacknowledged turn to a textualized nature – one reason the landscape could be "restored" to the way it looked to Europeans was that those Europeans wrote and drew descriptions of it – than the way in which this attempt to recover a past involved a conscious effort to remove everything that stood between us and that moment. That is, those behind this park project constructed the past in the present by attempting to remove the intervening history of this particular place, both its accretions and its losses. Oddly, this place was to become the site of a kind of time travel, a spot of time through which we could be transported back to that moment when Europeans first walked on Floridian soil.

Of course, this project announces through its very self-description its inability to give us the past immediately, a lesson learned – perhaps too well – by various recent historicisms.[1] While the presuppositions of this

I

project – that one is interested in Florida as it appeared to Europeans, that the nature found in key verbal or pictorial descriptions is "natural," and so on – were perhaps unconscious ones, it has become a rigorous ritual of historicizing criticism that it announce its preconceptions, define the positionality of its author, sometimes proclaim our inability to know the past in the very act of writing about it. Such confessions are important, but so too is the work undertaken both in attempting to remove the accumulations of temporal junk, the material and mental barriers between us and the past, and in seeking to reintroduce to our sense of the past lost populations, lost groups. On the one hand, we must realize, for example, that the very turn to this swamp as a "natural" backdrop to history depends upon a specific historical intervention – European colonization – which construes life prior to European conquest as "prehistory," as "natural"; since that spot already and always exists in other times, the decision to return from the "now" of our latest look at the swamp to the "then" of a "first" European gaze reenacts intellectually the colonization that brought the swamp into European history in the first place. On the other hand, our very self-consciousness about this putting into history might enable us truly to see – if not the "prehistory" we eradicate in the very act of distinguishing "history" from some "natural" land before time – at least the past moment that inaugurates our historical investment in this place: we cannot find behind the murk of history the "swamp" as thing-in-itself, but we can perhaps, avoiding the bog of presentism, discover at least *a* past to this place. Our inability to tell the total history of this spot does not mean we cannot tell a history of it. We may not be able to know a "nature" independent of our constructions of it, but we may still be able to know a history precisely because we recognize, after Vico or Marx, that it is something we have made.

   That is, admitting our preconceptions is not enough, since what we must then do is attempt to see beyond them; after all, the point of recognizing our own historicity lies in the hope that by doing so we can then self-consciously see the past as something more than a projection from the present. Even if we are finally trapped in some sort of modern historical amusement park, looking through windows of our own devising on pasts at least in part of our own construction, I would still argue, beyond the epistemological issues, that the attempt to know the past has an ethical claim upon us; we must try to know the past just as we must try to know the Other – or, less pretentiously, just as in life we try to let other people be themselves and not just some projection of our fears and desires.[2] As the example of the restored swamp was meant to suggest, this turn to the past is not an act of wise passiveness, not some naive hope that the past will speak for itself if only we suppress our own point of view. The turn to the past is an act in the present determined by a particular history, but we can, in remaining historically self-conscious, attempt to make it an act of clearance and reclamation rather than an act of colonizing the past by the present. In this book, I attempt to clear from our view of the cultural landscape of post-Napoleonic England some of the critical "debris" that has masked its contours and to reintroduce into our sense of the scene some "lost" figures, while remaining aware that what is debris for me may be a rich tradition to others, who may also wish that the figures I work to recover would remain forever lost.

The drive of historicisms, new and old, has been to let the past be the past not only so that we can recognize the lives of others different from us but also so that, if even for only a self-conscious moment, we can lift ourselves from our embeddedness in the present and thus perhaps glimpse a potential future also different from our time. Even if the search for such glimpses is like the work of those reclaiming the swamp – a turn to a particular past over against others because it serves present needs – it still might enable us to make our future, to convert the swamp into the utopian space of the park. We are in need of such glimpses and the hope they offer just now, when a "postcommunist," "postideological," "postmodern" world seems to offer only more selfishness, greed, oppression, bigotry, and obscurantism. For me, at least, such glimpses come in trying to re-present the work of writers at a "post-Napoleonic," "postrevolutionary," "postclassical" moment, writers who, unlike too many today, did not fall prey to cynicism and despair – "despondency" in the Wordsworthian terminology of their day – but who banded together as a group opposed to the powers-that-be and their embrace of the "spirit of money-getting," "superstition," and outmoded cultural visions. These writers formed the group around Leigh Hunt, the group labelled in conservative attacks as the Cockney School.

II

"I propose an association" – with these words Percy Shelley opens his *Proposals for an Association of Philanthropists Who Convinced of the Inadequacy of the Moral and Political State of Ireland to Produce Benefits Which Are Nevertheless Attainable Are Willing to Unite to Accomplish Its Regeneration* (1812). While this title suggests a very particular mission for the association, Shelley makes it clear that it will have a much wider scope: "I conceive that an assembly of men meeting to do all the good that opportunity will permit them to do must be in its nature as indefinite and varying as the instances of human vice and misery that precede, occasion, and call for its institution."[3] Certain that such an association will be opposed by the government, the aristocracy, and the priesthood, Shelley still believes that a group provides the best vehicle for cultural and political reform. In fact, it is in the freely associating group that Shelley sees the best hope of resisting such institutionalized associations as state, church, and class.

Shelley was not alone in desiring a group. Keats wrote to Benjamin Robert Haydon (10 January 1818, *KL*, I: 202), "I will be with you early next week – to night it should be, but we have a sort of a Club every Saturday evening," a reference to a group that gathered around James Rice. Rice was part of another group which included John Hamilton Reynolds and Benjamin Bailey and a group of young women in Essex. Reynolds, Rice, and Bailey were also members of the Zetosophian Society, "a literary, cultural, and social club composed of fourteen young men, most of them 'of very considerable genius.'"[4] Reynolds had earlier been part of the Breidden Society in Shropshire, which held an annual festival on Breidden Hill with feasting, poetry, singing, and dancing – and the crowning of the *poet ferneat*, there being ferns but no laurels available. We could continue to multiply the groups. Keats was once a member of a circle around George Felton Mathew. Horace Smith was part of an expatriate group at Versailles[5] similar to the one Shelley attempted to create at Pisa when he sought to bring together Byron, Hunt, and even the ill Keats. Benjamin Robert Haydon, the painter of the group, wrote at the time Keats, Shelley, and Hunt came together, "My great object is to form a School" (31 October 1816, *Diary*, II: 64). Byron and Hobhouse once proposed a "Couplet Club,"[6] and Byron belonged to the Whig Club and the Hampden Club. Keats's supporters Richard Woodhouse and John Taylor at one time founded a Philological Society.[7] These men all turned to associations as a means of cultural production and also as a site of opposition. They sought in a group both an immediate audience not unlike earlier manuscript circles, where one could share one's thoughts and ideas with a coterie, and a cultural, social, and political project not unlike that pursued by later explicitly avant-garde movements. It will be the argument of this book that what we call the second generation of romantic poets is not merely a temporal gathering of distinct voices but a self-consciously defined group, an association of intellectuals that centered on Leigh Hunt and that came to be known as the Cockney School. The visionary company of Shelley, Byron, Keats, Hunt, Reynolds, Smith, Hazlitt, and others may never have formally incorporated itself, but it was defined both internally and externally as a group working to reform culture and society.

What is a group? While I recognize that it is for me in part a strategically slippery site for analysis, it is certainly the case that I associate it with certain words – circle, coterie, even clique – and not with others – corporation, organization, establishment. It appears that the use of the word group in relation to an assemblage of persons arises in the eighteenth century (the *OED* cites 1748 as its first such use) at the moment when modern forms of collective association such as "party" were being defined. It is also interesting that the first uses of "group of people" appear to suggest "confused aggregation." This is, of course, in contrast to the earliest sense of the word in English, where "group" is used in the fine arts to designate a composed gathering of figures forming a design. On the one hand a formal design and on the other a human happening, a group might appear as a spatial order – as in a group photograph – but is more a temporal project – as in the development of Surrealism.

What is clear to me is that I deploy the concept of a group to avoid certain other locales from which to begin the study of literary culture. To emphasize the group as the site of literary production is, of course, to move away from the idea of the abstract individual as the producer of literary texts; it is even to move away from the more complicated intersubjective model of creation that arises when one discusses close partnerships – Wordsworth and Coleridge, in particular, but also Shelley and Byron or, to use a far less well-known example, James and Horace Smith.[8] Pairs do not comprise groups. Again, while it may make sense to talk about Wollstonecraft, Godwin, and the Shelleys as part of a family of writers,[9] family units, in which relations are a given, do not necessarily form groups in my sense. To begin at the opposite pole from the individual, we also need to see that certain key categories in our contemporary analysis of literature such as race, class, and gender also do not define groups. If it is true that one can betray one's class but never leave it, then "class" does not define a group in my sense; for "class" points to a subject position always already given, whereas the group defines an intersubjective collectivity always in the process of being imagined. Again, there certainly are gendered groups, but there is no group comprising all women or all men. It is not simply or definitively a matter of scale, though I do think that size matters when one is discussing a group as supporting literary production. It is also a question of one's relation to the collectivity under consideration. One finds oneself already part of a race, a class, a gender; these may very well be humanly constructed categories, but they are certainly not constructed by me when I find myself placed in this or that category. The group, on the other hand, is constructed by those who are affiliated with it. When Shelley sees his association opposed by the government (the nation), the aristocracy (class structure), and the priesthood (religion), he also poses the group against such given, institutionalized affiliations. He refuses to be defined by his nationality, class, or religious upbringing; he will choose with whom he will associate. The group names an "elective affinity." Goethe's use of the phrase suggests two linked aspects of belonging to a group. First, one's membership in a group is self-conscious; it is an act of willed identification – one elects to be part of a group. Second, however, one is also elected to a group, selected by both its members and by one's preexisting affinities. Becoming part of a group is an act of self-fashioning that necessarily occurs through the other. It is, in fact, through such affiliations, such self-conscious identifications, that one creates an identity beyond that set by the given categories into which one is cast. It is in the group, in this subjectivity in/as collectivity, that we can find a sense of personhood and the personal that is reduced to neither an empty autonomy nor an abstract difference. While we must never forget that groups are also defined by exclusion – that for there to be a group of "us," some "you" has to be left out – and while (as is clearly the case in the Hunt circle) the dynamic nature of a group means that individuals join and leave, are included and expelled, find themselves sometimes attached to the group, sometimes disgusted with it, finally, for me, the group embodies a project, perhaps utopian, in which a community is both imagined and lived beyond the limits of given collectivities such as those of family or nation.

The suggestion that we examine romantic poetry as a group activity will not sound so strange as it once might have. Given the work of scholars as different as Jerome McGann and Donald Reiman, Jack Stillinger and Marjorie Levinson, Marilyn Butler and Stuart Curran, Nicholas Roe and Susan Wolfson, we no longer necessarily view the romantic poet as the solitary singer declaiming alone on the mountaintop or sitting in isolation, pondering a bird's song. We have come to see the poetry of the romantic period as being a social product, with the text being forged by a collaborative process involving author, editor, typesetter, publisher, critic, and reader, and the author herself being conceived as a nexus of interpersonal, cultural, social, and economic forces. I am interested in this book in poetry as a social product in a quite mundane – ordinary and worldly – way; that is, I see the poetry of second-generation romanticism arising from the social interchange of a particular group of men and women. This group I will refer to not by the more usual names of the Keats Circle or the Shelley Circle but as the Cockney School or the Hunt circle, for it was Leigh Hunt who was actually at the center of the group – though, of course, by center I do not mean a fixed point equally distant from all the points on the spatial figure of a circle but a moving person unequally close to all of the people involved in the temporal project of a circle.

Hunt himself clearly saw writing as a social activity or even what we would call an ideological activity. In "Politics and Poetics," first published in Hunt's journal the *Reflector* (1.2 [1811]) and reprinted in the second edition of *The Feast of the Poets* (1815), Hunt offers a socialized scene of writing. He depicts himself writing not in splendid isolation, alone with nature, but at a desk in the city surrounded by historical and political texts. While he might long for a quiet tête-à-tête with his muse, he finds his writing shaped by many external pressures: by financial concerns, as "the punctual fiend, that bawls for copy" (l. 114), waits for him to finish the journalism he writes to earn a living; by political worries, as he remains aware that the government watches, ever ready to prosecute anything it can label seditious or libellous; even by physical pressures, as exhaustion, headaches, and the "Blue Daemon" (l. 28) of depression threaten him. As he places himself (in the original version) in the company of such public and politicized writers as Gifford, Sheridan, Canning, and Scott, Hunt sees his writing being shaped as much by editors' pens and government writs as it is by some internal muse.

For Hunt and for poets such as Shelley and Keats who entered his circle, poetry was a social activity in an immediate way, as they wrote for the highly politicized *Examiner*, as they penned occasional verse to one another, and as they participated in Hunt's much-maligned sonnet-writing contests. The *Examiner* is, in a sense, the textual home of the group, setting forth common ideological positions and publishing the verse of the circle's members; it also defines the project of being a group, distinguishing the *Examiner*'s writers and readers from organization by party – the weekly's motto is "Party is the madness of many for the gain of a few" – and suggesting that while the opponents of the group may be tagged by reductive because collective names – i.e., "borough mongers," "pensioners," "apostates," and "toad-eaters" – those within the group are both so particularized and so fully integrated within the circle that one can allude to them without naming them, certain that they will be recognized by the "knowing ones." Later chapters will attempt to detail the work of this circle. At this point, I want to suggest why I conceive of the group as an important focus for an attempt to construct a literary history.

III

Historical thinking works against abstraction; literary history works against abstracting literary texts from the larger range of human activities of which they are a part. As that old historicist Hegel notes, abstraction is a process of isolation, of drawing something away. Abstraction is often defined in opposition to particularity – the abstraction is too far removed from the rich details of life. Hegel sees it in opposition to totalization – the abstracted detail has been removed from the rich totality of which it is a part. Historicist resistance to abstraction and its attendant reductionism follows both paths, towards the particularity of "thick" description and towards the totality summed up in Fredric Jameson's account of "Hegel's great dictum, 'the true is the whole,' [which] is less an affirmation of some place of truth which Hegel himself (or others) might occupy, than it is a perspective and a method whereby the 'false' and the ideological can be unmasked and made visible."[10] Abstractions can be dissolved into details that escape containment within the abstraction, or abstractions can be seen as strategies of containment that can be revealed as limited only from the perspective of a totality that escapes containment. Abstractions can be shattered against the particular or the whole. Either way, they are found to be procrustean resting points for the mind.

While the move towards detail and that towards the whole seem opposed, we ideally want a method that will unite the quiddity of the particularized with the perspective of the totalized. We gesture towards such a method in, for example, discussing the merger of psychoanalysis and Marxism, in proclaiming that the "personal is the political," in finding the transcendent in the local, in identifying history as "ground" and "horizon." As Jameson suggests, no one can keep in mental play the vast dialectical power that would be needed to pay attention to all the details and to forge them into ever fuller approximations of the totality, to fill our abstractions with ever more particulars while opening them up to ever larger constructions of the whole. The truth of the matter is that in practice we tend towards one or the other pole; in simple terms, when we do literary history, we are likely to move, on the one hand, towards the biography of discrete individuals and the anecdote (the biography, as it were, of the discrete event) and, on the other, towards an analysis based on extremely large categories such as class or race or gender. When one makes the move towards the particular individual, the unique text, the striking event, one can be accused of replacing history with biography, of offering another formalism, or of hiding grand narratives within only seemingly random stories. When one moves towards totalization, one is likely to be seen running roughshod over the minutiae of the event, the text, the individual and thus of being not totalizing but totalitarian. And these are the objections that historical scholars themselves bring against historicist work, including their own: no one is harder on historicizing than historicists. In a real sense, what historical scholarship teaches us is skepticism, a doubt of grand narratives and a concern that in fact the devil is in the details and he is doing something we do not like.

It strikes me that there is a certain plausibility in starting somewhere in the middle, with neither the supposedly individual subject, individual fact, or individual text nor the hypothetically totalized community, history, culture. Alan Liu, in critiquing the "romanticism of the detail," has suggested that "what may be the single most promising, if also problematic, front of cultural criticism [is] its exploration of the communally 'parochial,' 'local,' and 'regional'"; he offers "'localism' as the underexplored zone between the discretely individual and the massively collective."[11] There are clearly many entry points into this middle ground, as we can see in studies ranging from the collective institution of the Renaissance theater to printing houses in the nineteenth century, from women's coterie circles to the construction of the institution of slavery and thus of "race." For me, the best way into this "underexplored zone" when discussing the second generation of romantics is through the notion of the group. Of course, this middle ground of the group – located somewhere between, say, the biographical subject and, say, the nation – occupies conceptually the same place as does abstraction lying between the particular and the whole. However, I would propose the group as a dynamic position and project that through its ties to both the individual and the collective, the particular and the whole, stands in for abstraction in order to allow us to stand beyond it. Put another way, any formulation of a group may itself be an abstraction, but thinking through the group, as it now presents highlighted subjects and now suggests widening associations, offers tactics for resisting even one's own abstractions.

Offering a model of such an approach, Jean-Paul Sartre, in *Search for a Method*, sought in the notion of a group a point of mediation between a class-based definition of an ideology and an individual's espousal of that ideology. Using the example of the idea of nature in the eighteenth century, Sartre explains the relationship between an idea as it is held within a general cultural moment and the same concept as it is held by an individual defined as a member of a group:

> Outside of precise acts of ideation, of writing, or of verbal designation, the Idea of Nature has no material being (still less an existence) in the eighteenth century. Yet it is real, for each individual takes it as something Other than his own specific act as reader or thinker insofar as it is also the thought of thousands of *other* thinkers. Thus the intellectual grasps his thought as being at once *his* and *other*. He thinks *in* the idea rather than the idea being *in* his thought; and this signifies that it is the sign of his belonging to a determined group (since its functions, ideology, etc., are known) and an undefined group (since the individual will never know all members nor even the total number).[12]

Keats, for example, is both part of a particular group – the Hunt circle – and of a series of ever larger undefined groups – writers, students of medicine, the "middle" class, men. When he engages a particular ideological issue – say, attitudes towards sexuality – he is not merely expressing a personal position but espousing notions that can be tied to the interests of both his particular group and other larger groups. We may never be able to reconstruct in full detail what the individual Keats thought about sex or usefully totalize the ideology of sex held by early-nineteenth-century bourgeois men, but we can come to understand the collective position affirmed by Keats and those with whom he allied himself as they define themselves in opposition to others within their historical moment, as they identify themselves as part of a group by, for example, espousing a particular sexual ideology. Remembering Sartre's warning about the status of the idea of the group – "the *group* never has and never can have the type of metaphysical existence which people try to give it. We repeat with Marxism: there are only men and real relations between men" (p. 6) – we can still work towards a fuller understanding of Keats's texts by placing him and them within the concrete network of human (which, of course, includes intellectual and literary) relations and oppositions surrounding Hunt.

Whether or not groups are a significant feature of differing historical moments as we find differently configured coteries, schools, movements, cenacles, and simply collections of friends, there were certainly preced- ents, including relatively immediate ones, for the gathering around Hunt. This gathering of writers and artists who at times imagine themselves the "unacknowledged legislators of the world" echoes the dream of a "republic of letters" that moved many in early-modern Europe, as Donald Dickson reminds us, from the famous Academia Platonica organized around Ficino at the Medici villa to the Society of Antiquaries founded in 1572 by William Camden and Robert Cotton under the patronage of Matthew Parker, the archbishop of Canter- bury.[13] From learned organizations such as the Royal Society to gather- ings of antiquarians and collectors such as the Society of Dilettanti and on to secret societies, we repeatedly find collectivities devoted to cultural work. Margaret J. M. Ezell has reminded us of the importance of coterie circles to seventeenth- and eighteenth-century literature.[14] Following upon Habermas's interest in them as the foundation of a "public sphere,"[15] eighteenth-century coffee houses, salons, and periodicals have attracted considerable interest. Hunt, at times, seems to draw directly upon such traditions: he named his journal the *Examiner* after the early-eighteenth-century periodical; his uncle Benjamin West pro- vided a link to the traditions of the Royal Academy; Hunt was a sometime member of the gathering that had been Joseph Johnson's circle in the 1790s – and his friends such as Hazlitt, Godwin, and Horace Twiss provided other links to earlier radical and dissenting groups.

Still, there is a different relationship between the Hunt circle and many earlier sites for cultural production, a difference marked, for example, in their mocking designation as the Cockney School, with the idea of the School paralleling them to older centers of cultural power but with the Cockney label attempting to deny them any cultural capital.[16] Where learned societies stood at the center of established culture, where eighteenth-century gatherings of writers such as the Scribblerians or the Kit-Cat Club offered themselves as competitors for the heart of Lon- don's public life, the Hunt circle was seen as more localized or particu- larized, as embodying only Cockney culture or literally marginalized in Hampstead. For the defenders of official culture, the Cockney School seemed less like the Kit-Cats than like Grub-Street hacks who, no longer the subject of high cultural disdain, have instead organized themselves into a powerful literary movement; again, they might appear to threaten the ideal of the "republic of letters" by insisting upon its radical democ- ratization. The Cockneys occupied an interesting space, usefully

thought of through their sometime designation as sub-urban, for while
the Cockney label (not to mention the office of the *Examiner* and other
haunts) tied them to urban London, they were both removed from the
established centers of London's power and considered beneath the
urbane culture of the elites. Of course, for Hunt and his group, this
apparent marginalization was a guarantee of their resistance to established power, as Hunt defined the *Examiner* apart from all party politics
and as the Cockneys conceived of themselves as opposed to the Lakers
"in and out of place," as Byron put it; they participated in both the
isolation and the liberation that marks an avant-garde. Like various
earlier cultural gatherings, the Hunt circle conceived of itself as a model
for society as a whole, but this was an oppositional model; that is, their
group becomes a site not for the identification with conventional culture
and the society it supports but for the struggle to create a reconfigured
social space built upon a new – Cockney – cultural literacy.

Thus, while it may seem odd to turn to the group in a period that is
conventionally designated as alternatively the Age of the Individual and
the Age of Nationalism, the group offers a way of thinking beyond such
cliched formulations in order to reconceptualize second-generation
romanticism. I have already tried to suggest the desire for a group on the
part of writers such as Shelley and Keats, a longing not surprising given
the status of those writers called "romantic" as a cultural avant-garde,
both distant from large portions of the public's taste and questing for a
position beyond the hegemony of official culture. It is also important, as
I will argue most fully in chapter 1, that they were defined by others as
being part of a coterie, the Cockney School; and it is significant that
both their self-definition and the attacks by their enemies defined them
as a group in opposition to other groups, particularly the Lake School.
By studying a group rather than individual writers, we see literary and
other intellectual work not as unique, isolated objects but as the products of forces of both affiliation and cultural warfare. The work we
identify with Keats or Shelley defines not abstract sensibilities but lived
positionalities. Put simply, Keats will be understood better when read
through Hunt, Shelley, Reynolds, and Byron and through Lockhart,
Wordsworth, or Southey as well. The text is an act within a collective
practice defined as it enters into an arena of competing practices. The
hope is that in examining the work of a group, defining individuals as
they are part of collective practices and the group itself as only one set of
practices within a larger cultural repertoire, one avoids both abstract
particulars and too easily achieved totalizations.

This book is an essay at defining the work of the Hunt circle. I begin with an account of the group's definition, both their internal sense of themselves as a group and their opponents' assault upon them as a coterie, as the Cockney School. My goal is to retrieve the group and its collective practice from both the negative formulation offered by *Blackwood's* and the defensive reaction of romantic scholars who have sought to isolate the poets so as to negate the force of the earlier attacks. The first chapter attempts to decenter our standard notions of the second generation of romantics by insisting that we read them as a group and by recentering their network of interrelations on Leigh Hunt. The second chapter offers a fuller portrait of the group's activities, its shared practices and positions. I am also concerned here with defining the mode of literary production in the circle as collective and collaborative; examining the group's collective work in commonplace books, collaborative projects, and "contest" poems, as well as in their major efforts, I draw upon the work of seventeenth-century scholars on coterie literature to show how the mode of literary production in the Hunt circle is bound up with manuscript circulation, with the "interactive," collaborative nature of coterie writing described by Margaret Ezell. We can find the traces of the group's communal project in the very ways in which they create texts.

Drawing upon this working definition of the group and arguing that we should see the group not so much as a context lying outside canonical works as the site within which they are produced and which they in turn produce, I turn in the third chapter to Keats's *Poems* of 1817, which can best be understood once it is situated firmly in the collective project of the Hunt circle, once it is seen as an exemplar of the group's stylistic and ideological practices and as a manifesto issued in the culture wars following the fall of Napoleon. The chapter ends with an account of "I stood tip-toe upon a little hill," the opening to *Poems*, which I argue is also an opening salvo in a battle with Wordsworth as Keats, Hunt, Hazlitt, Byron, and Shelley all contest the vision of the *Excursion*.

These first three chapters provide a sense of the Hunt circle through its affiliations and its oppositions. The final three chapters demonstrate more particularly how reading their poetry in the context of the group's project adds to our understanding and appreciation of the work of Shelley, Keats, and others. Chapters 4 and 5 offer two attempts to use the idea of the group to explore the literary work of the period. Chapter 4 takes up a particular genre, the experimental plays penned by Hunt, Mary Shelley, Percy Shelley, and Horace Smith. In a sense, the chapter

offers a simple point: a work such as *Prometheus Unbound*, when considered apart from the work of the Hunt circle, is likely to be seen as a
uniquely original poem, comparable – despite its dramatic form –
perhaps only to Blake's visionary epics; however, when Shelley's play is
placed within the project of the circle, we suddenly realize that it is part
of a set of generic experiments and ideological arguments he shares with
writers such as Hunt and Smith. Chapter 5 discusses the style and
subject matter usually defined as romantic classicism; here I want to
show that what might be seen as a turn away from both contemporary
subject matter and the "modern" style – a turn often defined through
Keats's "Ode on a Grecian Urn" – is in fact the epitome of Cockney
poetics and polemics. The final chapter not only returns to some of the
vexing relations within the group – in particular, problems with money
– but also reads *Adonais* – and other poems on the death of Keats,
Shelley, and Hunt – as first attempts to write a history or offer a
summary vision of the Hunt circle.

There is clearly much else in the work of the Hunt circle that could be
explored: the group's Italianate work from Hunt's *Story of Rimini* to
Keats's and Reynolds's abandoned Boccaccio project and even Byron's
Don Juan; the circle's collective efforts with the essay, literary, occasional,
and political; the considerable accomplishments of the women in the
circle that might lead through Mary Shelley to a consideration of the
novel, to which Peacock, Horace Smith, and even Hunt (*Sir Ralph Esher,
or Adventures of a Gentleman of the Court of Charles II*) contributed, or that
might take us via Elizabeth Kent and her *Flora Domestica* to new insights
into the poetry of a group that produced Hunt's *Foliage* and the flower-
filled verses of Keats. My book will have accomplished its purposes if
others come along to flesh out our account of the Hunt circle, thus
revealing how finally abstract my study, like any other, necessarily is.

Of course, I like to think of this book as avoiding some of abstraction's
pitfalls in order to move us closer to understanding the ways in which a
literary work is a complex social act as both a product and producer of a
web of human relations, relations that are both local and wide-ranging,
from the personal link a seduction poem may both draw upon and forge
with the person being seduced to the more distant connection a text
makes when a reader, contemplating the work long decades after it was
written, is himself or herself moved to write about it. I am most
interested in how and why particular literary texts arise in particularized
interpersonal circumstances and how these texts gain the cultural power
to engage ever widening circles, ever changing affiliative groups includ-

ing those of which I am a part. Put simply, I believe that if we attend to the Hunt circle the individual works produced within it will speak to us more fully as we hear them speak to and for the group.

CHAPTER I

The Cockney School attacks: or, the antiromantic ideology

I

QUEEN-BEAUTY of the Night – pale and alone –
  Eye not so coldly Love's brief happiness;
But look as once when thou didst leave thy throne,
  In garb and gait a sylvan huntress,
And with bright, buskined limbs, through dew and flowers,
  Lightly, on sprightly feet and agile, bounded,
With fawn-like leaps, among the Latmian bowers;
  While the wide dome of farthest heaven resounded
With the shrill shouts of thee and thy nymph-rovers,
When the hard chace of victory was won,
  And changed Actaeon by his hounds was torn.
But then thou hadst not seen Endymion,
  Nor knew the pain and coldness of his scorn; –
Yet, if thy love was dear to thee, be dear to lovers!

Coming across these lines without any identifying mark, one might reasonably wonder with Sidney Colvin whether one had found a previously unknown poem by Keats or perhaps an uncollected sonnet by Leigh Hunt.[1] The story of the love between Endymion and the goddess of the moon was a favorite of Keats's, treated both in the opening long piece of his *Poems* of 1817 and in his longest poem, *Endymion* (1818). This sonnet – with its "Latmian bowers," with its somewhat jarring compound coinage "nymph-rovers," with its description of a mythological subject in what could be called slangy diction, as when the goddess is seen "In *garb* and gait a sylvan huntress," and with its argument for the erotic joy of "Love's brief happiness" – might very well strike us as the work of the early Keats. It was, after all, for writing such poetry that Keats was ridiculed in the *Blackwood's* Cockney School attacks. It is for writing such poetry that the early "weak-sided" Keats, seen as too much the follower of Leigh Hunt, is still criticized. What such criticism both then and now reveals – as does the closeness of this sonnet to something Keats might have written – is that Keats, along with many other writers of his day, was in fact part of a school or circle around Hunt.

This sonnet was not, of course, written by Keats or Hunt but by another figure in their group who shared their poetic procedures and ideological interests, Cornelius Webb, who included these lines in his *Sonnets, Amatory, Incidental and Descriptive; with Other Poems* (1820). Born perhaps in 1789 and dying most likely after 1848, Cornelius Francis Webb or Webbe is virtually unknown, yet he played a part in a key moment in the reception history of what we call the second generation of romantic poets, who were then known as the Cockney School.[2] Webb himself was a minor but extremely active writer during the period, a contributor to such journals as the *New Monthly Magazine*, the *Literary Gazette*, the *New European Magazine*, the *Gentleman's Magazine*, and the *London Magazine* as well as the author of *Heath Flowers* (1817), the above-mentioned *Sonnets, Summer; An Invocation to Sleep; Fairy Revels; and Songs and Sonnets* (1821), and some later books of verse and prose, including a volume with the appropriately Cockney title of *Glances at Life in City and Suburb* (1836).[3] Despite some success – as George Marsh notes, the reviews were generally good and his poems frequently republished, indicating "a certain popularity" – Webb would turn from poetry to other literary labors. The "Note – To the Reader" in *Sonnets* complains that "Circumstances unfavourable to literary studies have compelled the Author to lay down his pen," but "If these few pieces are received favourably, it will induce the Author to publish some larger poems"; in other words, like John Hamilton Reynolds or Horace Smith or, for that matter, Keats, Webb felt a tension between his commitment to poetry and his need to earn a living. Seeking in poetry a professional career open to talent, Webb is typical of the poets in the circle of which Keats was a part.

When we read Webb and hear something of Keats or when we read, say, Horace Smith and find something of Shelley, we begin to realize that these writers were part of a collective poetic practice, a shared cultural project. We can see such links in other aspects of Webb's literary work. Webb's early books of poetry look like Keats's *Poems* of 1817 or Hunt's *Foliage* of 1818. (Keats apparently gave Webb a copy of his 1817 poems as a gift, and Webb wrote a typical Hunt-circle response in "To John Keats, on His First Poems.")[4] Like these better-known books, Webb's are organized by genre and touch on many of the same subjects and images as more famous volumes: there is an "Invocation to Sleep" that could be linked to Keats's "Sleep and Poetry"; there are sonnets on a nightingale, on the grasshopper, on indolence, and on Italy; there are many Keatsian bowers in these poems and numerous Huntian nymphs. A volume announced in February 1817 (and reviewed in the *Theatrical Inquisitor* [April 1817] but so far undiscovered) was given the title *Heath Flowers*, which is reminiscent of Hunt's later *Foliage*, as is Webb's 1832 *Lyric Leaves*.

Webb's literary career was linked to the work of the circle around Hunt, and not just by the *Blackwood's* attack.[5] Hunt included a series of sonnets by Webb in his *Literary Pocket Book* for 1822 that later appeared in *Lyric Leaves*; Hunt, of course, also published Keats, Shelley, and other members of their group such as Bryan Waller Procter ("Barry Cornwall"), Charles Cowden Clarke,[6] and Charles Ollier in his pocket books. Webb's second volume of poetry was issued by Charles Ollier and his brother, who had published volumes by Keats, Hunt, and Shelley. Later, Webb would be taken up by another acquaintance of Hunt's, for Douglas Jerrold would adapt a play from a story in Webb's *Posthumous Papers – Two Eyes between Two; or, Pay Me for My Eye: A Tale of Baghdad: A Broad Extravaganza, in One Act* (performed at the Royal Coburg, 1828). As late as 1836, Webb was still being attacked as a Cockney (*Monthly Review* n.s. 3 [October 1836], 223–30), but most of his reviews were surprisingly favorable. Interestingly, in an issue of the *Monthly Magazine* (50 [1 September 1820], 166), Keats's famous 1820 volume and Webb's *Sonnets* are reviewed on the same page, the journal finding Keats to be "equally high in the estimation of poetic opinion, as the author of Rimini [Hunt], or as he (Barry Cornwall) of the Dramatic Scenes," while saying of Webb's poems that "There is much fancy and strong poetical enthusiasm displayed in some of these sonnets, which has rarely been equalled, and by no means surpassed by any of our living poets."

Despite such contemporary praise, the only piece of verse by Webb that anyone today is likely to know did not appear in these early books but on the pages of *Blackwood's Edinburgh Magazine* as the epigraph for the infamous Cockney School attacks – attacks, of course, that placed Keats, as well as Shelley and Byron, in a context that included Webb, Hunt, Cornwall, Reynolds, and Smith. Keats, concerned about the insults in *Blackwood's*, wrote to Benjamin Bailey (3 November 1817, *KL*, 1: 180) of "one Cornelius Webb Poetaster – who unfortunately was of our Party occasionally at Hampstead and took it into his head to write the following – something about – 'we'll talk on Wordsworth Byron – a theme we never tire on' and so forth till he comes to Hunt and Keats. In the Motto they have put Hunt and Keats in large letters." In praising his colleagues in strong terms, Webb brought down abuse upon himself and them, for *Blackwood's* and its conservative allies could not allow a claim for cultural power by the liberal Hunt circle to go unchallenged. The lines as quoted in *Blackwood's* are as follows:

> Our talk shall be (a theme we never tire on)
> Of Chaucer, Spenser, Shakspeare, Milton, Byron,
> (Our England's Dante) – Wordsworth – HUNT, and KEATS,
> The Muses' son of promise; and of what feats
> He yet may do.   *Blackwood's* 2 (October 1817), 38

John Gibson Lockhart, writing as "Z." in *Blackwood's*, used these lines in order to ridicule Hunt and Keats, who would often be mockingly referred to as the "Muses' son of promise." Webb – or "Corny Webb" as *Blackwood's* sometimes calls him – was never the subject of a full-blown assault in the review, despite Z.'s proclamation to Hunt that he would "relieve my main attack upon you, by a diversion against some of your younger and less important auxiliaries, the Keateses [*sic*], the Shellys [*sic*], and the Webbes" ("Letter from Z., to Mr. Leigh Hunt," *Blackwood's* 2 [January 1818], 415).

Z., in fact, used the series primarily to attack Hunt along with Hazlitt and Keats, but *Blackwood's*, the *Quarterly Review*, and many other journals of the day kept up the assault on the larger group of writers who came to be known as the Cockney School, a group organized around Hunt that was in various pieces seen to include besides Keats and Hazlitt, Mary and Percy Shelley, sometimes Charles Lamb, Benjamin Robert Haydon, Vincent Novello, "Arthur Brooke" (John Chalke Claris), "Barry Cornwall" (Bryan Waller Procter), and even Byron. Thus, *Blackwood's* called Hazlitt the "Cockney Aristotle" (5 [April 1819], 97) and viciously attacked him for his *Liber Amoris*, labelling him "a COCKNEY and 'a LIBERAL'" (13 [June 1823], 645). While in 1818 *Blackwood's* found that "Mr Lamb's Parnassus is not in the kingdom of Cockaigne" (3 [August 1818], 599), it later labelled Lamb a "Cockney Scribbler" (5 [November 1820], 208), and, in ridiculing Lamb's response to Southey's attack on his religion, claimed that "even cockneys blush for you" (14 [October 1823], 505); Nicholas Roe has transcribed two letters from Alaric Watts to William Blackwood in which Lamb is again linked to the Cockneys, in one of which he is listed with "Procter, Hazlitt, Hunt, Peacock, Chas Ollier, Talford, Reynolds *cum multis aliis*," who "boast of their freedom

from the shackles of religious sentiment of every kind."[7] The painter
Haydon was referred to as the "Cockney Raphael" by *Blackwood's* (5
[April 1819], 97); Haydon, Novello, and Keats are named Hunt's execu-
tors in an attack upon Hunt in which he is imagined to be dead (6
[October 1819], 70–76). Claris, a friend of Hunt and Horace Smith, was
attacked for his elegy on Shelley, dedicated to Hunt, in the *Weekly
Literary Register and Review of the Fine Arts, Sciences, and Belles Lettres* (21
September 1822, n.p.). "Barry Cornwall" was repeatedly targeted as a
Cockney, as in a review of his *Flood of Thessaly* volume in *Blackwood's* (13
[May 1823], 532–41). Cornwall and Hunt were denigrated as "Metro-
politan poets" in *Honeycomb* (5 [15 July 1820], 33–37), while Cornwall was
lumped together with Hunt and Keats by the *Imperial Magazine* (3
[November 1821], 969). In a review of Mary Shelley's *Valperga; or, The
Life and Adventures of Castruccio, Prince of Lucca* (1823) in *Blackwood's* (13
[March 1823], 290), her portrayal of female characters is linked to the
work of a "certain *school.*"[8] Byron was repeatedly grouped with the
Cockneys in, for example, attacks on the *Liberal* (e.g. "On the Cockney
School. No. VII. Hunt's Art of Love," *Blackwood's* 12 [December 1822],
781) as well as in parodies of the *Liberal*, the *Illiberal*, and the *London
Liberal*, or the attack on Cantos VI–VIII of *Don Juan* that contends "his
lordship must have taken the Examiner, the Liberal, the Rimini, the
Round Table, as his model" and claims that his rhymes begin to remind
them of Barry Cornwall, Keats, and Hunt (*Blackwood's* 14 [August 1823],
88, 91).

In other words, *Blackwood's* and the other conservative reviewing
journals of the day sought to define what we call the second generation
of romantics as the Cockney School headed by Leigh Hunt. The
centrality of Hunt will perhaps surprise the modern reader, but so will
the contemporary insistence that these writers – whom we see as
offering different visions and verse – were part of a single school. Still, I
do not believe we can dismiss these attacks by simply referring to the
wildly partisan nature of reviewing during the period. Jerome McGann
and Marjorie Levinson have shown us how appropriate, in fact, many
features of the Cockney label are in the case of Keats's poetry.[9] One
function of this book is to argue that there was a Cockney School: a
group (in the sense I have outlined in my introduction) of writers, artists,
and intellectuals organized loosely around Leigh Hunt and his various
journals – primarily the *Examiner*, but also the *Indicator* and the *Liberal* –
that conceived of itself as a coherent circle, something in between the
kind of manuscript coterie circle that had once dominated literary

production and the kind of self-consciously avant-garde movement that
would mark much later literary and artistic effort. This was a circle that,
at different times, included an even larger group than that identified by
the reviews: Hunt himself and his family, including his brothers John
and Robert and his sister-in-law Elizabeth Kent, Keats, Percy and Mary
Shelley, Byron, Benjamin Robert Haydon, John Hamilton Reynolds,
Charles Armitage Brown, the Ollier brothers, Horace and James Smith,
Charles Cowden Clarke and his future wife Mary Novello, Procter,
Vincent Novello and his wife, Thomas Alsager, Thomas Barnes,
Thomas Love Peacock, Hazlitt, Edward Holmes, Godwin, Thomas
Richards, the Gattie brothers, Charles Wells, Charles Dilke, P. G.
Patmore, John Scott, Walter Coulson, Lamb, Barron Field, Joseph
Severn, perhaps Douglas Jerrold and Thomas Noon Talfourd, and
Cornelius Webb, as well as many family members and more ephemeral
participants. With Hunt as their chief organizer, they formed an intelligentsia, with the *Examiner* as their organ, with reform, anticlericalism,
and joyful paganism as their platform, and with shared enthusiasms
such as Mozart, vegetarianism, and myth. The question was not of the
existence of this group but of its definition. The most influential attempt
to label them – both then and now – was the Cockney School campaign,
with deleterious effects on the reception of these poets – both then and
now.

II

'Tis not your work they criticize, but you.
By politics alone, they try and tear ye,
And as you love or hate Lord Castlereagh, so fare ye!
London Magazine, May 1820

What though, for showing truth to flatter'd state,
Kind Hunt was shut in prison, yet has he,
In his immortal spirit, been as free
As the sky-searching lark, and as elate ...
Who shall his fame impair
When thou art dead, and all thy wretched crew.
Keats, "Written on the Day that Mr. Leigh Hunt left Prison"

The Cockney School attacks launched by *Blackwood's* in 1817 constituted
an enormously powerful act of cultural definition that still influences our
understanding of what we call the second generation of romantic writers

– Hunt's fame is still impaired by that "wretched crew," and scholars continue to work hard to separate other poets, Keats in particular, from the maligned Hunt. One sign of the power of these attacks is that they displaced another attempt to represent the collective efforts of writers such as Keats, Shelley, Hunt, John Hamilton Reynolds, Hazlitt, and Horace Smith. For it was Hunt himself who first announced the presence of a new school – in his 1816 *Examiner* review of the "young poets" Keats, Shelley, and Reynolds, in his longer review of Keats's *Poems* of 1817, and in his many occasional poems celebrating the group, often published in the *Examiner* and gathered together in his volume *Foliage* of 1818. The group had already made a collective appearance: *The Round Table: A Collection of Essays on Literature, Men, and Manners* (1817), while usually considered only in studies of Hazlitt, who wrote most of the pieces, was in fact originally conceived as a textual embodiment of the group, a meeting on the pages of the *Examiner* between Hazlitt, Hunt (who introduced the series and wrote twelve of the fifty-two pieces before Napoleon's return forced him to turn wholly to political writing), Lamb, Barnes, and another unknown collaborator.

The *Blackwood's* attacks were literally reactionary, a conservative response to a preexisting positive presentation of the group; each feature of the attack – its abuse of Hunt and his friends on social, sexual, stylistic, and ideological grounds – re-presents as a failing a key aspect of the circle's poetic project. It is emblematic that the Cockney School reviews opened by quoting Webb's lines praising the group, for even if Z. wished to ridicule these verses, the quotation recognizes the priority of the positive image that must be undermined. These attacks were in fact a counterattack, an act of recognition by ideological enemies of the gathering of writers around Leigh Hunt.[10] For example, a correspondent – perhaps John Wilson, shortly to be attached to *Blackwood's* – writing to the conservative *Anti-Gallican Monitor* (8 June 1817) admits that Hunt's "Young Poets" piece in the *Examiner* is the impetus behind his ridicule of the "school of poetry, that is adduced in the article... There are sundry *Genii* yclep'd – Leigh Hunt, John Keats, John Reynolds, Percy Shelley, and I believe I may add a few &c.'s &c.'s &c.'s at the head of this desperate gang – Mr. Hunt, the high Priest of Oppollo [*sic*] *nemcon*, in the Chair."[11] The piece goes on to recognize Hunt's power, to complain about the coterie nature of the group, and to ridicule Keats in particular. *Blackwood's*, too, feels the need to denigrate this group not because it can easily be dismissed (as Lockhart sometimes pretends), but because conservatives were concerned about its cultural authority. The more one reads *Blackwood's*, the clearer it becomes how obsessed the journal was with Hunt and his friends.

The Cockney School articles come, then, rather late in the day, after poets such as Keats had rallied to Hunt's side and after Hunt had sought to create a positive identity for the circle.[12] Writing in the *Examiner* for 1 December 1816, Hunt recognized "a new school of poetry rising of late, which promises to extinguish the French one that has prevailed among us since the time of Charles the 2d"; this school – as Hunt already identifies features central to twentieth-century criticism of the poetry of the period – is marked by an "aspiration after real nature and original fancy" (p. 762). Citing evidence that the new school is on the rise, Hunt refers to the *Edinburgh Review*'s admission that the "old school" was exhausted and to Byron's turn in *Childe Harold* III to nature, the "Noble Poet" having "renounced a certain leaven of the French style." As his later review (*Examiner*, 1 June, 6 July, 13 July 1817) of Keats's 1817 volume makes clear, Hunt credits the "Lake School" and Wordsworth in particular with having inaugurated a new age in poetry, but "like most Revolutionists, especially of the cast which they have since turned out to be, they went to an extreme, calculated rather at first to make the readers of poetry disgusted with originality and adhere with contempt and resentment to their magazine common-places" (p. 345). Hunt is interested in arguing that what we call the second generation of romantic poets form a school that has learned from the Lake Poets but is ready to go beyond them. While allying Byron to these efforts, he in particular wishes to announce three young poets, Percy Bysshe Shelley, John Hamilton Reynolds, and John Keats, "who appear to us to promise a considerable addition of strength to the new school" (1 December 1816, p. 762).

As Hunt points out in his review of *Poems*, Keats makes a similar argument in his "Sleep and Poetry," which as we will see in chapter 3 is a kind of poetic manifesto for this new school; in that poem, Keats, like Hunt, castigates the French school,[13] and, while preferring the Lake School, he finds its poets absorbed by the cultural despondency of the day, "the morbidity that taints the productions of the Lake Poets," to use Hunt's phrase (*Examiner*, 13 July 1817, p. 443). Reynolds, usually separated from Hunt in discussions of Keats and his friends, voices a similar position in his review of *Poems*, where he argues that Keats will "make a great addition to those who would overthrow that artificial taste which French criticism has long planted amongst us" (*Champion*, 9 March 1817, p. 78).

It was, of course, not just the criticism written by the group but their poetry itself that announced their allegiance to one another. *Poems* – with its dedication to Hunt, with its poems to Charles Cowden Clarke, Haydon, and Hunt, and with its sonnets written for Hunt's poetry-writing contests or in response to other moments within the group such as the reading of Chapman's Homer with Clarke – seeks to represent in verse the group and its life. The same can be said of Hunt's later volume, *Foliage* (1818), which offers poems to Keats, Shelley, Hazlitt, Lamb, Vincent Novello, Horace Smith, Haydon, John Hamilton Reynolds, and others associated with the Hunt circle, including Byron; Hunt includes poems celebrating the music made with Novello ("To Henry Robertson, John Gattie, and Vincent Novello"), the poetry created with Keats ("On Receiving a Crown of Ivy"), and Haydon's paintings ("To Benjamin Robert Haydon"). One can adduce many more examples of moments when these writers announce in print their connections within this circle: we might think of Shelley's dedication of *The Cenci* to Hunt or Hunt's dedication of his translation of Tasso's *Amyntas* to Keats; of John Hamilton Reynolds's sonnet praising Hunt's *Story of Rimini* (*Champion*, 8 December 1816, p. 390) or Hunt's answering sonnet published in *Foliage*; of Hunt's reviews in the *Examiner* and *Indicator* of Shelley and Keats or Keats's *Examiner* review of Reynolds's *Peter Bell*; of Horace Smith's acknowledgment of Hunt's influence on his *Amarynthus, the Nympholept* or his turn to Shelley in responding to "Ozymandias" in the sonnet "On a Stupendous Leg of Granite"; and of Shelley's *Adonais* with its praise of Keats and portraits of Byron and Hunt or "Arthur Brooke"'s *Elegy on the Death of Percy Bysshe Shelley* with its dedication to Leigh Hunt. Anyone familiar with the poetry of the day would have been aware of the complex interconnections of this group around Hunt. Anyone, like the *Blackwood's* crew, who opposed the politics of Hunt would be concerned about the potentially powerful presence of this "coterie" on the literary scene.

But why *Cockney* School? It was, in fact, a brilliant choice; for as we can see from the *Dictionary of the Vulgar Tongue* (1811 edition), the word cockney provided Lockhart not only with a place name for the new school – useful in contrasting it with the Lake School – but also with the suggestions of sexual libertinism and effeminacy that would be a major part of the assault upon Hunt, Keats, and their colleagues: "Cockney" is a

nick name given to the citizens of London, or persons born within the sound of Bow bell . . . The king of the cockneys is mentioned among the regulations for the sports and shows formerly held in the Middle Temple on Childermas Day, where he had his officers, a marshal, constable, butler, &c. ... Ray says, the interpretation of the word Cockney, is, a young person coaxed or conquered, made wanton; or a nestle cock, delicately bred and brought up, so as, when arrived at man's estate, to be unable to bear the least hardship.[14]

The Cockney School attacks use all of the elements found in this definition. For example, Hunt's detractors named him the "King of Cockaigne,"[15] presumably referring to the carnivalesque tradition of naming a Cockney King of London, though *Blackwood's* may also have taken its inspiration from Hunt and Hazlitt's collaborative project the *Round Table*, for in the first number of the Cockney series, Z. – quoting Hunt's introduction to their essays – states that when Hunt "talks about chivalry and King Arthur, he is always thinking of himself, and '*a small party of friends, who meet once a-week at a Round Table, to discuss the merits of a leg of mutton, and of the subjects upon which we are to write*'" (2 [October 1817], 39). In any event, Hunt is seen presiding over a court or coterie, as in this letter from Z. to Hunt, "King of the Cockneys":

Your Majesty, the King of the Cockneys, having signified your royal resolution to preserve an inviolable silence towards me, the unfortunate Z., who am said to "think the green leaves black," and to be "ignorant of all noble theories," (I refer your Majesty to one of your late edicts in the Cockney Court-gazette,) I shall notwithstanding, as it becomes a good and faithful subject to do, continue to pay a little further homage to your Majesty; and I therefore now seek, with a fitting tribute, once more to approach your throne. In the first place, then, I humbly suggest, that you give yourself too many of those regal airs so natural to a crowned head, and that you conduct yourself, at your court at Lisson Grove, with a stateliness and hauteur that may be considered, by the youthful nobility of Cockaigne, a perfect model of monarchical dignity, but is, in fact, risibly characteristic of your plebeian origin and education. (3 [May 1818], 196)

Recognizing that there is in fact a circle around Hunt, these attacks attempt to denigrate it. We get a mock court, with the *Examiner* as court gazette, Hunt's home at 13 Lisson Grove as the castle, and such figures as Keats and Hazlitt as courtiers. *Blackwood's* seeks to make the Hunt circle, portrayed as a sycophantic and subversive cabal, into a kind of demonic parody of the very court life which Hunt and his fellow writers frequently criticized in the pages of the *Examiner*. Of course, *Blackwood's* is also mocking what it sees as the pretensions of the Cockney group, its assault upon what it claims to be the social climbing of a "lower"-class coterie being a major part of its satiric campaign.

In the link of the word cockney to wantonness and weakness, we have two more features of the Cockney attacks: that Hunt and his circle are libertines and that they are also weak, "effeminate." (Of course, one wonders why anyone would question the potency of an opponent unless that opponent's power was in fact feared.) We see the first charge levelled repeatedly against Hunt, whom *Blackwood's* once described as "the most irresistible knight-errant erotic extant" (12 [December 1822], 775): "The extreme moral depravity of the Cockney School is another thing which is ever thrusting itself upon the public attention ... [Hunt's] poetry resembles that of a man who has kept company with kept-mistresses" (*Blackwood's* 2 [October 1817], 40); Hunt's "politics were debased by a noxious and disgusting mixture of libertinism and jacobinism" (*Gazette* 4 [25 May 1822], 49); Hunt was affected with "a most depraved taste" (*Déjeuné, or Companion for the Breakfast Table*, 27 October 1820, p. 47); another attacks "the nauseous overflowings of Mr. Leigh Hunt's perverted imagination" (*Honeycomb* 5 [15 July 1820], 36). Keats is a particular recipient of the second attack, as Marjorie Levinson has shown;[16] for example, she quotes the claim by *Blackwood's* that Keats "outhunted Hunt in a species of emasculated pruriency, that ... looks as if it were the product of some imaginative Eunuch's muse within the melancholy inspiration of the Haram" (18 [January 1826], 26). Levinson works from such comments on the sexual quality of Keats's poetry to develop her astonishing account of the implicit difficulties Keats faced in social and sexual self-fashioning, but I am more interested in the way these attacks point to an explicit erotic ideology that Keats espouses in conjunction with Hunt, Shelley, and others in the group. While the Cockney School attacks seek to make sex into a private problem for Keats, it was of course a public issue open to varying ideological constructions; and the vision of sexuality offered by the Hunt circle – in poems ranging from Hunt's *Story of Rimini* to Keats's *Endymion*, Shelley's *Epipsychidion*, and Horace Smith's *Amarynthus, the Nympholept* – was seen as dangerous by *Blackwood's* and its ideological companions.

Levinson connects the attack on Keats's "masturbatory exhibitionism" (an assault also made by the aristocratic Byron in his epistolary comments on Keats) with the class-based insults directed by *Blackwood's* towards both Keats and Hunt; McGann too reminds us of the class significance encoded in the word cockney and its use by *Blackwood's* and others to suggest that those in the lower classes should not be suffered to write poetry.[17] While Gareth Stedman Jones, in an important survey of successive constructions of the cockney from the eighteenth century onwards, reminds us that in the early nineteenth century the category of the "cockney" was formulated to emphasize "a difference not between middle and lower, let alone working, class, but between the citizen and the courtier, the plebeian and the patrician, the vulgar and the genteel,"[18] we can locate in these attacks an attempt to isolate the Hunt circle as an other in terms of status, rank, and cultural literacy. We have already seen the reference to Hunt's "plebeian" background; and in the attack on Keats there are the infamous lines on the impact of the success of Burns and Baillie which "has had the melancholy effect of turning the heads of we know not how many farm-servants and unmarried ladies; our very footmen compose tragedies, and there is scarcely a superannuated governess in the island that does not leave a roll of lyrics behind her in her band-box" (*Blackwood's* 3 [August 1818], 319). As one sees particularly in reviewers' attempts to detach Shelley and Byron, the aristocrats in the group, from the rest of the circle, there is behind the *Blackwood's* assaults a premise that poetry is best left to gentlemen. They are disturbed by what appears to them as a democratization of literature. The attacks are again reactionary, for their fear seems to be generated by what they see as the group's considerable success in coming together across social rank and despite class tensions (discussed in the next chapter), in capturing an audience (there are constant admissions that Hunt has a following), and in defining contemporary literature.

Jones suggests that various constructions of the cockney reflect "cultural and aesthetic notions of inclusion and exclusion" (p. 279), with *Blackwood's* in particular using the term for the purposes of both aesthetic and political expulsion: cockneys as the "vulgar spoke 'cant' because they thought 'cant' and they thought 'cant,' not least because they possessed no yardstick of comparison [outside of London life]. They were hence incapable of art and not fit members of the political nation" (p. 284). The Cockney style was a sign for both aesthetic and political inadequacy. McGann, too, links issues of class or rank to questions of style (as does Levinson in a different way), but he shows us how the Cockney School designation points to something admirable about the style of a Keats. He quotes from a review of Keats's 1817 volume found in the *Edinburgh [Scots] Magazine* (2nd ser., 1 [October 1817], 254–57), which identifies Keats as "a particular friend of Messers Hunt, the editors of the Examiner, and of Mr Hazlitt" and describes Hunt's and Keats's style as "vivacious, smart, witty, changeful, sparkling, and learned." As McGann points out, where we find the early Keats to be "self-indulgent, mawkish," early reviewers found him and his school to be mannered, "too full of conceits and sparkling points."[19]

We find similar comments running throughout the commentary on the Hunt circle. The *Monthly Review* (2nd ser., 92 [July 1820], 306) again tackles Keats: "Mr. Keats is a very bold author," marked by "peculiarities both of thought and manner" learned as "a disciple in a school in which these peculiarities are virtues: but the praises of this small *coterie* will hardly compensate for the disapprobation of the rest of the literary world." In defending Keats's 1820 volume, the *London Magazine* (2 [September 1820], 315–21) still complains of the "frequent obscurity and confusion of his language" (and, we should note, this is said of the odes, "Lamia," "Isabella," and so on and not, say, *Endymion*) and asserts that "We cannot help applying the word *insolent*, in a literary sense, to some instances of his neglectfulness, to the random swagger of occasional expressions, to the bravado style of many of his sentiments." The other *London Magazine*, published by Gold and Northhouse, attacked Shelley's *The Cenci* for being written in the "new-fangled style of poetry, facetiously yclept the Cockney School," marked by "an inordinate share of affectation and conceit" along with "a prodigious quantity of assurance" and "a contempt for all institutions, moral and divine" (1 [April 1820], 401), as we see stylistic issues again sliding into ideological ones.

These reviews correctly identify the Cockney style as both smart and abrasive (I am tempted to call it, using in good Huntian style one of our contemporary slang expressions, "smart-ass poetry"). There is something "bold" and assured about this poetry, something challenging and thus potentially "insolent," even something arrogantly annoying in its contempt for commonly held notions. The Cockney style is part of the assault, analyzed by Olivia Smith, upon a class-based notion of what constitutes "proper" or "pure" language over against the "vulgarity" of the working and even merchant classes;[20] the Hunt circle asserts that Cockney "vulgarity" can ascend to the same heights as traditional, "correct" poetry. The Cockney style is witty, allusive, intelligent, and it also possesses an urban and at its best urbane arrogance. With its diction shifts, its "new-fangled" feel, its odd juxtapositions, it was an attempt to capture the pulse of modern city life.

It is important always to stress the urban nature of the Cockney School, for it was a necessary if not sufficient cause for this appellation that the poets around Hunt were identified, from the first Cockney School piece on, as being London – as opposed to Lake District – poets. The importance of the link between Hunt's circle and London can be seen in the fact that it is repeated even in less contentious formulations, as when the writers around Hunt are referred to as the "metropolitan poets" (see, for example, "Portraits of the Metropolitan Poets, No. I: Leigh Hunt," *Honeycomb* 5 [15 July 1820], 33–37; also in *Imperial Magazine* 3 [November 1821], 969–76, and 3 [December 1821], 1068–73); or when Byron, who has complicated relations with the group, refers to the "Suburban School" (letter to John Murray, 7 August 1821, *L&J*, VIII: 172);[21] or when the *Imperial Magazine* talks of Hunt, Keats, and Barry Cornwall as "Cit poets" (3 [August 1821], 696); or when the *Monthly Magazine* (50 [August 1820], 65) comments in a review of Hunt's *Amyntas* on the "limited but sparkling genius of our modern metropolitan poets," a group that is seen to include Hunt, Keats, and Barry Cornwall.

Hunt would try to turn the tables on his attackers when, in a review of Shelley's *Rosalind and Helen*, he contrasts Shelley's poem with Wordsworth's *Peter Bell*, which Hunt had reviewed in the preceding issue of the *Examiner*, finding "The Poet of the Lakes" entangled in "his egotism and 'saving knowledge'," which leads him to "plant himself by the side of the oldest tyrannies and slaveries"; Shelley, on the other hand, is "our Cosmopolite-Poet [who] would evidently die with pleasure to all personal identity, could he but see his fellow-creatures reasonable and happy" (*Examiner* [9 May 1819], 302).[22] The contrast is not between the poet of "nature" and the city writer but between parochial prejudice and an urbane vision. The sense that an urban and cosmopolitan outlook is preferable to the egotistical provincialism of the Lake Poets is not unlike Byron's argument in his then unpublished dedication to *Don Juan* where he criticizes the narrowness of the Lake Poets, who "by dint of long seclusion / From better company have kept your own / At Keswick, and through still continued fusion / Of one another's minds at last have grown / To deem as a most logical conclusion, / That Poesy has wreaths for you alone; / There is a narrowness in such a notion, / Which makes me wish you'd change your lakes for ocean" (ll. 33–40). It is important that both Hunt and his ideological enemies define the poetry of the circle against that of the Lake School; for whatever poetic debts Hunt or Keats or Shelley owed to Wordsworth, Coleridge, and Southey, there is no doubt that they were engaged on opposite sides of a series of key cultural battles, with supporters of the Lake Poets seeing them as offering a Burkean embrace of nature as an anchor for conservative politics and with the Hunt circle seeing urban life as the ground for a cosmopolitan urbanity and liberalism.

The contrast between the Hunt circle and the Lake Poets was most often used to complain that the Cockneys, as urban poets, had no sense of nature.[23] *Blackwood's* began this line of attack: "Mr. Hunt is altogether unacquainted with the face of nature in her magnificent scenes; he has never seen any mountain higher than Highgate-hill, nor reclined by any stream more pastoral than the Serpentine River. But he is determined to be a poet eminently rural" (2 [October 1817], 39). We find the same complaints made elsewhere: "What a plague had the poets of Cockney to do with nature; the very air they breathe is artificial, and the circumstance of dwelling in a city presupposes a relinquishment of all rural notions and perceptions. Have they not Covent Garden market? What would they do with Arcadia?" (*Gazette of Fashion, and Magazine of Literature, the Fine Arts, and Belles Lettres* 5 [1 June 1822], 65); again, the *Literary Journal* (20 March 1819, p. 192) offered a parodic "Pleasant Walks; A Cockney Pastoral, *In the manner of Leigh Hunt, Esq.*" by "Beppo," where Hunt and Keats seek a "heath – / A lovely one – (and not / One like Hampstead's up-and-down pathy spot)" where they can find air able to dispel "From off our lungs the city's filthy soot, / And smoke to boot." What is interesting about such criticisms is that they accept a kind of simple-minded, vaguely Wordsworthian attempt to redefine pastoral poetry as a form of natural speaking about immediate nature, ignoring the fact that – from Theocritus in Alexandria to Virgil in Rome and Spenser in London – the traditional pastoral had always been an urban poetry. The Cockneys actually did write a great deal of pastoral poetry – that is, poetry written by urban poets about natural settings – from Shelley's *Rosalind and Helen, a Modern Eclogue* to Horace Smith's *Amaryn- thus, the Nympholept: A Pastoral Drama.* As Stuart Curran suggests, there is in the Cockney attacks "an implicit assumption that the pastoral genre is no more than a fantasy spun by city dwellers – Cockney poets."[24] *Blackwood's* and its comrades – not always admirers of Wordsworth – use the Lake School to attack the Cockney pastorals for being artificial, for being a suburban fantasy of Hampstead rather than an accurate por- trayal of the "real" nature found in the Lake District. While their complaints connect to a traditional sense of the Cockney as a Londoner who knows only the environs of the city, what truly bothers them is that the Hunt circle uses the pastoral as a means for criticizing their society – seen as dedicated to war and money-getting and prone to superstition and despondency – and for imagining a utopian alternative of freedom and love. *Blackwood's* must refute this reformist version of pastoral.

Thus, behind all of the various features of the Cockney School assault is the basic fact that *Blackwood's* and the other conservative reviews

disliked Hunt's politics and therefore suspected anyone who was associated with him. It is always important to remember – against continuing claims that "*Blackwood's* strictures were not politically motivated but
derived from literary tastes and social class prejudices"[25] – that the
Cockney School attacks were ideological and that one major bond
between poets as different as Hunt, Shelley, Keats, and Byron was that
of political (over class) allegiance. Or, rather, we should resist, with
Hunt, the attempt to divide the political from the circle's social, cultural,
and literary concerns. No one then doubted the importance of politics to
poetry. For example, Byron's one-time doctor, Polidori, in his volume
Ximenes finds poetry allying itself to power: "There was a time, when
poetry, contented in the sylvan shade, sought but to please. – Now, since
even Lords have become desirous of wreathing the bay around their
coronet, poetry has dared more – it has crouched into a footstool for
ambition to tread upon while aiming at power."[26] Hazlitt's famous
Examiner review (15 December 1816) of a production of *Coriolanus* may go
the furthest in linking poetry and power, but there was the general
assumption that there was a link between poetic vision and political
debate. As the quotation from the *London Magazine* that opens this
section suggests, poetry was judged on political grounds; put simply,
one's reception was dependent upon one's views of the government of
Castlereagh, Sidmouth, and Eldon. Hunt's critique of the *Quarterly
Review*'s attacks notes that the entire group's work has been read as
political pronouncements:

They dare not say a word till they know a man's connexions and opinions. If his
politics are not of the true cast, they cannot discover his poetry. If his faith is not
orthodox, how can he have any wit in him? ... I believe that the Quarterly
Reviewers have never said a word, good or bad, about Mr. Barry Cornwall ...
It is enough for Mr. Gifford that he is praised by the *Edinburgh Review* and the
Examiner. The same critic endeavoured to crush the young and exuberant
genius of Mr. Keats, for no other reason than his expressing a different view of
politics, and being first mentioned by that newspaper. Mr. Hazlitt, a man of
greater powers of thinking than all the Quarterly Reviewers put together, they
affect to consider next kin to a fool ... [To them] Mr. Hazlitt was a mere dealer
in slang, and Mr. Shelley a mere dealer in obscurity and nonsense. (*Examiner*, 9
June 1822, p. 356)

Faced with his period's insistence on the ideological valence of cultural acts, Hunt made a virtue of necessity. As he wrote in the first issue
of the *Reflector* ([1811], 5), "Politics, in times like these, should naturally
take the lead in periodical discussion, because they have an importance

almost unexampled in history, and because *they are now, in their turn, exhibiting their reaction upon literature, as literature in the preceding age exhibited its action upon them.*" In the *Examiner* (24 March 1811), commenting on the open chancellorship at Cambridge, Hunt notes that those who deny the "connection between politics and literature" either reduce politics to "their common-place light of news and party-struggles" or have been deceived by the "utter neglect with which the English Ministers have treated" the arts; he contends that "no doubt" of such a connection "was ever entertained on the subject by men of enlarged minds" (p. 177). For Hunt, politics is less about the daily struggle for party control of the government (the *Examiner*, with its motto "Party is the madness of many for the gain of a few," distances itself from both Whig and Tory) than it is about the total, complex set of relations between people that includes, among many other things, religion, the organization of sexuality, and culture. He sought an integrated vision of life that brought together the political, the social, the cultural, as when he argued in the preface to the first issue of the *Liberal* for a link between the "liberalities in the shape of Poetry, Essays, Tales, Translations" and liberal, even radical political opinion.

Of course, from Cobbett's claim in the *Political Register* (28 [1815], 196) that Hunt "kissed the rod with the most filial weakness" after his imprisonment, to Kevin Gilmartin's recent argument in his excellent *Print Politics* that Hunt by 1830 represented "the end of radical opposition" in the press,[27] Hunt's critics have found him at some point failing to match radical credentials with Wooler or Carlile or Cobbett himself. While it is true that by the passage of the Reform Bill in 1832 Hunt believed many of his political battles won, and while it is the case that he wrote to and for an urban intelligentsia rather than for a plebeian public sphere, I find no wavering in Hunt's political stand during the years that his circle was active, that is roughly between 1816 and 1822. If anything, Hunt was further radicalized by moments such as Peterloo (when he supported mass meetings and defended Richard Carlile) and by his involvement with Shelley and Byron in the *Liberal*. Gilmartin skillfully analyzes the tensions in Hunt's positions – between opposition to governmental power and his belief in a reformed government, between his hatred for "money-getting" and his defense of a kind of middle-class professionalism, between his principle of independent opposition and his need to connect with a political community, and, most important, between his desire to write straightforwardly and honestly about politics and his penchant for a mannered, allusive literary style. For Gilmartin,

Hunt, caught in these tensions, descends into an apologist for the middle class, for its political reforms, its economic gains, its literary taste. For me, Hunt, during the years between Waterloo and the deaths of Keats and Shelley, aspires to a resolution of these tensions through the group itself, as a site where the independent, detached examiner finds a community, where his mannered style could speak across class lines as a "Cockney" poetics that could still engage the aristocratic Shelley, where the circle itself – with its embrace of liberty, sociality, sexuality – could model a utopian republicanism. While it is somewhat easy now to laugh at Hunt's supposedly shabby genteel dilettantism and his suburban radicalism, at the time the Hunt circle was perceived as a threatening political force. *Blackwood's* was appalled by the Hunt circle's views on political reform, its attitude towards religion, its handling of sexuality, and its assault on traditional literary style and the hierarchy of genres. These linked issues will be explored, with regard to the poetry produced by the group, elsewhere in this book; here, though, it will be useful briefly to rehearse these attacks on the group in order to see that they do in fact point to important features of the circle's vision.

The most visible issue of the day was reform of Parliament, and Hunt's circle and the *Examiner* made clear their commitment; as Hunt said as late as his often tempered *Autobiography*, the *Examiner* "began with being of no party; but Reform soon gave it one" (p. 214). While the journal is now often found to be a bit too moderate, it was a powerful voice for the left at the time; as Edmund Blunden says of John Hunt, who ran the *Examiner*, he "was a reformist no less courageous though less conspicuous than Cobbett,"[28] and Shelley writing to Peacock on 24 August 1819 – when the *Examiner* was supposedly more timid, less radical – says, "The Examiners I receive. – Hunt as a political writer pleases me more & more" (*SL*, II: 115). Attacking corruption in the army, flogging in the navy, Methodism, the Regent, and anything else that smacked of oppression, superstition, and canting pretension, the *Examiner* was repeatedly prosecuted by the government, eventually leading of course to the imprisonment of the Hunts. *Blackwood's* recognized its ideological enemy in saying of Hunt's politics that it was "a crude, vague, ineffectual, and sour Jacobinism" (2 [October 1817], 39).

One popular way of questioning Hunt's politics was to link him with his namesake, Henry "Orator" Hunt of Bristol, as in a piece in the "Christopher North" series, where "Hampstead Hunt" is decried as a Cockney poet while "Bristol Hunt" is attacked as a Cockney politician (*Blackwood's* 5 [September 1819], 640). The attack on Keats notes that

"Keats belongs to the Cockney School of Politics, as well as the Cockney School of Poetry" (*Blackwood's* 3 [August 1818], 524). When Keats published his second volume, *Endymion* too was found to be "jacobinical" by the *British Critic* (N.S. 9 [June 1818], 652).[29] Gold's *London Magazine* (1 [April 1820], 401–7) complains that "Among the professors of the cockney school, Mr. Percy Bysshe Shelly is one of the most conspicuous" in that he has "contempt for all institutions, moral and divine, with secret yearnings for aught that is degrading to human nature, or revolting to decency."

Equally upsetting to their ideological opponents was the Hunt circle's treatment of religion and their use of mythological materials. *Blackwood's* again sounded the charge, attacking Hunt's religious position as "a poor tame dilution of the blasphemies of the *Encyclopaedie*" (2 [October 1817], 39). The *Imperial Magazine* (4 [1822], 1139–40) was appalled by the "irreligion" of Byron, Hunt, and Shelley's *Liberal*: "The Liberal is a publication which assumes this name, because its benevolence is extended to infidelity – to licentiousness of manners – to the open ridicule of what is awful and sacred – and to the destruction of moral principle." I will discuss at greater length in chapter 5 and throughout the book the use to which these writers put classical materials, but we need to see how ideologically charged their use of Greco-Roman myth was. The sexual message of Hunt's school of poetry, already mentioned, was immediately connected with the group's attitudes towards religion and its use of pagan myth. The *Quarterly Review* (18 [January 1818], 327), in attacking Hunt's *Foliage* and in particular his sonnet "On the Degrading Notions of Deity," addressed to Shelley, fulminated against the effort by "many of those with whom [Hunt] has recorded his sympathy and agreement in this volume" to bring about a "systematic revival of Epicureanism . . . Lucretius is the philosopher whom these men profess most to admire; and their leading tenet is, that the enjoyment of the pleasures of intellect and sense is not to be considered as the permitted, and regulated use of God's blessings, but the great object, and duty of life." The *Eclectic Review* (2nd ser., 10 [November 1818], 484–93) was also troubled by what it saw as Hunt's "creed of the heathen and the morals of the libertine" (p. 485). Again, it calls "childish" the mythological poems of the circle in its review (2nd ser., 14 [September 1820], 158–71) of Keats's 1820 volume: 'What better name can we bestow on the nonsense that Mr. Keats, and Mr. Leigh Hunt, and Mr. Percy Bysshe Shelley, and some of the poets about town, have been talking of 'the beautiful mythology of Greece'? To some persons . . . that mythology comes recommended chiefly by its grossness – its alliance to the sensitive pleasures which belong to the animal" (p. 169). Such critics were alive, as we have once again become, to the polemical, ideological charge of the myths used by the second-generation poets. The attacks do not so much reveal flaws in the poetry of a Keats or a Hunt as they uncover arenas of ideological conflict. This was not primarily a debate over aesthetics; it was a struggle over the definition of post-Napoleonic culture and society.

The problem is that the Cockney School attacks were extremely successful – then and now. They infuriated Hunt, who demanded in the pages of the *Examiner* that Z. identify himself; the assault worried Byron's London handlers concerning his links with Hunt; and the criticism hurt Keats, if not to the extent imagined by Shelley.[30] While I have focused on *Blackwood's*, the group also warred with the *Quarterly Review* – Hazlitt's *A Letter to William Gifford, Esq.* (1819) and Hunt's *Ultra-Crepidarius* (1823) were skirmishes in that battle – and many journals followed the lead of these powerful conservative reviews. The *New Monthly Magazine* (10 [September 1818], 162–63) not only borrowed from *Blackwood's* the designation of the group as the Cockney School but quoted at length from Z.'s article. Gold's *London Magazine* (2 [August 1820], 160) finds that the Keats of the 1820 volume "belongs to the Cockney School of Poetry – a school, we suppose, so denominated, from that fact of its writers having been educated in the city, and taking their pictures of rural life from its immediate environs." The *Literary Gazette* (4 [April 1818], 210), in reviling Hunt's *Foliage*, attacks the idea of any poetic school, "whether given to the watery, cockney, be-natural, or sentimental Bards of these times." Josiah Conder, reviewing Hunt's *Foliage* in the *Eclectic Review* (2nd ser. 10 [November 1818], 492), adopts the term cockneyism. The *Literary Register* (19 [July 1823], 40) refers to Hazlitt as the "Proteus of cockneyism." *John Bull* (98 [27 October 1822], 781) extends the attack to Hunt and Byron's *Liberal*, which is called an "Italianized Cockney Magazine" (which, of course, was true, for the *Liberal* published work by many members of the circle – Hunt, the Shelleys, Byron, Hazlitt, Horace Smith, Charles Armitage Brown, and Thomas Jefferson Hogg).[31] Such attacks were not, of course, simply a matter of literary rivalry or contention. They were part of a broader conservative attack on liberal and radical writers that led to the imprisonment of the Hunts, Hone, and Wooler, among others. Hunt was never in any doubt about the government's treatment of him. Writing to Henry L. Hunt from Italy, about sending the *Liberal* through the post "like a newspaper," he says, "As to their opening it, that they will always do; & doubtless they also open our letters. No matter. Our doings, literary & political, have always been open enough already, not to fear any scrutiny."[32]

The continuing impact of the *Blackwood's* articles is seen, I believe, in the struggle of Keats scholars in particular to distance their poet from the "King of the Cockneys." It has become so important to prove that Keats developed, both personally and poetically, away from Hunt that we forget that he returned to live with the Hunts in the summer of 1820 when he was so ill, that at this time Keats and Hunt worked together on the *Indicator* and that Hunt issued his translation of *Amyntas* with its dedication to Keats; we, unlike Keats's contemporaries, have been unable to see the Cockney features that persisted into the 1820 volume. While it has been less of an issue in Shelley and Byron criticism to separate them from Hunt, for no one has ever accused them of being Hunt's "élève," it has been the case that Shelley's friendship with Hunt, perhaps the most important in his life, has not often enough been seen as having a profound impact on his poetry or his thought; and Byron has been seen as condescending nobly when dealing with the plebeian poet in terms that would surely please the *Blackwood's* hatchetmen. However, from Byron's becoming inspired to write his first volume of poetry after reading Hunt's *Juvenalia* to his visit to Hunt in prison until his departure for Greece, from Shelley's first letter to Hunt as editor of the *Examiner* until his death, these two poets were also deeply tied to Hunt. Shelley, like Keats, turned before he died to Hunt, bringing him to Italy to edit the *Liberal*. And Byron, who clearly came to dislike Hunt,[33] tried to make the *Liberal* work and turned from his publisher of long standing, John Murray, to have Hunt's brother publish the final cantos of *Don Juan*.

The strategy of isolating Hunt was already used by *Blackwood's* and other reviews, which lamented Byron's links to Hunt, opined that Shelley as an aristocrat must surely have more genius than his Cockney connections, and even suggested that Keats might improve if he divorced himself from Hunt.[34] It was, in fact, in the changing treatment of Keats by contemporary conservatives that the pattern of the future reception history of these poets and their group was set. As Keats, then Shelley, then Byron died, *Blackwood's* and other reviews had to begin moderating their venom. They also had to respond to Shelley's *Adonais*, which I will argue in the final chapter celebrates in poetry his failed attempt to recreate at Pisa the London Hunt circle, and to Hunt's *Lord Byron and Some of His Contemporaries* (1828), also an attempt to view the second-generation romantics collectively. As G. M. Matthews argues in reviewing the treatment of Keats by *Blackwood's*, "In 1828 it was wise to begin changing the line a little, and Haydon had recently supplied a new one. 'That poor youth' had been ruined, not by his enemies, but by his friends."[35] Matthews quotes John Wilson from his response to Hunt's memoir: "But we killed Keates. There again you – lie. Hunt, Hazlitt, and the godless gang, slavered him to death. Bitterly did he confess that, in his last days, in language stronger than we wish to use" (*Blackwood's* 25 [September 1829], 525). In response to Shelley's myth that Keats was killed by the conservative reviewers, *Blackwood's*, drawing upon an unpublished essay by Haydon attacking Hunt, created a countermyth in which Keats was undone by his friendship with Hunt. To rebut Hunt's attempt to link himself with Keats, Byron, and Shelley as members of a unified group, *Blackwood's* had to argue that Byron, Shelley, and even Keats rose above the Cockney School. The dead Keats, along with Byron and Shelley, is saved in order to continue the attack upon the living Hunt.

The denigration of the Cockney School in the service of praising individual great poets continues, but we need to see that one of the greatest creations of these writers was the group itself which in turn inspired and nurtured their writing. We still do not have an adequate sense of the importance of this group, of the Cockney School, to both the creation and the reception of what we, more neutrally, call second-generation romantic writing. One goal of this book is to retrieve the Hunt circle from the Cockney School attacks and even from the praise of the more benign critical inheritors of the *Blackwood's* essayists.

CHAPTER 2

The Hunt era

I

You will see Hunt – one of those happy souls
Which are the salt of the Earth, and without whom
This world would smell like what it is, a tomb –
Who is, what others seem – his room no doubt
Is still adorned with many a cast from Shout,
With graceful flowers tastefully placed about,
And coronals of bay from ribbons hung,
And brighter wreaths in neat disorder flung,
The gifts of the most learn'd among some dozens
Of female friends, sisters-in-law and cousins.
And there is he with his eternal puns,
Which beat the dullest brain for smiles, like duns
Thundering for money at a poet's door.
Alas, it is no use to say, "I'm poor!"
Or oft in graver mood, when he will look
Things wiser than were ever read in book,
Except in Shakespeare's wisest tenderness.–

Shelley, "Letter to Maria Gisborne," ll. 209–25

In the fall of 1816, Keats and then Shelley joined a group already gathered around Leigh Hunt. The Hunt circle can be thought of as this group of individuals, as a series of locales and linked activities comprising the true Land of Cockaigne (i.e. Hunt's cottage in Hampstead, the Novellos' home on Oxford Street near Hyde Park, Shelley's Marlowe house, the office of the *Examiner*, Hampstead Heath, the British Museum, the London theaters), and as a body of texts (i.e. Keats's 1817 *Poems*, Hunt's *Foliage*, Hazlitt and Hunt's *Round Table*, Shelley's *Adonais*). As a collection of friends, the circle was the result of the coming together of particular individuals over shared beliefs and practices. As a literary school and cultural movement, it was the response to the particular historical moment defined by the fall of Napoleon, by hopes for reform and the actuality of reaction, by Waterloo and Peterloo, by contested definitions of religion, sexuality, nation, right.

As Hunt himself had proclaimed a year before the *Blackwood's* attacks, there was a school of poets gathering around him – what Keats interestingly calls in his letter about Webb a "Party," suggesting perhaps both its social and political dimensions. Keats himself arrived in October of 1816, being introduced to Hunt by his friend and schoolmaster's son, Charles Cowden Clarke. Shelley appeared at Hunt's cottage in the Vale of Health, Hampstead, during December, seeking to renew a brief 1811 acquaintance with Hunt, most likely on the advice of Byron, with whom he and Mary had, of course, spent time during the summer just past. While we have no complete record of the meetings between the three poets and the larger circle during this period, we know that they were often together, at Hunt's cottage and elsewhere, and that there was an active exchange of ideas and poetry.[1] We can get some sense of what this convivial period at Hampstead meant to Shelley from his later letter to Peacock (24 August 1819, *SL*, II: 114), where he considers leaving Italy for England: "What are mountains trees heaths, or even the glorious & ever beautiful sky with such sunsets as I have seen at Hampstead to friends? Social enjoyment in some form or other is the alpha & omega of existence." We can get some sense of what Hunt meant to these men from Keats's response to the news from Clarke that he, Keats, would meet the editor of the *Examiner*: "'t will be an Era in my existence" (9 October 1816, *KL*, I: 113).[2]

Hunt – editor of one of the period's most important periodicals, the author of the popular and controversial *Story of Rimini*, and a political martyr for the left – occupied in the crucial years between 1815 and 1820 a unique position of cultural significance. Byron was more popular and respected, but he was in exile. Wordsworth, though his reputation was still very much in dispute during this period, was seen by knowledgeable critics as the most likely candidate for poetic "greatness," but he and his fellow Lake Poets had come to be seen, fairly or not, as establishment figures, the "Lakers in and out of place" of Byron's *Don Juan*. Other writers – Hunt's Hampstead neighbor Joanna Baillie, for example, or Thomas Campbell or Samuel Rogers – had perhaps sold more volumes than Hunt and were clearly more acceptable to establishment reviewers, but their very respectability points to their eschewal of the kind of wide-ranging cultural critique that distinguishes Hunt and his group. When Keats entered into the London literary world and Shelley returned to it, Hunt was the leader of the literary left. He was not, perhaps, a Keats, a Hazlitt, or a Cobbett, but he combined poetical, critical, and political skills in a way no one else did.

Part of Hunt's power was social: he brought together the figures we identify as second-generation romanticism. His hospitality, genial wit, and enthusiasm for company and collective activities are testified to by all who met him. Clarke, for example, wrote of Hunt, "His manner – fascinating, animated, full of cordial amenity, and winning to a degree which I have never seen the parallel – drew me to him at once, and I fell as pronely in love with him as any girl in her teens falls in love with her first-seen Romeo" (*Recollections*, p. 16). Hazlitt, not known for warm praise, said of Hunt in *The Spirit of the Age*, "His natural gaiety and sprightliness of manner, his high animal spirits, and the *vinous* quality of his mind, produce an immediate fascination and intoxication in those who come in contact with him" (*CWH*, XI: 176). Writing to Charles Cowden Clarke and his sister, Isabella Towers, Hazlitt says that Hunt is "my most excellent friend – I like his foibles (if he has any) better than the best virtues of many others."[3] Again, Haydon, who would have his difficulties with Hunt, wrote in October 1816, "The greater part of my time has been spent in Leigh Hunt's society, who is certainly one of the most delightful companions on Earth – full of Poetry & wit & amiable humour. We argue always with full hearts on every thing but Religion & Buonaparte, and we resolved after a little never to talk of them" (*Diary*, II: 62). Shelley addressed Hunt in letters as "My dearest friend," and his dedication to *The Cenci*, addressed to "MY DEAR FRIEND," praises Hunt as the most "gentle, honourable, innocent, and brave" person he knows and as a man in "patient and irreconcilable enmity with domestic and political tyranny" (*Shelley's Poetry and Prose*, pp. 237–38). While we tend to admire the solitary genius or at least the genius working in solitude and to find something dilettantish about convivial culture, the Cockney School of second-generation romantics would never have been formed without Hunt's ability to bring very different people together.

In recalling Hunt's geniality, we should also remember the courage of a man who was willing to go to jail for his beliefs. While much is made of his financial needs, as he borrowed from everyone he could, his friends commented on his poetic generosity. Procter puts it this way: "He was essentially a gentleman in conduct, in demeanour, in manner, in his consideration for others – indeed, in all things that constitute the material of a gentleman. He was very good tempered; thoroughly easy tempered. He saw hosts of writers, of less ability than himself, outstripping him on the road to future success, yet I never heard from him a

word that could be construed into jealousy or envy; not even a mur-
mur."[4] We also need to recognize that he was often seen by his friends as
a source of comfort and strength. Byron noted of Hunt's support during
his struggles with his wife, "When party feeling ran highest against me,
Hunt was the only editor of a paper, the only literary man, who dared
say a word in my justification . . . I shall always be grateful to him for the
part he took on that occasion."[5] Shelley, in the midst of his troubles after
Harriet Shelley's suicide, wrote to Mary, "Leigh Hunt has been with me
all day & his delicate & tender attentions to me, his kind speeches of you,
have sustained me against the weight of the horror of this event" (16
December 1816, *SL*, 1: 520); to Byron, Shelley wrote of Hunt as a "most
friendly, and excellent man" who was willing "to stand by me as yet by
his counsel, and by his personal attentions to me" (17 January 1817, *SL*, 1:
530). When Keats was seriously ill in 1820, it was to Hunt's home that he
returned. Hunt was both a man of enormous conviviality and someone
his friends depended upon; for all his denigration as a shabby genteel
poseur or a Skimpole, he was the emotional center of the group and an
emotional support for Shelley, Keats, and Byron.

Hunt was also a much stronger cultural figure than we now allow; as
Donald Reiman has argued, "Leigh Hunt was one of the dozen most
important British writers of the Romantic period."[6] While Hunt has
been securely relegated to his status as a second-rate poet, at the time he
would often lead the way in the attempts of the second generation of
romantic poets to tap alternative cultural resources. His *Story of Rimini*,
with its assault upon established poetic convention in the stronghold of
the heroic couplet, not only pushed further Wordsworth's innovations
in prosody but also paved the way for *Endymion* and *Epipsychidion*. *Rimini*
also stands behind the Italianate poems of John Hamilton Reynolds,
Keats, and Barry Cornwall, just as Hunt's interest in reworking Dante
precedes that of Shelley, Keats, and Byron. Again, he began work on a
set of mythological poems in the fall of 1816 that scout out ground more
thoroughly explored by Keats and Shelley. As I hope to show in chapter
4, there would not have been a *Prometheus Unbound* without the model of
Hunt's *Descent of Liberty*. Hunt in many ways defines the modes of
second-generation romanticism that are then developed by Keats and
Shelley in ways we find more interesting. His contemporaries certainly
recognized their links to him, as can be seen in the dedications to Hunt
by Shelley (*The Cenci*), Keats (*Poems*), "Arthur Brooke" (*Elegy on the Death
of Shelley*), and Thomas Barnes (*Parliamentary Portraits*).

No one has ever doubted the critical acumen of Hunt, who very early on recognized the greatness of Keats, Shelley, Tennyson, and Dickens. His critical writings were impressive. William Archer calls him "the first English dramatic critic." George Saintsbury praises him for "having transformed the eighteenth century magazine." Kenneth Neill Cameron argues that the "ancestry of the magazine article of today can be traced more readily to Hunt than to any other English writer; and the intellectual periodical of today stems from *The Examiner*."[7] E. P. Thompson reminds us that the "*Examiner* served with brilliance as the weekly of the Radical intelligentsia."[8] Charles Cowden Clarke and his father are representatives of that intelligentsia in their "revelling in the liberty-loving, liberty-advocating, liberty-eloquent articles of the young editor" of the *Examiner* (*Recollections*, p. 16). Donald Reiman enumerates the many journalists of the nineteenth century who owed a direct debt to Hunt: Thomas Barnes at the *Times*, John Chalk Claris at the *Kent Herald*, Laman Blanchard, W. J. Fox, S. C. Hall, and George Henry Lewes, among others;[9] he could have also included the radical Scottish journalist William Tait, who dedicated the first issue of *Tait's Edinburgh Magazine* to Hunt.

The *Examiner*, while lacking the cultural authority of the *Edinburgh Review* (though, in retrospect, having in Hazlitt and Hunt two of the most powerful critical voices of the day), the vicious panache of *Blackwood's* (though certainly able to give as well as take in the battles with its ideological enemies), or the truly radical credentials of the *Black Dwarf* or the *Republican* (though *Blackwood's* 3 [July 1818], 453, found Hunt to be a truly radical "firebrand" stirring up the "vilest passions of [the] mob"), is to my mind the best weekly journal of its day. It was also one of the most popular, having in 1812, for example, higher sales than any of its competitors. Whether pursuing government oppression, religious prejudice, and the "spirit of money-getting," offering dramatic reviews by Hunt and Hazlitt, providing commentary on the visual arts by Robert Hunt and Haydon,[10] or publishing poems by Hunt, Keats, Shelley, Byron, Wordsworth, Lamb, Reynolds, and Smith, the *Examiner* was consistently lively and interesting and continually committed to its program of "Reform in Parliament, liberality of opinion in general (especially freedom from superstition), and a fusion of literary taste into all subjects whatsoever" (*Autobiography*, p. 214). While some have found the *Examiner* rather tame – particularly after the imprisonment of the Hunt brothers – Hunt himself notes that the weekly was "charged with Bonapartism, with republicanism, with disaffection to Church and State, with conspiracy at the tables of Burdett and Cobbett" (*Autobiogra-*

phy, p. 215); in its pages Hunt took on such issues as the national debt, the continuing wars in India, Catholic Emancipation, the struggle for freedom in the Americas, the rights of the poor, child labor, the slave trade, the freedom of the press, reform of military discipline, and prison conditions. It is also true that the Hunts would continue to challenge the government in print, even when, as in their defense in 1819 of Richard Carlile, it threatened the financial survival of the *Examiner* itself or when, as in 1821, the *Examiner*'s attacks on George IV and Castlereagh during the Queen Caroline affair brought about a second prison sentence for John Hunt, convicted of political libel.

One indication of the power of the *Examiner* is the strong reactions it elicited. Conservatives hated Hunt: Southey, for example, saw Hunt as another Voltaire or Rousseau making way for Henry Hunt as the French thinkers had made way for Marat and Hébert; he recommended to Lord Lonsdale, Wordsworth's patron, that Cobbett and Hunt be transported.[11] The left read Hunt avidly, and this readership included, not surprisingly, his poetic friends. Keats first came to admire Hunt largely through his reading of the *Examiner*, to which he was introduced by Clarke while he was still at school at Enfield. His letters make it clear that he continued to be a regular reader of the *Examiner*, which he arranges to have sent to him when out of London and which he also regularly sends to his brothers (e.g. *KL*, I: 137ff., 199; II: 11, 213). Shelley was also an ardent reader of the *Examiner*; settling in Italy, he announces to Peacock, "I have determined to take the Examiner here" (5 June 1818, *SL* II: 218). Byron read the *Examiner* at least during his friendship with Hunt prior to leaving England (e.g. letter to Hunt, 4–6 November 1815?, *L&J*, IV: 332). While literary critics have tended to prefer Hunt's other ventures – the *Indicator* and the collaborative effort of the *Liberal* – the *Examiner* was the voice of the second generation of romantics, the organ of the Cockney School.

Hunt's journals and his social gatherings brought together an impressive range of talents. At Hunt's home in the Vale of Health, Keats and Shelley would have found in the fall of 1816 an active circle already gathered. Hazlitt, Hunt's fellow at the Round Table, was there, as was Robert Benjamin Haydon, the painter who would come to love Keats but not Shelley. The musician Vincent Novello was a key member of the group who at his own home supplied Italian music to an audience that ranged from Lamb and Hunt to less well-known members of the circle such as John Gattie and Henry Robertson – musical friends (Robertson wrote opera reviews for the *Examiner*) celebrated in a Hunt sonnet – not to mention John Nyren, a famed cricket player.

Novello's wife, Mary Sabillia Novello, was one of a number of remarkable women in a group that included Mary Shelley, Mary Lamb, Claire Clairmont, and Mary Novello Clarke. Charles Cowden Clarke celebrates his mother-in-law as a bright, accomplished woman, who he feels should be as well known for her conversation full of "spirit and brilliancy" as for her famous meat pie and wassail bowl (*Recollections*, p. 25). She suggested the title of the *Indicator* to Hunt, supplied a paper to that journal entitled "Holiday Children" (signed "An Old Boy"), and later wrote for Hunt's *Tatler*, offering among other pieces an unfinished novel in letters. Hunt's friend Horace Twiss proclaimed Mary Sabillia Novello "as the next among women to Mary Wollstonecraft, with whom he was notedly and avowedly 'deeply smitten'" (*Recollections*, p. 25). There was also Elizabeth Kent, Marianne Hunt's sister, as described by Thorton Hunt: "though coming with little better than a dame-school education, she had so much natural faculty for study as to master two languages, a wide range of history, fiction, and poetry, with a technical knowledge of woman's favourite science, botany; which she illustrated from the library by really graceful writing"; her works include *Flora Domestica; or, The Portable Flower-Garden* (1823) and *Sylvan Sketches; or A Companion to the Park and the Shrubbery: With Illustrations from the Works of the Poets* (1825), published by Taylor and Hessey, and virtual anthologies of Cockney School verse, with passages from Hunt, Keats, Shelley, and Byron as well as Hunt's favorite Latin, Italian, and British poets.[12]

At Hunt's, the new arrivals also met Horace Smith, the financier-poet, of whom Hunt would write, "A finer nature than Horace Smith's, except in the single instance of Shelley, I never met with in man," and of whom Shelley said, "he writes poetry and pastoral dramas, and yet knows how to make money, and does make it, and is still generous" (*Autobiography*, pp. 231, 232). Hunt had come to know Smith and his brother James through Thomas Hill, dry-salter, book collector, and the proprietor of the *Monthly Mirror*, for which Hunt once wrote; in Hill's company, Hunt also met with the *Mirror*'s editor Edward Dubois, Thomas Campbell, Barron Field (a drama critic for the *Times*, a future judge, and sometime author, publishing some verse in the *Examiner* and in *First Fruits of Australian Poetry* [1819], reviewed by Lamb in the *Examiner* [16 January 1820]), Horace Twiss (nephew of Mrs. Siddons, a wit, and minor writer), the dramatist and novelist Theodore Hook, and the comic actor Charles Mathews (this is the same set that Keats mentions being introduced into by Horace Smith in his famous "negative capability" letter [21, 27 ⟨?⟩ December 1817, *KL* I: 193]). Hunt included in his circle various newspaper men – Thomas Alsager, financial writer for the *Times*, a lover of music, a member of the Surrey Institution involved in arranging for Hazlitt's lectures in 1818 and 1819, and the owner of the folio of Chapman's Homer that would later inspire Keats; Thomas Barnes, a school friend of Hunt's who contributed to the *Reflector* and the *Examiner* and later became editor of the *Times*;[13] and John Scott, editor of the *Champion*, where Reynolds and Keats would publish.

Hunt had also acquired extensive connections in political circles. Hunt was early on identified as an important voice for reform, and he was a key supporter of reform politicians and the "Philosophic" re-formers. Hunt had put the voice of the *Examiner* behind Sir Francis Burdett during his struggles with the government in 1810, even though Hunt claims he never met him (*Autobiography*, p. 215); he was also a supporter of the prison reformer Samuel Romilly. The Whig politician Henry Brougham, who was to become Hunt's lawyer, was also a friend who shared the poet's interest in Voltaire and Catullus (see *Correspondence* I: 56–68). Brougham would, of course, advise Shelley on his Chancery case in 1817, as would another literary lawyer attached to Hunt's circle, Basil Montagu, the friend of Wordsworth and Godwin, who was part of the early appreciative audience that listened to Keats's verses in manu-script. Brougham also encouraged Jeremy Bentham to seek out Hunt, and Bentham thus began a correspondence with the editor of the *Examiner*, invited Hunt to his Hermitage, and later visited him in jail. As Woodring points out, Hunt was a major popularizer of the utilitarian ideas of Bentham, held also by Brougham and by John Hunt.[14] Hunt was, however, also sympathetic to the ideas of Bentham's intellectual competitor, Robert Owen, the visionary reformer whose *New View of Society* took up where Godwin's *Enquiry concerning Political Justice* left off.[15]

Hunt also included Godwin as one of his longtime friends, and Hunt came to know many of Godwin's old radical acquaintances. While we tend to think of Godwin's relation to the younger romantics arising from his connections to the Shelleys, Hunt was friends with Godwin years before Shelley joined the circle in 1816, and, of course, Godwin had long been acquainted with Hazlitt and Lamb as well. In his *Autobiography*, Hunt tells us that he met Godwin at dinners held by Rowland Hunter, the bookseller who took over Joseph Johnson's radical salon from the 1790s: Hunt writes that he knew the "survivors of the literary party that were accustomed to dine with his [Hunter's] predecessor, Mr. Johnson. They came, as of old, on the Friday. The most regular were Fuseli and

Bonnycastle. Now and then, Godwin was present: oftener Mr. Kinnard, the magistrate, a great lover of Horace" (p. 234). Hunt and Godwin had, then, known each other for years, Godwin had visited his friend in prison, and Hunt, after meeting Keats, read to Godwin, Hazlitt, and Basil Montagu some of the then unknown John Keats's poems at a dinner party. Godwin is an important influence not just on Shelley but on many of the younger writers, including those such as Charles Wentworth Dilke, whom Keats could refer to as "a Godwin perfectibil[it]y Man" (letter to the George Keatses, 14 October 1818, *KL*, I: 397). The interest was mutual, for Godwin was clearly aware of the work of the Hunt circle, reading in 1817 Peacock, Hogg, Hunt, Keats, Hazlitt, and Byron.[16]

Hunt would also have introduced Shelley and Keats to Charles Lamb, whom Hunt had come to know when he edited the *Reflector* (1810); he had drawn on Lamb's talents as well as those of George Dyer (friend to Lamb and author of *Poems* [1792]), Thomas Barnes, Thomas Mitchell (Hunt's schoolmate who translated Aristophanes), James Scholefield (another schoolfellow, a professor of Greek, and like Mitchell later a "Quarterly Reviewer"), Octavius Gilchrist (grocer, fellow of the Society of Antiquaries, and part of the Bowles/Pope controversy), and Dr. John Aikin (friend of Priestley, Darwin, and John Howard) and his family, which included Anna Laetitia Aikin Barbauld and Lucy Aikin.[17] Charles Cowden Clarke, who brought Keats into the circle, had been one of Hunt's many visitors during his imprisonment; in fact, his guest list is part a membership roll for the Hunt circle, part a catalog of reform-minded intellectuals: Hazlitt, Tom Moore,[18] Jeremy Bentham, Byron, Thomas Alsager, Thomas Barnes, Maria Edgeworth, James Mill, Haydon, the Lambs, Barron Field, and Henry Brougham. Apparently, John Hamilton Reynolds also met Hunt while he was in prison;[19] after being introduced to Keats through Hunt, Reynolds would induct the younger poet into another circle that included James Rice and Benjamin Bailey, Charles Wentworth Dilke and Charles Armitage Brown. Thomas Love Peacock and Thomas Jefferson Hogg would also be introduced into the group when, in the spring of 1817, Shelley moved to Marlowe – where he was visited by members of the circle such as Hunt, Smith, Walter Coulson (writer, later lawyer, and friend to Hunt, Lamb, and Bentham), and Godwin. While we think of these new additions only as the friends of Shelley, after Shelley went to Italy Hunt reported that "Hogg and Peacock generally live here over Sunday ... and we pass very pleasant afternoons, talking of mythology, and the Greeks, and our old friends" (to Mary Shelley, 9 March 1819, *Correspondence*, I: 127). Hunt's circle was in fact a meeting point for a set of other literary and political connections and circles: Hunt knew everyone from William Wordsworth to William Hone.

All three of the figures who comprise canonical second-generation romanticism were allied to the Hunt circle and to Hunt himself, a fact that has been obscured by an emphasis upon these writers as unique geniuses as well as by accounts of their lives that finally overstress the real strains that at times existed between them. While Hunt and Byron or Shelley and Keats seem now to be unlikely companions, the Hunt circle provided a space within which they could come together despite differences in rank, education, or temperament. While we cannot ignore the tensions that occurred at times within the circle, the Hunt group existed in order to imagine a society that could overcome the divisions of, among others, rank or status. In recognizing the difficulties that arose between, say, Hunt and Byron, we cannot ignore their attempt to live through and beyond such problems.

By the time Keats and Shelley joined Hunt's circle, Byron was, of course, in exile, but he stood as a kind of corresponding member of the group. Byron was always present to the circle in his verse and in memory, and he was increasingly linked to the Cockney School in conservative attacks;[20] if Shelley's plans for the *Liberal* had come to full fruition, Byron would have become a complete member of the circle now transported to Pisa. He had long been friends with Hunt – the "wit in the dungeon" – and Byron, of course, formed an even deeper attachment to Mary and Percy Shelley beginning in the summer of 1816. Charles Robinson has given us our best account of the complex cross-influences in Byron and Shelley's relationship, reminding us that "they were personally acquainted for six years, spent in excess of two hundred and fifty days together during that time, read and reacted to all of each other's major works, and exchanged fifty letters" and noting that we find direct allusions to Byron in Shelley's *Julian and Maddalo*, "Lines Written among the Euganean Hills," "The Two Spirits: An Allegory," *Epipsychidion, Adonais, Hellas*, and "Sonnet to Byron" and to Shelley in *Don Juan*.[21]

Still, before Shelley had ever met Byron, Hunt had become rather close to the noble poet. Byron journeyed to Hunt's prison and ex-changed calls with him after his release; Byron provided source material for Hunt's *Story of Rimini*, corrected the poem in manuscript, and recommended that Murray publish *Rimini*, which Hunt then dedicated to him; Byron sent Hunt a rare copy of *English Bards and Scotch Reviewers* with manuscript corrections; and Hunt was a major defender of Byron during his struggles with Lady Byron. Hunt made his admiration for Byron's verse clear – he published a significant number of Byron's poems in the *Examiner* during 1815–16 and printed his own celebration "To the Right Honourable Lord Byron, on His Departure for Italy and Greece"[22] – but we forget that Byron wrote in his journal for 1 December 1813 (*L&J*, III: 228), "Hunt is an extraordinary character... If he goes on *qualis ab incepto*, I know few men who will deserve more praise or obtain it."[23]

Byron never had such feelings about Keats, whom he never met – although it is clear that he read Keats's verse and had a strong, and largely negative, reaction to it.[24] On Keats's side, we find a persistent sense of Byron's power: there is poetry showing the influence of Byron, from the early "Sonnet to Byron" (1814) to the late "Jealousies" (1819), not to mention the fact that as a medical student Keats "used to go with his neck nearly bare à là Byron" and that along with his early enthusiasm for Spenser, "Byron was also in favor" (Henry Stephens to G. F. Matthew, March 1847, *KC*, II: 211, 209).[25] We can see the impact of Byron throughout the work of the group, for example in the poetry of Reynolds, who dedicated his oriental tale *Safie* (1814) to him.

It is another dedication to Byron – that of *The Story of Rimini* to "My Dear Byron" – which suggests both some of the strengths of the group and one of its key tensions – that of rank or, to use another vocabulary, class. Class is a slippery term to use in analyzing the group in part because, as Raymond Williams, Asa Briggs, or Harold Perkin show, the division of society into wage laborers, capitalists, and landlords was being historically enacted and conceptualized during this period; alternative formulations and social formations existed, as some would talk of rank or order and others of multiple classes (i.e. the working class*es*), or as some would pit the rich against the poor, others the "productive classes" against a privileged class, and still others the "People" against the government.[26] There are difficulties in offering a class definition of either Cockneyism or of the Hunt circle: both the negative label and the actual group blur our demarcations between classes, as *Blackwood's* attempts to denigrate a group coming from varying backgrounds by consigning all of them to a "lower" Cockney order and as the group seeks to live beyond what we would identify as class divisions.

This is not to deny the distinctions blurred in these moves. *Blackwood's* would seek to drive what we would see as a class wedge (though Z. uses different terms) between Hunt and Byron in the first of the Cockney School attacks (2 [October 1817], 38–41), where Z. allows that he is aghast at Hunt's attempt to declare himself to be the friend of Byron: "We dare say Mr Hunt has some fine dreams about the true nobility being the nobility of talent, and flatters himself, that with those who acknowledge only that sort of rank, he himself passes for being a *peer* of Byron. He is sadly mistaken. He is as completely a Plebeian in his mind as he is in his rank and station in society." While there is no indication that at the time Byron took Hunt's dedication amiss, the gap between the peer and the plebeian would widen in Italy when, after Shelley's death, the two men found not only that they could not work together but that their styles of life were opposed. Hunt would later seek his revenge upon what he saw as Byron's slights in his unflattering portrait of the aristocratic poet in *Lord Byron and Some of His Contemporaries*.[27] Hunt and his *Examiner* could claim to be above party ("Party is the madness of many for the gain of a few" was the *Examiner*'s motto), but he could not escape the differences we identify with class.

We can also find class tensions between Keats and Shelley and different ones between Shelley and Hazlitt. Keats's decision to keep his distance from Shelley so that "I might have my own unfettered scope" (letter to Benjamin Bailey, 8 October 1817, *KL*, I: 170) – which might be accounted an indication of poetic competitiveness and anxiety – is in part a sign of the already existing distance between the apothecary, on the lower edges of the middle class, who struggles to finance his desire to be a poet and the son of the baronet, who can be a poet while awaiting the opportunity to reform the world. As I will discuss in chapter 6, the tensions between them were revealed in their final exchange of letters as the ill Keats planned his voyage to Italy, where a discussion of poetry rapidly slides into a dispute over money. This is not to say that Shelley played the lord with Keats, as perhaps Byron did in Italy with Hunt: Shelley was, in Byron's words to Moore, "the *least* selfish and the mildest of men" (4 March 1822, *L&J*, IX: 119); again, Hazlitt wrote in the *Edinburgh Review* (40 [July 1824]; *CWH*, XVI: 267), "in spite of an aristo-cratic education, he retained in his manners the simplicity of a primitive apostle." Still, Hazlitt, arising from the culture of Dissent, had his own class-related problems with Shelley, revealed in this same negative review of *Posthumous Poems*, where it becomes clear that he is concerned that Shelley's brand of radicalism – theoretical, all-encompassing, with-out reserve – is finally an aristocratic indulgence (his "unbelief" in established ideas is linked to "his presumption" [p. 266]) that does damage to the cause of reform: "The worst of it however was, that he thus gave great encouragement to those who believe in all received absurdities, and are wedded to all existing abuses: his extravagance seeming to sanction their grossness and selfishness, as theirs were a full justification of his folly and eccentricity" (p. 268). Here, the aristocratic free-thinker and the aristocratic proponent of Old Corruption become secret sharers.

There were, then, in the Hunt circle certainly perceptions of differences in rank (i.e. Keats's "You see what it is to be under six foot and not a lord") and actual differences in the source and amount of income that ground class distinctions. However, consciousness of such distinctions might have been vague in a group where Keats, after all, wrote poetry while living on an inheritance and Byron earned considerable amounts of money from the profession of writing. The group's shared disenchantment with both the government and its organized opposition, their collective heterodoxy on matters of religion, and their conception of themselves as a fellowship of poets and thinkers provided ways for them to view themselves as a coherent community joined by their embrace of a cosmopolitan culture and by their opposition to Old Corruption, Superstition, and the "spirit of money-getting." Thus, Hunt's dedication to the Right Honourable Lord Byron still reveals the group's attempt to live through divisions of rank, as he evokes a solidarity of poetry and friendship beyond class origins: "My dear Byron, You see what you have brought yourself to by liking my verses. It is taking you unawares, I allow; but you yourself have set example now-a-days of poet's dedicating to poet; and it is under that nobler title, as well as the still nobler one of friend, that I now address you." As I argued in my introduction, the group forms itself beyond such givens as class in seeking affiliative relations. Hunt's (and Keats's) doctrine of sociability, Hazlitt's theory of disinterestedness, Percy Shelley's radical egalitarianism, or Mary Shelley's feminism may arise from differing class positions, but they all seek to imagine a community not limited by the divisions of class interest and distinction. The circle was able, however uneasily, to hold together an astonishing group of people despite class tensions, personal rivalries, and the sometimes petty disputes that plague intimates. In their most idealizing moments, they imagined themselves as something like the model of a rankless or even classless society, and I think we should honor this vision, as long as we recall with Jon Klancher that "In the nineteenth century, the idea of classlessness could arise only out of an initial, compelling class awareness";[28] that is, their vision of a classless ideal, arising as it does out of a recognition of the differences in status that might divide them, does not negate the reality of social distinctions. Such a vision might in Hunt or even Keats appear as merely the attempt to offer an emerging idealization of the middle class as the one true alternative to the decadent lords of privilege on the one hand and the mob on the other, but we make a mistake when we project a Victorian sense of the middle class onto the social scene during the years between Waterloo and Peterloo and when we too easily dismiss the attempt of Hunt to ally "middle-class" intellectuals with plebeian movements or Shelley's appeal to all the "Men of England" that, as Neil Fraistat has shown, would be heard by both radical and "polite" audiences[29] or, more broadly, the group's attempt to imagine a space where one can examine society free of party or interest.

Whatever the problem, the group always struggled to regroup. For example, even in his quite hostile review of Shelley, Hazlitt turns to celebrate him, Keats, Byron, and Hunt as "poets, patriots and friends" as he eulogizes the dead Shelley and Keats, turning last to the recently deceased Byron, who has joined "this band of immortals," a "martyr to his zeal against tyrants" (*CWH*, XVI: 269). Hazlitt and Hunt had quarrelled earlier about Hazlitt's attitude towards Shelley, revealed in the piece "On Paradox and Commonplace" in his *Table Talk* (where "On People with One Idea" also targeted Hunt), but they moved quickly to reassert their friendship, with Hazlitt writing, "My dear Hunt, I have no quarrell with you, nor can I have. You are one of those people that I like, do what they will" (21 April 1821, *Letters of William Hazlitt*, p. 204), and with Hunt responding, "I have often said, I have a sort of irrepressible love for Hazlitt, on account of his sympathy for mankind, his unmercenary disinterestedness, and his suffering" (quoted in *ibid.* p. 206). When they met again in Florence in 1825 (where they considered starting a new collaborative journal), Hunt delayed dinner one evening to have Hazlitt read over an account of his faults, to which Hazlitt replied, "By God, sir, there's a good deal of truth in it."[30] These were bonds not easily cut, as we see too with Thomas Barnes, who had difficulties with Hunt at times but maintained their friendship throughout his life, saying, "I cannot bear to lose Hunt's friendship, for there is hardly a man I love so much."[31] Again, as we will see, Keats and Shelley may have disagreed over poetry and finances in their final letters to one another, but the real subject of those letters is Shelley's invitation to Keats to join him in Italy – generosity and group solidarity win out. In one sense, the attempt by *Blackwood's* to reduce the complexities of the group's actual social status to a single class category – with even Shelley and Byron being labelled Cockneys – is a sign of their success in forging a group solidarity beyond originary class positions. What was frightening about the Hunt circle was that it appeared to live beyond both residual and emerging social divisions. While such sociality might seem a tame political program, it was in fact a lived example of *fraternité*.

As in any circle of friends, there were many quarrels – between Hunt and Haydon, between Haydon and Keats, between Keats and Hunt – and there were many kinds of tension – the class ones I have been discussing, sexual tensions between Claire Clairmont and Mary Shelley or Marianne Hunt and Elizabeth Kent, religious disputes between Shelley and Haydon. There has, I think, been a scholarly tendency to emphasize the disputes (often described by Haydon in his journal and also alluded to by Keats, as in his satirical "comedy" of a literary and musical evening [to the George Keatses, 18 December 1818, *KL*, II: 14]) over the continuing theme of friendship, but we need to see Hazlitt and Hunt persevering through numerous controversies or Keats returning to the Hunt home at the end of his life, after, we are usually told, he had broken utterly with his one-time mentor. Again, our interest in the circle tends to wane as the "major" figures move away from its immediate orbit, but the survival of the group as a communal project was not dependent upon any single individual; for example, where we might imagine the group dissolving by 1819 with Shelley and Byron in Italy and Keats keeping his distance from Hunt, Hunt wrote to the Shelleys of gatherings with Peacock, Hogg, Coulson, the Novellos, the Gliddons, the Lambs, Alsager, Hazlitt, Procter, Curran, and Godwin (to Mary Shelley, 9 March 1819, *Correspondence*, I: 127–29). While it would be a mistake to accept the idealizing portrait of the group that its members would sometimes offer, it would equally be an error to see only petty coterie squabbling in their efforts to forge within their own community the kind of reformed society they sought to create in the world at large. They could not will into being a classless society or emancipate desire or settle once and for all often divisive questions about humanity, but we should respect their attempt to live beyond their class prejudices, to free love from jealousy, to question freely and with tolerance.

When members of the circle reflected on their time together, they always stressed the sociability of the group. Hunt remembered, for example, the time spent with Keats: "We read and walked together, and used to write verse on an evening upon a given subject. No imaginative pleasure was left unnoticed by us, or unenjoyed; from the recollection of the bards and patriots of old, to the luxury of a summer rain at our window, or the clicking of the coal in winter-time" (*LB*, p. 247). Clarke writes of the pastimes of the group:

Evenings of Mozartian operatic and chamber music at Vincent Novello's own house, where Leigh Hunt, Shelley, Keats and the Lambs were invited guests; the brilliant supper parties at the alternate dwellings of the Novellos, the Hunts and the Lambs, who had mutually agreed that bread and cheese, with celery, and Elia's immortalized "Lutheran beer" were to be the sole cates provided; the meetings at the theatres, when Munden, Dowton, Liston, Bannister, Elliston and Fanny Kelly were on the stage; the picnic repasts enjoyed together by appointment in the fields that lay spread in green breadth and luxuriance between the west end of Oxford Street and the western slope of Hampstead Hill – are things never to be forgotten. (*Recollections*, p. 19)[32]

Procter remembered meeting Lamb, Hazlitt, Peacock, and Walter Coulson at Hunt's suppers: "Hunt never gave dinners, but his suppers of cold meat and salad were cheerful and pleasant; sometimes the cheerfulness (after a 'wassail bowl') soared into noisy merriment. I remember one Christmas or New Year's evening, when we sat till two or three o'clock in the morning, and when the jokes and stories and imitations so overcame me that I was nearly falling off my chair with laughter."[33] The group was not solely occupied by appreciation and celebration, however. The Hunt circle was a site for both enjoying and creating culture: the group not only appreciated poetry with Hunt, music with Novello, and art with Haydon but made music, painted pictures, and wrote poetry, including the sonnets drafted together in Hunt's notorious contests.[34]

Inevitably, political discussions occupied much of their time. Haydon tells of the moment of hearing of Waterloo: "Read the Gazette again; I know it now actually by heart. Dined with Leigh Hunt. I give myself great credit for not worrying him to Death at this news. He was quiet for some time, but knowing it must come by & by, so putting on an air of indifference, 'Terrible Battle this, Haydon.' 'A glorious one, Hunt.' 'Oh, certainly.' To it we went" (25 June 1815, *Diary*, 1: 458). Hunt writes of Shelley asking him to explain the national debt (*Autobiography*, p. 325). Mary Shelley tells us of the mixture between art and politics when she notes that "Several of Hunt's acquaintances come in the evening – Music – after Supper a discussion until 3 in the morning with Hazlitt concerning monarchy & republicanism."[35] Procter has an interesting comment on the discussions that ran between Hunt, Hazlitt, and Lamb, which acknowledges the intellectual disputes while asserting the ultimate camaraderie of the circle: "each of them understood the other, and placed just value on their objections when any difference of opinion (not infrequent) arose between them. Without being debaters, they were accomplished talkers. They did not argue for the sake of conquest, but to strip off the mists and perplexities which sometimes obscure truth."[36] Productive debate, not universal agreement, was the group's goal.

The subject of such discussions might also be religion and might not be so congenial, as in Haydon's famous story about a dinner at Hunt's in 1816:

In a few minutes Shelley opened the conversation by saying in the most feminine and gentle voice, 'As to that detestable religion, the Christian –' I looked astounded, but casting a glance round the table easily saw by —'s expression of ecstasy and the women's simper, I was to be set at that evening *vi et armis*. No reply, however, was made to this sally during dinner, but when the dessert came and the servant was gone, to it we went like fiends.[37]

Sexuality was another subject upon which the group debated and disagreed. Hazlitt, for example, strongly disliked Hunt's notions about marriage; Procter reports, "Hunt has a crochet or theory about social intercourse (between the sexes), to which he never made any converts... This used to irritate Hazlitt, who said, 'Damn him; it's always coming out like a rash. Why doesn't he write a book about it, and get rid of it.'"[38]

Of course, just as they did not merely appreciate but also produce art, so did the circle move beyond discussions of politics: Hunt's *Examiner* itself is the clearest example of their intervention in politics, but we should also note the work of Hazlitt and Godwin, the journalism of Reynolds, Hazlitt, Barnes, and others for the *Examiner* as well as such venues as the *Champion* and John Hunt's *Yellow Dwarf*, the political pamphlets – "A Proposal for Putting Reform throughout the Kingdom" and "'We Pity the Plumage, but Forget the Dying Bird': An Address to the People on the Death of the Princess Charlotte" – that Shelley wrote during 1817, and, as I hope to show, much of the "literary" work of the group.

The group arose, in fact, at a moment when the relations between culture and politics, between art and society were being renegotiated and were thus the subject of much self-conscious and contentious debate. We need only think of the links between art and society made in the *Defence of Poetry*, of the mixture of culture and politics in Hunt's journalism and Hazlitt's essays, or of the bringing together of poetical and political argument in Byron's *Don Juan*. The group's opponents also talked politics and culture in the same breath, most notably in the Cockney School articles themselves but also in a piece such as Southey's *Quarterly Review* essay (16 [January 1817]) "The Rise and Progress of Popular Disaffection," which purported to review a number of texts, including Shelley's "Hermit of Marlowe" 1817 pamphlet proposing a vote on reform: Southey argues that while "poets and philosophers, as well as the divines, have ever reckoned an exemption from cares of this kind [political concerns] among the first blessings to be desired by those who would live well and wisely," given the events of 1816 – not to mention those of the earlier revolutionary period – "when questions are at stake in which the great interests of mankind, or the safety, honour, and welfare of their own country are nearly concerned, it is no longer fitting that they should look on as indifferent observers" (p. 512). The period of late 1816 and 1817, when the Hunt circle was at its most cohesive, was one, everyone agreed, that called for a cultural response to political events.

The defeat of Napoleon had not brought freedom with peace, as Hunt had hoped in the *Examiner* and Keats had envisioned in his 1814 poem "On Peace." Not only had the grand visions of the revolutionary era been destroyed, but even the more limited hopes for a society freed from war's burdens – economic and psychological, social and cultural – had proved barren. The Restoration staged by the Holy Alliance had already revealed its oppressive power. England's government, capable of massive mobilization for the war against revolutionary France, had no interest in girding up its loins to tackle its own internal problems. The year following Waterloo, as the Hunt circle came together, was one of economic depression and growing political anger. As E. P. Thompson describes it, "The autumn of 1816 was a period of extreme misery and post-war unemployment... In Spitalfields alone, it was alleged, there were 45,000 in want of food, and clamouring to enter the work-houses."[39] Neither the economic needs of the people nor their demands for political reform were being heeded by Parliament; the government instead handed out equal measures of repression and religion (in 1818, Sidmouth budgeted one million pounds for churches in seething industrial towns).

As for the opponents of the government, there were increasing agitations for mass demonstrations, even mass action, as Cobbett and "Orator" Hunt tried to mobilize the forces of "radical" reform to support universal manhood suffrage and as some groups imagined truly radical changes, with the Spencean Philanthropists, for example, pursuing a platform of agrarian socialism in journals such as the *Theological Inquirer* (1815), with which Shelley may have been associated, and the *Axe Laid to the Root* (1817). Spa Fields (November 1816), the March of the Blanketeers (March 1817), the Pentridge "rising" (June 1817), Peterloo (August 1819), the Cato Street Conspiracy (February 1820) – these are the signs of the long struggle for reform and sometimes for more than the reform of the franchise, but they also – along with Castle, Oliver, the suspension of habeas corpus, the Seditious Meetings Bill, the arrests of Hone and Wooler, and the "Six Acts" – name moments in the counter-revolutionary actions of the government. Some have found the reform movement in disarray in the years following Waterloo, with what were seen – at least through the lens of government propaganda – as violent attempts to overthrow the government, from Spa Fields to Cato Street, alienating middle-class liberals from the popular fight for reform.

For the Hunt circle, these years also provided moments of hope – witness Keats's exultation in the victories of Hone and Wooler set forth in his "negative capability" letter (to George and Tom Keats, 21, 27 ⟨?⟩ December 1817, *KL*, I: 191–94) or Byron's desire to return to England if "King Ludd" should rise again: "Are you not near the Luddites! By the Lord! if there's a row, but I'll be among ye! How go on the weavers – the breakers of frames – the Lutherans of politics – the reformers?" (to Thomas Moore, 24 December 1816, *L&J*, v: 149). However, members of the group also worried about the course of reform during these years, about whether the movement could hold together those who might break frames and those who considered themselves more moderate reformers. Shelley, for example, in many ways the most radical thinker of the group, still wrote to Byron during the time of Spa Fields (20 November 1816, *SL*, I: 513) that, while he hoped for "a most radical reform of the institutions of England," he worried about "the import-ance which the violence of demagogues has assumed," presumably expressing his concerns about Henry Hunt and Cobbett, with whom the *Examiner* also had differences. In a real sense, what the Hunt circle sought to do was to keep the hope for reform and even, perhaps, revolution alive during a period that saw the defeat of Napoleon, the apparent victory of the restored monarchies and "Old Corruption," uncertainty within the reform movement, and the government's con-certed efforts to divide and destroy its opponents.

This message of hope was offered as part of a struggle for the hearts and minds of the *liberally* minded in both senses of the word – that is, both those who at least leaned left and those who were interested in liberal learning.[40] In a sense, it was a battle to shape the ideology of what we would call the intelligentsia and what Coleridge called the clerisy, and it was thus a struggle in which the cultural and the political were deeply intertwined – as they always are, but never more so than during a period in which Burke, setting many of the terms for debate, called the French Revolution a "revolution in sentiments, manners, and moral opinions" and declared that the real political issues facing England were the defense of the spirit of established religion and the spirit of the patriarchal gentleman wrapped in the cloak of chivalry: the battle on the page over "sentiments" and "opinions" could be as fierce as the struggles in streets and fields.[41] This cultural war came in many ways to be understood as a poetic duel between the Lakers and the Cockneys. The Cockneys wrote at a time when many in the clerisy portrayed themselves as bewildered, even depressed, by recent events. Wordsworth in the *Excursion* had already defined the age's dis-ease: despondency over the unfulfilled hopes of the French Revolution. The *Excursion* and the response it drew from the Hunt circle (which I will discuss most fully in relation to Keats's *Poems* in chapter 3) make it clear that the melancholy, even morbidity, that is often found in the poetry of the period, from "Alastor" to *Manfred*, from "Darkness" to the "Ode to Melancholy," is not a symptom of any individual psychological disorder but a sign of a cultural crisis. Cultural despondency is almost the master theme of their epoch. However, where Wordsworth argued that this despair was the necessary punishment for revolutionary hubris that could be combatted only by a quietist return to nature and nature's God, the Hunt circle would attempt to combat despondency with continued revolutionary hope.

Hunt clearly worried about cultural malaise, concerned that people would despair under the new repression of the Holy Alliance; he sees writers such as Coleridge in his *Lay Sermons* encouraging despondency: "For what should induce the people of Europe to put up with weak promise-breakers [the Allies] when they would not with powerful ones [i.e. Napoleon]? Mr. COLERIDGE says, Hopelessness;– for such is the sum and substance of his late pamphlet" (*Examiner*, 12 January 1817, p. 17). Writing of Shelley's preface to *The Revolt of Islam* with its argument against despair in the face of the setbacks to reform and revolution, Hunt said he would recommend it to the Lake Poets were they "not as dogmatic in their despair as they used to be in their hope" (*Examiner*, 22 February 1818, p. 122). Shelley offered a diagnosis of the age that clearly looks to the *Excursion* as both a story of revolutionary despair and an embodiment of contemporary despondency:

on the first reverses of hope in the progress of French liberty ... many of the most ardent and tender-hearted of the worshippers of public good have been morally ruined by what a partial glimpse of the events they deplored, appeared to shew as the melancholy desolation of all their cherished hopes. Hence gloom and misanthropy have become the characteristics of the age in which we live, the solace of a disappointment that unconsciously finds relief only in the wilful exaggeration of its own despair. This influence has tainted the literature of the age with the hopelessness of the minds from which it flows.[42]

For Shelley, Wordsworth has become a symptom of the disease he sought to cure, while Hunt and his circle came to combat this despondency through their cultural work. As Keats wrote in *Endymion*, they sought "A thing of beauty" that is able to wreathe "A flowery band to bind us to the earth, / Spite of Despondence" (I, ll. 7–8).

Of course, this pursuit of "A thing of beauty" to oppose to massive political and social problems has struck many as exactly the hallmark of Huntian dilettantism, of Hampstead parlor radicalism. Or to use other terms, the Hunt circle's espousal of hope might seem to be pursuing idealization and displacement rather than confronting the real problems faced by the people. However, despondency was a "real" problem for the people, connected with their financial distress, as the radical *Gorgon* (28 November 1818) made clear: "To abridge the necessary means of subsistence of the working classes, is to degrade, consequently to demoralise them; and when the largest and most valuable portion of any community is thus degraded and demoralised, ages may pass away before society recovers its former character of virtue and happiness." Hunt shared this concern that if the proponents of reform became demoralized, the forces of reaction would win by default. Of course, his audience was not the "working classes" but their potential allies among the "middle classes." While the *Examiner* would, for example, support mass meetings after Peterloo, it served a different function in the reform movement than did the journals of Cobbett or Wooler; as E. P. Thompson says in contrasting the styles of Cobbett and Hazlitt, "It is a question of roles."[43] The Hunt circle worked to keep middle-class radicals and reformers allied with the larger movement for reform, and it did so by keeping the hope for change, a vision of an alternative future, alive, believable.

Still, there is within the group a turn to a kind of visionary cultural radicalism that, from some perspectives, can appear ineffective at best and a distraction from the real work of reform at worst. This was, for example, Hazlitt's concern about Shelley's brand of radicalism in "On Paradox and Commonplace" in *Table-Talk* (1821):

Just after the final failure, the completion of the last act of the French Revolution, when the legitimate wits were crying out, "The farce is over, now let us go to supper," these provoking reasoners got up a lively hypothesis about introducing the domestic government of the Nayrs into this country as a feasible set-off against the success of the Boroughmongers. The practical is with them always the antipodes of the ideal; and like other visionaries of a different stamp, they date the Millennium or New Order of Things from the Restoration of the Bourbons. (*CWH*, VIII: 150)

Hazlitt worries that in the wake of Waterloo radicals of Shelley's stamp will worry less about fighting against rotten boroughs than about impractical schemes for sexual liberation, as is suggested by his allusion to James Lawrence's *The Empire of the Nairs; or The Rights of Women* (1800; London, 1811), a book advocating free love that was popular among some of Godwin's followers, including Shelley. Hazlitt might well worry about how Shelley's notions on sex would strike middle-class supporters of reform, how they could play into the hands of those conservatives who argued that there was an identity between liberalism and libertinism. He might be concerned how attacks on religion-as-such would sit with reform-minded Dissenters. Even the Hunt circle's internationalism could be at odds with a public long bombarded with wartime nationalist propaganda. This split between an agenda of practical, "lunch-bucket" issues and a wide-ranging critique of culture has arisen within radical movements then and now.

However, we must not forget the ongoing commitment of the Hunt circle to the immediate issue of the reform of Parliament, a commitment that Hazlitt or Godwin never lost, a commitment pursued rigorously by Hunt's *Examiner*; Shelley may have been taken to task by Hazlitt as a disruptive visionary, but his *Philosophical View of Reform* is a cogent *and* practical analysis of the hierarchical structures of political, economic, and cultural power and of the means to effect a reform of them. One can see the Cockney's interest in issues beyond the immediate one of the franchise as a distraction, but it was also an attempt to turn present defeats into the hope for future victories. The Hunt circle believed that one could subvert power not only by confronting it directly on the ground but also by undermining the intellectual, emotional, ideological grounds for its appeal. If one could not literally assault the Bank of England, one could raise questions about the use of paper currency and ultimately the economic system it underwrote (as we will see in chapter 6). If one could not take the Tower, one could uncreate the idea of a "legitimate" government it stood for. If one could not behead the king and disestablish the church, one could ridicule the regent and question religious authority. What the Hunt circle did was to weaken "Old Corruption" by contesting the social and cultural instruments of its power. More than that, they offered a new vision of hope, of pagan joy in life and love at a moment of violence and despondency. In a society which increasingly stressed the values of *private* enterprise – of the abstract individual struggling against all others in an economic war – the group sought to embody the principles of generosity, of communality. In a culture marked by serious religious division and a strong conservative religious revival, the Hunt circle sought to combine free thinking with considerable tolerance, with this combination sometimes producing a fair amount of volatility, as when the deeply believing Haydon – who was still, importantly, welcome in this rather skeptical group – would argue religion with Shelley or Hunt. In a society that had been at war for a generation and that thus had built all of the necessary cultural supports for militarism, the Hunt circle and its voice the *Examiner* consistently stood out against violence, both that of governments and that of their opponents, with Shelley's advocacy of passive civil disobedience in the *Mask of Anarchy* and elsewhere representing the best of their thought. Finally, they sought to change society by creating a better community for themselves. Through a kind of prefigurative radicalism, they sought an image in their circle of the reformed world they imagined. Against violence in society and despondency in culture they pitted sociability: the bonds between them offered the hope of a society unbound.

Understood in the framework developed by Raymond Williams, the Hunt circle, facing in 1816 a moment of hegemonic reaction when governmental and social institutions and their cultural allies all sought to argue that the post-Waterloo period was some grand but simple return to a pre-Bastille era, created itself as what Williams terms a "formation": "within an apparent hegemony, which can be readily described in generalizing ways, there are not only alternative and oppositional formations (some of them, at certain historical stages, having become or in the process of becoming alternative and oppositional institutions), but, within what can be recognized as the dominant, effectively varying formations which resist any simple reduction to some generalized hegemonic function."[44] The circle around Hunt offered itself as an ideological vanguard, using its varied cultural practices to call into question cultural and institutional power, challenging (again using Williams's terms) the dominant ideology by offering a new or emergent vision, though one often backed by appeals to residual ideological elements – a move I will seek to explore in the group's turn to the classics for the authority to argue for liberty and above all for erotic liberation. The very things that bothered the Cockney School's critics – its attacks upon the government and organized religion, its celebration of sexuality, its very status as a coterie – identify it as a countercultural movement, rejecting established authority, embracing eroticism rather than violence as a means for revolutionizing life, and offering in its own communal organization a model for a society remade.

One might say that for this group, "as in Wordsworth, naive millennialism produced mainly declamation, but the shattered trust in premature political revolution and the need to reconstitute the grounds of hope lay behind the major achievements";[45] however, it is not so much that they engaged in a "shift to spiritual and moral revolution" over social and political revolt as it is that they found that they could best contribute to the struggle to change their society through cultural acts: this is a shift or an escape only if one believes cultural acts stand wholly apart from politics, while the Hunt circle clearly believed not only that politics shape poetics but that poetry can alter ideology. What the Hunt group offered was not so much a "displacement and poetic conceptualization whereby the actual human issues with which the poetry is concerned are resituated in a variety of idealized localities"[46] as it was a vision of that most idealized locality, utopia, but a vision grounded, perhaps even "proved upon the pulses," in the actual human issues that they confronted daily as part of an actual human community, the circle around Hunt. If we find, say, Shelley's *Mask of Anarchy* displacing and even suppressing real popular revolutionary energies by staging a figure of "Hope" that elides the moment in which power as Anarchy is, perhaps violently, overthrown rather than seeing, with Michael Scrivener,[47] Shelley offering a hopeful vision of passive, nonviolent resistance as a practical tactic for mass action that could still appeal to the "polite" allies of reform, then I think we are going to find any cultural act – as opposed to, say, registering voters or manning picket lines – to be escapist and diversionary. In a historical moment when the political and cultural are deeply interconnected, when cultural signs and symbols are essential to the preservation of power, when the government would call upon any and all "ideological state apparatuses" from religion to reactionary reviews, then cultural intervention has political and social consequences. *Blackwood's* was right: the Cockney School did exist, as both a community and as an educational project, the goal of which was nothing less than a radical reform of England brought on not by violence but by poetical and political instruction.

II

An Album! This! Why, 'tis for aught I see,
Sheer wit, and verse, and downright poetry;
A priceless book incipient; a treasure
Of growing pearl: A hoard for pride and pleasure
    Hunt, "Albums, Lines Written in the Album of Rotha Quillinan"

Mr Hunt cannot be *at home* at Hampstead, without having his Johnny Keatses and his Corny Webbs to cram sonnets into his waistcoat pockets. (*Blackwood's* 5 [April 1819], 97)

Blackwood's and its ideological companions not only found the politics of the Hunt circle distasteful; they also objected to the modes in which the group did its cultural work. They disliked its communal activities – such as Hunt's sonnet-writing contests repeatedly held up for ridicule – and its sense of group loyalty – attacked, for example, when one member of the group would write in support of another.[48] We find the group referred to as a "coterie" in a negative sense: they are seen as a small, self-important cabal intent upon mutual "puffery." Their verse is defined as essentially "private," not worthy of public distribution in print, as when the *Monthly Magazine and British Register* (45 [May 1818], 346) claims of *Foliage* that Hunt should have "reserved the principal part of this volume as *memoranda* for his portfolio, their appropriate place." However, such practices as the sonnet contests and the circulation of poems in manuscript in a port-folio or commonplace book in fact point to the social, communal nature of the circle's poetry. Moreover, such coterie practices need to be seen not as a sign of poetic weakness but as an attempt to create an alternative cultural practice, as a means to acquire new cultural power. Simply put, the Hunt circle pursued a coterie mode of literary production that resisted at the concrete point of literary work the subordination of culture to private and privatizing enterprise that they also attacked in the content of that work; faced with an increased sense of the author's isolation in relation to a distant public of purchasers, they sought to forge a collective literary practice and to communicate that communal sensibility through even their printed works.

I have no wish to set up some simple opposition between print culture and the coterie manuscript culture that preceded it, an opposition in which print can appear as the engine of alienating modern forces, distancing reader and author and commodifying culture. Print was also a democratizing medium, and one that allowed someone like Hunt

access to considerable cultural power. No doubt, the Hunt circle ultimately understood their writing in relation to print and to a potentially
large reading public. After all, Hunt prepared a weekly newspaper. His
writings rarely remained solely in manuscript. Hunt, Hazlitt, and even
Byron were part of an emerging profession of writers. Reynolds, Smith,
Webb, Barry Cornwall all published regularly. While Shelley might
caution Keats about rushing into print with the 1817 volume, there was
never any question but that Keats should ultimately seek to see his
poems in print – and, in fact, Shelley would help him find a publisher.[49]
Shelley's concern about his readership – particularly when he compared
himself with Byron – evidences his sense of himself in relation to an
audience for printed books.[50]

However, in the practice of the circle itself we also find modes of
literary production that appear much closer to the older procedures of
seventeenth- and eighteenth-century manuscript circles as they have
been reconstructed by such scholars as Arthur Marotti, Harold Love,
and especially Margaret J. M. Ezell.[51] This practice involves simultaneously a return to a residual, primarily aristocratic mode of literary
production as they seek to construct an aristocracy of poetic talent, a
turn against their sense that key contemporary professional writers –
particularly Southey but also, for Hunt, most literary reviewers – had
been "bought," and a turn towards an experimental practice that marks
them as an emerging avant-garde. While we have tended to equate
literary success with being in print, we need to see what coterie authors
lost when a piece of cultural work became a printed text. What had been
an immediate, shared piece of work becomes a manufactured commodity with all the attendant loss of control, over both its production and its
reception. While, as Ezell argues,[52] coterie manuscript production offered a means of communal, interactive cultural work, the printed text is
a collective product in a more distanced and abstract way: printer's
errors are not the same thing as a friend's corrections on a manuscript.
Where a coterie provided an immediate, responsive, and largely friendly
audience, the audience for printed texts is, as Lyotard argues, defined
not by "networks of reception" but by "economic networks," so that the
writer "no longer knows for whom he writes."[53] Certain of the group's
practices that were criticized make sense as a response to this situation.
What might seem to be coterie puffing was a way of combatting a world
of hostile, politically driven reviewing. What might seem a kind of
aesthetic escapism in, say, "Ode on a Grecian Urn," was a means of
protesting the status of cultural objects in a world of mechanical repro-

duction, as I will suggest in chapter 5. What might seem the dilettantism of Hunt's sonnet contests was a way of insisting on the literally social nature of literature. Again, the Hunt circle did not seek to oppose these practices to print culture but rather to infuse the sometimes alienating medium of print with the communal values of coterie production. In detailing the alternate mode of literary production pursued by the group, I want not only to bring attention to some misunderstood or neglected practices and texts but also to suggest that even the printed work of the Cockney School to which I will turn in later chapters needs to be understood as an attempt to extend to a larger audience the socialized mode of cultural literacy identified with manuscript circles.

Ezell has demonstrated for earlier periods that, as print began to dominate literary production in the seventeenth century, the coterie practices of manuscript circles survived into the eighteenth century, particularly in the work of women trying to give voice to their own emergent visions:

> For women writers in general, three forms of manuscript exchanges were available. They could produce manuscript books, circulate individual items in loose sheets which might also be preserved in commonplace books and manuscript miscellanies, or they could engage in correspondence. Obviously, these three modes are related – a poem or essay could begin in a letter, be copied and circulated, and finally end up either in a printed text or in a manuscript volume. Moreover, for some of these manuscript items, using one of these forms was a prelude to printing it. Others, however, were intended only for manuscript circulation.[54]

Ezell shows how these practices, all of which can be found in the work of the Hunt circle, create a socialized, collaborative, interactive mode of writing. Ezell's work on earlier groups can help us to understand the positive sense in which the poets around Hunt formed a coterie; that is, they engaged in a collective project signalled in the very nature of their texts and in the modes of literary production that brought them into the world. Put another way, the communal nature of the group's cultural work can be discovered in various traces of practices that link the texts of individual artists back into a socialized scene of writing; the group's writerly corpus embodies at a textual level their communal life.

One way to make this point is simply to observe how much of the group's work is occasional – how much of their verse arose against a particularized interpersonal background, how much they wrote directly to one another, how often they responded to the work being done by other members of the group, how their poetry was part of a social interaction which included not just attempts to clothe immortal ideas in deathless verse but also efforts to win admiration, to best a rival, perhaps to seduce. As I will argue most fully in discussing Keats's 1817 *Poems* in the next chapter, their verse records their life together. Again and again, we find poems arising for particular occasions within the group, with specific moments often being captured in the poems' titles: we need only think of Keats's "Written on the Day That Mr Leigh Hunt Left Prison" or "To a Friend Who Sent Me Some Roses" or "On Seeing the Elgin Marbles" or for that matter the Chapman's Homer sonnet; again, we find Shelley's "Marianne's Dream," Hunt's "To Henry Robertson, John Gattie, and Vincent Novello Not Keeping Their Appointed Hour," Reynolds's "Sonnet to Keats, on Reading His Sonnet Written in Chaucer," and Webb's "To John Keats, on His First Poems." There seemed to be little gap between life and art, as striking moments seemed to call forth verse immediately. For example, Keats's " Lines on Seeing a Lock of Milton's Hair" was written extempore during an occasion at Hunt's. As Keats wrote Bailey, "I was at Hunt's the other day, and he surprised me with a real authenticated Lock of *Milton's Hair*. I know you would like what I wrote thereon – so here it is" (to Benjamin Bailey, 23 January 1818, *KL*, 1: 210); as coterie writing created for his friends, Keats's lines were drafted in a notebook belonging to Hunt, then sent in a letter to Bailey, and never published. Again, Hunt told the story of talking with Shelley "one day (probably in or about 1817) concerning Love-Songs; and Shelley said he didn't see why Hate-Songs also should not be written, and that he could do them; and on the spot he improvised these lines of doggerel ['A Hate-Song (improvised)']."[55] We tend not to rate occasional verse very highly, but the Hunt circle used verse to respond in an immediate way both to public occasions – i.e. Byron's "Lines to a Lady Weeping" or Shelley's *Mask of Anarchy Written on the Occasion of the Massacre at Manchester* – and to private ones – i.e. Shelley's late lyrics to Jane Williams or Hunt's "To T. L. H., Six Years Old, During a Sickness." The occasional nature of so much of even the group's best verse is a sign of how deeply embedded their poetry was in day-to-day life, whether personal, social, cultural, or political.

Hunt's sonnet contests – seen by *Blackwood's* as "This fashion of firing off sonnets at each other . . . prevalent . . . among the bardlings"[56] – were a particularly strong example of the group's sense of poetry as a social activity. The practice involved a group engaging simultaneously in sonnet-writing on a set theme within a given period of time, at the end of which the poems would be read aloud to the assembly; the sonnets were written together, read together, and often published together. We know with certainty of the contests that produced Hunt's and Keats's poems on "The Grasshopper and the Cricket" and poems on the Nile by Hunt, Keats, and Shelley; I would follow Stillinger in seeing Keats's "Written in Disgust at Vulgar Superstition" as the product of one of these contests, perhaps linking it with Hunt's "To Percy Shelley, on the Degrading Notions of Deity."[57] Reiman and Powers suggest that Smith and Shelley engaged in a sonnet contest to produce their Ozymandias poems, and Joan Coldwell argues that there was a sonnet contest, with the sun as the set topic, involving Horace Smith, Charles Cowden Clarke, and Charles Ollier.[58] Keats's "On Receiving a Laurel Crown from Leigh Hunt" and Hunt's "On Receiving a Crown of Ivy from the Same [Keats]" also appear to be the product of a sonnet competition, as they were both written during the incident in which they crowned one another with laurel.[59]

While such contests, striking the modern reader as dilettantish, can be seen to reduce poetry to a parlor game, I think they suggest instead the deep connection between the verse of the Hunt circle and lived life. Hunt's, Shelley's, and Keats's participation in such contests also indicates the close ties between the verse written by the various writers within the circle; as Hunt would write of the grasshopper-and-cricket sonnets he and Keats penned, they were written in "companionship" rather than competition.[60] Poetry was not some separate solitary activity but a practice that flowed through their daily lives, connecting them to one another, as when Keats stepped briefly aside from a party to pen the dedicatory poem to his 1817 volume upon learning that the printer needed the verses immediately (*Recollections*, pp. 137–38).

This socialized scene of writing, this sense of writing as a bond between members of the group, is embodied in the very form of the group's work, since it is marked by coterie practices. The simplest form of coterie literary production mentioned by Ezell is the circulation of single sheets in manuscript. While there are far too many such examples to be discussed easily, it is important to remember how often the writers around Hunt circulated poems in manuscript, sometimes as a prelude to putting them into print, sometimes as a form of what Harold Love, following upon Ezell's insights, has called "scribal publication." Keats, for example, began as a member of a manuscript circle, circulating his poems in draft through first Clarke and then Hunt to an ever widening group that came to include Horace Smith, Godwin, Basil Montagu, Shelley, and Reynolds. Or, to take an example where the material moved in the other direction, Horace Smith loaned Keats "his manuscript [now held in the Essex County Record Office] called 'Nehemiah Muggs, an exposure of the Methodists,'" which Keats then excerpted in a letter to his brothers, since it was not in print (14 ⟨?⟩ February 1818, *KL*, I: 227); portions of the poem later appeared in the *London Magazine* (3 [February, March, June 1821], 200–202, 280–82, 648–50).

Another means of circulating verse was through letters, as Ezell notes. The epistle provides a meeting point between the public and the private spheres, between an informal, improvisatory communication and a form with a long literary tradition, including the contemporary example of Tom Moore, who in *Two-Penny Post Bag* (1813), edited by "Thomas Brown," pretends to have intercepted a series of letters by Tory supporters, a device used again in *The Fudge Family in Paris* (1818). The epistle was both a key coterie form for the Hunt circle – we need only think of the central place Keats's letters hold in his canon – and one of its more widely used public poetic modes – seen in Hunt's or Keats's printed verse epistles and in prose epistles such as Godwin's *Letters of Verax* (1815), begun as a letter to the *Morning Chronicle* (25 May 1815) in response to the declaration of war against Napoleon after his return from Elba, and Hazlitt's *Letter to William Gifford, Esq.* (1819), which Keats – pursuing a coterie mode of reproduction – would copy out at length in a letter to the George Keatses (13 March 1819, *KL*, II: 71–76). Correspondence, in both prose and verse, provided a key means for maintaining connections and solidarity within the group. It was a way of holding the group together on the page even when they were apart, it was a means for asserting within the coterie shared interests and values, and of course it was also a mode for producing texts for a sympathetic audience. The group, moreover, used the public epistle to draw upon the power generated in the coterie to present to an often hostile reviewing public an already united front, work already validated by having been accepted by others. The letter is a key means for demonstrating that the coterie is not a "private" realm set against a "public" one, but a counterculture set against an oppressive but empty official culture.

Of course, a poem did not necessarily have to be handed about on loose sheets or sent in a letter; one could copy a poem into someone else's album or commonplace book or even compose a new piece for it. Hunt wrote the poem "Albums" quoted at the head of this section for just such a volume, which he calls a "priceless book incipient," a book but not a print commodity. Such verses could exist in a range of formats: Keats copied his sonnet "To Sleep" into a lady's album (now in the Berg

Collection, New York Public Library), Reynolds published a poem called "Stanzas Written in an Album" in his *Garden of Florence* volume (1821), and Charles Lamb produced an entire volume entitled *Album Verses* (1830). Mary Frogley had a number of Keats's poems copied into an album by Kirkman, a cousin of George Felton Mathew's (poems later copied by Woodhouse into his book of transcripts). Keats's own habit of writing out verses in his fellow students' medical notebooks is merely an extension of this practice (see *KC*, II: 210). Reynolds, Bailey, and Rice often placed items in the volumes of the interesting Leigh sisters of Slade Hall, Sidmouth, who offer an important, because especially full, example of coterie practices.[61] In fact, the poetry of Bailey and Rice largely survives in the books kept by the women at Slade, and they also contain forty-six unpublished poems by Reynolds, who was at the time a rising writer; there is even an unpublished sonnet, "Written at the Close of Eve," by Hunt in a commonplace book kept by the Leighs' cousin Maria Pearse (LBL 16/KH 540, p. 62), to whom it was apparently shown in manuscript by Reynolds. Of course, some of these poems are copied into more than one of the women's books, and in the case of Reynolds's unpublished "Written in a Sister's Album," the poem is copied into three different volumes as well as into the Reynolds–Hood commonplace book, discussed below.[62]

Such modes of circulating poetry allow for the distribution of one's work outside the commercialized sphere of print; or, to put it another way, the group can complete what Robert Darnton, in analyzing print, calls the "communications circuit" – from writing through text production to reading – within the confines of the circle.[63] A poem handed by the poet to a friend in manuscript, rather than sold to a stranger in print form by a bookseller, appears to be a gift rather than property, to draw on Cixous's terms.[64] This feature is most obvious in manuscript poems prepared as presentation copies. One example of such "scribal publication" is a very elegant six-page octavo manuscript of Hunt's translation of Catullus Carmen 61, "The Nuptial Song of Julia and Manlius," with the Latin and the English translation presented side by side.[65] Byron sent Hunt a rare copy (because out of print) of *English Bards and Scotch Reviewers* with "some M.S. corrections," noting "it is however the only gift I have made of the kind this many a day" (letter to Hunt, 18 October 1815, *L&J*, IV: 318). Again, we often find manuscript poems added to gifts of printed volumes, as in the copy of *Poems* that Keats gave to Reynolds that included his never published sonnet on the laurel crown together with "To the Ladies Who Saw Me Crown'd," or in the copy of

Hunt's *Literary Pocket Book* (1819) that Shelley gave Miss Sophia Stacey with manuscript versions of "Time Long Past," "Good Night," and "Love's Philosophy," or in the copy of *The Feast of Poets* Hunt gave to his sister-in-law Elizabeth Kent where he inserted additional sonnets numbered so as to continue the group already in the printed text.[66] Charles Cowden Clarke had a manuscript volume of Keats's poems made as a gift for his sister Isabella Jane Clarke Towers. The volume has the title page "Poems / by / John Keats / with several, never / yet published / ... London / written by J C Stephens [the copyist] / for I J Towers. / 1828" and an inscription "I J Towers. / a little Birth day gift from her Brother / 5 October / 1828"; it includes the poems from the 1817 volume, six additional poems included by the copyist from periodicals and manuscripts held by Clarke, and two poems later added by Isabella Towers, one from a manuscript in Clarke's possession and one from Galignani's edition of Keats's work, the open-ended nature of such manuscript volumes being a key feature.[67]

Such gift-giving extended to the group's printed works in the obvious sense that they often gave each other copies of their books. Presentation copies offered another mode of circulation within the group, as in Hunt's gift of his *Literary Pocket-Book* (1819; held at Keats House) to "John Keats from his friend Leigh Hunt" that Keats then gave to Fanny Brawne, or the copy of Keats's 1820 volume sent to Shelley and loaned to Claire Clairmont, or Hunt's copy of the same volume that was with Shelley when he died, or Byron's annotated copy of *English Bards* sent to Hunt. This generosity is also seen in their habit, probably adopted from Byron, of dedicating their volumes to one another. Examples include Shelley's dedication of *The Cenci* to Hunt and of *Peter Bell the Third* to Moore; Hunt's dedication of his translation of *Amyntas* to Keats, of *The Descent of Liberty* to Thomas Barnes, of his translation of *Bacchus in Tuscany* to his brother John Hunt, and of *The Story of Rimini* to Byron; Thomas Barnes's dedication of *Parliamentary Portraits* (1815) to Hunt; Reynolds's dedication of *Safie* to Byron and of *The Naiad* to Haydon; Keats's dedication of *Poems* to Hunt; and Elizabeth Kent's of *Sylvan Sketches* to Marianne Hunt. Dedications were, of course, not only gifts of thanksgiving and praise but also a means of identifying oneself with the group: one announced one's ideological allegiances through such affiliations, as we will see most clearly in the case of Keats's *Poems*.

Members of the group did not just share their work upon its completion; one purpose of circulating poems in manuscript was to get comments from others, to allow them to share in the work. As Ezell has argued, coterie circles engage in a kind of communal creativity, with recipients of a manuscript feeling free to comment on it and even to change it. Hunt's image in his verses on albums at the head of this section is suggestive of this process of accretion, as each reader/writer adds to a growing text: even poems published over a single name are revealed as collaborative projects. Keats's poems, as Stillinger notes, often bear the influence of another's hand, as when Reynolds or Taylor helped Keats with *Endymion*; Stillinger shows that "Isabella" in particular was corrected by Reynolds and that "Woodhouse and Taylor between them are responsible for the title (Keats's own heading was 'The Pot of Basil,' which became the printed text's subtitle), for most of the punctuation and other 'accidentals' throughout, and for some of the wording of about sixty of the 504 lines – roughly one line out of every nine in the poem."[68] We find a similar case when Shelley revised *Laon and Cythna* into *The Revolt of Islam* with the help of a "literary committee" composed of Charles Ollier, Mary Shelley, Claire Clairmont, and Peacock.[69] Byron among others read Hunt's *The Story of Rimini* in manuscript and made corrections to it.[70] We see another kind of response, very common in the group, when Keats received a manuscript of Thomas Moore's "The Wreath and the Chain" (1801) copied by George Felton Mathew's cousins and wrote "On Receiving a Curious Shell, and a Copy of Verses" in response. Manuscript circulation produced both commentary and new verse, as we can also see in epistolary exchanges such as that between Reynolds and Keats, where Reynolds sent two sonnets on Robin Hood in a letter to Keats, to which Keats responded (3 February 1818, *KL*, I: 225) with a letter containing "Robin Hood" and "Lines on the Mermaid Tavern" marked "To J. H. R. In answer to his Robin Hood Sonnets."[71]

There is, in fact, an extraordinary amount of verse written in response to poems penned by someone else in the circle which creates a kind of immediate, lived intertextuality. There is an important difference between selecting an established classic, say, Horace, as one's intertext and choosing a contemporary such as Hunt. While, as I will argue in chapter 5, even allusions to the Latin classics were ideologically complex, there is a more immediate political charge in linking oneself to a controversial contemporary. Such synchronic intertextuality also invites the reader to reconstruct a living group by tracing these allusions; one is sent in search of contemporary texts, periodical information, even literary gossip in order to construe fully the ties between the poems. In a sense, a recognition of the existence of the Cockney School is a necessary ground for reading these poems; one must accept the group's collective project (and engage its collective ideology) in order to read an individual poem. While I am primarily interested in the way in which such coterie practices create a community within the group and offer a communal experience to readers, it is obviously the case that such procedures will also potentially alienate those who do not share the group's project, who reject its vision or who simply do not wish to unravel the group's coterie connections: the bonds that tie the group together can also establish boundaries others do not wish to cross.

We see such bonds being created in the many responsive, interactive poems written by the group. When Keats sent Haydon his sonnet "Great spirits now on earth are sojourning," which celebrates Haydon, Wordsworth, and Hunt – "He of ... The social smile, the chain for Freedom's sake" (included with a letter to Haydon, 21 November 1816, *KL*, I: 118–19) – Haydon immediately showed the sonnet to Reynolds, who wrote his own poem (published in *Champion*, 24 November 1816), noting that he wished a copy sent to Keats, "& say to him, how much I was pleased with his."[72] Again, Keats, visiting Clarke and finding him asleep over the supposedly Chaucerian "Floure and the Leaf," wrote a sonnet (appropriately entitled "Written on a Blank Space at the End of Chaucer's Tale of 'The Floure and the Leaf,'" *Examiner*, 16 March 1817, p. 176) – "which was an extempore effusion, and without the alteration of a single word" (*Recollections*, p. 139); when Reynolds saw the sonnet, either in a manuscript shared with him by Keats or in Clarke's Chaucer, he wrote in response, "Sonnet to Keats, on Reading His Sonnet Written in Chaucer" (27 February 1817). While Reynolds wrote a sonnet to Hunt praising *The Story of Rimini* and published it in the *Champion* (8 December 1816, p. 390), Keats wrote his own "On *The Story of Rimini*" in March 1817 and copied it into Hunt's copy of the just-published *Poems*; Hunt responded with a sonnet later included in *Foliage*. (Shelley also drafted "Lines to Leigh Hunt" in the summer of 1816 after reading *Rimini*, these multiple poems of praise indicating how popular Hunt's poem then was.) Horace Smith wrote his poem "On a Stupendous Leg of Granite, Discovered Standing by Itself in the Deserts of Egypt, with the Inscription Inserted Below" most likely after reading Shelley's "Ozymandias" in the *Examiner*.[73] The most famous of these responsive poems, *Adonais*, offers, as we will see in the final chapter, a reading of Keats's verse and of his 1820 volume in particular.

At the very least, these links send the reader out to read a precursor text that is also a piece of contemporary work, creating a synchronic intertextuality that bolsters the power of each text within the network of developing influences. At its strongest, such intertextuality recreates in the text the bonds – personal, poetic, political – that held the group together in life. The Hunt circle is linked in a material way on the page, most literally when poems by different authors appear together on the same manuscript sheet or in the pages of the *Examiner*. Dedications, some already noted, are another textual trace of links within the circle. Again, titles often signal a connection to another work, as in Reynolds's "Sonnet to Keats, on Reading His Sonnet Written in Chaucer," the sonnet probably by Woodhouse entitled "The House of Mourning Written by Mr. Scott," Horace Smith's "To Percy Bysshe Shelley, Esq., on His Poems" in *Amarynthus*, or Lamb's "To the Author of Poems Published under the Name of Barry Cornwall" (1820) and his "To My Friend the Indicator" (*Indicator*, 27 September 1820), which addressed Hunt as "Wit, poet, prose-man, party-man, translator." Hunt included in *Foliage* a whole series of poems addressed to Shelley, Keats, Haydon, Smith, and Reynolds, and there is a similar gathering in Keats's *Poems*. It is striking how often members of the group tie their poems together, given the pervasive anxiety over borrowings and possible plagiarisms (see, for example, Shelley's prefaces to *Prometheus Unbound* and *The Cenci*) that arises with a stress on originality and the ownership of texts.

The group battled this anxiety most directly through collaborative work. To take one simple case, we find on page 137 of a manuscript volume owned by Thomasine Leigh of Slade (LBL 6/KH 530) a poem in triplets with alternating lines being written by Bailey, Rice, and Reynolds. Bailey describes the scene of writing in a letter to Sarah Leigh:

> I told you in my letter of yesterday that we kept or were to keep your birthday at my rooms... Reynolds late in the Evening regretted that we had not sooner thought of writing a poem on the occasion in *triplets* Each person writing a line. I liked the thought, and my dear Sarah, I would not (could not?) let it pass "like idle wind." I there fore immediately produced the paper, and wrote the first line. [MS torn] we should have copied it fairly out before we sent it; but as we did it out of the *easiness* of our confident affection for you, we send you it exactly as we scratched it out originally.[74]

This incident – with its collaborative work, with its sense of occasional, social verse, and with the "scratched" version sent to one sister which is then recopied into the commonplace book of another – stands as a small exemplum of the coterie practices outlined by Ezell.

Larger projects also called forth a communal, collaborative spirit. Keats and Reynolds planned a volume of versified tales from Boccaccio, though of course Keats completed only "Isabella," which he placed in his 1820 volume, and Reynolds published his "Garden of Florence" and "Ladye of Provence" in *The Garden of Florence and Other Poems* (1821). Reynolds also mentions a plan for Keats to publish "Hyperion" with a mythological poem by Hunt, perhaps "Hero and Leander" or "Bacchus and Ariadne."[75] While we might think of Hunt and Keats as particularly interested in group projects, Marilyn Butler has described the work of Peacock and Shelley on "Arimanes" and *Laon and Cythna* as a "joint enterprise."[76] Mary and Percy Shelley collaborated on her two mythological dramas, *Proserpine* and *Midas*, for which he provided the lyrical passages. They also regularly read and commented on each other's works, which might develop side by side in notebooks they both used. Of course, Mary Shelley's most famous work, *Frankenstein*, arose as part of a collective attempt among the group with Byron in the summer of 1816 to write ghost stories. To continue to expand the list: Keats wrote *Otho the Great* as well as the lines "On Some Skulls in Beauley Abbey, near Inverness" with Charles Armitage Brown, Reynolds composed *Odes and Addresses to Great People* (1825) with Thomas Hood, and Horace Smith wrote the *Rejected Addresses* (1812) and *Horace in London* (1812) with his brother James.

Hunt also thought of his periodicals as social and interactive texts, necessarily collaborative, as in this comparison of the *Examiner* and the *Indicator* published in the latter journal (2 [20 October 1819], 9): "In the one he has a sort of public meeting with his friends; in the other, a more retired one. The Examiner is his tavern-room for politics, for political pleasantry, for criticism upon the theatres and living writers. The Indicator is his private room, his study, his retreat from public care and criticism, with the reader who chuses to accompany him." The very nature of periodical publication – in that it requires work by several hands, in that it seeks to create something like a coterie connection between the persona that, say, Hunt adopts with his indicating hand and its readership, and in that it is open to response from others through letters to the editor – corresponds to the collaborative, communal goals of the group. When the poetry of the group appeared in one of these journals, it immediately became part of a collaborative project, standing side by side with political essays by Hunt, theatrical reviews by Hazlitt, and commentary on art by Haydon. The *Liberal* was a later Italian joint effort involving Byron, Shelley, and Hunt as well as Mary Shelley,

Hazlitt, Charles Brown, and Hogg; significantly, all the works were issued anonymously, as if emanating from the group rather than an individual. There was even a purely coterie journal, the "Inspector," a manuscript journal produced by Reynolds and his friends for about six months in 1810.[77]

The group's commitment to "scribal publication," to the distribution of work within the circle through manuscript copies, is most fully seen in the production of manuscript volumes; these range from commonplace books to notebooks containing drafts of future work to the kind of complete manuscript book discussed by Ezell. As can be seen from marginal comments in various hands and poems copied from one volume into another, the women at Slade used their commonplace books as a way of sharing favorite verses and intriguing ideas. One of Thomasine Leigh's volumes of extracts from different authors (LBL 6/KH 530) offers an impressive gathering of contemporary verse. Beside pieces by the "house" poets Bailey, Rice, and Reynolds, it has extracts from Scott, Mrs. Opie, Charlotte Smith, Wordsworth, Coleridge, Southey, Moore, Hunt, Hazlitt, William Drummond, and Lamb. Woodhouse's interleaved copies of *Poems* and *Endymion* might be included here as manuscript annotated editions that provide commentary and variants for the printed texts. Another volume (LBL 3/KH 528), marked "Tamsine Leigh / Slade Valley / From a Friend & Brother" [Benjamin Bailey] and entitled "Extracts from various authors Vol. 1," is set up as a manuscript anthology complete with a table of contexts, section titles, and, in the case of a Burns poem (p. 81), notes explaining various dialect terms. The volume contains works by such established writers as Moore, Burns, and Charlotte Smith and a section entitled "Original Pieces" featuring Rice, Bailey, and Reynolds. Such volumes, always open to both additional copies and new verse, are examples of what Hunt calls a "book incipient," which is never a completed commodity to be passively consumed but an ongoing project ever being created by a community of reader/writers.

This feature of manuscript volumes can be seen even more clearly in commonplace books kept by active poets. Hunt's commonplace books, like the notebooks kept by Percy and Mary Shelley, are for the most part given over to notes and drafts of his own projects: one, for example, contains the draft for *Ultra-Crepidarius* along with a journal of his voyage to Italy and attempts at a poem on Shelley's death; another commonplace book – given to Hunt by Novello – contains notes for Hunt's *Byron and Some of His Contemporaries*, though devoting most of its space to what appears to be a projected book on mythology which would have used passages from Shelley, Keats, and Hunt himself; and a third volume has some notes for a play and for an unpublished book on great historical figures.[78] A commonplace book kept by Charles Cowden Clarke stands first as a compilation of passages that, as John Barnard argues, identify various enthusiasms of the group; there are, for example, extracts from various progressive histories, from the *Examiner*, from various oppositional political tracts, from Barbauld and Wollstonecraft, and from William Browne's *Britannia's Pastorals*, a group favorite.[79] In addition, Clarke copied work by members of the group – i.e. published political pieces by Byron and Hunt and two sonnets by Charles Ollier – and he also apparently composed a number of then unpublished poems in the volume. The literal context of these poems – verse by friends, selections from valued precursors and sources – materially reproduces the exchange of poetry, politics, and ideas within the circle.

Such volumes could also provide a site for collective work. Keats's early literary friend George Felton Mathew's circle kept a manuscript book called "The Garland: consisting of Poetical Extracts both ancient and modern" into which various members would copy poems.[80] The so-called Reynolds-Hood commonplace book – kept over a long period of time (Reynolds dates the volume 1816; Frances Freeling Hood signs the flyleaf with the date January 1847) and used by Reynolds himself, by his sister Charlotte, by Frances Hood (who contributes most to the volume), and by Thomas Hood – is another collaborative volume.[81] Mingled among newspaper clippings, extracts from authors ranging from Herrick to Tennyson, an abortive journal by Reynolds, and other traces of the ongoing life of the volume's creators are autograph poems by Reynolds, Rice, and Bailey, and later Hood. We also find sixteen transcribed poems by a little-known member of the circle – "I.C.T" – who has been identified by Kaufman and Leonidas Jones as being Isabella Jane Clarke Towers, Charles Cowden Clarke's sister.[82] Towers, who published three books of tales for children, *The Children's Fireside* (1828), *The Young Wanderer's Cave and Other Tales* (1830), and *Devils in the Woods* (1835), is another member of the group who found her way into print in journals edited by Hunt; her "Stanzas to a Fly That Has Survived the Winter of 1822" appeared in the *Literary Examiner* (13 December 1823), and "To Gathered Roses. (In Imitation of Herrick)" was printed in Hunt's *London Journal* (10 September 1834). Another section of the volume is devoted to "Manuscript Poems John Keats," perhaps, as Kaufman claims, "transcribed directly from autograph manuscripts of Keats," perhaps, as Stillinger argues, largely copied from one of Woodhouse's books of transcripts (W^2), but in any event another example of the complex ways in which poetry in manuscript travelled in the circle.[83] Again, this collection provides the poetry's living context, most immediately when we find a Reynolds sonnet ('Sweet Poets of the gentle antique line") dated "8 Febry 1818" followed by a Keats sonnet ("Blue! – 'Tis the life of Heaven") also dated "8 Feb 1818" and marked as an "Answer" to the preceding poem; when Reynolds printed his poem in his *Garden of Florence*, he transcribed Keats's sonnet into his personal copy, preserving for himself the manuscript context of the published work.

There are a number of volumes produced in the group that stand as completely original manuscript books. Bailey produced for his women friends at Slade a manuscript pamphlet of his "Introductory Address to the Zetosophian Society" (LBL 45/KH 545), this being Bailey's inaugural performance before the literary and cultural club to which he along with Rice and Reynolds belonged.[84] (There are other manuscript pamphlets that were circulated within the group, such as Clarke's manuscript lecture on *Hamlet* and *A Midsummer Night's Dream* with commentary by Hunt or Bailey's "Essay on Moral Principle";[85] and we should remember how many of Shelley's essays – including the *Defence of Poetry* – remained in manuscript during his lifetime.) In 1814, Bailey collected a number of poems for Sarah Leigh in a volume (LBL 46/KH 546) which includes a preface celebrating the friendship within their coterie: "It is unnecessary to remind the persons who are alluded to in the following lines, that the occasion, on which they are written, is the commemoration of extremely happy days spent in the rational enjoyment of the sublime beauties of nature. It will also, I trust, awaken and keep alive the active energies of a friendship which was formed on the firm basis of pure and virtuous affection." Bailey makes explicit here a point implicit also in album verse or responsive poems: that this circulation of verse within the group is a textual embodiment of the ties of friendship that bring them together; this poetry is often the product of a group's social attachments, and it is in turn productive of the affiliative bonds that hold the group together.

Bailey also created two copies of a manuscript book, "Recollections of the Heart" (LBL 47/KH 547, given "To my dear sisters, Mary, Sarah, & Tamsine" on 5 June 1815; and LBL 48/KH 548, given to Sarah Leigh on 24 August 1815). The book – with a title page, dedication, epigraph (from Wordsworth), and an index – follows Wordsworth's "Poems on the Naming of Places" (which the group had been reading) to provide a series of poems on seven rocks along the Dunscombe Cliffs which the group at Slade had seen, with one rock named for each member of the group and the seventh, "from whence we view the whole ... named '*Union Rock*,' as applying to all of us" (p. 2).[86] Bailey wrote most of these poems, though the one entitled "Sarah's Rock" (p. 5) is followed by the initials "J.H.R.," indicating that Reynolds penned this piece. Reynolds was not, however, part of the initial tour of the rocks, and thus there is no poem to him in the June manuscript – a piece entitled "Reynolds' Rock" (not in Bailey's hand) being added to the August manuscript (p. 8). There is also in the June volume a piece on a loose sheet entitled "The Happy Valley" and marked "For the 'Recollections of the Heart' to come after 'The Vale of Memory'"; this piece is included in that place (p. 24) in the later manuscript book.

Such additions to manuscript volumes – indicating the dynamic, developing nature of what Hunt imagines as the book as pearl – might provide a context for emendations of printed texts as well, say of Byron's revisions of *The Giaour* or Hunt's constant tinkering with *Feast of Poets*. While print appears to present a fixed text, the coterie context of Cockney verse suggests how even published volumes are open to change, as new lines are penned, and to recontextualization, as a new piece is inserted into a collection. Importantly, this is not a solitary practice but work undertaken in the light of readers' responses. Such responses are sometimes recorded directly in the manuscripts, most simply when, say, Byron corrects Hunt's *Rimini*. There is also manuscript commentary. For example, Benjamin Bailey's "Sonnet to Lord Thurlow on His Poem of Moonlight," which had been printed in the *Morning Chronicle* of 9 February 1814, is transcribed in a commonplace book kept by Sarah Pearse Leigh (dated 22 March 1815 [LBL 10/KH 534, p. 117]) with a series of footnoted corrections to the printed text, as well as a note that "this was written at the time of the Newspaper attacks on Lord Byron on account of his lines to the Princess Charlotte ["Lines to a Lady Weeping" included in Byron's *Corsair*], as an indirect defence of him." Again, a signed copy of Reynolds's *Eden of Imagination* (LBL 21/KH 549) sent to Maria Pearse by Rice, has corrections and additions, along with a positive evaluative note, signed "BB" for Benjamin Bailey. Such emendations by another hand suggest that the circle considered poems open to constant correction, even after they were in print, and, more important, that they felt free to correct one another's work, giving us a sense that they viewed their poetic productions as at least in part

collaborative. Again, in Thomasine Leigh's "Extracts from various
authors Vol. 1." (LBL 3/KH 528), opposite page 54, a missing stanza from
a Burns poem is included; across from Moore's "To Julia, Weeping,"
someone has noted, "Lord Byron has the same thought as the last stanza
of this Poem in The Bride of Abydos" (p. 25). We get a sense of the
interactive nature of these volumes when, on the page facing another
Moore poem (p. 37), Thomasine's sister Sarah has penned lines dated
"Nov.br 18th 1815" celebrating the time "when kind friendships cordial
smile / And social chat the time beguile." In "Recollections of the
Heart," we get further examples of such immediate social interaction.
For example, next to the poem that Bailey wrote for his own rock, where
he has written "This Rock is mine, unworthily mine," another hand has
inscribed "most worthily," and when he says, "My rude appearance is
my only claim," the response is "not true" (LBL 48, p. 7). That his
self-deprecating remarks and the responses may have been feints in a
flirtation between Bailey and Thomasine Leigh is exactly to the point:
these verses are not mirrors held up to life but actions taken as part of
life.

The most elaborate of these manuscript books is "Poems by Two
Friends." Containing poems by Reynolds and Bailey, this quarto volume of 212 pages (LBL 2/KH 542) given to Thomasine Leigh has a
dedication from Bailey, a title page complete with epigraph and date,
guide words at the bottom of each page, and an index with each poem
being identified as being by "B" or "R." In other words, this manuscript
volume looks in many ways like a printed text. However, where a
printed text is presumably complete when it is offered for sale, this
volume given as a gift is left open: pages i–liv and 188 to the end were left
blank so that Thomasine, Bailey, and perhaps others could enter other
poems and extracts. With the volume divided into poems and sonnets
and with the verse addressing the standard subjects of the Hunt circle,
this book looks very much like Keats's *Poems* or Hunt's *Foliage*.[87] Again,
Bailey's "Recollections of the Heart," which includes longer meditative
poems – "Invocation to Memory" and "The Vale of Memory" –
bracketing two sets of inscriptions and which closes with a set of sonnets,
looks very much like Keats's 1817 publication, which has a group of
sonnets, a section of epistles to members of his group, and a set of
miscellaneous poems, largely occasional, all bracketed by two longer
meditative poems, "I stood tip-toe upon a little hill" and "Sleep and
Poetry." Or, perhaps more precisely, printed books such as *Poems* and
Foliage resemble these coterie manuscript volumes: providing occasional

verse, linked poems, and tributes to members of the circle and remaining open in presentation copies to additions and corrections, these print volumes maintain the coterie practices we find in the manuscript materials.

Moreover, one could argue that the circle sought to transform the business of publication into an extension of the coterie, as it controlled both publishing outlets and reviewing venues – the group is engaged at every point in Darnton's "communications circuit." Hunt's journals and *Literary Pocket-Books*[88] published Hazlitt (who also appeared in John Hunt's short-lived *Yellow Dwarf* of 1818), Byron, Shelley, Keats, Smith, Clarke, Lamb, Reynolds, Procter, and Hunt himself. Charles Ollier, who had been a friend of Hunt's since 1811, brought out such volumes as Keats's *Poems* (1817), Hunt's *Foliage* (1818), *Poetical Works* (1819), and *Literary Pocket-Books*, Peacock's "Four Ages of Poetry" (which appeared in *Olliers Literary Miscellany* [1820]), Mary Shelley's *History of a Six Weeks' Tour* (1817), Hazlitt's *Characters of Shakespeare's Plays* (1817), and most of Percy Shelley's mature works from *Laon and Cythna/The Revolt of Islam* (1818) to *Hellas* (1822). Taylor and Hessey, also a part of the circle, published Reynolds's *Naiad* (1816) and *Peter Bell* (1819), Keats's *Endymion* (1818) and his 1820 volume, and Elizabeth Kent's *Flora Domestica* (1823).[89] Through the *Examiner* and the *Indicator* in particular, but also through such journals as the *Champion* and even the *Edinburgh Review*, Hunt, Hazlitt, Reynolds, and other members of the circle also supplied reviews for their friends and colleagues.[90] Histories of the group, such as Hunt's *Lord Byron and Some of His Contemporaries* or Clarke's *Recollections of Writers*, were later attempts to secure the circle's place before the public. From first draft to retrospective account, the cultural work of second-generation romanticism arose in the context of the Hunt circle, and their texts proudly bodied forth their interconnections.

We can view the continuity between manuscript and print in a little-known volume, Charles Cowden Clarke's *Carmina Minima* (London: Simpkin, Marshall, 1859). This is clearly a coterie volume: for example, there is a poem to Vincent Novello that celebrates friendship, and there are many occasional verses, including poems to accompany a presentation copy of Mary Novello Clarke's book of tales from Chaucer, a poem by Mary Clarke (again indicating the collaborative nature of such volumes), and a longer unfinished piece entitled "The Burial of the Soldier" that is reminiscent of Horace Smith's sonnet on Ozymandias. The volume begins with the poems written from 1816 to 1818 in Clarke's commonplace book, mentioned before, that either were influenced by or influenced Keats. In his preface, Clarke describes his efforts as moving from the desire to please a close group to the hope for a larger audience: "This knot of 'unconsidered Trifles' . . . was intended only for private circulation,– as a keepsake and memorial of old and sweet friendships, of cordial acquaintances, and of abounding hospitalities"; however, he hopes there may be "numerous unrecognized friends among my audiences" for his lectures, and "I therefore determined upon the usual, open form of publication." Clarke, as he traces the history of his verses from occasional pieces kept in a commonplace book for close friends to published works in a printed book offered to an anonymous readership, provides us with a model for the way in which verse moved from the Hunt circle out into the public sphere of print.

Carmina Minima, then, along with Keats's *Poems* and Hunt's *Foliage*, arising within a manuscript circle, sought both to preserve the occasional nature of their creation and to praise the coterie which nurtured them. The coterie volumes preserved by the Leigh women repeatedly celebrate the bonds of friendship that gave rise to them, and so do the volumes by Clarke, Keats, and Hunt – or a verse epistle such as Shelley's "Letter to Maria Gisborne," quoted at the opening of this chapter, that imagines the Gisbornes in London meeting Hunt, Godwin, Hogg, Peacock, and Horace Smith. As we have seen, titles, dedications, and occasional allusions all take the reader back into the group: part of the pleasure of such occasional communal verse is that – as we recognize a name, uncover an allusion, or clarify some other previously obscure link between poems and poets – we come to share in the interactions of the circle. As Ezell has argued, coterie practices when used in print texts seek to maintain with their readers a closer, more interactive relationship than is possible in the rather distanced relationship between an author and the readers of printed materials. We become, in a sense, part of the group when, say, we read an epistle from Hunt to Byron or Keats to Clarke and we become both the "I" sending the letter and the "you" who receives it; as in Tom Moore's "intercepted" letters, we are made privy to the "private" communications within the group, invited to join its collective activities and beliefs.

Many modern scholars, I think, still share with *Blackwood's* a skepticism about poetry conceived within a coterie. We still see coterie writing as an essentially "private" practice and value instead the quite different private enterprise of selling books. What we need to see about the Hunt circle is that both its coterie writing and its book publication were collective, collaborative enterprises: their modes of literary production

exemplify their vision of community. As we turn in the next chapter to
Keats's *Poems* of 1817, we will see that this coterie context provided vital
support for a rising poet, and that his text in turn offered a polemical
manifesto on behalf of the group's cultural project. The Cockney School
was not a defensive enclave for weak poets or an adolescent phase in the
maturation of future great writers but a rallying point for those oppositional writers we call second-generation romantics. We need to remember that the simplest result of the coterie links between these poems and
poets was to signal to the reading public their allegiance to one another
and particularly to Hunt, the leader of the literary left. More than that,
these coterie practices sought to recreate on the page for the reader the
generosity, the camaraderie, the collective inquiry, the communal celebration of life that the group offered as the ground for a new society.
The coterie nature of their writing is both a sign of and a support for
their oppositional stand.

CHAPTER 3

John Keats, coterie poet

I

The first volume of Keats's minor muse was launched amid the cheers and fond anticipations of all his circle . . . Alas! the book might have emerged in Timbuc-too with far stronger chance of fame and approbation . . . The whole commu-nity, as if by compact, seemed determined to know nothing about it. The word had been passed that its author was a Radical; and in those days of "Bible-Crown-and-Constitution" supremacy, he might have had better chance of success had he been an Anti-Jacobin. (Clarke, *Recollections*)

Keats's *Poems* of 1817 has never fared well, not with critics in his own time or with scholars in ours.[1] The concerns of modern Keats scholars may seem distant from those of the *Quarterly* reviewers or the *Blackwood's* crew, but as I tried to suggest in the first chapter, modern scholarship's defense of Keats shares much with his first calumniators. While Mar-jorie Levinson has argued that the *Blackwood's* attacks identify a feature of Keats's poetry that has been lost to modern criticism ("The most casual survey of this commentary (1817–1835) reveals a response so violent and sustained, so promiscuous in its blending of social, sexual, and stylistic critique, and so sharply opposed to mainstream modern commentary as to imply a determinate insight on the part of Keats's contemporaries and a determined oversight on the part of his belated admirers" [p. 3]), I think that in fact Keatsian scholars have learned the lessons of the Cockney attack too well. To defend their poet, they have constructed a Keats who frees himself from the Cockney label, as Levinson at other points indicates:

we put what the contemporary reviews called Keats's "vulgarity" under the sign of psychic, social, and textual unself-consciousness: roughly, the sign of sensuous sincerity. Further, by the providential tale of intellectual, moral, and artisanal development we find coded in Keats's letters, we put the vulgarity which cannot be so sublimed in the early verse and show its gradual sea-change into the rich, inclusive seriousness that distinguishes the great poetry. (P. 2)

As Levinson suggests, Keats's career has been mapped as an aesthetic education in which he is tutored by Hunt in the Cockney School before moving on to a "higher" education from Shakespeare and Milton.[2] Keats's life and work is read as the story of a young poet who acquires a bad model in Hunt, whom he fortunately outgrows in order to become, almost overnight, a major writer; we can thus largely dismiss the 1817 *Poems* and *Endymion* as Huntian apprentice work, while marvelling at how Keats could come so quickly to write the odes or the "Hyperion" fragment. In an inversion of what happens in Wordsworthian criticism to save the "good" early and presumably radical Wordsworth from the "bad" increasingly conservative Wordsworth, we construct a "bad" Keats of the poetically and politically reformist Cockney School who luckily graduates to become the most Wordsworthian poet of the second generation. In order, then, to save from Cockney contamination "Hyperion," the odes, and the later narrative poems, Keatsians have been willing to see Keats's "early" work – and particularly his *Poems* of 1817 – as an unfortunate adolescent flirtation with Hunt's muse or, more simply, as bad poetry.

"Bad poetry" is an especial problem for a poet such as Keats, who has been relentlessly constructed as a writer concerned with "art" (the aesthetic) rather than "life" (including the ideological), with loading every rift in his verse with lyric ore rather than worrying over the cultural or social "purpose" that a "modern work it is said must have" (letter to Shelley, 16 August 1820, *KL*, II: 322–23). John Barnard, writing of Keats's early poetry, speaks for many Keatsians in saying, "The origins of Keats's ambitions were wholly literary"[3] – though some would amend this to origins *and* aims. From the new criticism to deconstruction, from Walter Jackson Bate's claim that Keats's "primary inspiration ... is intensely literary" to Paul de Man's sense that his "experience is mainly literary,"[4] we have been offered a poet who cared about books and little else. Even a recent historicizing account, Andrew Bennett's intriguing *Keats, Narrative and Audience*, is finally more interested in Keats's struggle with narrative than in his relation to any actual audience. Keats's *Poems* of 1817 are not likely to please those who are looking for an aestheticized, writerly Keats: the poems have struck modern readers as both too immaturely arty (as Barnard puts it, "art too often stands between Keats and life" [p. 15]) and simply not good enough art. In an effort to "save" him from such "immature" efforts, the "mature" Keats has then been constructed as a writer who successfully creates his art primarily for the sake of art.

This is not to say that there has not recently been an attempt to create a political Keats; we need think only of the 1986 special issue of *Studies in Romanticism* on Keats and politics, edited by Susan Wolfson, *Keats and History*, edited by Nicholas Roe, and Roe's *Keats and the Culture of Dissent* (Oxford, 1997).[5] However, there has been a tendency to equate the political with the bad in Keats, to find the achievement of Keats in his ability to escape or to transmute (depending on one's own ideology of the aesthetic) political, social, even cultural issues. In a way, everyone, formalist and cultural critic alike, sees politics as infiltrating or contaminating[6] the supposedly pure realm of the aesthetic; this can be a cause for lament or celebration, but I think an increasingly prevalent position is that of George Levine: "In the current critical scene, literature is all too often demeaned, the aesthetic experience denigrated or reduced to mystified ideology."[7] In the case of the early Keats, however, we have to see that his poetry has been demeaned by having his ideological experience denigrated or reduced to mistaken aesthetics; that is, ideological gestures in *Poems* are read as aesthetic errors.

The case against Keats's early, Cockney poetry as bad poetry also has a biographical version: to learn how to outgrow the influence of Leigh Hunt, he had to break with his one-time mentor. Considerable energy has been spent in denying that Keats remained tied to Hunt even though – as I have already suggested and will note again in the final chapter – they were close enough so that Keats returned to live with Hunt during his final illness. It is as if in order to deny that Keats's poetry is political – that it is concerned with the ways men and women organize themselves in society – Keats scholars have had to remove him from the immediate social context which nurtured his poetry, the circle around Hunt; the poet who matures to write poetry independent of political content is also seen as the young man who grows into an adult independence – as if great art was finally only about art and true maturity was finally about being able to be alone with oneself. We need to see that Keats's early poetry is social poetry, arising from a concrete social context and engaging debates over cultural, religious, and social issues that we would see as political or ideological.

While Hunt would acknowledge some aesthetic weaknesses in Keats's first volume, he knew that the reaction to *Poems* was not simply a response to infelicitous word choice or jarring rhymes: "there were political opinions in the book; and these not according with the opinions of the then government authorities, the writer was found to be a very absurd person, and not to be borne" (*LB*, p. 250). For Hunt, as for Clarke in the passage quoted above, the rejection of Keats's initial volume was not a matter of aesthetic judgment but political conflict. What Keats's friends understood and what *Blackwood's* in its primarily ideological rather than stylistic attacks also indicates is that Keats's early verse needs to be seen not as part of some private poetic development but as a contribution to a larger ideological project. As William Keach puts it in his excellent account of the politics of Keats's couplet writing, "the stylistic choices and performances of the 1817 and 1818 volumes *are* political choices and performances."[8] To see Keats as part of the Hunt circle is to reveal the self-consciously ideological content of his poetry – in particular, to see that Keats's *Poems* of 1817 demands to be read not as weak apprentice work for the future odes but as a key statement in 1817 of the Hunt circle's project and self-definition. To return Keats's *Poems* to their immediate context in the Hunt circle and the cultural battles of their day is not to diminish their aesthetic qualities but to credit the larger cultural project that Keats shared with the Hunt circle. It is to see Keats's involvement in the Cockney School as a political as well as poetic education and his growth as an ideological as well as a stylistic development.

II

Keats's Cockney political education began before he met Hunt, through Hunt's and Keats's common acquaintance, Charles Cowden Clarke, who introduced Keats to the *Examiner*. Clarke tells us that "Leigh Hunt's *Examiner* – which my father took in and I used to lend to Keats – no doubt laid the foundation of his love of civil and religious liberty" (*Recollections*, p. 124).[9] Hunt's weekly enabled Keats to acquire an initial sense of ideological self-definition, a fact revealed in such early poems as "On Peace" (April 1814) and "Lines Written on 29 May, the Anniversary of Charles's Restoration, on Hearing the Bells Ringing" (1814 or 1815) which, as Miriam Allot has shown, echo positions adopted in the *Examiner*.[10] "On Peace," for example, reflects Hunt's attitudes towards Napoleon and the peace of 1814 ("he was a great soldier, and little else ... The *Examiner*, however much it differed with the military policy of Bonaparte's antagonists, or however meanly it thought of their understandings, never overrated his own or was one of his partisans"

[*Autobiography*, pp. 215–16]), positions also embodied in Hunt's *Descent of Liberty* written in 1814 while he was in prison and published in 1815.

It is not too much to say that Keats became a poet through a series of distant and then close encounters with Hunt. Present as Keats first swims into our ken, Hunt and the circle which gathered around him are central to Keats's poetic career. In August of 1816, in our earliest, fragmentary letter by him, Keats writes a verse epistle to his brother George in which he refers to Leigh Hunt as "Libertas" (*KL*, 1: 105), the name he uses for Hunt in a number of poems. In the first complete letter we have by him (9 October 1816), Keats is again concerned with Hunt, as he opens a letter to Charles Cowden Clarke, "The busy time has just gone by, and I can now devote any time you may mention to the pleasure of seeing Mr Hunt" (*KL*, 1: 113). Clarke had been a weekly visitor to Hunt's jail cell during Hunt's imprisonment for libel after his attack on the Prince Regent, bringing baskets of fruit to Hunt and carrying back to Keats tales of Hunt's prison gatherings with the likes of Bentham and Mill, Thomas Moore and Byron. When Hunt was freed, Keats penned "Written on the Day that Mr. Leigh Hunt Left Prison" (2 February 1815) and gave it to Clarke, who was on his way to visit Hunt – this being one of the first poems Keats shared with an outsider (Clarke later wrote, "How clearly do I recall the conscious look and hesitation with which he offered it!" [*Recollections*, p. 127]). Keats's first published poem, "O Solitude" appeared over his initials in Hunt's *Examiner* (5 May 1816). When it came time for Keats to meet Hunt, he wrote to Clarke, "'twill be an era in my existence." And it was: for in becoming a member of Hunt's circle during October of 1816 Keats, who could have begun his practice as surgeon-apothecary after 31 October, decided to be a poet.[11]

Clarke remembered first showing Keats's poetry – including "How many bards gild the lapses of time" – to Hunt and his circle and being pleasantly surprised by the enthusiastic response of Hunt and Horace Smith (*Recollections*, pp. 132–33). Hunt later wrote, "I shall never forget the impression made upon me by the exuberant specimens of genuine though young poetry that were laid before me" (*LB*, p. 247). Sometime shortly after the ninth of October 1816, Keats and Hunt finally met. Clarke tells us, "This was a red letter day in the young poet's life, and one which will never fade with me while memory lasts ... The interview, which stretched into three 'morning calls,' was the prelude to many after-scenes and sauntering about Caen Wood and its neighbourhood" (*Recollections*, p. 133). Hunt's account is similar: "We became intimate on the spot, and I found the young poet's heart as warm as his imagination." Keats became a regular visitor at Hunt's cottage in the Vale of Health near Hampstead Heath as they entered into a season of continual talk and writing; as Hunt remembered it, "We read and walked together, and used to write verse on an evening upon a given subject. No imaginative pleasure was left unnoticed by us, or unenjoyed; from the recollection of the bards and patriots of old, to the luxury of a summer rain at our window, or the clicking of the coal in winter-time" (*LB*, p. 247). Keats was fully immersed in the Hunt circle's round of physical pleasures, poetic enjoyments, and political conversations.

As we saw in the preceding chapter, when Keats in October 1816 joined the Hunt circle and met such men as Horace Smith, Hazlitt, Haydon, and Lamb, he entered a world of sonnet-writing contests, of debates on religion pitting Shelley and Hunt against Haydon, of musical evenings at the Novellos' or Lambs', of political discussions involving the Shelleys, Hunt and Hazlitt, of picnics on Hampstead Heath. It was both an exciting world and a generous one, with Keats, as Clarke tells us, "suddenly made a familiar of the [Hunt] household and . . . always welcome"; Hunt immediately began to circulate Keats's verse, and when Hunt shared some early poems with such a difficult audience as Godwin and Hazlitt, "they were pronounced to be as extraordinary as I thought them" (*LB*, p. 248). Keats entered a social group for whom sociability itself was a key value. As Hunt's dedication and preface to *Foliage* would argue and as Keats would suggest in his 1817 *Poems*, such sociability – the cheerful bonding of men and women – was a key to reforming a society divided by war, "money-getting," and religious sectarianism – this "war and money-injured land," as Hunt puts it (p. viii). Sociability, particularly when Hunt argues for it under the heading "Cursory Observations on Poetry and Cheerfulness," has struck many as a rather trivial solution to the period's pressing problems, but for Hunt and his circle sociability was a way of reclaiming the social and thus the political from what they saw as religious bigots, narrowly nationalist patriots, and money-driven misers. Sociability was a first step in healing the fissures in the commonwealth, in restoring what Wordsworth saw as the lost "confidence in social man" (*Excursion*, IV: 261) that he felt the French Revolution had destroyed, and thus in reclaiming society's ability to transform itself.

Welcoming Keats, Hunt became his key supporter, using the *Examiner* to make Keats's reputation as a poet. Keats published his first poem there, he was first reviewed there, and Hunt printed a large number of

Keats's poems during the period between their initial meeting in October of 1816 and the publication of Keats's first volume in early March 1817: "On First Looking into Chapman's Homer" (1 December 1816), "To Kosciusko" (16 February 1817), "After dark vapors have oppress'd our plains" (23 February), "To Haydon, with a Sonnet Written on Seeing the Elgin Marbles" and "On Seeing the Elgin Marbles" (9 March), and "This pleasant tale is like a little copse" (16 March). Since the *Examiner* did not print much verse, this is a remarkable amount of space to be given to an unknown poet, comparable to that given to Byron in the heyday of his friendship with Hunt in 1815–16 or to that given to Hunt himself. Moreover, this list is not a complete account of Keats in the *Examiner*, since it only includes poems first published there. Hunt would sometimes reprint Keats's poems, as when he placed Keats's sonnet "On the Grasshopper and the Cricket" – produced in a sonnet contest and published in Keats's *Poems* – together with his sonnet on the subject in the 21 September 1817 *Examiner*. Hunt would also at times quote from Keats in the midst of an article; to take one example, he cited stanzas 26–30 from the manuscript of *Jealousies* in the 23 August 1820 *Indicator*. We should also note that Keats published two poems – "To Ailsa Rock" and "Four seasons fill the measure of the year" – in Hunt's *Literary Pocket-Book* for 1819 (1818) and two more in the *Indicator* – "La Belle Dame sans Merci" (10 May 1820) and "As Hermes once took to his feathers light" (28 June 1820). Since Keats placed only three other poems in periodicals – "On the Sea" in the *Champion* (17 August 1817) and "Ode to a Nightingale" (July 1819) and "On a Grecian Urn" (January 1820) in the *Annals of the Fine Arts* – his involvement with Hunt's journals is significant, and it carries through Keats's life: the sonnet derived from Dante published in the *Indicator* is the last poem Keats saw published (his 1820 volume came out the same week). We need to stress Keats's connection with Hunt's journals in the face of comments that suggest that the completely isolated publication of "To the Sea" in the *Champion* represents some kind of defection by Keats from the *Examiner*.[12] Rather than seeking to separate Keats from Hunt's periodicals, we might, in fact, think of Keats as the house poet of the *Examiner* during late 1816 and early 1817, the period during which he came to be part of Hunt's circle. When he collected such early poems for his first volume, it was inevitable that they reflect his sense and celebration of the group around Leigh Hunt.

When a contemporary reader opened Keats's *Poems* of 1817, she would first have met a dedication to Hunt and then have turned to a long poem with an epigram by Hunt before moving on to two attempts at romances in a Huntian style and a number of other poems that name Hunt or bear his influence, before coming to a final poem invoking the Hunt household and circle. Everything about the book marks it as a coterie volume. As contemporary reviewers noted, Keats adopted Hunt's style. Keats's heroes in the volume – whether literary ones such as Spenser[13] or political ones such as Kosciusko – were also those of the Hunt circle. Even the organization of the book, with its opening and closing long poems and its sections of epistles and sonnets, resembles Hunt's coterie volume *Foliage* or the manuscript volume "Poems by Two Friends" produced by Benjamin Bailey and John Hamilton Reynolds, discussed in the last chapter.[14]

Keats's early work, then, insists upon his links to Hunt. Since Keats came into the literary world first as a poet of Hunt's *Examiner* and then as the author of a volume announcing his allegiance to the Hunt circle, his later identification as a member of Hunt's Cockney School was literally correct. Lockhart recognized another ideological enemy in reading the 1817 *Poems*, with the volume announcing in its very epigraph – the lines from Spenser "What more felicity can fall to creature, / Than to enjoy delight with liberty" – its commitment to a Cockney version of life, liberty, and the pursuit of happiness. We need to see how this volume is a product of the Hunt "party," as Keats termed it (letter to Bailey, 3 November 1817, *KL*, I: 180), in both senses of the word: that is, we need to see the coterie nature of this book, and then we need to examine its espousal of an ideology that Keats in large measure shared with other members of the circle such as Hunt, Shelley, Hazlitt, and Smith.

III

While Wordsworth perhaps was "not used to make / A present joy the matter of a song" (*Prelude*, I: 46–47), Keats's verse is overwhelmingly occasional. The immediacy of his poetry not only contributes to its "new fangled" quality, its urgent freshness, its embrace of a Huntian "now" that marks the Cockney style; it will also, as opposed to providing a retrospective account of failed or lost social vision in the past, announce a commitment in the present to a particular social group – the Hunt circle – and its vision of sociality and thus of society. The pieces that make up Keats's *Poems* celebrate members of the Hunt group, respond to their work, sometimes compete with it. Interestingly, the verse included in the volume which does not have some connection with the

Hunt circle tends to have arisen within the circle around George Felton Mathew. And beyond the poetry of this volume, we need only think of his poems to Fanny Brawne, of the verse written during his walking tour of 1818, or of the many poems included in letters or written as letters. Keats's is social poetry and thus poetry about society, politics, in a literal sense.

We should first note Keats's inclusion in *Poems* of pieces about Hunt and other members of the group. I have already referred to his early "Written on the Day that Mr. Leigh Hunt Left Prison"; once he had joined the group, Keats celebrated his first meetings at Hunt's cottage in poems such as "Keen, fitful gusts are whispering here and there," where Keats proclaims himself "brimfull of the friendliness / That in a little cottage I have found," and "On Leaving Some Friends at an Early Hour," which, according to Woodhouse's partial shorthand note, was written about "(Reynolds Hunt and [?]) in a hackney coach."[5] When through Hunt Keats met Haydon, he soon composed a sonnet praising Haydon, Wordsworth, and Hunt as the three "Great Spirits" of the age (19 or 20 November 1816). This sonnet is a good example of the collective, interactive nature of the group's work: it was the second of two Keats poems to Haydon, the first of which, "Addressed to Haydon," was a response to Wordsworth's "To B. R. Haydon," published in the *Champion* (4 February 1816) and the *Examiner* (31 March 1816); Hunt also wrote a poem to Haydon, published in the *Examiner* (20 October 1816) as "Written in a blank leaf of his Copy of Vasari's Lives of the Painters"; Keats knew both Wordsworth's and Hunt's poems, and his poem in turn inspired Reynolds's sonnet "To Haydon."

Hunt himself is omnipresent in *Poems*, from the dedicatory poem to the closing evocation of the Hunt household in "Sleep and Poetry." He appears as "Libertas" in "Specimen of an Induction to a Poem" and the verse epistles "To My Brother George" and "To Charles Cowden Clarke," poems modelled in part on Hunt's verse letters to Moore and Hazlitt. Hunt's *Story of Rimini* is the main influence on "Specimen of an Induction to a Poem" and "Calidore: A Fragment," and the sonnets "To one who has been long in city pent" and "To a Friend Who Sent Me Some Roses" have been linked by Allot (p. 45) to Hunt's Hampstead sonnets. The volume, then, asks to be identified as the work of a colleague of Hunt, and, of course, *Blackwood's* would oblige. Other comments make it equally clear that readers understood the author's desire to be identified with Hunt. The *Edinburgh Magazine and Literary Miscellany* (1 [October 1817], 254), for example, stated in its review of

Poems, "Of the author of this small volume we know nothing more than that he is said to be a very young man, and a particular friend of the Messrs Hunt, the editors of the *Examiner,* and of Mr. Hazlitt." Again, John Taylor, in deciding to become Keats's publisher, wrote to his father (16 May 1817) to defend the decision to print a writer made controversial by his associations with Hunt, agreeing "in finding much fault with his Dedication &c."[16] Unlike later Keats scholars, Keats's contemporaries understood that *Poems* proclaimed a political as well as aesthetic allegiance to the leader of the liberal intelligentsia.

Even poems that do not refer directly to the group arose from its practices and interests. The scene of writing for many of Keats's poems lies inside the circle, the most obvious being "On the Grasshopper and Cricket," written in a sonnet contest with Hunt. The most famous example is probably the sonnet "On First Looking into Chapman's Homer," written after a now celebrated literary evening involving Keats and Charles Cowden Clarke, who tells us, "A beautiful copy of the folio edition of Chapman's translation of Homer had been lent me ... and to work we went, turning to some of the 'famousest' passages, as we had scrapily known them in Pope's version . . . it was in the teeming wonderment of this ... first introduction that, when I came down to breakfast the next morning, I found upon my table a letter with no other enclosure than this famous sonnet" (*Recollections,* pp. 128–30). This interest in Chapman's Homer was not restricted to the two friends. The folio edition being examined by Keats and Clarke belonged to Thomas Alsager, Hunt's comrade and financial editor of the *Times;* Hunt and Lamb were admirers of Chapman; and Godwin had defended the translation of Homer in his *Lives of Edward and John Philips, Nephews and Pupils of Milton. Including Various Particulars of the Literary and Political History of Their Times* (1815).[17] Godwin's account of translation reads like a defense for Keats's reading of Homer through Chapman, which has of course been criticized. Godwin argues that while one should avoid contemporaneous translations, "obsolete translations" are

precious to the man of taste, the man of feeling, and the philosopher. In the old English Homer for example, I have some pleasure, in as much as I find Homer himself there; but I have also an inestimable pleasure added to this, while I remark, and feel in my inmost heart, the venerable and illustrious garb in which he is thus brought before me. This further pleasure I have, which I could not find even in the original itself. The translation of Homer, published by George Chapman, in the reign of queen Elizabeth and king James, is one of the greatest treasures the English language has to boast. (Pp. 241–42)

Godwin goes on to praise Chapman at Pope's expense. And in writing of Thomas North's translation of Plutarch, he sounds much the way Keats does in his sonnet: "and yet I must confess, till this book fell into my hands, I had no genuine feeling of Plutarch's merits, or knowledge of what sort of a writer he was" (p. 245). Keats's sonnet not only celebrates an evening of communal appreciation of poetry but also strokes a touchstone for the group as a whole. It is not surprising that this was the poem selected by Hunt to stand for Keats in his *Examiner* review "Young Poets" (1 December 1816), or that he cites it again in *Lord Byron and Some of His Contemporaries*, where he notes that "Modern criticism has made the public well acquainted with the merits of Chapman" (p. 248).

The dedicatory sonnet to Hunt that opened *Poems* also arose in a communal, coterie setting, as Clarke's story of its composition reveals: "on the evening when the last proof sheet was brought from the printer, it was accompanied by the information that if a 'dedication to the book was intended it must be sent forthwith'"; Keats, who was among several of his friends, then "drew to a side-table, and in the buzz of a mixed conversation ... he composed and brought to Charles Ollier, the publisher, the Dedication Sonnet to Leigh Hunt" (*Recollections*, p. 138). Other poems written at this time but not included in the volume responded to similar moments of collective activity and friendly companionship: for example, Keats wrote a sonnet in Clarke's copy of their mutually beloved Chaucer and composed verses after delighting in the Elgin Marbles with Haydon.

Of course, a number of the poems in the 1817 volume were written before Keats came to know Hunt personally, but, as indicated above, his literary and ideological influence was often still felt. And even those poems that do not relate to Hunt or his circle still bear the marks of coterie production, this time the circle being that of George Felton Mathew. Beyond the epistle "To George Felton Mathew," there are "To Some Ladies" and "On Receiving a Curious Shell and a Copy of Verses from the Same Ladies," written to the Mathew sisters, cousins of George Felton. One should also place here the sonnet stanzas of "Woman! when I behold thee flippant, vain" which Mathew singled out for praise (while damning the Chapman's Homer sonnet) in his review of the 1817 volume (*European Magazine* 71 [May 1817], 434–37). There are also poems connected with Keats's brothers: the verse epistle "To My Brother George," the sonnets "To My Brother George," and "To My Brothers,"[18] "To Georgiana Augusta Wylie" (a sonnet to George's future wife), and the two poems – "To****" ("Hadst thou liv'd in days of old")[19] and "To –" ("Had I a man's fair form") – that were written at George's request as valentines to Mary Frogley (cousin to Woodhouse and a member of the Mathew circle). "O Solitude," with its mention of "two kindred spirits" (l. 14), was written either to George Keats or to George Felton Mathew.[20] There are still more occasional poems – "To Charles Cowden Clarke," the third verse epistle in the volume, and the sonnet "To a Friend Who Sent Me Some Roses," addressed to Charles Wells, schoolmate of Tom Keats and friend of Hunt and Hazlitt. In fact, both the volume's sonnet section and that devoted to epistles insist upon the coterie nature of Keats's verse.

In invoking the life and values of the Hunt circle, Keats's section of sonnets is linked to similar gatherings in other Cockney School volumes. I have already noted Reynolds's and Bailey's "Poems by Two Friends," the manuscript volume prepared for the Leigh sisters with its marked section of sonnets. Horace Smith's 1821 *Amarynthus* volume includes in its selection of "Sonnets, and Other Poems" the sonnet that Smith wrote in response to or perhaps in competition with Shelley's "Ozymandias" and the sonnet "To Percy Bysshe Shelley, Esq., on His Poems," as well as such occasional pieces as "On Unexpectedly Receiving a Letter, with a Sum of Money" and "On the Spanish Revolution." Reynolds's *Garden of Florence; and Other Poems* (1821) includes in those other poems three sonnets on Robin Hood ("Sonnet to — With the Two Following"), two of which had been sent in a letter to Keats; "Sweet Poets of the gentle antique line," which inspired Keats's "Blue!– 'Tis the Life of Heaven" in response; and "Sonnet on the Picture of a Lady," which takes up the story of Isabella and her pot of basil that Keats had tackled for the Boccaccio volume planned with Reynolds. The volume that most insistently uses the sonnet to invoke the group is Hunt's own *Foliage* with its verses to Keats, Shelley, Haydon, Novello, and Smith and its pointedly occasional titles such as "To — — , M. D. on His Giving Me a Lock of Milton's Hair."

Keats's sonnets also indicate their occasional, social nature in such titles as "Written on the Day That Mr. Leigh Hunt Left Prison," "To a Friend Who Sent Me Some Roses," and "On Leaving Some Friends at an Early Hour"; the fact that some of the poems (two of the sonnets and all of the epistles) are marked by dates is another textual indicator of their circumstantial, worldly existence. Moreover, these poems revel in sociability; there is little of the solitary singer or the escapist fantasist here. I have already mentioned the "friendliness" found at Hunt's cottage in "Keen, fitful gusts." Again, the roses sent to Keats by Wells

"Whisper'd of peace, and truth, and friendliness unquell'd" (l. 14). The first sonnet included, addressed to George Keats, ends its description of ocean and moon with the question "But what, without the social thought of thee, / Would be the wonders of the sky and sea?" While this is less powerful than Shelley's close to "Mont Blanc" – "And what were thou, and earth, and stars, and sea, / If to the human mind's imaginings / Silence and solitude were vacancy?" – Keats's poem does suggest the importance of community, of connection to his imaginings. Even in calling out in a sonnet to "Solitude," Keats turns to companionship, finding it "the highest bliss of human-kind, / When to thy haunts two kindred spirits flee" (ll. 13–14); and when he writes "On Leaving Some Friends at an Early Hour," he finds his spirit is "not content so soon to be alone" (l. 14). Other sonnets immortalize communal moments – his brother Tom's birthday ("To My Brothers"), reading Chapman's Homer with Clarke, writing sonnets with Hunt. Taken as a group, the sonnets – in both their compositional history and in their arguments – firmly circumstance Keats's poetry in the vital social life of his family and friends.

Keats's verse epistles – which should be linked to the seven "Epistles" in Hunt's *Foliage*, the "Epistle to . . ." which follows the sonnets in Reynolds's *Garden of Florence*, and Moore's volumes of "intercepted" letters – announce their social, communal nature by their very genre. Serving as actual letters, they are of necessity occasional. The epistle to George Felton Mathew, whom Keats identifies as his "Too partial friend" (l. 11), originated as a response to the celebration (later published in *European Magazine*, October 1816) of Keats in Mathew's "To a Poetical Friend." The other two epistles were both posted from Margate, where Keats spent August and September of 1816. They are also occasional in that they address Keats's immediate concerns as he considers becoming a poet: in "To George Felton Mathew," Keats worries that "far different cares" (l. 17) will keep him from the poetry that he is sure surrounds his friend; in "To My Brother George," he fears "That I should never hear Apollo's song" (l. 9), while in "To Charles Cowden Clarke," Keats explains "Why I have never penn'd a line to thee: / Because my thoughts were never free, and clear, / And little fit to please a classic ear" (ll. 22–24). Centering on Keats's worries about his poetic abilities, each epistle finds consolation and inspiration in turning to a friend who is imagined as having something the poet lacks; they possess a dynamic of generosity not unlike Coleridge's "conversation" poems. These poems celebrate the ways in which Keats's poetry is nurtured within a

social sphere, with "To George Felton Mathew" imagining a brotherhood of poets, "To My Brother George" praising the perfect reader,
and "To Charles Cowden Clarke" celebrating the ideal mentor.

The earliest of these epistles evokes Keats's pre-Hunt association with
George Felton Mathew: what Keats hopes will be a collaborative
partnership. The poem opens with the call to create "a brotherhood in
song" to rival Beaumont and Fletcher, the "brother Poets" "Who with
combined powers, their wit employ'd / To raise a trophy to the drama's
muses" (ll. 2, 5–7). The two earlier dramatists – whose "partnership
productions" were praised by Reynolds in the *Champion* (7 January 1816,
pp. 6–7) – stand almost as the patron saints of the kind of collaborative
work that Keats sought. Hunt would also invoke Beaumont and
Fletcher, in the epigraph ("In the fields, or by the fire. Beaumont &
Fletcher")[21] he gave to his manuscript version of the grasshopper-and-
cricket poem he wrote in competition with Keats – the epigraph suggesting that this sonnet "contest" was not so much a competition as a
collaborative social act between "brother" poets.

As McGann, Allot (p. 25), and ultimately Mathew himself (*KC* II: 186)
show us, the epistle hinges on a contrast between Keats's day-to-day
entanglements in his work "walking the hospitals" and Mathew's freedom to write. The problem that some have with such a poem, however,
is exactly that we must have this occasional – "insider" – knowledge in
order to appreciate it; it would seem not only that such poetry is coterie
writing but that its meaning is restricted to those who are privy to the
secrets of the group. McGann argues that the poem contains not only a
"generalized reference . . . for the public at large" but also a "personal
reference . . . available only to what Byron used to call the 'knowing
ones.'"[22] McGann posits a level of "personal reference" and presumably private knowledge opposed to the "generalized reference" of, say,
the poem's allusion to Milton, which is open to the public. This suggests
that the poem, at least at some points, speaks in a way only accessible to
someone like Mathew who was aware of Keats's daily experiences.
While I would first question whether the poem is open in some special
way to Mathew (in any event, when he wrote about the poem to Milnes
in 1847, he found "What he [Keats] says more is at present involved in
obscurity"; *KC*, II: 187), I would also argue that once the poem appears
in print the public at large not only responds to the "generalized
reference" but is also made aware by the poem's very genre that it is
listening in on a more specific conversation. Generic conventions, which
are obviously shared by Keats's readership at large, send us in search of

information which is not ultimately "private" but simply in the possession of a smaller community. That is, what we get here is not a private meaning opposed to a public one, but a concrete social act – a conversation between two poets – being shared with a larger social group, the readers of Keats's *Poems*. We are, in fact, being asked to join the group in reading the poem; in a sense, we come to embody the "brother poets," for as we read we become both the "I" speaking the poem and the "you," the "Mathew" addressed in it. Moving the poem from manuscript to print, Keats uses its coterie nature not to exclude potential readers but to bid us to become part of the coterie itself.

The poem is able to invite us into the communion it imagines exactly because it is an imagined community. That is, it is not at all clear that Mathew in fact shared with Keats the values embodied in the poem that the author clearly hopes his readers will embrace. The epistle offers three linked alternatives to the cares that beset the poet and threaten his muse. He will pursue his inspiration in nature (ll. 31–52), seeking to escape "this dark city" and its "contradictions" by finding a "flowery spot, sequestered, wild, romantic"; in poetry (ll. 53–65) with its "soft humanity"; and in the histories of those who fought for liberty (ll. 65–71), such as King Alfred, William Tell, and William Wallace.[23] Keats's Huntian trinity of the physical world, beautiful poetry, and political liberty would not have been that of the far more conventional Mathew. As he wrote to Milnes, Keats "was of the sceptical and republican school. An advocate for the innovations which were making progress in his time. A faultfinder with everything established. I, on the contrary, hated controversy and dispute – dreaded discord and disorder – loved the institutions of my country – believed them founded in nature and truth – best calculated to uphold religion and morality – harmonising on the one hand with the Theocracy of heaven, and on the other with the paternal rule at home" (*KC*, II: 185–86).

Mathew endorses the interlocking hierarchies of patriarchal family, monarchical government, and institutionalized religion that were rejected by Keats, repeatedly attacked by Hunt, and embodied by Shelley in the figure of the villainous Count Cenci. It is not at all surprising that Mathew ends his discussion of his ideological disagreements with Keats by indicating that "At this time Keats was on intimate terms with Leigh Hunt." Keats – skeptic and republican, according to Mathew – stands on quite different ground from the friend to whom he is writing and closer to Shelley, who reportedly in the summer of 1816 signed himself in hotel registers as a democrat, a philanthropist, and an atheist. Keats and

Mathew are brother poets not in some private space but in the imagined social space of the poem into which we can then enter.

This moment in the poem suggests two problems for the project of the Hunt circle. First, while I have been arguing for the inclusiveness of their poetry, it must again be admitted that it includes only those who want to be included, those who in this case share the values of the poem. This brotherhood would not appear welcoming to Lockhart and his ilk. We can see this difficulty in, for example, Hunt's dedication of *Foliage* to Sir John Edward Swinburne, who is praised through a series of contrasts that exclude as much as they include even as Hunt announces the book's object as "a love of nature out of doors, and of sociality within":

You are not one of those who pay the strange compliment to heaven of depreciating this world, because you believe in another: you admire its beauties both in nature and art; you think that a knowledge of the finest voices it has uttered, ancient as well as modern, ought, even in gratitude, to be shared by the sex that has inspired so many of them; – a rational piety and a manly patriotism does not hinder you from putting the Phidian Jupiter over your organ, or flowers at the end of your room. (P. viii)

Swinburne is praised at the expense of those who, in Hunt's view, deprecate this world through religious conviction, who demean women, who endorse an irrational patriotism. The group believes its values – sociability, cosmopolitanism, religious tolerance, some sense of sexual equality – are inclusive, but clearly they do not include the individual who wishes to uphold king, church, and the patriarchy. Any community, defined by its values, its practices, its pleasures, is of necessity going to exclude someone. Of course, the Hunt circle's hope is that they will attract or convert their readers rather than excluding them.

The second problem arises through Keats's attempt to overcome such exclusions in an imagined community, which is, of course, also an attempt to broaden the appeal of the group's vision beyond the immediate circle – not everyone can literally be a member of a particular coterie. The group wishes to celebrate the local, the particular, the lived experience of the community, but they also wish to speak to a much larger audience, to become the (un)acknowledged legislators of the world (this is to restate in other terms the tension between their use of coterie manuscript practices and their ultimate goal of appearing in print). The circle's use of coterie practices in printed works and their evocation of a particular group as a model for an alternative society are parts of an attempt to negotiate the movement from the circle to society.

It is imaginative sympathy – the ability to care for others one does not know directly and to envision a community, a world different from the given one – that is the vehicle for this crossing, but the Hunt circle – Keats and Shelley in particular – are aware of the vicissitudes of the imagination as the move from the concrete to the envisioned can lead one not to a vision shared by a growing circle but to the waking dream of the eccentric self. Questioning the imagination so as to refine it is part of the quest for a renewed society that must be imagined before it can be made.

Keats's concern about lost imaginative inspiration is more, then, than a worry over his own poetic abilities, and it is essential to the poem's quest for community that he work to recover imaginative power, as he does most clearly in his rather wild account of the transformations Mathew has supposedly undergone. Mathew provides another of his circumstancing comments in discussing Keats's account of this Ovidian metamorphosis: "My transformation to 'a fish of gold' may refer to my having been devoted to a secular and uncongenial employment, in which I was engaged at the time he knew me" (*KC*, II: 187). We have here an occasion when the recipient of the letter, and of any private allusions it might have, proves himself to be a less than accurate reader of the verses. While Keats did complain when one of his friends found his occupation getting in the way of his poetry (see, for example, his concern that "Reynolds is completely limed in the law: he is not only reconcil'd to it but hobbyhorses upon it" [letter to the George Keatses, 19 March 1819, *KL*, II: 78]), in this poem he is contrasting his own involvement in work to Mathew's devotion to the muse. While Keats is "oft in doubt whether at all / I shall again see Phoebus in the morning" (ll. 20–21), he is certain that for Mathew the muse "will thy every dwelling grace, / And make 'a sun-shine in a shady place,': / For thou wast once a floweret blooming wild, / Close to the source, bright, pure and unde-fil'd, / Whence gush the streams of song" (ll. 74–78). Cast into a rivulet by "chaste Diana" as a gift for her brother Apollo (ll. 79–83), Mathew as flower was then changed into a golden fish by Apollo (ll. 85–86) before becoming a "black-eyed swan" and only then a man (ll. 85–89). These transformations – looking forward to passages in "I stood tip-toe," in *Endymion*, and beyond – provide Mathew with a poetic lineage as he passes from Helicon, home of the Muses, through the hands of Diana – Keats's "Maker of sweet poets" ("I stood tip-toe," l. 116) – and the god of poetry, Apollo, to become a swan with its famous song before resolving into a human poet. Of course, in arguing that Mathew is a true poet, in granting inspiration and genius to his friend, Keats too finds his reward, his poetic voice. Interestingly, that voice, even before Keats met Hunt, was already a Cockney one: this passage, filled with the "flashy expressions," the allusions (here, to Spenser, perhaps Chatterton, and Greco-Roman myth), the energy, and the familiarity that as I have noted were seen to mark the Cockney style, represents exactly the kind of verse that infuriated the reviewers with the *Quarterly* and *Blackwood's*. But what they hear here is, I think, not just a style they dislike but also a lifestyle, an oddly open and democratic coterie, where anyone can write about the classical myths, where anyone may have experienced "travels strange" (l. 90), where anyone (in the language of the epigraph to the "Epistles" from *Britannia's Pastorals*) can become the next "young" "Shepheard" ready "to fit his quill." The brotherhood of poets evokes a larger sense of *fraternité*. The close but not closed coterie is a model for a larger transformed community.

"To My Brother George," a poem more literally on brotherhood, also voices Keats's concerns about his abilities as a poet: "Full many a dreary hour have I past, / My brain bewildered, and my mind o'ercast / With heaviness; in seasons when I've thought / . . . That I should never hear Apollo's song" (ll. 1–3, 9). Keats's deprivation is contrasted with what is given to "those that love the bay," and here he has Hunt, "Libertas" (l. 24), particularly in mind. Poets such as Hunt are able to discover poetry in everything (ll. 21–22), to experience an imaginative vision of life that goes beyond the everyday (ll. 25–52), and finally to transform the world outside of poetry by inspiriting the "patriot" (ll. 73–76), the "sage" (ll. 77–80), and lovers (ll. 81–109), as poetry has a cultural and political impact. Keats again finds he can write poetry in praising the poetic abilities of others, and he resolves his problem by again imagining a social setting for his writing, here his brother's response to reading his verses:

> As to my sonnets, though none else should heed them,
> I feel delighted, still, that you should read them.
> Of late, too, I have had much calm enjoyment,
> Stretch'd on the grass at my best lov'd employment
> Of scribbling lines for you.   (ll. 117–21)

Where the poem to Mathew ended with an exercise of Keats's poetic fancy, the verses to his brother close upon what Hunt would call a "Now," a description of the things that occupy Keats's immediate consciousness: "E'en now I'm pillowed on a bed of flowers"; "Now 'tis I see a canvass'd ship, and now / Mark the bright silver curling round her prow"; "Now I direct my eyes into the west" (ll. 123, 133–34, 139). While mainly occupied with flowers and the sea, Keats is aware of more sinister aspects of the landscape, for the poppies with their "scarlet coats" are "So pert and useless, that they bring to mind / The scarlet coats that pester human-kind" (ll. 128–30), a reference to the troops bivouacked across England during the Napoleonic wars to guard against both potential invasion and internal uprisings. Keats had seen a depot for troops during his stay as Carisbrooke, "which disgusted me extremely with Government for placing such a Nest of Debauchery in so beautiful a place . . . In the room where I slept at Newport I found this on the Window 'O Isle spoilt by the Mil*a*tary'" (to John Hamilton Reynolds, 17 April 1817, *KL*, I: 131–32). Keats grants his "private" communion with his brother a "public" significance: the false society of the military, disruptive of the larger community, stands in contrast to the communion between the two brothers, evoked again in the poem's closing lines: "Why westward turn? 'Twas but to say adieu! / 'Twas but to kiss my hand, dear George, to you!" (ll. 141–42).

"To Charles Cowden Clarke" is based on the same opposition between Keats, who is seen as losing his way "Whene'er I venture on the stream of rhyme" (l. 16), and Clarke, who is presented as one who has read deep in the classics, Spenser and Tasso, Shakespeare and Milton (ll. 24–41). Perhaps even more important, Clarke has had the advantage of friendship with Hunt the political martyr – "wronged Libertas" (l. 44) – and the author of *Story of Rimini*, who has told Clarke stories "Of troops chivalrous prancing through a city, / And tearful ladies made for love, and pity: / With many else which I have never known" (ll. 46–48). Keats is willing "For you to try my dull, unlearned quill" (l. 51), because it is Clarke who has taught him to love literature, from Spenser to Milton, from the epigram to the epic. Clarke has also instructed him in history, teaching him to love the heroes of liberty such as Alfred, Tell, and Brutus (ll. 68–72). Most important, he feels he can write to Clarke because he knows Clarke to be a social man, one who delights in life; it is with Clarke that he has enjoyed the music of Mozart, Arne, and Handel, with Clarke that he has "revell'd in a chat that ceased not / When at night-fall among your books we got," with Clarke that he himself has learned to appreciate not just art but life – " 'Life's very toys / With him,' said I, 'will take a pleasant charm'" (ll. 109–29). Keats again finds his inspiration in imagining the gifts given another and locates his poetry in a moment of social exchange.

The epistles and the sonnets, then, evoke, celebrate, and ultimately promulgate a coterie life, a communal sense of poetry as a shared joy in life. These poems praise members of the Hunt (and Mathew) group and recount moments spent together. They describe life within the circle and find in that life the inspiration, the content, and the audience necessary to Keats's art. In the end, these poems invite their readers to join the world they evoke, urging them to become members of the coterie, to share in the Cockney delight in literature and liberty. Not only are the communalism, the liberality of these poems linked to a liberal politics set against an ideology of private "money getting" and social divisiveness, but this invitation is embodied in the very form of the verse; for its sometimes slangy diction, its use of classical and other allusions not for intimidation but enticement, and its "new fangled" rhythms and rhymes all sought to bring to poetry a new audience – the middle-class readers on the rise and the artisans ridiculed by *Blackwood's*. The imagined coterie of writer and readers, like the real Hunt circle, is offered as a point of mediation with traditional cultural capital. We can better appreciate the power of the aesthetic playfulness and generosity of these pieces when we realize that they are part of a party platform, an invitation to enroll in the Cockney school of song, which in the longer opening and closing poems is revealed to be the Cockney school of politics as well.

IV

Keats's volume becomes something more than a simple record of the circle through its opening and closing poems, which set forth a manifesto for the group. Of course, even some of the short poems announce Keats's links to specific aspects of the *Examiner* group's ideology. "To Kosciusko," one of the last poems written for the 1817 volume, shows Keats's ties to stands taken in the *Examiner*, for it celebrates one of Hunt's heroes (i.e. *Examiner*, 12 January 1817), the Polish patriot who fought in the American War of Independence and in his own country's revolt against Russia in 1791. Hunt had a bust of Kosciusko in his cottage at the Vale of Health (as Keats notes in "Sleep and Poetry," ll. 387–88), and he also wrote a sonnet on Kosciusko, "who took part neither with Bonaparte in the height of his power, nor with the Allies," which was published in the *Examiner* (19 November 1815) and later in *Foliage*. Again, Keats's sonnet "To Haydon" attacks "money mong'ring" (l. 8) in an echo of the *Examiner*'s repeated assaults on the "spirit of money-getting."

Keats's "To Hope," written in February 1815, during the period in which he was writing such clearly political poems as the one on Hunt's release or the sonnet on the anniversary of Charles II's restoration, takes up the issue of Wordsworthian "Despondency" (l. 9) and seeks to defeat it by writing poetry – "sigh[ing] out sonnets to the midnight air" – and by appealing to "the patriot's high bequest, / Great Liberty!" (ll. 28, 37–38). Far from seeking an apolitical aesthetic, Keats's volume continually links poetry to politics, literature to liberty.

Keats's commitment to the Hunt circle's vision is most fully developed in "I stood tip-toe" and "Sleep and Poetry." The better known "Sleep and Poetry," the volume's closing poem, evokes life at Hunt's cottage in order to follow Hunt in announcing a new school of poetry. As Clarke tells us, "It was in the library at Hunt's cottage, where an extemporary bed had been made up for him on the sofa, that he composed the framework and many lines of the poem" (*Recollections*, pp. 133–34).[24] The poem's bibliographic code signals its status as coterie verse: the epigraph is from the pseudo-Chaucerian *The Floure and the Leafe*, so admired by the group (see *Examiner*, 3 September 1815) that it prompted the verses by Keats in Clarke's copy of the text and a responding sonnet from Reynolds; it adopts Hunt's couplet style, as Keach has shown, and uses Huntian images and diction; it invokes Hunt's muse, who will account as "poet-kings" those "Who simply tell the most heart-easing things" (ll. 267–78); and it celebrates Hunt himself as one of the saviors of contemporary poetry (ll. 226–29). "Sleep and Poetry" is Keats's announcement that he has found himself as a poet in joining the Hunt circle.

It also embraces a Huntian program: that poetry is a "friend / To soothe the cares, and lift the thoughts of man" (ll. 246–47), a position taken by Hunt in his "Preface" to *Foliage*, "Including Cursory Observations on Poetry and Cheerfulness." "Sleep and Poetry" is a call for inspiration, an outline of a poetic project, and a sketch of poetic history. In setting forth Keats's program for poetry, it is in a sense a response to the worries about Keats's status as a poet voiced in the epistles (and sometimes here, as he must still fight off a sense of his own immaturity and the threat of "despondence" [l. 281]). He has discovered the "end and aim of Poetry" in a "vast idea" of life which enables him to "glean / Therefrom my liberty" (ll. 290–93) as he commits himself to the values set forth in his volume's epigram. This poetic project, which voices Keats's desire to overwhelm himself in poetry so that he can produce first erotic pastoral romances and then a poetry of the "nobler life, / Where I may find the agonies, the strife / Of human hearts," is a Cockney version of the Virgilian progress from pastoral to didactic to epic poetry.

With its celebration of earlier English poetry, its attack on the "French" school, and its praise for Hunt and Wordsworth (his admiration for the latter modified by concern over what Hunt calls in his review of the poem "the morbidity that taints the productions of the Lake Poets"), Keats's history of poetry is similar to that offered by Hunt in his "Young Poets" review and in his piece on Keats's volume itself. It also echoes in its comment about the couplet as a "rocking horse" that displaces Pegasus (ll. 185–87) Hazlitt's attack on the heroic couplet ("Dr. Johnson and Pope would have converted his [Milton's] vaunting Pegasus into a rocking horse": *Examiner*, 20 August 1815, p. 542). We should also note that Keats joins here other members of the group who wrote verse histories or criticism of verse, the most famous being Byron's *English Bards and Scotch Reviewers* (1809), but we could also include Hunt's *Feast of Poets* (1811 in *Reflector*; 1814), Reynolds's *Eden of the Imagination* (1814), and the Smith brothers' *Rejected Addresses* (1812); in prose, we could think of Hazlitt's *Lectures on the English Poets* (1818), Peacock's "Four Ages of Poetry" (1820), Shelley's *Defence of Poetry* (1821; 1840), and Reynolds's "The Pilgrimage of Living Poets to the Stream of Castaly" (1816). Having adopted the Hunt circle's view of past literary history, it is no surprise that Keats celebrates the poetry it is writing in the present: in praising the birth of a poetic "myrtle, fairer than / E'er grew in Paphos" (ll. 248–49), Keats rejoices in what Woodhouse calls the "coming age of poetry" and "the approaching generation of poets" (*Annotated "Poems"*, p. 212, for ll. 248–50) and in what Allot has seen as more specifically Hunt's poetry (p. 80).

The poem closes and thus ends the volume with an evocation of the life of the Hunt circle, its "brotherhood, / And friendliness, the nurse of mutual good" (ll. 317–18). It celebrates the sonnet contests, that often ridiculed feature of Huntian literary sociability, as Keats speaks of "The hearty grasp that sends a pleasant sonnet / Into the brain ere one can think upon it; / The silence when some rhymes are coming out; / And when they're come, the very pleasant rout" (ll. 319–22). The Hunt circle provides the social setting for the production of poetry sought in the verse epistles. Keats finds inspiration in Hunt's home as he admires the books available at Hunt's cottage, enjoys the music that fills the house, prizes the prints, busts, and portraits collected by Hunt. Importantly, most of these works of art are mythological celebrations of pleasure and the erotic, but there are also images of poetic precursors such as Sappho and Petrarch and of political heroes such as Alfred and Kosciusko. Hunt himself appears as the poet "who keeps the keys / Of pleasure's temple" (ll. 354–55). Quite simply, the poem describes life in the Hunt circle and uses that life as the ground from which to build Keats's vision of poetry and his own career. While the subject of the poem may seem to be his own poetic development, the process of becoming a poet is placed in a fully socialized scene of writing. The poem arises not from lonely inspiration but from shared daily rituals and pleasures. The function of poetry is not to offer private insight or consolation but to transform a culture of despondency into one devoted to the hopes of a world reformed.

The volume's opening poem, "I stood tip-toe upon a little hill," has received little attention,[25] although it plays a part in Marjorie Levinson's fascinating attempt in *Keats's Life of Allegory* to place Keats within a middle-class aesthetic. She explores the poem's relationship to what she sees as the double tradition behind it: poetry offering an objective topography descending from Gray and Thomson, and that providing a landscape of the mind deriving from Dyer's "Grongar Hill." She finds that Keats fails to master either set of conventions, for he does not objectively possess the aristocratic landscape (Caen Wood) he describes and lacks the full subjectivity needed to explore an inner space (pp. 235–45). In commenting on the opening line of the poem, she explicitly contrasts Keats's attempt with a Wordsworthian one:

By the familiarity and ingenuousness of the word [tip-toe], Keats implies ... a delicate intimacy between reader and writer. The word alerts us to the pleasure Keats proposes to impart and to the pleasure he forgoes. Both the gravity and the gracelessness of the Wordsworthian contract are implicitly refused. In the rejection, one glimpses that widespread and quite consciously political antagonism Marilyn Butler has marked out between the poets of the first generation (fideistic, northern, gothic, ascetic) and those of the second (Liberal, southern, Renaissance, sensuous). (P. 239)

Levinson adds, "Or rather, one registers in Keats's opening line his exclusion from that cultural debate." It is here that a discussion of the poem needs to begin, for I will argue that "I stood tip-toe" is directly engaged in this debate, that the poem is not a topographical poem, whether objective or subjective, but a polemical account of myth set against that offered by Wordsworth in the fourth book of the *Excursion*.

"I stood tip-toe upon a little hill" opens with characteristic Cockney polemical swagger. The poem's first line, often seen as a strained attempt to acquire physical and poetic stature and used by Levinson to indicate Keats's exclusion from certain cultural power, strikes me as a Cockney parody of the Wanderer's claim in *Excursion* IV: 110–14: "it may be allowed me to remember / What visionary powers of eye and soul / In youth were mine *when stationed on top / Of some huge hill*, expectant, I beheld / The sun rise up" (emphasis added).[26] Keats, tiptoeing on his little hill, is not going to offer the sublime landscapes and grand moral theology of Wordsworth. Like Hunt – whose poem of sexual liberation, *The Story of Rimini*, supplies Keats with his epigraph – Keats creates instead a poetry of pleasure: looking over his landscape, "I was light-hearted, / And many pleasures to my vision started; / So I straightway began to pluck a posey / Of luxuries bright, milky, soft and rosy" (ll. 25–28). We get a typical Cockney near pun here on "posey" and Keats's favorite word for poetry, poesy, and this pun suggests that the organization of the poem is not so much that of the conventional locodescriptive surveyor of topography as it is that of the flower arranger.

The poem first offers a posy of plants and flowers, from the "bush of May flowers" through laburnum and violets in lines 29–34, to "A filbert hedge" with various trees in lines 35–46, "ardent marigolds" in lines 47–56, "sweetpeas" in lines 56–60, and "evening primroses" in lines 107–15. The poem advances by adding flora, an organizational device that would have been clearer had Keats not inserted lines 61–106, not present in what appears to be the first finished section of the poem (ll. 1–60, 107–14).[27] Still, these added lines – which describe a streamside scene before evoking a nymphlike maiden for Keats to admire – fit with the poem's program of pleasure. Then, at almost the exact midpoint of the poem (line 116 out of 240), Keats moves from his posy of flowers to poesy as he offers a group of poetic luxuries, the four myths – Cupid and Psyche, Pan and Syrinx, Narcissus and Echo, and Endymion and Cynthia – of the poem's closing section. These myths will provide Keats with a vehicle to set forth his difference from his precursor and his *Excursion*, for he will use the two central myths to analyze what he calls elsewhere the "wordsworthian or egotistical sublime," while the framing tales are offered as versions of Keats's own poetry of pleasure. When Wordsworth later found Keats in *Endymion* offering a "pretty piece of paganism," he recognized that the younger poet was engaged in a treatment of myth quite opposed to his in the *Excursion*.[28]

Ever since the publication of *Poems*, it has been recognized that Keats responded in his opening piece to the fourth book of Wordsworth's *Excursion*.[29] The Hunt circle was much taken with Wordsworth's account of mythology in this book. It was praised by Lamb as well as by Keats's critical mentor Hazlitt in his 1814 review. Hunt was rereading the *Excursion* in the fall of 1816 when he and Keats first met, and Wordsworth lies behind Hunt's own attempts at myth in "Hero and Leander," "Bacchus and Ariadne," and the "Nymphs." We learn from the commonplace books of the Leigh women discussed earlier that Reynolds provided them a kind of personal "Cliff Notes" version of Wordsworth's long poem.³⁰ When Wordsworth sat for Haydon's "Christ's Entry into Jerusalem" during December 1817, he read out loud the entirety of book IV, presumably knowing it would please his audience.³¹ Echoes of the *Excursion* can be found throughout the work of the group, from "Alastor" to *Childe Harold* III; from *Endymion* to *Laon and Cythna* and its source, Peacock's unfinished "Ahrimanes"; from Reynolds's "Romance of Youth" to Smith's *Amarynthus, the Nympholept*. This involvement with Wordsworth's poem is not a simple act of homage; instead, the group's engagement with the *Excursion* and the accelerating distinction being drawn between the Lakers and the Cockneys lead them to a collective effort to rewrite what was the central poem in their Wordsworth canon. We can understand "I stood tip-toe" as an early contribution to this larger effort to contest Wordsworth's containment of pagan myth in his account of man coming to God through nature.

Wordsworth's treatment of myth in book IV of the *Excursion* occurs when the Solitary's interlocutors seek to correct the "despondency" into which he has fallen, a despair that has arisen from his "Disappointment from the French Revolution" and his subsequent "loss of confidence in social man" (l. 261). The revolutionary belief that humankind could create a utopia on its own was both impious and unnatural, for this faith in humanity ignored "nature's gradual processes" to pursue radical change and thus represented an aspiration "Rashly, to fall once more," seizing the "false fruit" of self-reliance and self-determination offered to "overweening spirits" (ll. 288–91). In the section of the book which the prose Argument labels "Superstition better than apathy," Wordsworth contends that myth, even as superstition, is a defense against what he sees as the corrosive power of modern skepticism (represented here by Voltaire; ll. 995–1034). Wordsworth offers a lesson in comparative religion in which we learn that the Jewish, Persian, Babylonian, Chaldean, and Grecian modes of belief all offered a way for their people to connect with nature and ultimately with God. The most important passage for the Hunt circle was the one on "pagan Greece":

– In that fair clime, the lonely herdsman, stretched
On the soft grass through half a summer's day,
With music lulled his indolent repose:
And, in some fit of weariness, if he,
When his own breath was silent, chanced to hear
A distant strain, far sweeter than the sounds
Which his poor skill could make, his fancy fetched,
Even from the blazing chariot of the sun,
A beardless Youth, who touched a golden lute,
And filled the illumined groves with ravishment.

(Ll. 851–60)

Here and in other accounts of the creation of world myth, Wordsworth argues that an imaginative response to nature inevitably leads one to grasp the supernatural. There are many historically contingent paths that humankind has followed, but they all lead him through nature to God: "As men from men / Do, in the constitution of their souls, differ... So manifold and various are the ways / Of restoration, fashion-ed to the steps / Of all infirmity, and tending all / To the same point, attainable by all – / Peace in ourselves, and union with our God" (ll. 1106–8, 1112–16). When we come to the section on Greek myth (ll. 817–762, 847–87), we are to understand that the Greeks offer a particular historical version of a universal truth: we can find a way out of despon-dency and to the transcendent through an imaginative response to nature.

Moreover, natural religion offers the same political lesson throughout the ages. Greek myth is seen to stand "in contempt / Of doubt and bold denial hourly urged / Amid the wrangling schools" (ll. 733–35), just as Wordsworth's own myth of nature is offered to rebut the bold denial and doubt of the revolutionary era. Nature and the mythopoetic re-sponse to it are the guarantees of religiosity. If one abandons all attempts at social regeneration, despondency can be defeated through an imagin-ative response to nature that points beyond this world to the divine. Myth is a record of humanity's struggle to come to know God, a struggle fulfilled through Christianity and betrayed by the French Revolution with its turn to society rather than nature and nature's God. If one binds the mythopoetic imagination to a nature that leads through a glass darkly to the divine, then the imagination can create no "false" myths of liberty, equality, fraternity.

Wordsworth's direct ideological use of myth as a means of combat-ing the disorienting splendors and miseries of the age of revolution engages a larger cultural war over the meaning of myth. Wordsworth is most clearly responding to an Enlightenment assault on superstition which saw writers such as Voltaire and Hume constructing myth (and by extension religion itself) as a product of the savage mind to be debunked. When writers such as the Baron d'Holbach used pagan myth to attack Christianity and its institutions, Christian apologists felt the need to respond, offering accounts that tamed ancient myth, deriding it themselves as superstition or uncovering it as a degenerate version of biblical truths. Wordsworth is part of the second of these responses when he speaks of "those bewildered Pagans of old time" who looked "Beyond their own poor natures and above" (ll. 934–35). Of course, as Wordsworth himself recognized in having the Solitary suggest that this defense of paganism might lead one back to "Romish phantasy" (l. 908), there is a danger in this turn to myth. One might rescue myth for projects quite different from Wordsworth's. The Deist John Toland shared with Wordsworth a sense of connection between paganism and Christianity, but he located it in a primitive monotheism from which both are seen to be derived. In a more radical interpretation, Charles Dupuis uncovered a central solar myth beyond all religions.[32]

In Wordsworth's England, as Marilyn Butler and Marilyn Gaull note,[33] Richard Payne Knight's *Discourse on the Worship of Priapus* (1786, reissued in a chastened version in 1818) provided a key intervention in this argument, locating a pansexual key to all mythology and religion (he was supported by Sir William Hamilton, to whom we will return in chapter 5, who offered *An Account of the Remains of the Worship of Priapus* in 1777). Knight argues that humanity's symbol systems can be seen as deriving from the female and male genitalia. Sounding somewhat like an Enlightenment Lacan, Knight argues that the phallus is a master signifier, representing human and finally supernatural creativity, while the female genitalia are tied to the prehuman power of nature. His *Discourse*, complete with explicit illustrations, shocked his readers and was initially withdrawn because it was seen as an assault not only upon good taste but upon Christianity as well.

Myth, then, was not some neutral aesthetic device; the Cockney turn to myth resulted, as we have seen, in their being charged with libertinism and epicureanism. In its most general form, the ideological debate over myth occurs in the context of arguments over a varyingly defined pleasure, espoused by some as an organizing principle for life and society. We hear claims for pleasure's power in Blake's call for an apocalypse brought on "by an improvement of sensual enjoyment" and even in Wordsworth's claim that pleasure forms the "naked and native dignity of man." The liberal Bentham attempted to ground moral theory in people's desire for pleasure. Revolutionary politics called for the pursuit of happiness. Of course, the opponents of radical politics were certainly quick enough to link them to sexual transgression. Reactionary writers such as Burke or Polwhele sought to link revolution and the French Revolution in particular with sexual excess. Gaull has argued that any appeal for sexual pleasure had to have political implications in a society whose ruler George III issued proclamations against "vice" and which listened to Malthus's call for sexual restraint as a way of preventing overpopulation and its vicissitudes. More dramatically, Ronald Paulson has called the "act of love" "the quintessential act of rebellion in a patriarchal society."[34]

While the Hunt circle's engagement with myth is sometimes dismissed as a kind of aesthetic of rococo embellishment, they too found in paganism an ideology of sexual liberation. It is important to stress the connection between sexualized verse and political speech, particularly because Keats's own brand of eroticism has often been labelled escapist. The embrace of pleasure and the erotic as a gesture of political and cultural rebellion should not be unfamiliar. From the Ranters in the seventeenth century and the Hébertistes of the French Revolution to the counterculture of the 1960s, political and sexual liberation have often been linked. The appeal of sexual revolution seems particularly strong among those – such as many in the post-Napoleonic intelligentsia – who feel they have witnessed the collapse of a vital political movement or who are simply disenchanted with politics as usual. Basic economic, political, and social institutions may seem fixed, but erotic behavior still seems open to change, and that change is seen as perhaps carrying the power to revolutionize from below the institutions that oppress and repress sexual along with other behavior. From the perspective of a political program committed to changing the economic, political, ideological, and cultural apparatus of a society, this turn to the sexual will seem defeatist at best, reactionary at worst. Yet a more positive view can see the embrace of the erotic as a search for an energy capable of reforming a society where political action seems blocked; what is sought is a fulcrum in personal and interpersonal sexual relations that might be used to gain leverage on what appears to be an unmovable social order. For Hunt's Cockney School, the erotic could appear as a realm of freedom in a world where revolution had – at least for the moment –

failed and where new acts of political subversion were themselves being subverted by government spies and instigators.

As Butler has argued, these poets offered a "cult of sexuality" in opposition to Wordsworth's and the Lakers' "authoritarian, ascetic and life-denying ... Hebraic Christianity": "The crucial fact about the classicism of Shelley and Peacock is that it does evolve into paganism – not so much an aesthetic as an ideological cult, an interpretation of man's oldest beliefs which stresses first that they are inventions and second that they belong to a natural rather than a supernatural order. What is more – a significant advantage in a propaganda war – the cult of sexuality is celebratory and joyous."[35]

While Butler centers her discussion on the group gathered in 1817 at Marlowe, particularly Shelley and Peacock, I would see this meeting as an offshoot of the larger and earlier Hunt circle – and Hunt did spend a good bit of time in Marlowe in the spring of 1817. The key features of this "cult," its questioning of Christianity and its embrace of pagan myth as an exploration of the erotic, are already present in the 1816 Hunt circle; as Haydon commented during the period when the circle was coming together, "Hunt says he prefers infinitely the beauties of Pagan Mythology to the gloomy repentance of the Christians" (5 November 1816, *Diary*, II: 68). We can see the group's – and Keats's – involvement in the cultural debate over myth and religion in two poems that I have argued were the product of a sonnet contest conducted at the time Keats was completing "I stood tip-toe" – his "Written in Disgust of Vulgar Superstition" and Hunt's "To Percy Shelley, on the Degrading Notions of Deity."

Keats's sonnet has been called by Douglas Bush "unwontedly anti-Christian":[36]

> The church bells toll a melancholy round,
>   Calling the people to some other prayers,
>   Some other gloominess, more dreadful cares,
> More heark'ning to the sermon's horrid sound.
> Surely the mind of man is closely bound
>   In some black spell; seeing that each one tears
>   Himself from fireside joys, and Lydian airs,
> And converse high of those with glory crown'd.
> Still, still they toll, and I should feel a damp,
>   A chill as from a tomb, did I not know
> That they are dying like an outburnt lamp;
>   That 'tis their sighing, wailing ere they go

Into oblivion;– that fresh flowers will grow,
And many glories of immortal stamp.

Tom Keats's transcript dates the poem "Sunday Evening Decr 24 1816," which suggestively places the scene of writing on Christmas Eve. However, Sunday fell on December 22 that year, and Cowden Clarke tells us that the poem was written "one Sunday morning as I stood by his side" (*KC*, II: 154). Whichever dating we accept – and Stillinger argues for Sunday 22 December 1816 – the poem's polemical stand towards either the weekly or yearly Christian celebration is clear. As the turn through Milton's "L'Allegro" to "Lydian airs" suggests,[37] paganism is again offered as the antidote to a despondency that is seen to be the product not of revolutionary despair but of the misplaced Christian hope for another world. The sonnet is a kind of bitter "Sunday Morning," with its contrast between "other prayers, / Some other gloominess, more dreadful cares" and "fireside joys, and Lydian airs" presaging Wallace Stevens's juxtaposition of "Complacencies of the peignoir, and late / Coffee and oranges in a sunny chair" with "the dark / Encroachment of that old catastrophe" ("Sunday Morning," ll. 1–2, 6–7).[38]

Hunt's sonnet, addressed to the most religiously skeptical of the group, joins with Keats's to pit pagan joy against gloomy Christianity:

> What wonder, Percy, that with jealous rage
>   Men should defame the kindly and the wise,
>   When in the midst of the all-beauteous skies,
> And all this lovely world, that should engage
> Their mutual search for the old golden age,
>   They seat a phantom, swelled into grim size
>   Out of their own passions and bigotries,
> And then, for fear, proclaim it meek and sage!
> And this they call a light and a revealing!
>   Wise as the clown, who plodding home at night
>   In autumn, turns at call of fancied elf,
> And sees upon the fog, with ghastly feeling,
>   A giant shadow in its imminent might,
>   Which his own lanthorn throws up from himself.

Like Keats, Hunt sees Christianity as a cultural formation that has lost its usefulness: it is here merely a delusion and in Keats's poem an "outburnt lamp." Like Keats, Hunt contrasts a ghostly and ghastly Christianity with the nature and antiquity sought by the "kindly and the wise," though Hunt concentrates on an almost Feuerbachian or

Blakean analysis of the way in which people project an image of deity
from their own "passions and bigotries," a position he also maintained
against Haydon: "In an argument with Leigh Hunt, he said he was
convinced people believed Xtianity under the influence of terror" (19
October 1816, *Diary*, II: 57). Both sonnets participate in the larger assault
on organized Christianity launched by the Hunt circle that can be seen
in many pieces in the *Examiner*, in various poetical works from Shelley's
pre-Hunt *Queen Mab* to Byron's *Vision of Judgment* published in the *Liberal*,
and in such anecdotes as Haydon's about Shelley's quizzing of "that
detestable religion, the Christian."

While Bate suggests that Keats wrote "Vulgar Superstition" merely
at the instigation of and in a sort of false imitation of Hunt and Shelley,
Keats's skeptical sentiments were known at an earlier date to others – to
George Felton Mathew, as we have seen; to his fellow student at Guy's
Hospital, John Spurgin, who as an avid Swedenborgian argued with
Keats's freethinking at a period before Keats met Hunt and Shelley; and
to Henry Stephens, another fellow student on whose notebook Keats
wrote his doggerel lines praising "women, wine and snuff" as "My
beloved Trinity."39 Again, a year after the "Vulgar Superstition" sonnet, Keats gave voice to similar views in a letter to Benjamin Bailey
written upon learning that his friend had not secured his promised
curacy:

O for a recourse somewhat human independent of the great Consolations of
Religion and undepraved Sensations. of the Beautiful. the poetical in all things
– O for a Remedy against such wrongs within the pale of the World! Should not
those things be pure enjoymen should they stand the chance of being con-
taminated by being called in as antagonists to Bishops? Would not earthly thing
do? (3 November 1817, *KL*, I: 179)

This passage establishes Keats's embrace of the "poetical" as an ideological move against the Christianity of establishment bishops. It also
links Keats, seeking an earthly, human consolation, with Shelley and
Hunt in their quest for what Hunt in his sonnet calls the "old golden
age" that lives within "all this lovely world"; Keats asks long before his
inheritor Stevens, "shall the earth / Seem all of paradise that we shall
know?" ("Sunday Morning," ll. 40–41).

"I stood tip-toe" pursues the group's ideological deployment of myth
through a direct confrontation with Wordsworth. The section on myths
is introduced by an apostrophe to the moon as "Maker of sweet poets"
(l. 116), in which Keats seems to make a Wordsworthian argument, "For

what has made the sage or poet write / But the fair paradise of Nature's light?" (ll. 125–26). Literalizing his posy/poesy pun from the opening of the piece, he finds in the "calm grandeur of a sober line" the "waving of the mountain pine, / And when a tale is beautifully staid, / We feel the safety of a hawthorn glade" (ll. 127–30). Like Wordsworth, Keats finds this turn to nature a relief from the despondency that can claim us when we are beset by the world: nature or poetry "Charms us at once away from all our troubles: / So that we feel uplifted from the world, / Walking upon the white clouds wreath'd and curl'd" (ll. 138–40).

However, where Wordsworth finds a conservative and stoic message in nature ("O blest seclusion! when the mind admits / The law of duty; and can therefore move / Through each vicissitude of loss and gain"; ll. 1035–37), Keats discovers "luxuries," "pleasures," a "world of blisses" (ll. 26, 28, 54) until "The soul is lost in pleasant smotherings" (l. 132). Wordsworth wants to bind the imagination to nature to prevent it from creating dangerous abstract visions of social life: if we tie ourselves to nature, we will never try the social experiments that lead to despair when they fail. Keats finds a surfeit of pleasure in nature – 'There was wide wandering for the greediest eye" (l. 15) – that "charms" away despair and links us back to life, a point made more clearly in the opening to *Endymion*:

> A thing of beauty is a joy for ever:
> Its loveliness increases; it will never
> Pass into nothingness; but still will keep
> A bower quiet for us, and a sleep
> Full of sweet dreams, and health, and quiet breathing.
> Therefore, on every morrow, we are wreathing
> A flowery band to bind us to the earth,
> Spite of Despondence. (Ll. 1–8)

Where Keats and the rest of Hunt's circle follow Wordsworth in identifying despondency as their particular *mal du siècle*, they find his solution to revolutionary disappointment to be a deeper despair that they link to an otherworldly Christianity. Keats offers earthly pleasures that in fulfilling the imagination's dreams bind it back to nature in spite of despondency. It is in the communal celebration of pleasure that we will find a way to defeat the "egotistical sublime" that replaces the world with the soul's conversation with itself.

This is not to say, of course, that we need accept the attempt by Keats and his Cockney peers to cast Wordsworth and the Lakers as antisocial egotists, desponding solipsists; the Lake School was in fact offering its own complex, opposing social vision grounded in a sense of nation and a national church. The *Excursion* itself ultimately propounds a social vision; it is simply one in which one's identity is found in established institutions. It is not so much a question of choosing society or the self but of deciding between opposing visions of the social order. While the Cockneys offer themselves as the saviors of sociability as such, their status as a cultural avant-garde suggests how much of the accepted structure of society they chose to reject. Still, for them, the choice was between a new society founded on a communal concern for the other that embraces liberty, the commonweal, and pleasure and the existing order with its embrace of hierarchy, greed, and a religiously grounded rejection of earthly pursuits. As Hazlitt put it (*Examiner*, 15 December 1816) at the time Keats was writing his poem, "The love of liberty is the love of others; the love of power is the love of ourselves. The one is real; the other often but an empty dream" (*CWH*, VII: 152).

Keats's attack on Wordsworth's "egotistical sublime" is well known and forcefully stated in his letters. For example, in writing of Wordsworth to Reynolds on 3 February 1818, Keats objects to being "bullied into a certain philosophy engendered in the whims of an Egotist":

Every man has his speculations, but every man does not brood and peacock over them till he makes a false coinage and deceives himself – Many a man can travel to the very bourne of Heaven, and yet want confidence to put down his halfseeing. Sancho will invent a Journey heavenward as well as any body. We hate poetry that has a palpable design upon us – and if we do not agree, seems to put its hand in its breeches pocket. Poetry should be great & unobtrusive, a thing which enters into one's soul, and does not startle it or amaze it with itself but with its subject. – How beautiful are the retired flowers! how would they lose their beauty were they to throng into the highway crying out, "admire me I am a violet! dote upon me I am a primrose!" (*KL*, I: 223–24)

This passage echoes the sentiments of Hazlitt's review of the *Excursion* where he attacks the "intense intellectual egotism" that "swallows up every thing" and that refuses to "share the palm with his subject."[40] However, there also seems to be lurking behind Keats's attack on Wordsworth – the "peacock" poet who is so self-consumed that he himself replaces the flowers he should be describing – the myth of Narcissus, who fell in love with his own reflection until, dying in despair, he turned into a flower. (Hazlitt sees Wordsworth as a poet always gazing at himself, always "making every object about him a whole length mirror to reflect his favourite thoughts" [*CWH*, IV: 117].) The hint of autoeroticism – as egotistical poetry puts "its hand in its breeches pocket" – is completely appropriate to a myth of narcissism.

Narcissus is, of course, the third subject in the mythological section of "I stood tip-toe." Keats asks, "What first inspired a bard of old to sing / Narcissus pining o'er the untainted spring?" (ll. 163–64). Keats offers here a passage modelled on the creation of myth in *Excursion* IV, as his poet creates the myth of Narcissus from a natural scene just as Wordsworth's shepherd imagines Apollo in his response to nature. Keats imagines the bard sitting by a clear pool in the "pleasant cool"; "And on the bank a lonely flower he spied, / A meek and forlorn flower, with naught of pride, / Drooping its beauty o'er the water clearness, / To woo its own sad image into nearness" (ll. 171–74). The poet contemplates the scene until "Some fainter gleamings o'er his fancy shot" and he transforms the natural scene into the myth of Narcissus and Echo.

These lines also echo the opening of Keats's poem, where he is standing on his little hill, enjoying the morning that was "*cooling*" and watching the "sweet buds" that with "modest *pride*" "Pull *droopingly*" (ll. 1–4; my emphases). Watching the scene, Keats too creates a myth, though here he is the one transformed: "I gazed awhile, and felt as light, and free / As though the fanning wings of Mercury / Had played upon my heels" (ll. 23–25). Becoming like Mercury, Keats goes out to gather his posy of flowers and poesy. Keats's echoes work to establish a difference between himself and the poet of Narcissus. Where Narcissus, becoming a flower, "would not move; / But still would seem to droop, to pine, to love" (ll. 175–76), Keats, appreciating flowers rather than replacing them with his egocentric whims, will go out to pluck all the luxuries he can. The narcissistic poet, immobilized and fixated upon himself, ignores the beauties of the world and replaces the natural flower with his own blossoming egotism, but the poet of pleasure, granted the wings of Mercury, finds that the physical realm offers a "world of blisses."

In his questioning of Wordsworth's "intense egotism," Hazlitt argues that there is a danger in pursuing such intellectual egotism, for it "must check the genial expansion of the moral sentiments and social affections, must lead to a cold and dry abstraction, as they are found to suspend the animal functions, and relax the bodily frame" (*CWH*, IV: 117). That is, where Wordsworth argues that his retreat into nature leads one beyond the "loss of confidence in social man" to connect with nature and ultimately God, Hazlitt contends that Wordsworth's egotistical mode brings about this loss of social confidence as it destroys "social affections." Keats's poem – with its luxuriant flowers, its erotic evocations of women, its sensuous verse – tries to reconnect the imagination with the "animal functions" and to revivify the "bodily frame" that Wordsworth would lay to sleep so that we might become a living soul. Keats's poetry of pleasure has a social, political purpose: by reconnecting us with others and the world through desire, it would restore our "confidence in social man," so that we can imagine a world remade.

The myth of Narcissus offers a clear analogue to the idea of an "egotistical" poetry, but what of Keats's second myth, the story of Pan and Syrinx? (Of course, Pan's appearance may owe something to the fact that he is mentioned in the *Excursion*; he also has ties to two of the other myths, with the Keatsian source Lemprière reporting Pan's seduction of Diana while in the form of a white goat and also his courtship of Echo.) This myth gets brief treatment in "I stood tip-toe," where Keats speaks of a poet

> Telling us how fair, trembling Syrinx fled
> Arcadian Pan, with such a fearful dread.
> Poor nymph,– poor Pan,– how he did weep to find
> Nought but a lovely sighing of the wind
> Along the reedy stream; a half heard strain,
> Full of sweet desolation – balmy pain.　　　　(Ll. 157–63)

The story of Pan and Syrinx in which the god loses the woman but creates a new musical instrument that he names for her is almost a paradigmatic vision of art as a substitution for or sublimation of erotic pleasure: out of the loss of the woman Pan creates song. The story as it is found in Ovid is one of the sacrifice of the object to art, the woman for the pan pipe. Reality is frustrating, but art claims to heal the loss.

Pan, who deserts the physical for an imaginative substitute, can then be seen as an artist of the "egotistical sublime," a possibility reinforced by Keats's description of Pan in the stanzaic hymn from book 1 of *Endymion*, where the god is called the "unimaginable lodge / For solitary thinkings; such as dodge / Conception to the very bourne of heaven" (1: 293–95). The phrase "the very bourne of heaven," of course, reappears in the letter about Wordsworth, quoted above, where Keats complains of the older poet's attempt to impose upon us his vision when in fact such visions finally "dodge conception." Pan is made here the locus of the solitary thinking that the egotistical poet draws upon to impose upon the world. Together, the myths of Narcissus and Pan outline the kind of poetry (and, in turn, the kind of politics) Keats seeks to move beyond. Keats rejects a poetry that he feels turns from society to isolation in nature and a belief in the transcendent; and he objects to poetry in which imagination is used to replace reality, to offer fictive substitutes for real deprivations. His verse epistle to Reynolds asks, "is it that imagination brought / Beyond its proper bound, yet still confined,– / Lost in a sort of purgatory blind, / Cannot refer to any standard law / Of either earth or heaven?" (ll. 78–82). These lines detail the fate of the egotistical poet who rejects his earthly lot, his "proper bound," and seeks to replace what he sees as a flawed reality with a visionary ideal, just as Pan takes the pipe when he cannot have the woman. But this attempt is impossible. While the imagination draws one away from reality, one is still "confined" to this side of paradise regained; one may reach the "very bourne of heaven" but not heaven itself. Egotistical art finds life a hell, but seeking an imaginative heaven wins only the purgatory of illusion.

Keats contends (as "Ode to Psyche" suggests) that he, like Words-worth, lives after the great mythic systems of Classical culture and Christianity have lost their power. In the place of the gods and God, Wordsworth is seen offering the divine self, the almighty ego. For Keats, both the religious and the egotistical poet are imperialists of the imagin-ation, granting the power to create beauty to a single source; thus, it is finally no surprise that the poet of the egotistical sublime attempts to turn his poetry to the service of traditional religion and finally of traditional political power as well. In the *Examiner* piece (15 December 1816) entitled "On Modern Apostates," written as Keats finished "I stood tip-toe," Hazlitt asserted that Wordsworth and the Lakers have always placed the self above either poetic or political sympathy; he writes that "the secret of the Jacobin poetry and the anti-jacobin politics" of Wordsworth are linked, for "His lyrical poetry was a cant of humanity about the commonest people to level the great with the small; and his political poetry is a cant of loyalty to level Bonaparte with kings and hereditary imbecility ... he sympathizes only with what can enter into no competition with him, with 'the bare earth and mountains bare, and the grass in the green field.' He sees nothing but himself and the universe ... The Bourbons, and their processions of the Holy Ghost, give no disturbance to his vanity; and he therefore gives them none" (*CWH*, VII: 144–45). Where Wordsworth would reserve all greatness, all meaning, for the self, Keats argues for a return of meaning to all of the objects in the world; for when we again learn to delight in the world, we will revive our "animal functions" and thus our "moral sentiments and social affections." Keats's poetry of pleasure, like Hunt's poetry of cheerfulness, defeats despondency and its egotistical weakening of social

bonds by offering a "recourse somewhat human" that returns to this
world rather than turning from it.

Keats sets forth his poetics and politics of pleasure in the two other
myths found in "I stood tip-toe," both of which image the return of
meaning to the world through a merger of the divine and the human.
The first of these myths of erotic union is that of Cupid and Psyche:

> So felt he, who first told, how Psyche went
> On the smooth wind to realms of wonderment;
> What Psyche felt, and Love, when their full lips
> First touch'd; what amorous, and fondling nips
> They gave each other's cheeks; with all their sighs,
> And how they kist each other's tremulous eyes:
> The silver lamp,– the ravishment, – the wonder –
> The darkness,– the loneliness,– the fearful thunder;
> Their woes gone by, and both to heaven upflown,
> To bow for gratitude before Jove's throne.   (Ll. 141–50)

This passage is close to the Hunt of "Hero and Leander" and "Bacchus
and Ariadne" in its embrace of the "cult of sexuality." Keats is clearly
not interested in narrating the myth; the story is alluded to through a
series of nouns. Nor does this, the first of the myths in "I stood tip-toe,"
follow the pattern of myth creation in the *Excursion*. While the Pan and
Narcissus sections critiquing Wordsworth imitate Keats's precursor in
having the poet respond imaginatively to nature to create myth, here the
myth of Cupid and Psyche is simply presented as an opportunity to
celebrate their erotic union. Keats made clear the meaning of this union
when he returned to the myth in his later ode.

As the "Ode to Psyche" moves to the poet's closing dedication to the
goddess, Keats would seem to retreat from the external world into his
own consciousness, creating a temple of Psyche within "some untrod-
den region of my mind" (l. 51). Keats is often seen here, in a poem which
in many ways announces his mature project as poet, dedicating himself
to a Wordsworthian poetic of the self. However, at the end of its
description of an interior landscape, the poem turns outward again in its
final lines:

> And there shall be for thee all soft delight
>   That shadowy thought can win,
> A bright torch, and a casement ope at night,
>   To let the warm Love in!   (Ll. 64–67)

While most critics would see the Keats of this ode as a very different poet from the Huntian ephebe who wrote "I stood tip-toe," these lines echo Hunt's erotic tale "Hero and Leander," where Hunt's heroine also stands at a "casement's ledge" (l. 73) until the darkness comes, when she goes to the roof to signal with a "torch of gold" (l. 94) the path that Leander is to swim to reach her. More important, this is the point in Keats's poem where Keats connects most directly with the classical story of Cupid and Psyche as related in Apuleius' *Golden Ass*, where Psyche waits at night for Cupid to come to her through an open window – though in that version she must keep the room dark so that she will not recognize the god. Keats uses this moment and his inversion of the conventional story to gesture beyond the opposition between self and object, consciousness and world, that has beset the poem from its opening question of whether he saw Psyche with "awaken'd eyes" or merely dreamed that he saw her through his recognition that as a modern poet he lives far from the pagan sense of connection with the world, those days of "happy pieties" when "holy were the haunted forest boughs, / Holy the air, the water, and the fire" (ll. 41, 38–39). Keats offers here an image of a relationship to the world that would not leave the self in opposition to the object, that would instead bind it to the object in love, that would unite the psyche – the soul or mind – with love, with Eros.

And what is the offspring of this union of mind and love? Keats recalls here not only the *Golden Ass*, but also the *Faerie Queen*, and in particular the description of Cupid and Psyche in the Garden of Adonis, a description that concludes: "She with him lives, and hath him borne a chyld, / Pleasure, that doth both gods and men aggrate, / Pleasure, the daughter of Cupid and Psyche late" (III.6.50.7–10). Apuleius' version of the story closes on a similar note. As Cupid and Psyche celebrate their marriage with a great feast, we are told, "and thus Psyches was married to Cupid, and after she was delivered of a child whom we call Pleasure."[41]

This union of the mind and love to produce pleasure is the central myth behind Keats's commitment to the cult of sexuality and to a rejuvenated sense of social man. While the ode engages the modern poet's necessary turn to the self, it turns out from the self to engage the world in love producing pleasure. Keats gives force to his poetry of pleasure in two ways. First, he suggests that the connection between the mind and the world should be understood through the model of erotic union. While Wordsworth might have called for the marriage between the individual mind and the external world, Keats offers the wedding night. Sexuality, Keats suggests, is a mode of interaction with the world through which the self comes to see the other as truly present and beautifully desirable. Sex enacts the return of meaning to the world, finding supernal value in the physical, uniting the self with the other without collapsing the other into the self. Keats's poetry pursues not the autoeroticism of the egotistical sublime but a sexual encounter with the world. Second, Keats uses intertextual echoes to image this escape from the self through pleasure, for the engagement with other texts leads away from the self as surely as does a turn to the physical world. Echoes of other texts are the material traces of the poet's encounter with something outside his own head. They are the textual equivalents of Keats's sexual encounters, Keats's act of love for other poets.

"I stood tip-toe" closes with a celebration of the story of Endymion and Cynthia, "That sweetest of all songs, that ever new, / That aye refreshing, pure deliciousness" (ll. 182–83). In keeping with his commitment to pleasure, Keats identifies the lover and the poet ("He was a Poet, sure, a lover too" [l. 193]; importantly, this poet/lover stands on another hilltop, here "Latmos's top" [l. 194]). Keats hopes for the inspiration to create a poetry equal to this erotic union, calling "for three words of honey, that I might / Tell but one wonder of thy bridal night!" (ll. 209–10). Pursuing his notion that pleasure can revitalize and thus reform the social world, Keats explores the beneficent influence their coupling has upon their society. In a scene that parallels Shelley's vision of a world reformed through the union of Prometheus and Asia at the close of the third act of *Prometheus Unbound*, Keats imagines a world transformed by love and poetry as the healthy are filled with joy, the women are revealed as fully beautiful, and the sick are healed:

> Young men, and maidens at each other gaz'd
> With hands held back, and motionless, amaz'd
> To see the brightness in each another's eyes;
> And so they stood, fill'd with a sweet surprise,
> Until their tongues were loos'd in poesy.
> Therefore no lover did of anguish die:
> But the soft numbers, in that moment spoken,
> Made silken ties, that never may be broken.
> Cynthia! I cannot tell the greater blisses.
> That follow'd thine, and thy dear shepherd's kisses:
> Was there a Poet born? (Ll. 231–41)

The union of Cynthia and Endymion generates universal love and poetry. Importantly, it is through poetry that love is guaranteed, and reciprocally it is through the love of Cynthia and Endymion that a poet is created, the birth of the poet from this union of goddess and mortal paralleling the birth of Pleasure from the marriage of Cupid and Psyche. Here is the fulfillment of Keats's response to Wordsworth's *Excursion*. Wordsworth responds to the "loss of confidence in social man" in a solitary communion with nature that teaches the "law of duty" and thus a return to the traditional political and religious order. Keats, through the pleasure we take in the world and particularly in erotic contact, images the way back into a society made new through pleasure, a society remade through sexual love, not political violence.

The four myths in "I stood tip-toe" outline, then, Keats's sense of the dangers of an egotistical or narcissistic poetry and his celebration of sexuality as a way of connecting with the world that escapes the lures of the self. The opposition he establishes is not just between himself and Wordsworth. It is between an orientation towards this world and a turn from the world to the self, between a pagan celebration of life and a pietistic rejection of its social and sexual pleasures. It is, thus, also a statement of the difference between the Lake School and the Cockney School, between great poets who had become political and cultural "apostates" penning the *Excursion*, the *Lay Sermons*, and the *Poet's Pilgrimage to Waterloo* and a younger generation of rising radical writers. "I stood tip-toe" is not a poem of personal anxiety, whether in relation to Wordsworth or to class and culture. It is a polemical poem, a salvo fired in the culture war being waged in 1816.

Hunt later insisted upon the fact that "I stood tip-toe" arose from the life of the group. He tells us the poem was suggested to Keats "by a delightful summer-day as he stood beside the gate that leads from the Battery on Hampstead Heath into a field by Caen Wood." Hunt goes on to recall first receiving *Poems* from Keats: "It was in the beautiful lane, running from the road between Hampstead and Highgate to the foot of Highgate Hill, that, meeting me one day, he first gave me the volume. If the admirer of Mr. Keats's poetry does not know the lane in question, he ought to become acquainted with it, both on his author's account and its own. It has been also paced by Mr. Lamb and Mr. Hazlitt, and frequented, like the rest of the beautiful neighbourhood, by Mr. Coleridge; so that instead of Millfield Lane, which is the name it is known by 'on earth,' it has sometimes been called Poets' Lane, which is an appellation it richly deserves" (*LB*, pp. 249–50). This return of Keats's poem to the coterie is wholly appropriate to Keats's message, for the sociability espoused by and embodied in the Hunt group is another remedy against the "egotistical sublime" and the despondency and quietism it promotes. Like the erotic unions celebrated in "I stood tip-toe," the collective activities of the coterie were a way of restoring our faith in social man. As Raymond Williams reminds us, "the primary meaning of *society* was companionship or fellowship."[42] Williams notes that in the latter eighteenth century, "society" and "social" became increasingly abstract terms, as in Wordsworth's phrase "social man"; but the Hunt circle's ideology of sociability seeks to keep the idea of society closer to the older, particularized notion of companionship, of the kind of fellowship one finds within a coterie. Where Wordsworth pits an abstract individual – the "Solitary" – against what he perceives as the equally abstract social system of the French Revolution's "men of theory" in order to urge a return to the "organic" institutions of church and state, Keats and the Hunt circle are interested in the concrete moments when one is more than an isolated individual but less than a unit in some large aggregation – that is, in moments of erotic contact or on occasions of social communion set against a definition of the individual through either the "egotistical sublime" or the traditional structures of church and state. Keats's *Poems*, which finds the ground for a universal *fraternité* in the literal bonds between brothers, which seeks to rejuvenate our general social affections by awakening our pursuit of concrete erotic pleasure, which locates the hopes for a culture and society remade in the specific occasions of the collaborative, interactive work of the Hunt circle, both argues for and embodies coterie practice as a foundation for a communal act of reform.

In the lines quoted in the last paragraph, Hunt does not only locate both the production and the reception of Keats's first volume in the coterie that supported it and for which it speaks. More than that, he nominates Keats – along with Lamb, Hazlitt, and Coleridge – as the spirit of this place in Hampstead: offering tales of the poets, Hunt suggests an etiological myth of a name not known "on earth." With Christianity an "outburnt lamp" and the "happy pieties" of pagan Greece merely a "fond" memory, Hunt suggests that the "consolation somewhat human" Keats sought in attempting to return meaning from heaven to earth will be created through the communal activity of poets, Cockneys though they may be.

CHAPTER 4

Staging hope: genre, myth, and ideology in the dramas of the Hunt circle

I

How does a political prisoner in 1814 write a play about the abdication of Napoleon? While this situation – that of Leigh Hunt who was in prison at the time of Napoleon's fall in April 1814 as a result of his attack in the *Examiner* on the Prince Regent – might seem extreme, it is in fact paradigmatic for a number of writers in Hunt's circle as they turned to dramas on mythological subjects in pursuit of the cultural power to address and perhaps to liberate an audience when the forces of liberation had been routed and their own positions – in exile or on the Cockney borders of official culture – were variously defined by a certain powerlessness. The Hunt circle's turn to mythologizing drama was a collective effort that produced most famously Percy Shelley's *Prometheus Unbound* but also Mary Shelley's *Midas* and *Proserpine*, various "dramatic sketches" by "Barry Cornwall," and Horace Smith's *Amarynthus, the Nympholept* along with a number of relevant translations and abandoned projects.[1]

Hunt's immediate literary response to Napoleon's abdication was his "Ode for the Spring of 1814," printed in the *Examiner* on 17 April, Hunt's poem being written almost as quickly as Byron's better-known ode.[2] Hunt, however, was not done with the subject and began work on a drama, *The Descent of Liberty*, the dedication to which is dated 10 July 1814. Published the next year, the play was well received within the circle and without; Reynolds, for example, wrote to Dovaston (25 February 1815) that the play has "enraptured me!"[3] *The Descent* stands as a first attempt to answer the question of what form the drama should take as culture enters the post-Napoleonic, potentially postrevolutionary era. Hunt's surprising answer is that the imprisoned radical writing after the fall of Napoleon turns to a courtly form which flourished before the rise of Cromwell: he offered *The Descent of Liberty* as "A Mask."

What does it mean to write "a mask" in 1814? Similar questions can be asked of the other dramas on mythological subjects produced by the Hunt circle: *Prometheus Unbound* is called a "lyrical drama," Horace Smith's *Amarynthus, The Nympholept* is a "pastoral drama," Barry Cornwall's plays are labelled "dramatic scenes," with, for example, his *Lysander and Ione* being linked to the pastoral. What do these generic markers signify?

Today they are most likely to be read as a rejection of early-nineteenth-century theater. No one has doubted then or now that the theater of the early nineteenth century was in crisis: the theaters were felt to be too large for effective acting; spectacle, music, and special effects seemed to overwhelm the power of the word; royalty and the aristocracy had increasingly abandoned the drama for the opera; the "legitimate" dramatic forms were being displaced by new, popular dramatic types such as the melodrama. It has also been a matter of agreement – at least until some recent challenging work on the period's drama – that the response of the romantic poets to this crisis was a retreat from the stage to the closet, to a mental theater.[4] While this would seem especially to be true of such plays as *The Descent of Liberty* and *Prometheus Unbound,* I want to argue that the mythological plays of the Hunt circle are not a rejection of the stage but an attempt to remake it. They are in fact a kind of canon reformation with which we should be familiar, a struggle to derive new cultural power by turning from the "great" tradition – not to the artistic limbo of the closet – but to alternative sources of cultural authority. In these plays, we can see how artists work to acquire cultural influence for a countercultural message by seeking beyond established and ideologically stabilized forms for a generic site within which one can negotiate between tradition and innovation, authority and revolutionary gesture, necessary formal containment and desired ideological criticism. More specifically, Shelley, Hunt, and their circle see the collapse of the standard high genres of the drama – tragedy and the comedy of manners[5] – and then turn to two forms that had matured in the seventeenth century but which were still viable throughout the eighteenth century – the masque and the pastoral drama. Hunt led the way in his *Descent of Liberty*, with its learned prefatory essay on the history of the masque defining the generic tradition for others, and in his 1820 translation of a key pastoral play, Tasso's *Amyntas,* dedicated to Keats and accompanied by another encyclopedic essay.

II

We should not assume that Hunt's generic choice was eccentrically antiquarian. When Hunt turned to the masque, he knew that Milton's *Comus* was offered regularly during the eighteenth century in a somewhat altered form; it was revived at Covent Garden, with new scenery and costumes, on 28 April 1815, when it had an impressive run of fourteen nights and was reviewed by Hazlitt in the *Examiner* (11 June 1815), who used the opportunity to reopen the debate on the power of the word versus the power of spectacle in the masque as well as to contrast Milton as poet *and* patriot with the Lake Poets.[6] There were a good number of masques staged during the 1700s, particularly between 1700 and 1750,[7] some of which were very successful: for example, the anonymous *Cephalus and Procris* (premiered 28 October 1730) had a spectacular initial run of seventy-four performances during the 1730–31 season at Drury Lane and was revived over the next ten years; Colley Cibber put two masques on the Drury Lane stage in 1715, *Myrtillo* (5 November) and *Venus and Adonis* (12 March), the second having over thirty performances in five years; David Mallet's *Britannia* (Drury Lane, 9 May 1755) had twelve performances between 1755 and 1758; George Colman the elder, who was one reviser of *Comus* (Covent Garden, 16 October 1773), also adapted Jonson's *The Masque of Oberon* as *The Fairy Prince* (Covent Garden, 12 November 1771); and Richard Cumberland put his *Calypso* on stage at Covent Garden on 20 March 1779. There were others in the early nineteenth century who joined Hunt in experimenting with the masque. In 1807, the interesting Frank Sayers turned to the masque for his *Descent of Frea*, one of his "dramatic sketches of Northern mythology"; and Cornelius Neale published his *Lyrical Dramas* (1819) – *Rinaldo and Armida* and *Love's Trial* – clearly showing his acquaintance with masque conventions.[8] When Hunt indicates that his masque was intended for the stage, he was demonstrating not an ignorance of stage possibilities but a knowledge of a living tradition. Hunt's essay "The Origin and Nature of Masks" is also part of a larger scholarly effort devoted to the masque. Volumes of "old plays" regularly included masques; for example, Charles Wentworth Dilke, friend to Keats and Hunt, published a six-volume update of Dodsley's earlier collection in 1814–16 that includes Lyly's masque *Endymion, or the Man in the Moon* (1591) (it also includes Lyly's pastoral *Midas* [1592]), and Gifford's 1816 edition of Ben Jonson's plays gave one and a half volumes to his masques.

We can get an initial sense of the appeal of the masque to Hunt when we remember that the term covered a large cultural landscape, with one foot in the aristocratic and high cultural heritage of the Stuart courtly masque and another in the popular culture of the masquerades studied by Terry Castle. The history of the "mask" is further complicated by its use in the eighteenth century to designate English operatic forms over against Italianate ones and by its confusing links with the popular harlequinade (upon which Shelley will draw). Hunt, in his prefatory essay, is primarily concerned with the masques that were a part of late-sixteenth- and seventeenth-century court life, including the large body of masques written by Ben Jonson (plays he does not particularly admire) as well as key works by Beaumont (*The Masque of the Inner Temple and Gray's Inn*), Thomas Carew (*Coelum Britannicum*), William Browne (*The Inner Temple Mask or Circe*), and Milton (*Comus*); he also notes the use of masques inside other forms by Spenser and Shakespeare, *The Tempest* being another important site for the survival of the masque on stage. Hunt, while allowing some connection between the masque and classical drama and Provençal festivals, locates the origin of the form in Italy, arguing that it developed in England from Italian sources when private masquerades held in great houses to celebrate events such as a marriage or a birth were merged with the public pageants of the Tudor monarchs with their allegory and personification.

Hunt offers this definition of the masque: "A mixed Drama, allowing of natural incidents as of every thing else that is dramatic, but more essentially given up to the fancy, and abounding in machinery and personification, generally with a particular allusion" (*Descent of Liberty*, p. xxiv). In the masque, Hunt discovered a viable dramatic tradition that relies upon scenic show ("machinery") and could thus command the contemporary stage with its demand for spectacle, that uses classical materials in a fanciful way and could thus be a vehicle for his own mythologizing vision, and that uses personification and allegory to comment on an immediate event ("particular allusion") and could thus provide a practical way of offering ideological commentary. In calling the form a "mixed Drama" – a term used by someone such as the theatrical diarist John Genest as a way of attacking the hybridized nature of late-eighteenth- and early-nineteenth-century drama – and also in noting that it is given to "lawlessness" (p. xvi) and "license" (p. xxiv), Hunt recognizes the fact that the masque does not rest easily within the hierarchy of genres embodied in the repertoires of the patent theaters royal, that it is potentially "illegitimate," in the political as well as the theatrical and aesthetic senses of the word. When we link the masque to the masquerade, its countercultural appeal becomes even clearer, for the masquerade – which Castle describes as a "'strange Medley of persons' – a rough mix of high and low"[9] – offered the same confusion of hierarchy, the same license that Hunt seeks in the masque. Nicholas Roe's links between the form of Hunt's masque and that of French revolutionary fêtes suggest another way in which such a play invoked popular gatherings.[10] The masque offered a site for negotiating (to use Stephen Greenblatt's term) between various sources of theatrical, cultural, and social energy, drawing now on a particular set of spectacular stage effects common to the masque, the harlequinade, and the opera, now on the prestige of an older aristocratic form, now on the vitality of popular celebrations. The power of the masque for Hunt lies in the fact that it is part of an authorized, aristocratic tradition while at the same time it could appear as innovative, even insurgent, on the contemporary stage.

Hunt and his circle's work with the masque – linked to both popular and aristocratic cultures – reenacts a stylistic and ideological tension in their project as a whole. On the one hand, they wish to speak to and for the "people," to engage as wide an audience as possible. On the other hand, they want to maintain the values they find embodied in literate culture and the literary tradition, which leads them to embrace a literary style and a set of cultural references that potentially exclude many readers. (We might think here of the division between "esoteric" and "exoteric" writing in Shelley, for example.) On the one hand, they embrace much of the political program of the more radical, plebeian end of the reform movement. On the other hand, they offer a cultural program that some might define as elitist.[11] There are various ways to dismiss their efforts: the Cockney School attacks belittled the work of the group as social-climbing, as an assertion of a cultural literacy that Z. believes, given their ideology, they cannot have; attacks from a different ideological vantage point might criticize the circle as a combination of aristocratic would-be Napoleons who dream of leading but not mixing with the people, and middle-class dabblers in radical culture and politics who will ultimately betray their working-class allies. To return to the masque, it could be seen as a sign of the group's attempt to acquire a cultural authority they cannot have because of their "low" status or as an unconscious betrayal of their covert allegiance to a cultural tradition that cannot escape its aristocratic ideological imbrications. None of these criticisms, however, do justice to what the group attempted to accomplish in the masque. In the masque as in their circle itself, the group sought to find a site where the divisions based on distinctions of class and taste might be bridged, where we might find a "rough mix of high and low," a "lawlessly" mixed drama as well as social scene. What can be seen, from different points of attack, as Cockney cultural poaching or reactionary literary nostalgia might perhaps better be seen as an attempt to extend the cultural franchise, cultural literacy, across traditional boundaries. The promise of Cockney culture, and of the Cockney use of the masque, is not a rigorously plebeian culture or a purely aristocratic culture but a "strange Medley," a Bakhtinian heteroglossia.

Hunt's *The Descent* has a simple plot: Napoleon is represented by the Enchanter whose cloud hangs over the land only to be dissipated by another cloud that carries the geniuses of Prussia, Austria, Russia, and Britain, an action witnessed by a group of shepherds; Liberty then stages an elaborate procession in which peace, the arts, and various virtues are presented and celebrated. Hunt's debt to the masque form is perhaps clearest in the processional, where he presents through allegory his reading of Napoleon's defeat as the victory of Liberty and Peace.

When we read the stage directions for this section of the play – with its panoramas of cities wrapped in clouds and its gods enthroned on mountaintops – we tend to find *The Descent* hopelessly untheatrical; but in fact Hunt was drawing on stage machinery that had led to the success of many eighteenth- and early-nineteenth-century plays. For example, Lewis Theobald's pantomimic *Rape of Proserpine* (Lincoln's-Inn-Fields, 7 February 1727), popular throughout the century, includes a scene where the followers of Ceres build a trophy for Jupiter out of the debris of his war with the Titans only to have it destroyed by an earthquake that reveals Mount Aetna in flames from which a giant rises who is then dashed by a thunderbolt hurled by Jove. It is an intriguing paradox that the spectacular staging demanded by *The Descent* or by *Prometheus Unbound* strikes us as a sign of the untheatricality of these plays – their status as poems more than dramas – while in the context of the early-nineteenth-century stage such theatrical techniques in other plays were seen as signalling a victory of mere stagecraft over the poetic word. As early as the battles between Ben Jonson and Inigo Jones, the masque had offered an occasion to struggle over the relative power of language and spectacle in the drama. We see the same battle being fought through the masque in the eighteenth century, when the term came to designate an operatic form that was essentially a spoken drama which included an all-sung masque; for example, sung masques were introduced into *Macbeth*, *Timon of Athens*, and *Measure for Measure*. For its defenders, the masque became a way of preserving the power of the word against the onslaught of the continuous music of the Italianate opera, a form which Samuel Johnson saw as "an exotick and irrational entertainment, which has been always combated, and always has prevailed."[12] Hunt recognizes the tension in the masque when he notes that he has offered a "drama professedl y full of machinery" but "written expressly for the closet" and says that in his play he wished to make "the scenic and fanciful part of it predominant" while providing more "human interest, than is possessed by Masks in general" (p. lii). As we will see with other plays written by the group and most clearly in *Prometheus Unbound*, Hunt draws upon a strong theatrical tradition to imagine a stage beyond the theater ("a stage of his own in the reader's fancy" [p. liii]) where he can find a proper balance between word and stage effect.

Hunt's most important debt to the masque is in his use of the *anti*masque to dramatize Napoleon's defeat not as a victory for the allies' military force leading to a restoration of monarchical power but as a mass disenchantment leading to a utopia of liberty, peace, and pleasure. Hunt's *Examiner* (e.g. 23 September 1810) made it clear that it did not support Napoleon, but it refused to endorse his opponents either. As Hunt puts it in his preface to the play, "Let such of Bonaparte's enemies as had other qualities besides force to bring against him, receive their due reputation; – it is the popular Spirit, after all that had the main hand in the business" (p. viii). While in *The Descent* the allies are part of the final victorious procession, each is praised only insofar as he is committed to liberty. Prussia, for example, is enthroned after receiving the command to "Recollect for those you rule, / What you learnt in Sorrow's school, / And acquaint their homes with me, / Triumph-teaching Liberty" (iii.272–75), while Russia is instructed to free Poland (iii.303–25). Wishing to embrace the people and their values, Hunt plays off the conventions of the antimasque to celebrate the victory over Napoleon without endorsing any restoration of traditional power.

Stephen Orgel explains that the Jonsonian antimasque worked to prove that "the world of evil [embodied in the antimasque] is not real. It exists at all only in relation to the world of ideals, which are the norms of the masque's universe. So the antimasque is physically ugly, threatening but in fact dramatically powerless," as all of the antimasque figures disappear from the stage before the final celebration.[13] In Hunt's play, Napoleon functions as the antimasque figure, and he is defined merely as a perversion of the values Hunt celebrates, as "the great Apostate from Liberty" (p. v): "What choice has his been of these dark vexations, / These sullen heights, this flound'ring in Heav'n's worst, / This poor purblind acting of the god, / When by the same good gift of understanding / Thus devilishly abused, and by applying / To books of clearer wisdom, he had been / Blessing and blest" (II.14–20). Napoleon as the Enchanter becomes a kind of political huckster who has tricked the people into believing that he represents their values. His hold on power is essentially ephemeral, and thus his defeat is appropriately figured through the disappearance of the antimasque figure – here the dispersal of a cloud – as all come to understand that it is their belief in and fear of the Enchanter that has granted him dominion. Byron also spoke in his ode of Napoleon's "spell upon the minds of men" (III.5), and Shelley would follow Hunt in using the masque in *Prometheus Unbound* to recount the defeat of that greater tyrant, Jupiter, who loses power when "The loathsome mask has fallen" (III.193).

Of course, Hunt inverts the hierarchy of the traditional masque. From Beaumont's *Masque of the Inner Temple and Gray's Inn*, where the second antimasque offers a "Rurall daunce, consisting likewise not of any suted persons, but of a confusion, or commixture of all such persons as are naturall and proper for Country sports," to Milton's play with Comus and his crew, the antimasque embodied the "lower" drives and "lower" orders that are overcome by the ideal virtues of the court. Hunt redefines the antimasque in keeping with the popular harlequinade's portrayal of conventional order being defeated by the subordinate forces of desire and freedom. It is the court of Napoleon that is overthrown, and the values of the play are embodied in the lowly shepherds who could have appeared in the antic dance of the conventional antimasque. Against those who would see the defeat of Napoleon as the end of revolution, Hunt drew on the theatrical and cultural power of the masque to suggest that the hierarchical politics of power embraced by the traditional form have been a masquerade: when the masks that have enchanted the people are removed, it is not an immutable world of hereditary power that is revealed but a popular utopia of peace, art, and pleasure shared by the yeomanry, artists, and lovers who make up Hunt's final "Vision of Real Glory."

III

When Hunt selected shepherds to embody the positive values of his masque, offering an ideological reworking of Virgil's first eclogue of the kind studied by Annabel Paterson, he engaged another form important to the mythological dramas of his circle, the pastoral drama.[14] The members of the Hunt circle were deeply engaged with the pastoral drama; in fact, as Stuart Curran has suggested[15] and as I argued in the first chapter, the attacks upon Hunt, Keats, and others can be read as a rejection of their pastoralism – a poetry written about nature by city poets, by Cockneys. As one reviewer (*Honeycomb* 5 [15 July 1820], 65) said of the Cockneys, "Have they not Covent Garden market? What would they do with Arcadia?"

Their engagement with Arcadia and with the pastoral drama in particular is in fact quite clear. Hunt translated one of the two key representatives of the genre, Tasso's *Aminta* (1573), providing another essay that shows his command of the tradition.[16] Both Hunt and Peacock translated sections of the other major Italian pastoral drama, Guarini's *Il Pastor Fido* (1583). We know that Shelley read *Il Pastor Fido* and Tasso's *Aminta* (twice), as well as key English plays in the tradition such as Fletcher's *The Faithful Shepherdess* (1610) and Ben Jonson's *The Sad Shepherd* (1641), and that Horace Smith claimed as influences upon his pastoral drama *Il Pastor Fido*, *Amyntas* (in Hunt's translation), *The Faithful Shepherdess*, and *Comus*. Hazlitt proposed editing a volume, "The Old English Theatre," that would have included both *The Faithful Shepherdess* and *The Sad Shepherd*, plays he also addressed in lectures.[17] It is interesting in this context to note that the only Greek drama that Shelley translated in its entirety was Euripides' *Cyclops*, a play which had been considered the originary model for the pastoral drama since Rapin's "Dissertatio de carmine pastorali" that prefaces his *Eclogae Sacrae* (1659). Others argued that the pastoral drama arose out of the dialogues found in eclogues and idylls, and again it is significant that Shelley and Hunt translated key examples of those forms, with Hunt, for example, providing in his pastoral volume *Foliage* (1818) versions of both the Cyclops' love lament from Theocritus' *Idyll XI* and "The Syracusan Gossips" (*Idyll XV*).[18]

In his essay on the pastoral drama included as a preface to *Amyntas*, Hunt notes its possible sources in classical models but, connecting it to the masque, again gives the Italians credit for creating the form, identifying Agostino de Becarri's *Il Sacrifizio* (1573) as the first example of the genre and Tasso's *Amyntas* as the most influential (pp. xiii–xiv); he contends that by 1700 there were more than two hundred examples of the Italian pastoral drama, and he also notes the development of the English form from Fletcher's *Faithful Shepherdess* to Allan Ramsay's *Gentle Shepherd* (1725).

While the *Princeton Encyclopedia of Poetry and Poetics* (1974) confidently announces that Ramsay's 1725 play is the "last pastoral drama in England," one can find many later examples, including nine revisions of Ramsay's play, one as late as 1811, as well as such works as Garrick's adaptation of *The Winter's Tale* as *Florizel and Perdita* (Drury Lane, 9 February 1758), Charlotte Lennox's *Philander: A Dramatic Pastoral* (1758), Charles Dibdin's *Shepherd's Artifice* (Covent Garden, 21 May 1765), Hannah More's *The Search for Happiness: A Pastoral Drama* (1773), George Colman the Elder's *The Sheep Shearing; or, Florizel and Perdita* (Haymarket, 18 July 1777), with both Colman's and Garrick's plays perhaps owing debts to MacNamara Morgan's *The Sheep-Shearing: or, Florizel and Perdita. A Pastoral Comedy. Taken from Shakespeare* (Covent Garden, 25 March 1754), and T. Goodwin's *The Loyal Shepherds; or, The Rustic Heroine. A Dramatic Pastoral Poem* (1779) – not to mention Elizabeth Thomas's *A Dramatick Pastoral Occasioned by the Collection at Glocester on the Coronation Day. For Portioning Young Women of Virtuous Characters* (1762).[19] One could still find pastoral elements on the stage in Hunt's day, most often in some of Shakespeare's comedies; Hunt reviewed in the *Examiner* (9 June 1817, p. 248) a version of Ramsay's *Gentle Shepherd* that had been "cut down into a short afterpiece" for a benefit at Covent Garden. As in the case of the masque, the pastoral drama had ties to a wide range of cultural sites, from the prestigious and widely admired *Il Pastor Fido* to the controversial theatricals held by Marie Antoinette in her pastoral retreat at the Petit Trianon. While the pastoral drama clearly derived some of its cultural authority from its ties to the larger and more prestigious body of pastoral lyric and while pastoral drama shares with this poetry the exploration of the shape and limits of human freedom in an idealized natural setting, it was the pastoral drama's treatment of love and sexuality – which, again, ranges from the idealized treatment of chastity in *Comus* to the pornographic tradition surrounding Marie Antoinette – that appealed most to the Hunt circle, with their turn to what Marilyn Butler calls the "cult of the South," a celebration of sexuality, communality, and creativity.[20]

Horace Smith's *Amarynthus, the Nympholept: A Pastoral Drama, in Three Acts, with Other Poems* offers the Hunt circle's fullest engagement with the pastoral drama. As Stuart Curran has said of Hunt's *Foliage* volume, Smith's book is designed as a pastoral project. The volume's epigraph is taken from Virgil's *Georgics*,[21] the bulk of the volume is taken up by his pastoral drama, and it closes with "Sicilian Arethusa," a poem to the river nymph also celebrated by Shelley (in lines written for Mary Shelley's mythological play *Proserpine*) and Keats (book II of *Endymion*). (It is not a coincidence that Guarini's *Il Pastor Fido* uses the figure of Alfeo, or Alpheus, the lover of Arethusa, as its prologue.) The sonnets Smith includes in the volume provide such an obviously pastoral piece as "On the Statue of a Piping Faun," as well as a number of others that use pastoral images. The volume uses pastoral space to reject contemporary society's dedication to what Hunt called in the *Examiner* (e.g. 13 March 1816) the "spirit of money-getting" and to overturn the traditional pastoral drama's commitment to an ideology of female chastity in favor of a green world of love, pleasure, and imagination. To pursue these issues, Smith uses a double plot, one dealing with Amarynthus' nympholepsy and the other with the lovers Amarillis and Phoebidas.

The love plot is rather conventional, with the aging, rich Athenian Celadon – devotee of Plutus, "God of the foul / And sordid slaves of gold" (1.3) – standing for what Northrop Frye calls the "blocking" society opposed to the lovers.[22] The real threat to the lovers, however, comes from an ideal of chastity that had been celebrated in pastoral plays from *Il Pastor Fido* and *The Faithful Shepherdess* to *Comus*. In Tasso's *Amyntas*, for example, Sylvia, dedicated to Diana and the hunt, celebrates her chastity, which she calls her "honesty" and which she opposes to the hero's love. In Smith's play, we hear from the virtuous Theucarlia that the "lessons of cold chastity" cry "out against licentious love" (1.4), and Celadon plots to have Amarillis, who has spurned him, condemned to a life as a virgin priestess.

The play, however, rejects this attempt to force chastity upon Amarillis as she is liberated to celebrate her sexuality and her love for Phoebidas in act 3, scene 4, when the lovers are united with a call for the collected company to leave in order to celebrate "the nuptial rites, / With sportive cheer and festival delights," the kind of festive exit found at the end of many Shakespearean comedies. Smith links the ideal of chastity and the spirit of money-getting as parallel means of hoarding one's self, a selfish denial of communion and community. Smith offers his version of the Hunt circle's attack on an interlocked set of values which embraced the work ethic over a principle of pleasure, which conceived of women as property secured by the ideology of female chastity, and which enshrined what Shelley called "Mammon," "the principle of Self, of which money is the visible incarnation," over the outflowings of poetry and love (*Defence*, p. 503). Smith perhaps turns here in particular against the vision of female restraint found in *Comus*. Hunt in his preface to *Amyntas* had certainly found Milton's lady "too safe and contented in her own virtue" (p. xxii),[23] and Keats placed *Comus* in its ideological context, "who could gainsay his ideas on virtue, vice, and Chastity in Comus, just at the time of the dismissal of Cod-pieces and a hundred other disgraces?" (letter to John Hamilton Reynolds, 3 May 1818, *KL*, I: 281–82). *Comus* and its sexual politics had to be given a romantic rereading just as surely as did *Paradise Lost*.

Smith's second plot centers on Amarynthus, who in seeking a physical representation of an ultimate truth (the "Omnipotent Unseen" [III.5]) has convinced himself he suffers from nympholepsy, a madness brought on when a mortal beholds a nymph; he has, in fact, only seen Amarillis pretending to be a nymph to avoid being consigned to a life of chastity. Amarynthus is a figure not unlike the poet in Shelley's *Alastor*, and he is even more closely related to Keats's Endymion in his demand for a higher reality, a deep truth he cannot find in the pastoral world that surrounds him. At times, he appears as a kind of Greek Manfred, ready to plunge into the grave if it will give him the answers ("O let me leap alive into my tomb, / If there the secret is reveal'd to us" [II.1]). After calling upon a catalog of nymphs reminiscent of Hunt's poem of that name, he cannot accept the silence as he finds a voice is wanting: "What! is the world struck dumb? no sound, no sight? / O earth, or air, speak for the love of mercy. / My brain, my brain! I shall go mad outright" (II.4). Like Endymion, he is condemned to follow a dream from which only reality can save him; as Oenone, a prophetess cursed by Apollo, tells him, "From fancied visions he shall be / Reliev'd by their reality" (I.3). The plot is resolved as Amarynthus comes to realize that Amarillis is a mortal while at the same time he falls in love with the real nymph Dryope, whose own love renders her mortal as she dies into life for Amarynthus. The play ends with a celebration of love as the means through which our own spirits – and the world they inhabit – can be deified: "Let us but strive / To love our fellow-man as Heaven loves us, / (Which is true piety), and earth will seem / Itself a heaven" (III.5).

Smith conceives Amarynthus' search for an embodied absolute as arising in response to his cultural situation. In Athens, impressed by the powerful and beautiful forms of organized religion, he has come to need a physical representation of the spiritual, an error analyzed by the priest Chabrias in the play's opening speech on the history of religion. Chabrias tells us that "primeval shepherds," whose "yearning hearts required a God," created the abstract god "Pan" when they intuited a spiritual unity in all things. However, man mistakenly wished to give this "etherial spirit" a form, and "soon the heavenly archtype / In the terrestrial symbol disappears." In the place of an imaginative vision of universal connection, we find the "human capriform," the goat-god that man "deified, and impiously stain'd / With earthly lusts to satisfy their own" (I.I). Chabrias' speech – which traces a development from an imaginative response to nature, through an abstraction of natural force into a god set over against the world, and then to the creation of priestcraft, justifying its own desires by claiming divine sanction – seems very close to Blake's account in *The Marriage of Heaven and Hell* of how we come to forget that all deities reside within the human breast.

But, of course, it is not Blake's *Marriage* but Wordsworth's "spousal verse" of the *Excursion* to which Smith is reacting. In particular, he echoes here the discussion of mythology from book IV, "Despondency Corrected," that key passage addressed by Keats and others in the Hunt circle, as we have seen. Smith's awareness of Wordsworth's account of myth is made clear in his preface, where he offers a prose version of Wordsworth's description of the creation of Greek myth out of an imaginative response to daily occurrences: "Partial glimpses of some country girl, tripping, perhaps, through the twilight-grove to meet her lover, or stealing into the copse at day-break to bathe in its embowered waters, were quite sufficient to inflame the combustible fancy of a Greek" (p. vii). However, like Hunt in *Foliage* with its "Cursory Observations on Poetry and Cheerfulness" or Keats in *Poems* with its poetry of pleasure, Smith overcomes the Wordsworthian despondency arising from a "loss of confidence in social man" (IV.261) by embracing the "social mirth, / And unpolluted human happiness" (I.I) discovered by his lovers.

In his preface to the play, Smith agrees with Wordsworth that Greek mythology arose as an imaginative response to nature, but the question remains of how one is to interpret these pretty pieces of natural supernaturalism. For the Wordsworth of the *Excursion*, myth, even as superstition, is a defense against what he sees as the corrosive power of modern skepticism, a function he argues it also served in classical Greece. Smith too sees his era and that of his play marked by a skeptical turn of mind; as he makes clear in his preface, he sees Amarynthus and the religious skeptic Celadon (Urania describes him as "One who derides all holy things, denies / Th'existence of the nymphs of earth or sky, / And at the terrors of th'invisible world / Laughs" [III.3]) as embodying a particular moment of ideological crisis in Athens, when "religious scepticism and excitement ... producing doubt upon all points rather than conviction upon any, stimulated that insatiable curiosity for prying into the mysteries of nature, of which it has been attempted to delineate a faint outline

in the character of Amarynthus" (pp. ix–x). Smith finds in classical
Athens as in post-Enlightenment England a struggle between a Wordsworthian fideism that would finally give up this various and vexing
world in order to find the security of a unitary truth and a skepticism
that (in a Celadon) claims to see through all superstitious evocations of
the truth only to bow before Mammon and his gold.

Smith engages here the debate over myth discussed in chapter 3.
Myth for the skeptic is a product of superstition that should be revealed
as false. For the Wordsworthian fideist, it is a dark adumbration of
Christian truth. For Smith's Chabrias, myth is neither truth nor false-
hood but man's attempt to construct meaning. Myth for Smith is neither
credal belief nor fiction, and thus it can function for him not unlike the
category of the ideological in contemporary cultural critique. "Ideology" too occupies a shadowy ground between believed truth and revealed fiction, as Raymond Williams has explained: "'ideology' then
hovers between 'a system of beliefs characteristic of a certain class' and
'a system of illusory beliefs – false ideas or false consciousness – which
can be contrasted with true or scientific knowledge.'"[24] There is a
tension between a neutral definition of ideology which allows us to
respect the knowledge contained in a prior system of belief while
unveiling the illusion of its claim to completeness and a polemical
definition that contrasts prior systems of belief as false and fictional with
a "science" or "truth" in our possession. Caught in this productive
tension, ideology comes to stand for the fact that any set of ideas can be
placed within some group's interests; and thus to recognize the ideological is to indicate a freedom from it without having to deconstruct it
absolutely. To adapt Wordsworth, ideologies are "creeds outworn,"
beliefs we might still cherish but within which we can no longer live.

These differing conceptions of ideology were present during the early
nineteenth century, as McGann has shown in his brief history of the
term.[25] He distinguishes among French (or Enlightenment), German (or
Romantic), and Critical (or Marxist) ideology. The first two recapitulate
the tension formulated by Williams, with Critical ideology mediating for
McGann between their deconstructive and idealizing turns. The
"French" and "Romantic" theories of ideology were available to the
Hunt circle, the first through a long line of eighteenth-century French
thinkers and the second in Coleridge.

The French ideology undermines creeds. Its project is to rid the world
of superstition, to reveal the fictional basis undergirding traditional
systems of human belief. Its stand towards the past is polemical, since

the past of tradition is revealed as embracing false ideas, a false consciousness, debunked by a present natural science of ideas: concrete knowledge destroys false belief. The appeal of the French ideology to, say, Keats is suggested in the anecdote concerning his visit to Haydon's studio to see the painter's "Christ's Entry into Jerusalem" with its images of Wordsworth bowing to Christ and of Voltaire as a sneering scoffer; Haydon wrote that Keats went up to the picture, "placed his hand on his heart, & bowing his head, 'there is the being I will bow to,' said he – he stood before Voltaire!" (*Diary*, II: 317).[26] While Keats might, like Carlyle's Professor Teufelsdrockh, finally find Voltaire holding "only the torch for burning, no hammer for building," he clearly sides with the skeptic over against believers such as Haydon.

The romantic ideology, as defined by McGann through Coleridge's arguments in *The Statesman's Manual* (1816), seeks to reunite knowledge and belief. For Coleridge, this restoration is accomplished by turning the French ideology on its head. The Enlightenment (represented in *The Statesman's Manual* most clearly by Hume) is dismissed as abstract theorizing opposed to the concrete truths of the Bible, marked for Coleridge by "its freedom from the hollowness of abstractions." While enlightened thought offers "a shadow-fight of Things and Quantities," the Bible "gives us the history of Men" (p. 28). The ideologues are the ones caught in ideological false consciousness. The Bible is recovered as the actual history of man coming to a knowledge that is the same as belief: "principles, as taught in the Bible . . . are understood in exact proportion as they are believed and felt . . . For the words of the apostle are literally and philosophically true: WE (that is, the human race) LIVE BY FAITH" (pp. 17–18, quoted in McGann, p. 6). McGann emphasizes the orientation towards the past that marks the romantic ideology as it rediscovers the past not as the history of an error but as the story of humankind's concrete and thus limited, but still valuable, approaches to the truth. This orientation to the past in Coleridge is particularly pronounced, for it is an orientation towards a particular past, towards the special history of the Bible.

This unification of belief and knowledge would strike the Hunt circle as a masking by ideology of reality, what they would see as an obfuscation of real conditions by superstition. I do not, of course, want to argue that Smith and his fellow Cockneys liberate themselves from ideology, nor am I going to claim that they achieve what McGann calls a critical – that is, Marxist – theory of ideology, but I do want to suggest that in their treatment of myths – in Chabrias' account of the myth of Pan, for example – they outline a historicizing account of belief systems that granted them a skeptical, if not materialist, stance towards the kind of idealism embraced by Coleridge. Their distrust of Coleridge's position is evidenced in Hazlitt's attacks on *The Statesman's Manual*, in Byron's criticism of *Biographia Literaria* in *Don Juan*, or in Hunt's attack in *The Feast of Poets* (1815) where Coleridge is presented vexing Apollo "By his idling, and gabbling, and muddling in prose" (p. 288). Coleridge is seen as deserting the poetry of life for the prose of abstruse philosophy, as obscuring experience with abstraction, as betraying his youthful visions of a world remade to an increasing desire to return to a world that has perhaps been unmade. Keats's famous criticism of Coleridge comes in the "negative capability" letter: "Coleridge, for instance, would let go by a fine isolated verisimilitude caught from the Penetralium of mystery, from being incapable of remaining content with half knowledge" (to George and Tom Keats, 21, 27 ⟨?⟩ December 1817, *KL*, 1: 193–94). In concert with his fellow Cockneys, Keats performs on Coleridge the same operation Coleridge performs on the French ideologues: he turns him into an abstract theoretician for whom system is more important than the human experience of truth as half-knowledge.

But how to stop this endless game of ideological one-up-man-ship in which each attempt to move beyond a false belief is seen as an embrace of yet another illusory position? There is a contrary gesture in Keats's letter that moves him beyond a deconstruction of Coleridge. Keats does not want merely to dismiss Coleridge's insights as false ideas or false consciousness. Coleridge offers "half *knowledge*," a "*fine* verisimilitude," with my emphases accentuating the positive in Keats's formulations, as we should also do in the famous definition of "negative capability" – "that is when man is capable of being in uncertainties, Mysteries, doubts, without any irritable reaching after fact & reason" – where it is the irritability, the premature grasping, of the truth seeker and not truth and reason that are criticized. For Keats, Coleridge's problem is that he cannot accept the limited truths of our experience but must have Truth, or a knowledge we can believe absolutely. Keats places us all on the path of the "grand march of intellect" – we are all exploring the chambers within the "Mansion of Life" – but we have not reached the end of that march or explored very far in that house. He rejects any move that would leap ahead to offer final solutions. His skepticism, like that of Smith or Shelley, is not a rejection of the pursuit of "fact and reason," but a recognition that an individual in historical time can only have some of the facts and a partial conception of reason. Truth is not so much a goal that can be reached as a projected vantage point from which all isolated verisimilitudes claiming to be the truth can be revealed as isolated and limited, no matter how fine.

By deploying an analysis of myth as outworn creeds, Smith – like Hunt, Keats, and Shelley – seeks to understand and stand beyond past cultural forms, to free himself from the ideological power of these enchanting cultural objects. Moreover, in setting forth their own visions through myth, the Hunt circle signal their understanding of the limitation of their own cultural constructions. Casting their own beliefs as myths, they can seek to set forth truths without asserting they have found the truth.

Smith's play draws on the powerful resources of the pastoral tradition even as he remakes them. In stressing man's myth-making power as he confronts nature to discover not divine truth but human truths, Smith allies himself with the pastoral's continuing exploration of art conducted through a celebration of nature. His elevation of sexual love over chaste restraint unleashes the eroticism always lurking within the pastoral, the libertinism that nineteenth-century readers found in Fletcher despite his faithful shepherdess, the pleasures revealed in Carew's "Rapture" that sits behind his *Coelum Britannicum* and its celebration of sexual probity, the orgies – imagined or otherwise – that Marie Antoinette was said to perform behind the guise of a *fête champêtre*. While the pastoral drama might have been seen as a celebration of a simple natural order, including a supposedly natural female sexual reticence, Smith finds in the pastoral *human* nature, including the human construction of nature through myth and a celebration of human sexuality as a guarantee of the utopian possibilities of life.

IV

The mythological plays of the Shelleys are less tightly identified with the generic traditions I have been investigating, but they offer a more synoptic account of the Hunt circle's work in mythological drama. Mary Shelley's *Midas* and *Proserpine* offer a mythological diptych, and while Alan Richardson, in our best piece on these plays,[27] has stressed the gender differences between Mary Shelley's generic experiments in mythologizing and those done by male poets such as her husband, I am interested in the ways in which these plays continue the collective project undertaken by the Hunt circle.[28]

Shelley's *Midas* is a powerful attack on the money-getting also embodied in Smith's Celadon. The curtain rises on a pastoral world where even Midas is engaged in "rural tasks" (p. 48). However, Midas is almost immediately distracted by the appearance of Apollo with "crown of gold," "gold ... on your silken robes," "gold-inwoven sandals," and "golden lyre" (pp. 49–50). This fascination with gold, of course, fore-shadows Midas's decision – when offered by Bacchus any wish "from out the deep, rich mine / Of human fancy" (p. 68) – to ask that all he touches be turned to gold. His imagination being bound by his desire for money and power, it is appropriate that he be "wrapt / In golden dreams" (pp. 76–77) and that his most rhapsodic speech is a paean to all he can win through gold: he will raise "Innumerable armies" and "buy Empires:– India shall be mine"; and he will "change all earth to heaven," challenging even "Great Jove" for "who knows / If my gold win not the Cyclopean Powers" (pp. 72–73). Of course, the irony run-ning throughout the play is that, while Midas aspires to become a god and derides his subjects as "Earth-born, groveling dolts" (p. 75), he has been metamorphosed downward as Apollo gives him ass's ears for insulting him and Bacchus notes "You have the judgement of an ass" (p. 70). As with Amarynthus or, say, the Poet in "Alastor," the desire to leave behind the all-too-human results in a reduction to the less-than-human. Not only does Midas find that his golden powers alienate him from the pastoral world of natural riches that surrounds him, but the secret of his ass's ears isolates him from the rest of humanity as he threatens Zopyrion not to reveal his secret so that "now a smile / If Midas knows it may prove capital" (p. 59), truly an end to the sociability celebrated by Hunt or Smith. The play ends appropriately with Midas giving up his golden touch and turning to celebrate a pastoral world of simplicity and equality that might remind us of the values embraced at the close of Hunt's *Descent*: "I'll build a little bower of freshest green, / Canopied o'er with leaves & floored with moss:– / I'll dress in skins;– I'll drink from wooden cups / And eat on wooden platters – sleep on flock; / None but poor men shall dare attend on me" (p. 86). The truly golden world of arcadian simplicity can be created now that "we have lost / Man's curse, heart-bartering, soul-enchaining gold" (p. 89). *Midas*, like *Amarynthus* and much of the other work of the Hunt circle, concludes by finding that the true human heaven is earth.

Proserpine[29] also celebrates a pastoral world, here threatened by male sexual violence and the tyranny of a sky god, just as in *Prometheus Unbound* the zenith of oppressive power is signalled in Jupiter's threatened rape of Thetis. It is significant that this play takes place in Sicily, the birthplace of the pastoral (as Hunt puts it in his 9 March 1819 letter to Mary Shelley [*Correspondence*, 1: 129], "Didn't you go to Sicily while you were in the neighbourhood – the land of Theocritus, and Proserpine, and Polyphemus?"), and that a good portion of the play is given over to recounting the story of the nymph Arethusa, whose story had been tied into the pastoral drama by Guarini. Shelley's is a female pastoral world, where the tale of Aphrodite is "more pleasing" (p. 8) than that of Prometheus, already dramatized by Percy Shelley, and where even Jove sends a female messenger, Iris, rather than the customary Mercury who confronts Prometheus. Richardson usefully follows Susan Gubar[30] in seeing *Proserpine* as a play of female bonding. The contrasts with the male-dominated world of *Midas* are striking: where there is a contest between male poets in *Midas*, here the women share in communal storytelling; where Midas lives in his golden palace imagining himself at the center of an all-powerful court, Ceres laments leaving the pastoral enclave she shares with Proserpine for Jove's court, where "The golden self-moved seats surround his throne" (p. 6); where Midas wants to convert earthly things to gold, the women of *Proserpine* delight in the flowers of the earth; and where the society of *Midas* is marked by egotism, greed, and strife, the female society of *Proserpine* values community, gift-giving, and love. We might, in fact, think of the contrast between the worlds of *Midas* and *Proserpine* as that between the realm of the proper and of property and the realm of the gift set forth by Hélène Cixous.[31]

The female world is disrupted when Pluto comes to claim Proserpine as his property through a rape, an act of violence ratified by Jove, here as in *Prometheus Unbound* the voice, through his "dread decree" (p. 36), of oppressive power. While Mary Shelley does not stage a total liberation from Jove's power, she does subvert it. The Shade of Ascalaphus (cousin to the Phantasm of Jupiter in *Prometheus Unbound*) claims that Jove "is almighty! who shall set the bounds / To his high will?" (p. 40), but Ceres and Proserpine do in effect challenge his power, depriving Jove's world of their life-giving powers and finding their heaven in hell ("Elysium shall be Enna" [p. 39]). The play closes with the summary statement "Thus has black Pluto changed the reign of Jove, / He seizes half the Earth when he takes thee" (p. 44). As in *Midas* and other plays of the group, acts of appropriation and oppression result in a loss of the possibilities of human life embodied in the pastoral, possibilities still guaranteed here by the strong bonds between the women asserted in the face of masculine violence.

Percy Shelley's *Prometheus Unbound* is the culmination of the Hunt circle's exploration of mythological drama, engaging all of the forms and issues taken up in other works. It shares with Hunt's *Descent* an attempt to stage universal liberation, and in fact the basic rhythm of *Prometheus Unbound*, with its movement from tragic entrapment to a sudden and nonviolent reformation of the world and finally to a universal revel, would seem to be derived from Hunt's play. Shelley's Jupiter is a summary figure for all that the Hunt circle opposes, and his instantaneous defeat in the third act, brought on not by violence but through a change in imaginative perception, is allied with both Hunt's and Smith's sense that the oppression and despondency that threaten their world are mental errors, a granting of power to false idols. Shelley's drama, particularly in Asia's interview with Demogorgon (II.4), also deepens the analysis of myth creation that is found in Smith's *Amarynthus*. And if Shelley's fervent espousal of the imagination – where "Language is a perpetual Orphic song, / Which rules with Daedal harmony a throng / Of thoughts and forms, which else senseless and shapeless were" (IV.415–17) – offers a strong version of Smith's account of man's construction of the world through myth, then Shelley's grand celebration of love in *Prometheus Unbound* brings to fruition the promise of an erotic utopia set forth in Smith's *Amarynthus*.

Prometheus Unbound also takes up the dramatic genres reworked in other plays produced by the circle. While there is often a critical attempt to ally Shelley's work with the epic, *Prometheus Unbound* is insistently directed towards dramatic traditions. In fact, it seeks to encompass essentially the entire range of drama from tragedy to melodrama,[32] and thus it also engages both the pastoral drama and the masque. I even want to find Shelley playing off of the enormously popular harlequinade or pantomime, the English form of which was created in the early eighteenth century by men such as John Weaver and particularly John Rich; these early harlequinades have much the same rhythm as the masque – with the pantomime scenes serving as a kind of antimasque to the frame story – and they often treated stories from myth, with Weaver trying to link the form to classical precedents. We might see Asia as the harlequinade's "benevolent agent ... almost always female" who intervenes when a young woman (here, Thetis) is about to be forced into marriage (here, a rape) with an old, powerful man; Demogorgon can appear as Harlequin, defeating Jupiter as Pantaloon by enacting the kind of liberatory transformation for which the stage figure with his magic bat was famous; and the unmasking that occurs in *Prometheus Unbound* might parallel the removal of the "big heads" that disguise the characters at first within the pantomime.[33] We can see the appeal the harlequinade had to the group in Hunt's *Examiner* (5 January 1817) survey of the form, where Hunt praises the English harlequinade: "there is something *real* in Pantomime: there is animal spirit in it" (p. 140). Harlequins and Columbines remind Hunt of the Golden Age and force him to ask why people have "turned from the best things and virtues in it to the pursuit of all sorts of imaginary possessions, which only serve to set them against each other" (p. 143). The world is too much with us, but the popular pantomime can remind us what it is like to be suckled in the creed of the pagan Golden Age.

Of course, while there are such echoes in Shelley's work of the English theater's perhaps most-loved form, they are not likely to be heard in his play's complex orchestration of dramatic variations, and any appeal to popular drama is probably lost in his desire "to familiarize the highly-refined imagination of the more select classes of poetical readers" with "beautiful idealisms" that will awaken in them love, trust, and hope ("Preface," p. 135). He hopes, then, to do for these "select classes" what Hunt finds the harlequinade doing for the popular audience, and thus Shelley will particularly turn to the more refined forms of the masque and the pastoral.

As Stuart Curran has discussed most fully, the fourth act draws on the masque to stage a revel in which the entire universe joins.[34] Jupiter's reign is offered as a kind of antimasque similar to the one Hunt used to present Napoleon as the Enchanter in his *Descent*. One is even tempted to find *Prometheus Unbound* an inversion of a particular masque, Carew's *Coelum Britannicum*. Carew's masque imagines Jupiter, in imitation of the glories of the British court, reforming Olympus so that "the rebel flame is quench'd / In heavenly breasts," and the "loose embraces" of erotic love are forsworn. This distinctly un-Shelleyan ethos, a vision of life he might identify with his own Jupiter, is presented by Jupiter's messenger, Mercury, who is opposed by the figure of Momus, who calls himself "Momus-ap-Somnus-ap-Erebus-ap-Chaos-ap-*Demogorgon*-ap-Eternity" (emphasis added).[35] Whether Shelley knew Carew's masque or not (we do know he became interested in the masque in preparing his play on Charles I which opens on a scene in which a crowd watches the court gathering for a masked performance),[36] he has created a play in which his Demogorgon/Momus figure defeats Mercury and his patron Jupiter in order to revive eroticism and perpetual revolution. But whether Shelley knew of this particular play or not, he was certainly engaged, both in *Prometheus Unbound* and in *The Mask of Anarchy* (where the mask of

anarchs is unmasked as the antimasque), in the kind of revisionist use of
the masque that we have in Hunt's *Descent*: it is the courtly world of
Jupiter that is overthrown; it is the democratic world of the popular
masquerade that is celebrated ("The loathsome mask has fallen, the
man remains / Sceptreless, free, uncircumscribed – but man: / Equal,
unclassed, tribeless and nationless" [III.4.193–95]); and the revel that is
enacted at the end does not turn inward to a closed aristocratic world
but outward to embrace the universe.

Again, high Aeschylean tragedy gives way to pastoral celebration as
Prometheus is released from his chains in the mountains and he retires
with Asia to "A Forest" (III.4). This move suggests that the patterns of
repetition and confinement that mark tragedy and the vision of
creaturely sorrow, pain, and death it presents are not the summit of
human wisdom, that there is a pastoral world of liberation and pleasure
that can be won beyond tragedy. This is not to say that humanity
escapes "chance and death and mutability" – death too is in Arcadia –
but from the perspective of the pastoral enclave created by Prometheus
and Asia these are merely the "clogs of that which else might oversoar /
The loftiest star of unascended heaven" (III.4.201–3). Humanity's future,
"Life, Joy, Empire, and Victory," lies not in a tragic wisdom of limitation and destruction but in the hope preserved within the utopian vision
of the pastoral (IV.554–78).

V

In linking these dramas to what were living theatrical traditions, and
especially in remembering that these plays turn to the most sensory part
of the drama – the spectacle, the costumes, the music, and the special
effects that marked the pastoral drama and the masque – I hope to have
demonstrated that the dramatic work of the Hunt circle did not, as is so
often assumed, arise from an antitheatrical prejudice. However, they
did oppose the theater of their day, a theater in which the pastoral and
the masque would have appeared "unrealistic," as the stage was increasingly dominated by the moralizing melodrama. Against the contemporary theater and a putative realism, the Hunt circle offered a drama of
the realizable ideal – ideal because it is manifestly not the real of the
audience's present, and realizable because it is being enacted before us
and thus appears as a human possibility. In their ideological idealiz-
ations and extreme theatricality, these plays may seem displacements or
even retreats from real human problems, but I would argue that their

very improbability, their status as utopian fantasies and their demand for a renovated, imaginary theater mark them as attempts to liberate humanity from a false sense of limitation imposed on us by those very problems. Because as dramas these works demand enactment and because their performance would require a stage beyond the contemporary theater and by extension a society different from the one supporting the patent theaters royal, these plays offer visions of embodied possibility. The dramas on myth offered by the Hunt circle reject the contemporary stage not because they oppose the theater as such but because they reject the corrupt society that governs the stage of their time. Hunt, Smith, and the Shelleys turn to seventeenth-century essentially aristocratic forms to unlock a vision of civic and erotic liberty for their day; in the pastoral drama's links to a vision of arcadia (the ode to the Golden Age, for example, was the most admired passage in Tasso's *Amyntas*) and in the antimasque's potentially democratic and sexual forces, the Hunt circle found a version of utopia in the heart of an older ideology.[37] In the place of the violence and the selfish money-getting of their day, they offer a utopia of the erotic and the communal – but not a utopia that occupies "nowhere" but a hope that exists in the space of a projected theater that stands as an emblem of a re-visioned world.

Leigh Hunt, in prison, converted his cell into a pastoral nook and meeting place for his wide circle of friends. Suffering the realities of oppression, he sought to create – in life as well as in vision – a utopia of peace in a world at war, of pleasure in a culture of money-getting, of communality in a society deeply divided against itself. We tend to see something dilettantish in the imprisoned Hunt living in a room decorated with flowered wallpaper, his busts of great poets, his lute and pianoforte – a room Charles Lamb said could not exist "except in a fairy tale" (*Autobiography*, p. 294). I think we should see something heroic in this attempt to create – not just in a mental theater but in the space in which he lived – a pastoral stage upon which to act out the possibility of community, imagination, and love.

CHAPTER 5

Cockney classicism: history with footnotes

I

The great craze of the Cockneys at present, is to be Greekish... A Hottentot in
top-boots is not more ridiculous than a classical Cockney. (*Blackwood's* 13 [May
1823])

In 1783, the collector and connoisseur William Hamilton, who served as
the British envoy to the court of Naples, returned to his home country
with an ancient vase, then known as the Barbarini Vase but soon to be
called the Portland Vase (figure 1). Hamilton found that the state of his
finances forced him to sell what he considered to be the prize piece in his
collection; he wrote in praise of the vase that "Except the Apollo
Belvedere, the Niobes, and two or three others of the first-class marbles,
I do not believe that there are any monuments of antiquity that were
executed by so great an artist."[1] The vase went to the Duchess of
Portland, a woman whom Horace Walpole described as "perfectly
sober and intoxicated only by *empty* vases";[2] but she paid 1,800 guineas
for the piece, an extraordinary price when one considers that twenty
years later the entire Townley collection of classical sculptures went to
the British Museum for 20,000 guineas. Its attraction deepened by the
mystery of the subject matter depicted on its frieze, the Portland Vase
had then all the power and allure – what Walter Benjamin calls an
object's "aura" – of a great and unique work of art.[3]

However, what we might call its mode of cultural existence was soon
to change radically. The Duchess of Portland died within a year of
purchasing the vase, and thus it was put up for auction along with the
rest of her museum of curiosities. Her son, the third Duke of Portland,
secretly purchased the vase, and it was he who made two decisions that
shaped the vase's future history. In 1810, he decided to place the vase on
permanent loan with the British Museum, where it immediately became
a favorite attraction, where a regular visitor to the museum such as John

Fig. 1. The Portland Vase.

Keats could have seen it, and where his friend Benjamin Robert Haydon certainly did see it.[4] This unique art object, prized by an aristocratic connoisseur such as Hamilton, was thus given over to the more democratic gaze of the national museum.

More important, the Duke of Portland agreed upon purchasing the vase to loan it to Josiah Wedgwood for twelve months so that the master potter could copy it; while the first edition of the Wedgwood Portland probably ran to no more than forty-five copies, later editions – including an 1839 issue that covered the naked figures on the vase – multiplied the replicated images of the Portland. Moreover, there were many engravings made of the vase, the most interesting being the four, perhaps by Blake, that accompanied the lines by Wedgwood's friend Erasmus Darwin, who – inspired by the copy sent him as a gift – praised the vase in his *Botanic Garden* (1791). The unique art object suddenly existed in a host of reproductions.[5]

Susan Sontag, in her novel *The Volcano Lover*, imagines Hamilton's response to this endless reduplication of his beloved vase:

Pity the uniquely valuable objects whose destiny is to be made available, in toy form, to everyone... Such was the fate of the celebrated object [the Portland Vase] whose sale had been the Cavaliere's [Hamilton's] greatest coup as an art dealer ... [Hamilton] would surely have been startled by the progeny of the vase that the Wedgwood firm began turning out by the tens of thousands in the next century. Olive-green, yellow, pale pink, lilac, lavender-blue, grey, black, and brown Portland vases; Portland vases in many sizes, including small, medium and large. Everyone could have, should have a Portland vase – and however desired: that was the company's plan. It grew, it shrank, it could be any color. The vase became a notion, a tribute to itself.

Who can really love the Portland vase now?

The most valuable possession is always identical with itself.[6]

Of course, the Portland Vase later suffered another change in its mode of existence, for on the seventh of February 1845, a young man entered the room in the British Museum where the vase was exhibited and, using a Persian "curiosity in sculpture," smashed it into more than two hundred fragments.[7] When restorers came to reconstruct the vase, they had to rely on reproductions such as Wedgwood's for models. This unique work of art now exists only as it has been mediated through its duplicates. Hamilton's most valuable possession will never again be identical with itself.

II

Keats's "Ode on a Grecian Urn" was once thought to represent a particular, unique art object – the usual suspects include the Townley Vase, part of the Townley collection that came to the British Museum in

1805 and that Keats surely would have seen; the Sosibios Vase, which Napoleon had brought to Paris and which was reportedly traced by Keats out of a four-volume set of engravings from the Musée Napoléon; the Holland House Urn, which unlike the other candidates depicts a sacrifice, thus providing a possible model for stanza four; and the Borghese Vase, again in the Louvre but reproduced often. As Jerome McGann has pointed out, we are now somewhat embarrassed by the attempt to limit this supposedly universal poem to a specific prototype, but he also reminds us that the poem demands that we consider it as a representation of a concrete object. "Part of the poem's fiction," McGann argues, "...is that the urn it describes is an actual urn comparable to the Townley, Borghese, or Sosibios vases... The poem's fiction – that its *ideal* subject is an *actual* urn – asks its readers to try to visualize, in a concrete way, the urn of the poet's imaginings."[8]

We can see the aptness of McGann's analysis if we think of a number of the key features of the poem. The address to and interrogation of the urn create a dramatic situation in which we must imagine the poet facing a specific object. The depiction of the sacrifice in stanza four, often praised as particularly elusive, mysterious and thus somehow universal, actually provides the moment where the presence of the depicted vase is strongest, as we get the concrete description of the "heifer lowing at the skies, / And all her silken flanks with garlands drest" and the particularizing adjectives in the phrase "this folk, this pious morn." Whatever the ideals evoked in the poem, they are imagined as being embodied in a particular work of art.

McGann finds the resolution of this tension in the project of romantic classicism with its sense of Greek art as being simultaneously perfectly ideal and perfectly embodied. Romantic classicism was not, however, merely an aesthetic doctrine; it was also a practical project, perhaps best represented by Wedgwood's factory, Etruria, which had a classicizing – and romantic – name but made useful household products. Even the journal that first published Keats's ode, the *Annals of the Fine Arts*, which McGann identifies as one of the "chief ideological organs" of romantic classicism, strikes me less as a promulgator of an ideal of classical art than as a trade journal.[9]

With its lists of active London artists (including their addresses, for the aid of potential purchasers), its reviews of public exhibitions, its reports on the transactions of British and foreign academies and societies that patronize the fine arts, its lists of purchasers from various exhibitions, its reviews of various books on the arts, its catalogs of private collections, its news on works in progress, and its very politic dedications to various individuals and institutions that supported their efforts, the _Annals_ might appear to be a kind of _Chronicle of Higher Education_ for early-nineteenth-century artists. It is true that there are articles devoted to antique sculpture and Italian Renaissance painting – the classics of the art world – but there are also pieces on the superiority of "Gothic architecture over other styles for religious edifices" (2 [1817], 173), on domestic architecture, on the proposed Waterloo monument, on the panorama at Leicester Square, and on engravings of famous actresses and of views of the Bank of England and the Royal Exchange. The _Annals_ is as much a practical guide for the producers and consumers of art as it is a learned inquiry into the nature of the classic in art.

The appearance of Keats's ode in the _Annals_ as "On a Grecian Urn" (next to a sonnet by Barry Cornwall on Michelangelo) links the poem not just to an abstract romantic classicism but to a very real commercial-ized classicism and its transformation – as in Wedgwood's reproductions – of unique works of art into reproducible commodities. We need to remember that Keats lived in an era in which the organization usually called the Society for the Encouragement of the Arts had as its full title the Society for the Encouragement of Arts, Manufactures and Com-merce in Great Britain. The British Institution for the Development of the Fine Arts, whose exhibits are often praised during the period over against those of the Royal Academy, had as its mission "To improve and extend our manufactures by that degree of taste and elegance of design which are to be exclusively derived from the cultivation of the fine arts and thereby to increase the general prosperity and resources of the empire." Keats wrote at a time when only a few artists could make a living through individual paintings, but there was a thriving industry for engravers offering endlessly reproducible products. In early-nineteenth-century London, one could view an extraordinary range of reproduced art objects – not just Wedgwood vases but classical statues done in wax, ancient buildings modelled in cork, and paintings redone in colored wools on linen and hung in Miss Linwood's famous gallery of over sixty needlepoint reproductions of the masters. While Keats knew some art objects firsthand through visits to the British Museum and various exhibition halls, he was more likely to know them through reproduc-tions, such as those of statues and paintings in Leigh Hunt's cottage in the Vale of Health celebrated by Keats at the close of "Sleep and Poetry" or those of vases found in Kirk's _Outlines from the Figures and Compositions upon the Greek, Roman, and Etruscan Vases of the Late Sir William_

Hamilton; with Engraved Borders (2nd ed., 1814) or Henry Moses's *A Collection of Antique Vases* (1814).[10] We know that Keats, Hunt, and Shelley were taken with James Tassie's engraved enamel gems reproducing classical and literary subjects.[11] The situation of the "Ode on a Grecian Urn" is conditioned less by works such as the Elgin Marbles, with their supposed realistic idealism, than it is by the existence of reproductions of artworks such as the Wedgwood Portland Vase, with its ability to bring beauty – practically, commercially – into the actual lives of consumers. The first thing we must realize about Keats's poem is that it confronts the vicissitudes of a thing of beauty in the age of porcelain – and wax, cork, and needlepoint – reproduction.

Keats, of course, experienced these vicissitudes firsthand each time he ventured into print. As I have argued, Keats began as a coterie poet, showing his work to the members of the circle around Leigh Hunt and receiving the praise not only of Hunt but also of other participants in the group such as Charles Cowden Clarke, Horace Smith, and William Hazlitt. In manuscript, a Keats poem circulated among a controlled circle of friends who would treasure the work and offer support. However, once the poem was committed to reproduction in a published book, Keats lost control of its reception and its interpretation as it entered the commercialized, public space of print. As the poems that Keats first showed to the Hunt circle in manuscript came to be printed in his *Poems* of 1817 and *Endymion* of 1818, Keats exchanged his status as a coterie favorite for that of a target of the Cockney School attacks. His unique works of art were through a series of reproductions – the last being the reviewers' mocking quotations – reduced to parody.

I believe that Keats responded to this condition of authorship and this mode of cultural existence of the artistic object in the "Ode on a Grecian Urn" by attempting to recreate in fiction the "aura" – the power and attraction – lost to an object such as the Portland Vase. Walter Benjamin in "The Work of Art in the Age of Mechanical Reproduction" argues that the replication of an art object destroys its physical history, its provenance or history of ownership, and its original context or cultural history:

Even the most perfect reproduction of a work of art is lacking in one element: its presence in time and space, its unique existence at the place where it happens to be. This unique existence of the work of art determined the history to which it was subject throughout the time of its existence. This includes the changes which it may have suffered in physical condition over the years as well as the various changes in its ownership... One might subsume the eliminated element in the term "aura" and go on to say: that which withers in the age of mechanical reproduction is the aura of the work of art . . . One might generalize by saying: the technique of reproduction detaches the reproduced object from the domain of tradition. By making many reproductions it substitutes a plurality of copies for a unique existence.[12]

We can perhaps get a sense of what Benjamin's argument means for art in Keats's day if we look (as I too engage in the endless round of reproduction) at an engraving of the "Portland Museum," the Duchess of Portland's collection of curios and antiquities, including the Portland Vase (figure 2).

The vase occupies the central place in the composition, and a mirror is placed behind it in an attempt to re-present the vase as fully as possible. But the engraving cannot offer us the Portland Vase, and not only because three dimensions are collapsed into two; the contrast between the cobalt-blue glass of the vase and the milky-white glass of the relief is lost, the shape is altered, and the figures are not reproduced with accuracy. Moreover, what Benjamin sees as the vase's history as it is inscribed in the physical object is lost: not only are we unaware from the engraving that the figures' "surfaces [were] partially decayed by time," as Wedgwood noted (in deciding, with the concurrence of William Hamilton, to restore "their original smoothness" in his reproductions),[13] but also there is no way for us to see that the bottom of the vase had at some time been broken and replaced with a glass disk not belonging to the original (though the image on the disk is apparently reproduced as a drawing wedged under the vase). The history of its ownership is obscured as well: the very renaming of the vase as the Portland Vase reinvents it in the present, denying its status as a long-coveted object, formerly owned by and named for the Barbarini; the changes in its ownership are lost – not to mention its all-too-obscure origins – in order to celebrate the current owner. Moreover, the engraving removes the vase from any context that might help us to understand it in a historical sense; the vase is placed amongst a melange of odd, mainly natural, objects, and a piece of coral is placed in it (which, oddly, disappears in the mirrored reflection). The aura of the vase is destroyed as it loses its physical reality, its provenance, and its historical context. It comes as no surprise that this engraving was reproduced as the frontispiece to Mr. Skinner and Co.'s catalog for the auction of the Duchess of Portland's collection.

Keats's ode seeks to reverse this process. Addressing himself to the features that Benjamin finds lost in reproduction, Keats provides his urn

Fig. 2. Charles Grignion after Edward Francis Burney, *The Portland Museum*,
frontispiece to Mr. Skinner and Co.'s sale catalog, 24 April – 7 June 1786.
Etching and engraving. 8 April 1786.

with both a physical inviolability – it is "still unravish'd," unlike the Portland Vase with its lost bottom – and a life history, from its "birth" at the hands of its unknown creator through its status as the "foster-child of silence and slow time" to its future status as "a friend to man," "When old age shall this generation waste" (ll. 1–2, 46–48). If the reproduction is the object without history, Keats makes his vase into a "Sylvan historian" offering a legend. Keats would seem in his fiction to heal the damage done to real urns such as the Portland Vase. The great success of Keats's poem is that it convinces us that there is an urn behind it, that it is powerfully re-presenting a unique work of art with its aura intact.

It is finally stanza four, with its evocation of an unrepresented town that never can be represented because no one remains to remember it, that guarantees the aura of the imagined urn; for it is exactly the absence imagined here that cannot be reproduced. The aura of the work of art is dependent upon what is no longer there – its original physical form that has necessarily altered, its provenance which is here a lost origin, and its history in slow time. The very silence of the urn (at least until the closing lines) insures its aura by keeping within the potentiality of the absent what the poem demands be made present. And it is finally the possibility of its complete absence that guarantees the work of art its unique power. The Portland Vase, like any art object, was valuable because it could be ravished, because it could be – and was – shattered. The urn of the ode is "still unravish'd," but that very claim seems to imagine its ravishment, its destruction. It is the possibility of such loss, of our utter abandonment by the work of art, which is embodied in stanza four: "And, little town, thy streets for evermore / Will silent be; and not a soul to tell / Why thou art desolate, can e'er return" (ll. 38–40).

It would be wrong, however, to see Keats's "Ode on a Grecian Urn" as an exercise in cultural nostalgia, an attempt to recreate a lost aesthetic wholeness in his divided age. Keats is always aware of his distance from any idealized past; he knows he is what Schiller called a "sentimental poet," writing – as Keats put it in "Ode to Psyche" – "Too, too late for the fond believing lyre." Keats wants to rescue his urn and his art from the ravages of reproduction, but he does so not through invoking a unified, naive, pure, timeless art object but rather by writing an ironic, sentimental, eroticized, and historicized poem about such an object. Put another way, he creates the fiction of the unique object of romantic classicism – the perfectly embodied, realized ideal – through a poem that is paradoxical, elusive, and distanced. He grants the imagined urn its aura by recognizing that his poem cannot achieve such a state, a fact he recognizes in calling the urn a "Sylvan historian, who canst thus express / A flowery tale more sweetly than our rhyme" (ll. 3–4). "Ode on a Grecian Urn" is a work of what I want to call Cockney classicism that seeks to return passion and power – the aura of the classic – to art beyond the diminution of its power through endless imitation. But that beyond is a sign of the poem's own belatedness, of its own acts of imitation – and thus reproduction – of another poem and of a woman's performances.

III

The Portland Vase has itself never been a particularly popular candidate for the model behind Keats's "Ode on a Grecian Urn."[14] One reason for this is that the vase now appears to have been made during the reign of Augustus, probably by Alexandrian craftsmen working in Italy. Along with its peers in the late-eighteenth-century pantheon of classical art – the Apollo Belvedere and the Laocoön group – the vase has lost its artistic authority as it has come to be seen as a late and derivative piece. It is no longer good enough nor Greek enough to be Keats's model; we prefer to imagine him responding to the Elgin Marbles or at least to neo-Attic urns such as the Townley Vase. However, as Ian Jack notes, "Keats must have known the Portland Vase well... a work whose significance was frequently debated at this time, and which Erasmus Darwin refers to in *The Botanic Garden*"; and Keats's friend Haydon used a figure from the vase in his "The Raising of Lazarus."[15] Moreover, we need to remember that, at the time, the Portland Vase was considered one of the greatest of classical works and that – while called a vase – it was repeatedly identified as a "Sepulchral Urn," supposedly containing the ashes of the Roman emperor Alexander Severus and his mother, Mammea. Sir William Hamilton went further, linking it to Alexander Severus' more exalted and Greek prototype, Alexander the Great; Hamilton, after lauding the vase as we have seen, continues, "and I have no doubt of this being a work of the time of Alexander the Great, and was probably brought out of Asia by Alexander, whose ashes were deposited therein after his death."[16] For Hamilton, the Portland Vase was the greatest of Grecian urns, once containing one of the greatest Greeks.

While the main interpretive tradition surrounding the Portland Vase read its frieze as an allegory of life and death, no less an authority than Winckelmann as early as 1776 linked the images on the vase to the legend of Peleus and Thetis, a position developed by such later scholars as J. Milligen and W. Watkiss Lloyd, who in 1849 was the first to link the vase to a specific representation of this myth: Catullus 64, the "Epithalamium of Peleus and Thetis." Recently, Randall L. Skalsky has argued convincingly for ties between the Portland Vase and Catullus' poem, finding the vase offering the same kind of witty, learned manipulation of myth that marks Catullus' verse.[17] The vase, which I have been treating as an original, now appears as a cross-media reproduction, an attempt to recreate a poem in the form of an urn. Keats's ode – which, of course, seeks to recreate an urn in the shape of a poem – tries to recreate the aura of an imaginative Portland Vase by taking upon itself the belatedness of imitation, by making itself a reproduction of the vase's great poetic prototype, thus freeing the urn to stand perhaps for itself.

Whether or not Keats knew the arguments that linked the Portland Vase to the story of Peleus and Thetis, he almost surely knew Catullus' poem.[18] Catullus' poetry had sparked British imitators since the Renaissance, and the Hunt circle was clearly interested in the poet, though this influence has been overlooked. Hunt himself translated a number of Catullus' poems, among them two of the seven long poems including the "Epithalamium" grouped together in Catullus' volume – Catullus 61, "The Nuptial Song of Julia and Manlius," and Catullus 63, the "Atys," interestingly described by Hunt as an attack on the extremes to which religions, including Christianity, carry their practitioners (*Reflector* 1 [1811], 165). Hunt's brother John opened his *Poetry* (1824) with a translation from Catullus and included four more adaptations of the Roman poet. Byron called Moore the "young Catullus of his day" and wrote in a poem to Moore before their visit to Hunt in prison, "To-morrow be with me, as soon as you can, sir, / All ready and dress'd for proceeding to spunge on / (According to compact) the wit in the dungeon – / Pray Phoebus at length our political malice / May not get us lodgings within the same palace! . . . / And you'll be Catullus, the Regent Mamurra." Byron, Coleridge, Landor, Reynolds, and Frere all translated poems by Catullus. Catullus 64 may have been imitated by Shelley in *Queen Mab*, Frank Sayers translated part of 64 in his *Poems, Containing Dramatic Sketches of Northern Mythology* (4th ed., 1807), and George Lamb, Caroline Lamb's brother-in-law, published a translation of the complete poems in 1821, with an acknowledgment of Hunt's efforts on the "Atys." Even Wordsworth has a reference to Catullus 3 in his sonnet "To . . ." (1835), which opens " 'Wait, prithee, wait!' this answer Lesbia threw / Forth to her Dove," a Catullan moment incidentally also alluded to by Cornelius

Webb in his *Summer* (1821), where he speaks of "the Lesbia-love sparrow" (p. 9).[19] While we might locate the primary influence of Catullus on British poetry in the seventeenth century or in the Victorian era or in the modern age, he was a clear and present influence on the poets of the romantic era.

I believe that in encountering Catullus the Cockney poets engaged in a profound act of self-recognition. For Catullus too was part of a literary group attacked by the establishment, the "neoteric," or "new," poets who wrote during the late Roman Republic and were part of a hellenizing movement in Latin literature that led them to draw on Alexandrian models such as Callimachus. Neoteric poetry – with its self-conscious, playfully belated style, with its inversion of traditional myths, with its combination of learned allusions and slangy diction, with its evocation of the natural and the sensual by an urban coterie – almost provides the program for Cockney poetry;[20] the neoterics have also been seen as offering Renaissance writers "a way of legitimizing their social and convivial approach to poetry"[21] which would also appeal to the Hunt circle, with their social, communal sense of poetry. We can also find a Catullan spirit – the same combination of playfulness and erudition, of esoteric lore and low diction – in the style of much Cockney poetry, as we see in the opening of Peacock's *Rhododaphne*:

> The rose and myrtle blend in beauty
> Round Thespian Love's hypaethric fane;
> And there alone, with festal duty
> Of joyous song and choral train,
> From many a mountain, stream, and vale,
> And many a city fair and free,
> The sons of Greece commingling hail
> Love's primogenial deity.　　　　　　　(Ll. 1–8)[22]

The light, quickly moving verse runs up against a phrase such as "hypaethric [open to the air] fane"; the straightforward image of all Greece coming to a festival is complicated by the allusion to "Love's primogenial deity," which is soon divided into "Creative, Heavenly, Earthly Love" and which calls forth a long footnote from Peacock citing Plato, Aristophanes, Plutarch, and Lactantius. This is the style not only of the *doctus* Catullus but of the Doctor of Cockney Poetry, Leigh Hunt, as we have seen it defined in contemporary reviews. It thus comes as no surprise that Hunt's first major poem, *The Feast of Poets*, has as its motto a quotation from the neoterics' model, Callimachus, and that among its eight additional poems are three translations from Catullus.

Catullus 64 is our one great example of the Latin epyllion, or "little epic," one of the counterepic forms the neoterics cultivated (poems such as Cinna's *Smyrna*, Calvus' *Io*, and Caecilius' poem on Cybele do not survive). To a certain extent, the identification of Catullus 64 as an epyllion arises from an attempt by nineteenth-century scholars to find a classical precedent for a body of Renaissance narrative poems, usually on erotic subjects, that includes Michael Drayton's *Endimion and Phoebe: Ideas Latmus* (1595), the Hero and Leander poems of Marlowe (1593) and Chapman (1598), Lodge's *Scillaes Metamorphosis* (1589), Shirley's *Narcissus, or The Self-Lover* (1646), and Shakespeare's *Venus and Adonis* (1593).[23] Interestingly, these poems take up many of the subjects that run through the mythological poems of the Hunt circle, from Hunt's own "Hero and Leander" to Keats's *Endymion*, and there is some evidence of the romantics drawing upon such works.[24] In any event, Catullus' "Epithalamium" as an epyllion engages epic and heroic subject matter without adopting either epic form or a heroic ideology.

The eccentric narrative of Catullus 64 opens with the voyage of Jason and the Argonauts, only to have the mission left behind as Peleus and Thetis meet and decide to marry. As the wedding guests gather, we discover that one of the wedding presents is a tapestry depicting another hero, Theseus, though we see him at one of his least heroic moments as he abandons Ariadne, who is later swept up by Bacchus. The account of Theseus' abandonment of Ariadne, her lament for and curse upon her lover, and his father's death through the hero's carelessness actually occupies the largest section of the piece. The poem closes with a song by the Parcae, who detail the supposed glories of this marriage that will bring forth the "greatest" hero, Achilles, who is described (in Lamb's translation) as a killing machine who will choke the river Scamander with corpses, whose "valour oft, his ever dauntless breast / Shall mothers' grief o'er children's biers attest," and whose death will be mourned by the sacrifice of Polyxena (II: 43, 45).

The poem systematically undercuts the heroic. The Trojan War is imagined as a killing field commanded by Agamemnon, named only as the "perjured Pelops' grandson." Achilles' heroism raises itself upon slaughter, upon the tears of mothers and the sacrifice of the maiden Polyxena on his tomb. Again, Theseus returns as a hero to rule Thebes, but he can do so only by abandoning Ariadne. Even the marriage of Peleus and Thetis – the only marriage between a mortal and an immortal – is a result of force used against women, for Thetis is bound to marriage with Peleus once Jupiter learns from Prometheus that if he mates with her she will produce a child greater than himself, a fact importantly not revealed by Shelley's Prometheus to his Jupiter. Lawrence Lipking, in his account *Abandoned Women and Poetic Tradition* that includes Catullus 64, argues that "epics require abandoned women."[25] Catullus' epyllion rejects the epic, heroic tradition as a result. For set against the abandoned Ariadne, the sacrificed Polyxena, and the coerced Thetis is Ariadne after she discovers "wild ecstasy" with Bacchus. The only moment of joy in the poem comes as "Bacchus young," followed by dancing Satyrs and Sileni who play "timbrels," "cymbals," and "fifes," appears "With love for thee high raging in his heart, / Thee seeking, Ariadne" (II: 37). The poem indicts the heroic choice made by Theseus and Achilles of an epic career over a life of sexual and personal fulfillment, an indictment strong enough to call forth Virgil's reply in the Dido episode of his epic where, echoing in order to "correct" Catullus, he sought to demonstrate that it is the right choice to abandon one's love for the demands of country, home, and *pietas*. "Pius Aeneas" properly escapes Dido's bower of bliss to found Rome.[26]

The Peleus and Thetis story, with its ties to the Prometheus myth, to the adventures of Theseus and Ariadne, and to the story of Troy, holds a central place in the mythological imagination of the younger romantics, perhaps most importantly if mostly tangentially in *Prometheus Unbound*. Horace Smith has a poem that may owe some debt to Catullus 64 – it at least takes up some of the same subject matter – though it announces that it is "Suggested by a Passage in the second book of Apollonius of Rhodius." His "Shriek of Prometheus" (published in *London Magazine* 3 [June 1821], 608), imagines the Argonauts sailing and listening to Orpheus sing of Apollo and Pan (the subject of the lyrics Percy wrote for Mary Shelley's play *Midas*), only to be terrified by the sound of Prometheus' cries as he is attacked by Zeus' eagle. "Barry Cornwall" wrote but did not publish "The Song of Ariadne," which takes up another part of Catullus' poem, though here the debt is more likely to Ovid;[27] there is also "The Story of Prometheus Done into Doggerel" by J. H. Reynolds's one-time mentor John F. M. Dovaston.[28] However, we can perhaps best get a sense of the Catullan project of the Cockney movement through Hunt's mythological poems, in particular his "Bacchus and Ariadne."[29]

If the Dido and Aeneas episode of the *Aeneid* offered a response to the Catullan account of Theseus and Ariadne, Hunt's "Bacchus and Ariadne" – which appears to draw directly on the incident depicted in the tapestry from Catullus 64 – offers a Catullan counterresponse to

Virgil. At the point where Ariadne realizes she has been abandoned by her lover, Hunt interrupts to attack the possible explanations that could be offered for the behavior of a Theseus – or an Aeneas:

> Some say that Theseus took this selfish flight
> From common causes – a cloyed appetite;
> Others, that having brought her sister there
> As well, he turned his easy love to her;
> And others, who are sure to quote Heaven's orders
> For great men's crimes, though not for small disorders,
> Pretend that Bacchus in the true old way,
> A dream, advised him sternly not to stay,
> But go and cut up nations limb by limb,
> And leave the lady and the bower to him.   (Ll. 46–55)

In this account it seems most likely that Theseus, like Aeneas, has left his love in order to follow a course of war. The god Bacchus values the "lady and the bower," but the hero prefers to "go and cut up nations limb by limb," not unlike Catullus' Achilles.

With Theseus gone, Bacchus, followed by his celebrants, reveals himself to Ariadne. The arrival of Bacchus and his crew is heralded by the music they play, music described by Hunt in words that seem to echo Catullus 64: Ariadne "heard the noise / Which seemed fast coming, like a throng of joys: / And now she heard the sound of cymbals clashed; / And now, as if – cups were together dashed; / And timbrels then, and pipes, which fine crisp fingers / Seemed to be dancing on; and laughing singers" (ll. 147–52). Hunt's poem essentially continues the story of Bacchus and Ariadne from where Catullus' leaves off. Where Catullus returns to describe the wedding party of Peleus and Thetis, complete with an appearance from the gods, Hunt gives an account of the joining of Bacchus and Ariadne, together with the revels of his followers and a dance performed by the gods who come to bless their union. For her loss and pain, Ariadne receives abundant recompense, as we learn that Bacchus "gave and shared as much more happiness / Than Theseus, as a noble spirit's caress, / Full of sincerity, and mind, and heart, / Out-relishes mere fire and self-embittering art" (ll. 340–43). Theseus may have departed for epic glory, but Hunt's poem prefers to remain with Ariadne, glorying in her sexual union with Bacchus.

"Bacchus and Ariadne" had its origins in the response (discussed in chapter 3) of Hazlitt, Keats, and Hunt when Hunt reread the *Excursion* and its account of Greek myth in the fall of 1816. It is, in a way, written against Wordsworth's epic as a Catullan epyllion, celebrating love and sensuality over against the demands of duty, nation, and traditional family values. Again, Hunt's "Hero and Leander" seeks an action of epic worth in a love story, with the name of Leander's lover suggesting that there is something heroic in the erotic; the poem criticizes "foolish men" and "Their vice-creating ways," who render sex a sin, being "blindest / To what is happiest, loveliest, best, and kindest" (ll. 150–55). Poems such as Keats's *Endymion* and Shelley's *Witch of Atlas* can also be usefully thought of as epyllions, and while Byron's *Don Juan* adopts a different stance towards the epic, it too plays with the heroic tradition in order to celebrate the erotic. Hunt's "Nymphs" offers the kind of mythological revisionism and creativity we find in Catullus 64 and elsewhere. The group's penchant for esoteric myths, which has been noticed by Hungerford amongst others, echoes similar moves in Callimachus and Catullus.[30]

Keats, whose use of the classics was criticized in his time and has been in our own, is perhaps best served by making these connections between the Cockney project and a Catullan poetic. Throughout Keats's career, we can find him turning to such a poetic at key moments of self-definition – in, for example, "I stood tip-toe upon a little hill" that as we have seen serves as a kind of manifesto for his 1817 *Poems*, in the proems to *Endymion*, and in the turn from the Titans to Apollo in book III of "Hyperion." The opening of the second book of *Endymion*, for example, sounds a Callimachan and Catullan note when it rejects the epic subject matter of the "woes of Troy" to celebrate "Troilus and Cressid sweet." Keats cries, "Hence, pageant history," turning from stories of military exploits such as Alexander's and tales of adventure such as Ulysses', and preferring "Juliet leaning / Amid her window-flowers,– sighing,– weaning / Tenderly her fancy from its maiden snow, [which] / Doth more avail than these: the silver flow / Of Hero's tears, the swoon of Imogen, / Fair Pastorella in the bandit's den, / Are things to brood on with more ardency / Than the death-day of empires" (II.8–34).

As I have noted, Keats's engagement with Cockney poetry is usually seen as a juvenile attachment to Hunt which he abandons as he grows as a poet, but the late "Ode on a Grecian Urn" – as can be seen in its proliferating puns – uses the same "archly-thoughtful manner," the same "licentious brilliancy of epithet" that the *Edinburgh Magazine* (2d ser., 1 [October 1817], 256) found in Keats's poetry in 1817. Individual scholars often note a single pun in the poem – Ian Jack reminds us that the phrase "leaf-fringed legend" can refer to either a story or an embellished written statement; William Empson objected to the opening line of the last stanza as "very bad ... the half pun [of "Attic" with "attitude"] suggesting a false Greek derivation and jammed up against an arty bit of Old English seems ... affected and ugly"; and Paul Hamilton takes up the phrase "With brede / Of marble men and maidens overwrought" to point out that "overwrought" can be read as "the elevation of the 'brede' above the surface of the urn, the emotions of the 'mad pursuit' of 'men and maidens,' the transference of figures from one work of art 'over' to another, and the overarching umbrage, itself legendary, fringing the urn's narrative."[31] Pursuing Hamilton's point further, we might find the full statement taking up not only the way in which the figures are fashioned on the urn but also the breeding going on between overwrought or worked-up women and men stiffened into "marble."

There are many more puns – for example, "Thou still unravish'd bride of quietness," where "still" could refer to a motionless, quiet quality of the urn or function as a modifier of "unravish'd," indicating that the bride has yet to be ravished; "flowery tale," where we could have a tale embellished with floral designs, an ornate, overly poetic story, or simply a pastoral narrative; or the "desolate" city which is both abandoned and in despair. Even the original title of the poem in the *Annals of the Fine Arts* 15 (January 1820) – "On A Grecian Urn" – puns, for it could refer either to the poem about or on a Grecian urn or to what is being depicted that is on the urn. We need to be aware of such puns in this poem and elsewhere in Keats, for we do not necessarily think of him as a punster, and yet he is quite fond of such verbal quibbles, just as he is of oxymorons, coinages, new compound words, and other attempts to force language to do double duty. If we fail to notice the density of the punning in the ode, we lose a sense of the poem's playfulness, of the experimental, even quirky, nature of Keats's language to which Marjorie Levinson has pointed,[32] of the Catullan and Cockney delight in toying with what others consider serious in the name of a linguistic and also finally an erotic delight.

This witty, extreme, even odd, wordplay, so distinctive of Cockney verse, links Keats back – via Hunt, if not directly – to Catullus and the neoteric poetic, and particularly back to the "Epithalamium of Peleus and Thetis"; for I want to argue that the "legend" which "haunts about" the shape of Keats's urn is the same one depicted on the Portland Vase, that of Catullus' odd wedding poem. For example, we are told that the urn's legend is "Of deities or mortals, or of both"; whereas this might simply express an inability to read the urn, it might recall Catullus 64, with its account of the only marriage between a mortal and a goddess. The action imagined here – "the maidens loth," who "struggle to escape" from the men in "mad pursuit" – could be a reference to Thetis' initial rejection of Peleus and his need to pursue and win her against her will, a facet of their story introduced only elliptically in Catullus ("Nor Thetis *then* a mortal bridegroom spurn'd"; emphasis added) but made clear in such Keatsian source books as Lemprière's *Bibliotheca Classica*. The final line of the stanza ("What pipes and timbrels? What wild ecstasy?") can certainly be linked to the coming of Bacchus to Ariadne as he is accompanied by devotees with pipes, cymbals, and timbrels, a point made in both Catullus 64 and Hunt's "Bacchus and Ariadne." One is even tempted to find in Catullus' bizarre wedding song the source of Keats's equally unusual imagery of the bride awaiting ravishment, and perhaps then to see the urn, like the tapestry in Catullus 64, as a wedding present that tells a legend.

However, I believe that the strongest evidence for a link between the ode and the epyllion comes in stanza four, the most admired part of poem and one for which we have struggled to discover a model or prototype. Keats's description of the abandoned town is tantalizingly close to Catullus' account of the desertion of Thessaly as everyone journeys to attend the wedding of Peleus and Thetis:

> Thessalia's crowds with gifts the palace seek,
> And looks of greater joy than words speak.
> The throng from Tempe's vale, from Scyros roams,
> From Cranon's turrets and Larissa's homes,
> And seek from every side the rich Pharsalian domes.
> The earth's untill'd, the bullock's callous throat,
> Free from the yoke, regains its softer coat:
> The lowly vineyard knows no weeding rakes,
> Nor ox with sloping share the furrow breaks:
> No pruner lops the tree's incumbering boughs,
> And rust grows thick on the neglected ploughs.   (II: 22)

The pattern of Keats's stanza is the same, moving from a processional – in his case the sacrifice rather than a wedding – to a description of a town "emptied" of its people. We might even imagine Keats arriving at the notion of the eternally empty city of the urn from Catullus' distortion and acceleration of time as almost instantaneously equipment begins to rust, oxen go soft, and vines grow wild. In both poems, these passages gesture towards a loss, an absence, that underwrites the poems' more apparent argument.

It is not, however, so much specific connections between the two poems that are important as it is Keats's use of a Catullan style and his pursuit of a Catullan argument against the epic and the heroic. The urn is identified as a "Sylvan historian," suggesting almost oxymoronically that it is engaged with history – the realm of epic – and that it is from a pastoral world, a world we do not normally think of as having a history. Such an identification makes sense, however, when the ode is linked to the epyllion, with its ability to engage within a small compass the subject matter of epic while rejecting its ethos. Within the even smaller, lyric compass of the ode, Keats, offering a history of Tempe or Arcady rather than of wars and monarchs, turns back from epic history to the pastoral that was traditionally seen as merely a prelude to the epic in the kind of developmental pattern embodied by Virgil, followed by Spenser, Milton, and Pope, and in Keats's lifetime still invoked, though in an altered way, by Wordsworth, moving from *Lyrical Ballads* to the *Excursion*, or Southey, whose seemingly yearly epics, as Byron put it, "cram the creaking shelves" ("English Bards," l. 127). Keats continually veered from this pattern – for example in the proems to *Endymion*, as we have seen. Even when Keats seems to offer an epic, in his fragment "Hyperion," he ultimately rejects the traditional form as the third book turns from the Titans to Apollo, from the Miltonic style of the first two books to the Cockney style of Hunt, from epic strife to the pastoral isle on which Apollo resides:

> Thus in alternate uproar and sad peace,
> Amazed were those Titans utterly.
> Oh, leave them, Muse! Oh, leave them to their woes;
> For thou art weak to sing such tumults dire;
> A solitary sorrow best befits
> Thy lips, and antheming a lonely grief.
> Leave them, O Muse! for thou anon wilt find
> Many a fallen old Divinity
> Wandering in vain about bewildered shores.
> Meanwhile touch piously the Delphic harp,
> And not a wind of heaven but will breathe
> In aid soft warble from the Dorian flute;
> For lo! 'tis for the father of all verse.   (III.1–13)

Bate finds himself reminded "disturbingly of *Endymion*" here, and Allot comments, "This is true. The inferiority of Book III is marked."[33] But while they lament the move from Miltonic inversions to Huntian luxuries, Keats is seeking to make a point through this stylistic shift: in a sense, through the third book he recreates "Hyperion" not as a failed epic about a war in heaven but as a completed epyllion about the rejection of such "tumults dire" in favor of Apollo's quest to "die into life."

"Ode on a Grecian Urn" makes a similar turn. It is not going to tell us an epic "legend [that] haunts about thy shape" – we get no tales of Theseus or Achilles or brave Ulysses – but the ode is instead going to invoke a pastoral world defined by the "happy melodist," the "bold lover," and the "happy, happy boughs." Just as Catullus turns from war to love, so does Keats turn from the frenzied actions of men and gods to the silent "green world" of the second and third stanzas.

We need to remember that Keats could well have used the ode to engage an epic subject matter, what Keats calls in *Endymion* "the death day of empires," a phrase which, while used in a general statement about his advocacy of tales of love over war stories, surely invoked for his audience the fall of Napoleon and the death of his empire. The odal form had been repeatedly used to comment on Napoleon and his defeat; we need think only of Byron's "Ode to Napoleon Bonaparte" (1814) or Wordsworth's "Thanksgiving Ode" (1816). We should also remember that this particular ode might well have invoked empire and death, for when we think of an urn, even an urn such as the Portland Vase, we usually think of a funeral urn. As we have seen, the Portland Vase was thought to have contained the ashes of Alexander Severus or even Alexander the Great, commemorating death days in other empires.

Keats might have considered using this funerary urn to celebrate the dead of the Napoleonic wars, particularly because he placed the ode in the *Annals of the Fine Arts*, a site for the debate over war monuments. While Roe has found the poem haunted by the mass killings of June 1794 in Revolutionary France, while Tillotama Rajan argues that the urn contains the ashes of past culture as history itself is tossed on the ashheap of history, and while Daniel Watkins discovers the ashes of oppressed women in the urn,[34] this more immediate debate provides a more direct context for the ode. On 5 February 1816, Parliament voted in favor of erecting two monuments, one to celebrate Trafalgar, the navy, and Nelson, the other for Waterloo, the army, and Wellington. Whereas the Trafalgar monument was completed, the Waterloo memorial was abandoned because of its cost and disagreements over the design of the structure – not to mention that Wellington himself was a controversial figure, with, for example, Southey celebrating "how our great Commander's eagle eye, / Which comprehended all, secured the victory"

(*The Poet's Pilgrimage to Waterloo* [1816], III.32, 191–92) while Byron dismissed him as "Vilainton" (*Don Juan*, IX.1).

The *Annals of the Fine Arts* offered arguments on both sides of the debate over the monument. In the first volume (1817), John Galt argues that the monument should not be to Wellington. He rejects a pillar with a statue, for "it implies that the original was elevated by his merits, above his fellow citizens. Besides, it is not the skill of the commander, but the fortitude of an army that we celebrate; and an army could not be very well exhibited on the top of any column, either literally, or by an allegorical statue" (pp. 65–66). Also rejecting a triumphal arch as being intended for heroes, and an allegorical statue as being too difficult to interpret, Galt finally settles upon a giant sarcophagus ("companionable" form to the funerary urn) to represent both the scope of the victory and "the number of the slain" (p. 67). The desire for an antimilitaristic war memorial clearly predates the Vietnam War.

The second volume of the *Annals* a year later contained an essay by James Elmes, the editor: "The Most Proper Mode of Commemorating the Great Victories of the Late Wars." He argues in favor of honoring Wellington: "as history has scarcely had to record, since the days of the heroic Theseus, a more perfect hero or one blessed with more marks of quality than the hero of Britain, a country that has not inaptly been called the modern Greece, and as the world has never yet produced a more perfect work of art than the temple erected by Theseus at Athens" (p. 33), so England should erect a copy of the Temple of Theseus dedicated to Wellington.

The idea of Wellington as Theseus has an obvious appeal to me, as I want to establish Keats as his period's Catullan debunker of such a hero (and Keats does in a letter to his sister-in-law [13–28 January 1820, *KL*, II: 246] lump Wellington together with Castlereagh and Canning, who he feels should wear the nonsense refrain "'T wang-dillo-dee on their Backs instead of wearing ribbands in their Button holes"), but my point is not that Keats uses the ode to attack Wellington or to debate Waterloo. Rather, this context suggests the choices Keats does not make, his decision to focus the ode not on dead warriors but on eternal lovers. Refusing to identify the ashes in the urn, he turns from the pikes and tumbrels that marked the reactionary image of revolutionary history to embrace the "pipes and timbrels" of Bacchic ecstasy.

The ode's second and third stanzas offer a pastoral world that inverts the traditional economy of desire found in the epic. If epic requires men to abandon women, Keats imagines a world in which the beloved woman "cannot fade . . . / For ever wilt thou love, and she be fair!" (ll. 19–20). If Catullus's abandoned Ariadne is frozen by her grief and "Like some wild Bacchant's form in sculptured stone, / Looks on afar from ocean's barren side" (II: 24), Keats will freeze not the moment of rupture and loss but that of rapture and lust, as he depicts the "Bold lover" as a stone figure who "never canst . . . kiss, / Though winning near the goal," and whose love is thus "For ever warm and still to be enjoy'd, / For ever panting, and for ever young" (ll. 17–18, 26–27). While criticism of this poem often uses the static world of the urn – "All breathing human passion far above" (l. 28) – to criticize the dynamic world of human sexuality,[35] it seems to me that Keats's essential move here is not to criticize art or sex but to find in the erotic world which he identifies with the pastoral – and which he had invoked as early as "Sleep and Poetry," with its realm of "Flora, and old Pan" – the same cultural value found in epic accounts of war or tragic dramatizations of death, what Keats saw at the time of "Sleep and Poetry" as "a nobler life, / Where I may find the agonies, the strife / Of human hearts" (ll. 102, 123–25). Catullus sought to grant authority to his poetry of love by undercutting its epic competitors through Catullus 64. Hunt sought in "Bacchus and Ariadne" to establish the continuing power of Dionysian love through an etiological myth that explains a constellation as the crown of Ariadne that Bacchus flings into the heavens as an eternal commemoration of their love. Keats too seeks to create an image of eternal love, an icon of perpetual erotic excitement, in order to offer a Catullan answer to the denigration of sexual love by an ethos of the heroic career.

The epic pattern of abandonment traced by Lipking depends upon a contrast between male action directed towards a heroic career and female passivity expressed through either erotic longing or post-coital despair. Theseus must leave Ariadne, Aeneas must desert Dido, Antony should tear himself from Cleopatra, because the heroic male supposedly creates himself by separating himself from a feminized realm of love, longing, and loss. While this heroic move may be figured as a choice of the active over the passive, the public over the personal, the heroic project is in fact threatened by the possibility of personal romantic and erotic fulfillment; epic abandonment seems to rest upon a notion of limited human energy that can support either an erotic life or a heroic career but not both. It is out of a denial of the possibility of complete sexual gratification that the hero is propelled into a public realm of action defined through violence: rather than the feared loss of self in supposedly passive emotional enthrallment to the other, the hero seeks the exaltation of self – or nation or god – through the active, violent destruction of the other. As a result, the figure of the abandoned female does not just stand for the violence done to women by this heroic ethos; it also points to the self-maiming violence that the male carries out against himself and his desires in order to render himself ready for his public, heroic role. Virgil's Aeneas, for example, in order to become the founder of Rome must give up all that he desires and loves – not only Dido, but also his first wife, Creusa, whom he literally forgets in fleeing from Troy, and his beloved Troy itself, home to his family, his customary way of life, and his memories.

Keats's ode creates a countermyth of the eternal erotic in its first three stanzas, and then in stanza four it replaces the epic's abandonment of women with an abandoned community. It is not a woman who is sacrificed here, as, say, Dido is sacrificed; it is the heifer "lowing at the skies" (l. 33). It is not Ariadne who is abandoned but the "little town by river or sea shore, / Or mountain-built with peaceful citadel" that is "emptied of this folk, this pious morn" (ll. 35–37). The epic ethos that embraces heroic warfare over erotic play, the nation and piety over lovers and their pleasure, is finally seen as destroying the community it would mold into a nation as the "folk" are led from its "peaceful citadel" or "little town" to be taken to the sacrifice that those who wish to build nations, religions, or empires always demand. If "History is what hurts, it is what refuses desire and sets inexorable limits to individual as well as collective praxis,"[36] then Keats invokes the actual destructiveness of the histories of empire over against the mythic, epic celebration of nation-making as heroic. Keats's poem sides with the Ariadnes and the Didos, the mourning mothers (and fathers) against Theseus and Aeneas, Achilles and Wellington.

IV

Of course, such stories of love versus duty, of abandonment and sacrifice, were not played out only in classical myth; nor were Keats and the Cockneys the only ones engaged in creating an eroticized classicism. Keats's text leads us to another site where such issues were central. The final stanza of the ode opens:

> O Attic shape! Fair attitude! with brede
> Of marble men and maidens overwrought,
> With forest branches and the trodden weed;

Thou, silent form, dost tease us out of thought
As doth eternity. (Ll. 41–45)

I have already suggested that in these lines we hear a pun, that we think about the breeding between overwrought maidens and marble men: an interesting inversion of the Pygmalion story, in which it is an over-wrought man who falls in love with a marble maiden. This double entendre is called forth by an allusion that lies buried in the opening phrases of the stanza, "O Attic shape! Fair attitude," phrases dismissed by Empson and Bridges as an attempt at a bad half pun. Behind these phrases, however, stands a real woman known for her fair attitudes, for the silent form of her enactments of classical statues that gave bodily shape to the modern dream of Attic art: Emma Hamilton, wife of the one-time owner of the Portland Vase, Sir William Hamilton, and mistress of Admiral Nelson, the Aeneas who did not want to leave his Dido.[37] The art of her attitudes as she crossed class barriers to offer a new appreciation of classical culture provides an important context for Cockney classicism; the story of her loves suggests how the Theseus–Ariadne, Aeneas–Dido archetype was invested at the time with new cultural energy and why Keats would draw on it and on Catullus' version of it in particular.

Born Amy or "Emy" Lyon, the future Lady Hamilton came from poverty.[38] Her father, a blacksmith, died when she was young, and she was sent to live with her maternal grandmother, Mrs. Kidd, and then at a very early age put into service as a domestic. At some point, apparently with her mother, she moved to London. Trying various jobs, she finally came to work for James Graham, a Scotsman who had spent time in America dispensing massages, milk baths, and electrical treatments. In London, Graham established the "Temple of Health," which soon came to include its most famous attraction, the "celestial bed," de-scribed by Graham as follows:

On the utmost summit of the dome are placed two exquisite figures of Cupid and Psyche, with a figure of Hymen behind, with his torch flaming with electrical fire in one hand and with the other, supporting a celestial crown, sparkling over a pair of living turtle doves, on a little bed of roses . . . At the head of the bed appears sparkling with electrical fire a first great commandment: BE FRUITFUL, MULTIPLY AND REPLENISH THE EARTH.[39]

Graham claimed that the "Superior ecstasy which the parties enjoy in the Celestial Bed is really astonishing and never before thought of in this world." A couple having difficulty in conceiving a child or experiencing problems in sexual performance could rent this bed for the night. Attending the couple to the bed and apparently gracing it as well was a corps of "Goddesses of Youth and Health," and among their number was Amy, now Emma, Lyons. These goddesses appeared in scanty classical garb and assumed various provocative poses designed to inspire the couple – as Graham put it, "the barren must certainly become fruitful when they are powerfully agitated in the delights of love." It was apparently in the employ of Graham that Emma first learned to exploit classical costumes and poses for erotic purposes, skills she would put to use in creating her famous attitudes.

Emma took a number of lovers, perhaps being first seduced by a friend of the Prince of Wales, a ship's captain, John Willet Payne. Sir Harry Featherstonhaugh certainly took her as his mistress in 1781 until she became pregnant, at which point he dismissed her. She then became the lover of Charles Greville, the bachelor son of the Earl of Warwick and an art collector. They lived together for four years, apparently in happiness. Greville introduced her to the painter George Romney, who fell in love with her; she became his favorite model, as he painted her at least two dozen times. In demand as a model for other painters as well, she was usually portrayed as a figure from classical myth.

Greville, however, decided to end the affair, and he did so by sending Emma in 1786 to Naples, where his uncle, Sir William Hamilton, represented the crown. After lamenting the loss of her young lover, she eventually became the mistress and then the wife of the older man. While the fact that Emma became a confidant of the Queen of Naples made their somewhat unusual social situation in Italy still comfortable, back home in England the well-known Hamilton did not escape some satiric barbs. Peter Pindar wrote of the marriage:

> O Knight of Naples, is it come to pass,
> That thou hast left the gods of stone and brass,
> To wed a deity of flesh and blood?

In a note, Pindar added, "It is really true – the Knight is *married* to a beautiful *virgin*, whom he styles his *Grecian*. Her attitudes are the most *desirable* models for *young* artists." Horace Walpole, knowing of Emma's representations of famous classical statues, quipped, "Sir William has actually married his gallery of statues."[40]

Both men refer to Emma's famous attitudes, performances admired by everyone who visited Naples, including Walpole himself, who said that "her attitudes were a whole theater of grace and various expressions," and Goethe, who wrote:

He [Hamilton] has had a Greek costume made for her which becomes her extremely. Dressed in this, she lets down her hair and, with a few shawls, gives so much variety to her poses, gesture, expressions, etc., that the spectator can hardly believe his eyes. He sees what thousands of artists would have liked to express realized before him in movements and surprising transformations – standing, kneeling, sitting, reclining, serious, sad, playful, ecstatic, contrite, alluring, threatening, anxious, one pose follows another without a break... In her, he [Hamilton] has found all the antiquities... This much is certain: as a performance it's like nothing you ever saw before in your life.[41]

As Goethe makes clear, Emma, working within a kind of blackout box Hamilton had designed for her, would use shawls and handkerchiefs as her only aids as she shifted from one figure taken from classical myth to another, always freezing into a pose that recalled that of a famous statue. This early version of performance art enabled Emma to represent a wide range of emotions, moving rapidly from figure to figure. Such an evocation through essentially pantomimic techniques of a series of emotions might suggest a connection between her attitudes and the contemporary dramatic form, the monodrama, a form of drama where, in Tennyson's words, "successive phases of passion in one person take the place of successive persons." Goethe himself experimented with this form, as did Southey and Matthew Lewis in England. Rousseau seems to have created the monodrama in attempting to reform the opera; his monodrama was, interestingly enough, *Pygmalion*, the story of a statue coming to life, a play apparently known to Emma Hamilton and later translated in Leigh Hunt's *Indicator*.[42]

While Emma represented a great many figures and a wide range of emotions, she was particularly renowned for her figures of suffering, and one of her best-known attitudes was that of the abandoned Ariadne (see the related image, the *Bacchante couchée* by Vigée-Lebrun [figure 3]). Her performances were considered a bit scandalous, for it was rumored that they were enacted in a state of undress appropriate to the subjects represented. The supposed *Memoirs of Emma, Lady Hamilton* (which Mary and Percy Shelley read when it was published in 1815) offered this leering description of her performances: "Having once condescended to become the living representative of the most voluptuous characters of the Grecian mythology, she made no scruple of giving to each libidinous figure all the force and attraction of the naked truth."[43]

Emma Hamilton was not alone in practicing the art of the attitude, though she seems to be its originator; nor was she the only one to discover an erotic charge in classical images. In 1813, Giovanni Battista Belzoni performed as the "Roman Hercules," offering "several striking

Fig. 3. Elizabeth Vigée-Lebrun, *Bacchante couchée*. Also known as *Emma Hart,
the Future Lady Hamilton, as Ariadne*. Oil on canvas. 1790.

Attitudes, from the most admired antique Statues"; the great equestrian
Andrew Ducrow at about the same time initiated his *poses plastiques
équestres*, recreating such images as Mercury or a Roman gladiator while
riding his horse around the circus ring. *Tableaux vivants* also became
popular, so that in 1833, for example, we can find at Covent Garden a
presentation by T. Thompson of the "Grecian Statues, or Living
Models of the Antique." In 1845, Professor Keller began offering "Poses
Plastiques and Grand Tableaux Vivans," at first of biblical subjects but
increasingly of paintings of classical subjects that featured a great deal of
nudity. Madame Wharton's theater Walhalla offered similar fare, with
representations of Venus rising from the sea, of Edwin Landseer's Lady
Godiva, of Canova's *Nymph*, and of Raphael's *Bacchanalian Triumph*.[44]
While these performances were often advertised as a way of improving
art through a study of the human body and also as a means of bringing
art to the people, their appeal seems to have been largely that of an arty
strip show. Emma Hamilton had shown the way to generate an audience for the classics by making them sources of erotic titillation.

　　Emma Hamilton's erotic classicism was, however, turned against her as the Hamiltons' life in Naples took a surprising turn. Beginning in 1792, the revolutionary government in France began pressuring the Kingdom of Naples. As the only port of significance in the area still allied with the British fleet, Naples was important enough to be visited repeatedly by Nelson, who like many before him fell in love with Emma and began an affair with her that would last the rest of his life, leading to his separation from his wife and a scandal that threatened his career. When in 1798 a revolution backed by French troops drove the king and queen and their court, including the Hamiltons, into exile, it was Nelson who removed them to Sicily. From Sicily, Nelson helped the royalists plot counterrevolution; he sailed with them back into Naples in 1799 to retake the city, an action he took against orders; and he at least acquiesced in the counterrevolutionary terror that then took place.

England began to fear that Nelson cared more for Emma and her desires than for prosecuting the war, that he had become an Antony dallying in the bed of a Cleopatra (Hugh Elliot, the British ambassador in Saxony, called them "Antony and Moll Cleopatra").[45] Of course, the ultimate target of such concerns became Emma rather than Nelson: if Hamilton's beloved Portland Vase could be reduced by endless imitations, his beloved Emma could be traduced through repeated parodies. The beautiful Emma was now found to be too fat, a drunkard, and a gambler. Lady Elgin – whose husband's classical statues in the British Museum would become far more famous than Sir William Hamilton's urns and vases that had founded the museum's classical collection – visited Naples in 1799 and said of Lady Hamilton, "She is a Whapper! and I think her manner very vulgar. It is really humiliating to see Lord Nelson, he seems quite dying and yet as if he had no other thought than her."[46]

When Nelson and the Hamiltons journeyed to England in late 1800, they became the target of both caustic newspapers (the *Morning Herald* of 20 November 1800 remembered Emma's past in commenting that "Lady Hamilton's countenance is of so rosy and blooming a description that, as Dr. Graham would say, she appears so far a perfect '*Goddess of Health*'!") and the caricaturists. The relations between Nelson and the Hamiltons hover around a number of Rowlandson's images of aging husbands and young lovers, as Ronald Paulson has argued.[47] In *Modern Antiques* (figure 4), an aging antiquarian who could be Sir William prowls among ancient Egyptian artifacts – perhaps brought back after Nelson's successful Egyptian mission – while Emma and Nelson (the man is in a naval uniform) meet as the two young lovers inside a mummy case. Rowlandson produced an etching directly representing "Lady Hxxxxx Attitudes" (figure 5), in which the elderly Sir William displays the naked

Fig. 4. Thomas Rowlandson, *Modern Antiques*. Drawing. ?1811.

Fig. 5. Thomas Rowlandson, *Lady Hxxxxx Attitudes*. Etching. ?1791.

Emma (who interestingly rests her foot on a Grecian urn) to a young artist; in the background there is a statue of a satyr seizing a woman, and on the floor two classical statues kiss. Emma is seen as living in a world of eroticized classicism in which she is the final art object and her husband becomes an art dealer as pimp displaying her to the young man.

Gillray's images were even harsher. In *A Cognocenti Contemplating ye Beauties of ye Antique* (figure 6), the aging Sir William Hamilton – who had joined Richard Payne Knight in arguing for the centrality of priapic cults in ancient theology – looks at various Dionysian and priapic objects (including a cracked Grecian urn), in the middle of which stands a bust of Emma – as the *Morning Herald* put it, "Such, after ransacking Herculaneum and Pompeia, for thirty-eight years, is the Chief curiosity, with which that celebrated *antiquarian* Sir William Hamilton, has returned to his native country" (20 November 1800). On the walls are pictures of Naples's Vesuvius – the object of much study by Hamilton (Sontag's "volcano lover"), of Hamilton as the aging Claudius, who of course had married the insatiable Messalina, of Emma as Cleopatra, and of Nelson as Marc Antony. Here, the beauties of the antique collected by Hamilton are reduced to sexual prototypes of Emma, to sources for her attitudes; and she becomes the modern Cleopatra keeping England's Antony from battle while Sir William Hamilton becomes a doddering Claudius more interested in volcanoes than in his fiery young wife. It is as if the classical prototypes imaged on the wall have – like Emma's attitudes – come to life.

Gillray also depicted Emma at a moment of abandonment in his *Dido in Despair!* (figure 7). Nelson this time is Aeneas sailing off with his fleet, leaving Emma with the decrepit Sir William asleep in the bed, with Sir William's eroticized antiquities strewn about the floor and a book of "attitudes" open to a recumbent nude on the settee. In this etching, Gillray makes explicit the connection between Hamilton's classical collections, Emma's roles in her attitudes, and the part she played in life: she is cast in one more classical role, Dido left by her lover. This Ariadne is abandoned not to Bacchus and sexual fulfillment but to the ancient and apparently incapable student of Bacchic artifacts. Part of the power of Gillray's image is that it explores the confusion of the boundary between art and life in this romantic triangle: where does art end and life begin in this circle of role-playing attitudes developed from the classics but now apparently being played out in life? Of course, Gillray uses this power to try to reinforce the conventional economy of desire rejected by Catullus and Keats: women must be abandoned and real men must go to war if England is to be saved; the erotic world is left to dirty old men.

Fig. 6. James Gillray, *A Cognocenti Contemplating yᵉ Beauties of yᵉ Antique.*
Etching. 10 February 1801.

Fig. 7. James Gillray, *Dido in Despair!* Etching. 6 February 1801.

As Gillray's use of Emma's attitudes and Walpole's comment on the Hamilton marriage suggest, they fear that the struggle between duty and pleasure arises from a confusion between hard reality and the world of play that is art. It is because Emma Hamilton has made once-safe classical images come alive in the flesh that they have become eroticized. It is because she is capable of being Cleopatra or Dido in life that Nelson is in danger. Emma is the Pygmalion and Galatea myth become real, and these men find her frightening.

Rowlandson's *Pygmalion and Galatea* (figure 8) belongs with these other images, for it evokes Emma Hamilton's ability to provide her lovers with statues come alive, with idealized images made real – a fleshly romantic classicism. But if the print draws upon the same connections as Peter Pindar, Walpole, or Gillray, it does so to offer a different vision. As in *Modern Antiques*, we seem to be in a museum, surrounded by classical art objects, in this case a series of libidinous female statues and a huge urn on the base of which we see the mad pursuit of a maiden loth. The two central nude figures are presumably the artist and the awakened Galatea. The man lies back on some sort of couch while the woman mounts him, bending down to kiss him and grasping his sexual organ in order to couple with him. She is the bold lover who, frozen in Rowlandson's image, never can kiss or consummate her desire, though their genitals are winning near the goal. While Paulson sees the female figure as threatening – he writes, "As long as she was a statue on a pedestal she posed no threat; once alive, she proceeds to castrate him"[48] – this coupling, as opposed to the rape of a woman occurring on the urn in the background, would seem a more happy love, forever warm and still to be enjoyed, even if it is a breeding in which the woman is actively overwrought and the male, overcome by desire, is turned to hard marble. Here is the world of the eroticized classicism rejected by Gillray, a celebration of female sexuality absolutely opposed to the abandonment of women.[49]

This attempt to link Keats's words to Rowlandson's images might seem illegitimate, a trick of historicist juxtaposition, since there is no evidence that Keats knew anything about Rowlandson's work. However, I am less interested in a direct link between the ode and any of these images than I am in Keats's allusion through the phrase "fair attitude" to Emma Hamilton and the world of eroticized classicism she came to represent and which was attacked or celebrated in these prints. In the context of her attitudes and these images, the erotic power of Keats's ode is recharged, and its engagement in a struggle over sexual

Fig. 8. Thomas Rowlandson, *Pygmalion and Galatea*. Etching. Ca. 1800.

politics is rediscovered. It is important to remember that it was exactly for offering such titillating scenes from the classics that works such as Keats's *Endymion* were attacked; the Cockney School articles are at least in part an attempt to contest the Hunt circle's definition of classical culture as a pagan celebration of life, liberty, and the pursuit of erotic happiness. To *Blackwood's*, since a "classical Cockney" is a grotesque, a "Hottentot in top-boots" (13 [May 1823], 534, 541), Cockney interest in classical statuary must be pornographic: "Christopher North" claims that Hunt purchases reproductions of classical statuary in order to surround himself with "about a dozen nudities for the moderate sum of eighteen-pence a pair, rough and smooth" (*Blackwood's* 14 [August 1823], 243).

These attacks suggest that Cockney poetry, like Hamilton's attitudes and Rowlandson's prints, test the line between the erotic and the pornographic. Keats was very much alive to the potential erotic power of art; from an early programmatic poem such as "I stood tip-toe upon a little hill" and its celebration of the "pure deliciousness" of the union of Cynthia and Endymion, through *Endymion* itself, "The Eve of St. Agnes," and the "Ode to Psyche," and on to Keats's late poems to Fanny Brawne, we find Keats both using the erotic to grant his poetry power and reflecting through his poetry on the power of desire. If we return to his famous "negative capability" letter (to George and Tom Keats, 21, 27 ⟨?⟩ December 1817, *KL*, 1: 191–94), sometimes read as a defense of an art that rises above both the lived life of the passions and ideological argument, there we find that Keats links art to both political and erotic power. The letter opens with a report from Keats to his brothers about his reviewing activities, but it quickly moves to the recent acquittal of the radical journalist and publisher William Hone on charges of seditious libel and to an earlier court victory by Thomas Jonathan Wooler: "Hone the publisher's trial, you must find very amusing; & as Englishmen very encouraging – his *Not Guilty* is a thing, which not to have been, would have dulled still more Liberty's Emblazoning... Wooler & Hone have done an essential service." The letter concludes with a comment on the censorship of Shelley's *Laon and Cythna*, which had to be recast as *The Revolt of Islam*. The entire discussion of art that forms the heart of the letter occurs in a context of the state's attempt to control discourse; in a society that repeatedly seeks to censor, the political power of the word is clear.

Keats goes on to discuss a visit to an exhibition of Benjamin West's *Death on a Pale Horse*: "It is a wonderful picture, when West's age is considered; But there is nothing to be intense upon; no women one feels mad to kiss; no face swelling into reality. the excellence of every Art is its intensity, capable of making all disagreeables evaporate, from their being in close relationship with Beauty & Truth – Examine King Lear & you will find this examplified throughout." In the words of the "Ode on a Grecian Urn," art should "tease us out of thought." But how does art accomplish this? Not, I think, through the pursuit of a formal, abstract beauty that is often found to be the burden of this letter.

We can get a better sense of what Keats is arguing for here if we contrast his remarks with those of Joyce's Stephen Daedalus when, in the context of a discussion of classical nudes, he seeks to resolve a similar question of how tragic art treats the "disagreeables" of life while offering beauty: "The feelings excited by improper art are kinetic, desire or loathing. Desire urges us to possess, to go to something; loathing urges us to abandon, to go from something. These are kinetic emotions. The arts which excite them, pornographical or didactic, are therefore improper arts. The esthetic emotion (I use the general term) is therefore static. The mind is arrested and raised above desire and loathing."[50] Many readings of Keats's passage tend to conform it to the view expressed by Daedalus: art is seen as raising the mind above desire and loathing, above "disagreeables," in order to unite it with Truth and Beauty. However, we need to see that truth and beauty are for Keats didactic and pornographic, in the terms offered by Daedalus. For Keats, beauty in art offers women one is mad to kiss; that is, he asks for the painterly equivalent of a cheap thrill, pornographic titillation.[51] Where the spurious *Memoirs of Lady Hamilton* condemn her attitudes with the observation that "Lasciviousness in a picture cannot possibly be painted without correspondent ideas to those which it is intended to excite in the beholder" (p. 51), Keats wishes to celebrate those lascivious ideas and responses as beauty. And in a letter that begins with Wooler and Hone and ends with the censorship of Shelley's *Laon and Cythna*, it is hard to believe that Keats's truth is somehow a nondidactic, apolitical (and ultimately empty) abstraction.

I think part of our misunderstanding comes from a misreading of what is usually seen as the letter's key passage, the definition of negative capability, "that is when man is capable of being in uncertainties, Mysteries, doubts, without any irritable reaching after fact & reason – Coleridge, for instance, would let go by a fine isolated verisimilitude caught from the Penetralium of mystery, from being incapable of remaining content with half knowledge. This pursued through Volumes would perhaps take us no further than this, that with a great poet the sense of Beauty overcomes every other consideration, or rather obliterates all consideration." Sometimes taken for an art-for-art's sake rejection of any didactic element in poetry, this passage is instead, as I suggested in the last chapter, an assault on the "*irritable* reaching after fact & reason," not a rejection of fact and reason; it is a willingness to live in "half knowledge," not a despair over knowledge. Keats is rejecting a totalized conception of Truth, not the pursuit in art of contingent truths, fine verisimilitudes; he accepts that knowledge is limited, interested, what we would call ideological. Keats's beauty is not some Platonic abstraction; it finds its practical and paradigmatic embodiment in that which is erotically attractive, in that which provokes desire and which thus unites the desiring self with the provocative other. His truth is not some absolute sought by Coleridge, but the contingent ideological positions that one constructs as one seeks what Keats calls, in a passage discussed in chapter 3, "a recourse somewhat human independent of the great Consolations of Religion and undepraved Sensations. of the Beautiful. the poetical in all things" (letter to Benjamin Bailey, 3 November 1817, *KL*, I: 179). The beauty that evokes desire is the consolation offered in a world denied the truth; and in that this desire connects the self with an other beyond the self – in that it is the sign of a world beyond the self's illusions, a ground for the ideological – it also offers us all the truth we can know within "the pale of the world." In other words, "'Beauty is truth, truth beauty' – that is all / Ye know on earth, and all ye need to know."

Pace Stephen Daedalus, Keats finds beauty and truth kinetic – the beauty of attraction, the truth of ever changing approximations, verisimilitudes. One of the questions posed by Keats's ode is: How can art, which does appear static, capture such beauty and truth? How can a "Cold Pastoral" embody human passion? The central stanzas of the ode confront this question in examining the gap between the kinetic passion of the "wild ecstasy" that remains only a question directed towards the urn and the represented "happy love" that stands "All breathing human passion far above, / That leaves a heart high-sorrowful and cloy'd, / A burning forehead, and a parching tongue." The erotic – not unlike the romantic classicism that tried to invoke it in art – seems to promise an embodied ideal as sex is at once intensely, physically real and a playing out of desire's ideals. At the moment one finds a woman or man one is mad to kiss, when a face swells into the reality of sexual attraction, when one discovers someone to be intense upon, then "all disagreeables" do "evaporate." However, the reality even of this ideal breathing human passion is that it cannot be sustained forever, that one must reconfront the "disagreeables" of life. The project of Cockney classicism – to ground the ideal in the real, to find the beautiful in "undepraved sensations," to seek what had always been offered as a transcendental consolation in a secularized "recourse somewhat human" – must finally admit that what it offers is "breathing human passion," not a "more happy, happy love"; is earth, not heaven; is the real, not the ideal; is physical life and death, not an eternal moment. The danger to an erotic poet such as Keats is that faced with the contingency of lived sexuality – with its propensity to leave a "heart high-sorrowful and cloy'd" – one embraces an aesthetic simulacrum of the erotic that promises to arrest the mind and raise it above desire and loathing but that in fact offers the arrested sexuality we might with more justification than Daedalus identify with the pornographic. By countering the static pleasures of the second and third stanzas with the kinetic loss of the fourth stanza and in confronting the "Cold Pastoral" of poetry with the fleshly eroticism of Emma Hamilton's fair attitudes, Keats's ode – offering "all ye need to know" – returns us from art to earth.

Emma Hamilton – who through her attitudes embodied the ideal, who offered an erotic moment that through her art seemed to touch eternity – lived out the reality of breathing human passion as her beauty gave way to old age, drinking, and corpulence, as her role changed from Galatea coming alive for her lover to Dido abandoned by hers. The danger of an art less embodied than hers – and the danger posed by Keats's urn but not his ode – is that it can replace the beautifully contingent, fragile power of the lived and passing moment of human passion with a static and thus infinitely reproducible because not unique and passing aesthetic image. The images of the lovers in the second and third stanzas of Keats's ode, like the images in Rowlandson's etching of Pygmalion and Galatea or on many actual Grecian urns, move towards the infinitely reproducible world of pornographic sexuality – reproducible not only in the sense that pornographic images and texts endlessly repeat one another, providing the same acts, positions, variations over and over again, but also in the sense that one can always return to the pornographic text or image to discover the same sexual moment. Part of the appeal of pornography is that it is "All breathing human passion far above," that it offers forever the same arousal, it promises the same fulfillment free from the contingent complications of the disagreeables of lived life. While lived sexuality may be now satisfying, now frustrating, now full of love, now almost mechanical, now seemingly perfect, now frighteningly routine, a pornographic text offers the identical pleasure over and over again. Every time we turn to Rowlandson's print, we will see the same moment of foreplay; every time we read Keats's urn we will see the same love "ever warm and still to be enjoyed." If the mechanical reproduction of works of art threatens the aura of art, pornographic reproduction threatens the aura of sensual life itself. In refusing the status of the Classic, the True – which can be infinitely reproduced because it claims to be eternally the same independent of form or context – and in rejecting the appeal of the pornographic – with its endless reiteration of masculine satisfaction – Keats's ode, in its Cockney classicism of contextual contingency and of the embodied erotic of an Emma Hamilton, defends art and life against both reductions.

V

Keats's "Ode on a Grecian Urn" – with its Catullan wordplay, its erotic classicism, its sympathy with the Ariadnes and Emma Hamiltons of the world – is part of the Cockney School's attempt to define the classic as the pagan, the passionate, and the politically radical. It is thus part of the culture wars that raged after the defeat of Napoleon, a defeat that conservatism – aided by the Southey of the *Poet's Pilgrimage to Waterloo* and the *Lay of the Laureate* (his *Carmen Nuptiale*), by the Coleridge of the *Lay Sermons*, and by the Wordsworth of *The Excursion* – sought to see as the end of the revolutionary era. Part of this struggle was clearly over exactly how one was to define classical culture and the nineteenth century's relationship to it. In an era when Greece could again be equated with the struggle for liberty, when the classics could mean not only a traditional gentleman's educational heritage but also Sir William Hamilton's priapic cults, Shelley's Lucretius, or, for that matter, Catullus, the ideal of the classical was deeply contested.

The *Blackwood's* Cockney School attack on Keats praised Wordsworth as "the most classical of living English poets" (3 [August 1818], 520). If Wordsworth – who dismissed Keats's "Hymn to Pan" as a "pretty piece of paganism," who upon seeing at Christie's Canova's group of Cupid and Psyche kissing growled, "The *Dev-ils*," who criticized the eroticism of Dryden's version of Virgil's Dido and offered his own chastened lines ("Translation of Part of the First Book of the Aeneid," 1816, 1832), and who, most important, in *The Excursion* explained Greek myth as a shadowy adumbration of Christian transcendentalism – if Wordsworth is the "most classical" of writers, then Hunt, Keats, and Shelley clearly are not. But against the cold classicism of the author of *Laodamia* (1815), the Hunt circle sought a paganism ever warm, ever panting, and forever young. "Ode on a Grecian Urn" is part of a Cockney project of wresting the control of the definition of the classical from the conservative defenders of a deadening, urnlike tradition.[52]

Keats's poetry at the time was considered scandalous – and to do it justice, we must rediscover the scandal of a poem such as "Ode on a Grecian Urn." The great scandal of Catullus' love poetry was that in his affair with the older, married Lesbia he adopted the "feminized" position of longing and loss, rejecting the demands of the supposedly heroic and certainly civic, public, and warlike Roman ethos in doing so. When we are reminded by Marjorie Levinson of the sexual language in the contemporary criticism of Keats – where his verse is called "unclean," "profligate," "disgusting" – and when we are taught by Susan Wolfson to see again the nineteenth century's "feminized" Keats,[53] we find, I think, a similar concern: that Keats, who should be a productive member of society as an apothecary – "back to the shop Mr John," advises Z. – has instead joined Hunt and Shelley in imagining a life of democratized love and luxury; that Keats, in his friend Benjamin Bailey's words, has adopted "that abominable principle of *Shelley's* – that *Sensual Love* is the principle of *things*" (*KC*, I: 35). In a society that had been mobilized for war for two decades and that continued to imagine much of its culture as a celebration of military heroism and conquests, Keats joined with the Hunt circle to offer his pretty pieces of paganism in an attempt "to put a Mite of help to the Liberal side" (to C. W. Dilke, 22 September 1819, *KL*, II: 180). Keats aligns himself with Shelley, Byron, and Hunt – and with their precursor Catullus – as a poet of a radical eroticism.

CHAPTER 6

Final reckonings: Keats and Shelley on the wealth of the imagination

I

During June of 1820, Keats was living at 2 Wesleyan Place in Kentish Town, near to Leigh Hunt's lodgings at Mortimer Terrace. Keats came to Hunt's on 22 June after a serious hemorrhage; he met the Shelleys' friend Mrs. Gisborne and found that Hunt himself was ill. Still, the Hunts insisted on Keats moving in with them the next day. Keats remained with the Hunts until 12 August, when Mrs. Hunt – being otherwise occupied – gave a letter from Fanny Brawne to the maid to deliver to Keats; the maid, who left the next day, gave the letter to one of the Hunts' boys, who broke the seal, provoking an outbreak from Keats that led him to move to Well Walk and the Brawne household, though he would shortly apologize to Hunt for his "lunes" (13 ⟨?⟩ August 1820, *KL*, II: 316).

On the same day as this uproar, Keats received another and more famous letter; as Keats would write to his sister on 13 August, "Yesterday I received an invitation from Mr Shelley, a Gentleman residing at Pisa, to spend the Winter with him" (13 August 1820, *KL*, II: 313–14). On 27 July 1820 (*SL*, II: 220–21), Shelley had sent what Donald Reiman has called "probably the best known [letter] that Shelley ever wrote."[1] Directed to John Keats in care of Leigh Hunt at the office of the *Examiner*, the letter invited Keats, who had been ordered to Italy by his doctors, to join Shelley, who had heard of Keats's illness from the Gisbornes. The Gisbornes carried Keats's reply, dated 16 August (*KL*, II: 322–23), back to Italy along with Keats's volume of 1820, both of which were left with Claire Clairmont sometime around 10 October.[2] Hunt would write to Shelley on 23 August (*Correspondence*, I: 158) that Keats "is sensible of your kindness," and Keats himself wrote to Charles Brown on 14 August (*KL*, II: 320–21) commending both Shelley's offer and Hunt's help.

Shelley's offer and Keats's reply constitute perhaps the most famous two-letter correspondence in literary history,[3] but to understand it, we must return this exchange to its context in the complex interactions within the Hunt circle that I have been examining. With Shelley in Italy and Keats supposedly having broken with Hunt, the Hunt circle is rarely seen as relevant to the later, "mature," work of Keats or Shelley. The vitality of the group's connections, however, is indicated by Keats's return to Hunt's home. Charles Armitage Brown tells us of Keats that "It was his choice, during my absence to lodge at Kentish Town, that he might be near his friend, Leigh Hunt, in whose companionship he was ever happy" (*KC*, II: 74). Keats was with Hunt as his final volume was published in late June; he saw his last poem go into print as Hunt published "As Hermes once took to his feathers light" in the *Indicator* for 28 June 1820. At this time, Keats collaborated with Hunt on "A Now" for the *Indicator*, and Hunt dedicated his translation of Tasso's *Amyntas* to the younger poet, comparing Keats to Tasso as "equally pestered by the critical, and admired by the poetical," establishing already a theme of Shelley's *Adonais*.

Shelley himself, while in Italy, was in regular contact with Hunt, subscribed to the *Examiner*, and worked to reconstruct the Hunt circle in Pisa (where he also gathered round him Edward and Jane Williams, John Taaffe, Alexander Mavrocordato, Lady Mountcashel, Thomas Medwin, and Edward Trelawny) through his invitation to Keats and his plans for the *Liberal* that involved Hunt, the Shelleys, Byron, and perhaps Horace Smith (who made it only as far as Versailles but who wrote to Thomas Hill on 31 July 1822, that "I find there is a lying article in Blackwood & John Bull accusing me of being at Pisa with the triumvirate, organizing plans of Atheism & Sedition!").[4] Vincent Novello also contemplated travelling to Italy,[5] and Hazlitt later joined Hunt, so that most of the group's central members turned to Italy.

Keats and Shelley never left the Cockney School – as their continuing ties to Hunt and the critical reaction to their work attest – and they were brought together in this final exchange of letters again through the mediation of Hunt. There are, as we will see, real tensions in this exchange over money and poetic success, and perhaps lying behind them is the difference in class between the poets that might be bridged in the presence of the Hunt circle but could not be erased. Keats, as we will see, also voiced concerns about being independent and particularly about being unduly influenced by Shelley. In this exchange, we see divisions that did exist in the group (and one could offer a similar analysis of Hunt's relations to Haydon or Shelley's to Godwin), but even Keats's drive for independence is defined in relation to the group as he comes to a sense of his individuality only in and through the collectivity. Whatever disagreements there were in the Hunt circle, the bonds between them were stronger than the strains put upon them. The group remains vital as both a context for this exchange of letters and as the ground for the ideals Shelley will espouse in his oblique response in the *Defence of Poetry* and in the portrait of Keats in *Adonais* to which I will turn later: even the disagreements I will be tracing were productive, and Shelley and others demonstrate the desire to envision the group standing beyond any disagreements. While some might see any move by Keats away from the Cockney School as a positive act of maturation, Shelley finds Keats's drift away from the group to be questionable poetically, personally, and politically. *Adonais* will be written in part to assert that the best part of Keats, the part of him that lives on, is the part which was always at home in the Hunt circle: Shelley works to rescue Keats not only from the critics but from himself in order to return him to the ranks of the Cockney School.

II

In his letter to Shelley, Keats acknowledges Shelley's offer while doubting his own ability to act on it. Most of the letter, however, is devoted to a critique of Shelley's verse, a response to various comments Shelley had made on Keats's poetry, from the two poets' first meetings through Hunt at Hampstead in 1816 up to the letter Keats is answering. Keats's observations on Shelley – which have been seen as "trenchant," as a "famous" and "merited reproof," and as "critical wisdom"[6] – are worth quoting in full:

I am glad you take any pleasure in my poor Poem [*Endymion*];– which I would willingly take the trouble to unwrite, if possible, did I care so much as I have done about Reputation. I received a copy of the Cenci, as from yourself from Hunt. There is only one part of it I am judge of; the Poetry, and dramatic effect, which by many spirits now a days is considered the mammon. A modern work it is said must have a purpose, which may be the God – *an artist* must serve Mammon – he must have "self concentration" selfishness perhaps. You I am sure will forgive me for sincerely remarking that you might curb your magnanimity and be more of an artist, and 'load every rift' of your subject with ore. The thought of such discipline must fall like cold chains upon you, who perhaps never sat with your wings furl'd for six Months together. And is not this extraordina[r]y talk for the writer of Endymion? whose mind was like a pack of scattered cards – I am pick'd up and sorted to a pip. My Imagination is a Monastery and I am its Monk – you must explain my metap^{cs} to yourself. I am in expectation of Prometheus every day. Could I have my own wish for its interest effected you would have it still in manuscript – or be but now putting an end to the second act. I remember you advising me not to publish my first-blights, on Hampstead heath – I am returning advice upon your hands. Most of the Poems in the volume I send you have been written above two years, and would never have been publish'd but from a hope of gain; so you see I am inclined to take your advice now. (*KL*, II: 322–23)

I want to suggest that this letter is not so much a wise reproach to Shelley – a "telling criticism of Shelley's hortatory bent," as Aileen Ward puts it (p. 368) – as a settling of accounts with a poet whose development paralleled Keats's own, an attempt to control his personal and poetic relations with Shelley as they had evolved within the Hunt circle.

The Keats who received Shelley's invitation was a man with very little control over his life. He was dying and knew it. He was desperately in love with Fanny Brawne and could do nothing about it. He was also in serious financial difficulties. All of these troubles surface in the letter. The reference to his illness and expected death is the clearest as he predicts he will not live to join Shelley. Any mention of Fanny Brawne would have been lost on Shelley; Shelley did not know anything about her, Keats, of course, having kept secret his engagement even from friends such as Hunt.[7] Still, one wonders about the image of Keats's imagination as his monastery and of himself as a monk: is this a statement of his faith in his art or an ironic commentary on his inability to have a full sexual life, his forced cloistering from the world of the senses? As Keats says, "you must explain my metap[hysics *or* metaphor] to yourself."[8]

The financial references are the most insistent, riddling his central discussion of the nature of poetry with fiscal terms and images. Keats's use of economic imagery in his letter might have been inspired by Shelley's reference in his invitation to the "treasures" of *Endymion* that Shelley felt had been "poured forth with indistinct profusion," resulting in "the comparatively few copies which have been sold" (*SL*, II: 221). Or perhaps it was Keats's recent rereading of Spenser to mark passages for Fanny Brawne (*KL*, II: 302) that brought the image of Mammon to mind. This is not, of course, the only place where such images appear in Keats; the use of economic imagery in Keats's later poetry has been powerfully addressed by critics such as K. K. Ruthven, Kurt Heinzelman, and Marjorie Levinson.[9]

However, by the time Keats received Shelley's letter, finances were for him less the subject of figuration than of literal figuring as he found himself in debt following his brother George's visit in January of 1820. George needed to raise money for his family and his financial ventures in the United States. To his credit, George did manage to force their guardian Abbey to clarify some issues and received the rest of his own inheritance and his share of Tom's estate, for a total of approximately three hundred pounds. He needed more, however, and thus he apparently asked Keats to lend him his share of Tom's money.[10] While George would later deny that he had done anything improper (letter to C. W. Dilke, 10 April 1824, *KC*, I: 276–81), several of Keats's statements and the observations of such witnesses as Charles Armitage Brown, Fanny Brawne, and Keats's publisher John Taylor lead one to believe that George at the very least took advantage of his brother's willingness to help him and his family.[11] According to Taylor, George left Keats with seventy pounds, which could not even cover Keats's immediate debts of eighty pounds, with another seventy pounds of debt not taken into account at that point.[12] Keats found himself forced to borrow from Brown and Taylor. Increasingly ill, he was taken in first by the Hunts and then by the Brawnes. When the doctors told him that summer that he must voyage to Italy, he was faced not only with a long trip fighting his disease but the extreme difficulty in funding such an excursion in the first place. Hunt and others would try to help. Shelley's letter is his offer of assistance.

Keats could not have been surprised by Shelley's generous letter, which he told Brown was "of a very kind nature" (*KL*, II: 321). Shelley's generosity was well known in his circle of friends,[13] the person he had tried to help most being Leigh Hunt. The Hunts' financial problems are notorious, and Leigh Hunt's inability to handle money appears to be one of the things that bothered Keats about his mentor and benefactor. Hunt was an incessant borrower, and Shelley had been one of his main sources of income. As Hunt himself tells us (*Autobiography*, p. 323), "the princeliness of his disposition was seen most in his behaviour to another friend, the writer of this memoir, who is proud to relate, that with money raised by an effort, Shelley once made him a present of fourteen hundred pounds, to extricate him from debt."

As Hunt notes, "I was not extricated," and Shelley continued to try to find the means to help his friend. The large loan was made to Hunt at the end of 1816. In a letter to Hunt of 3 August 1817, Shelley was again trying to fix Hunt's finances, trying to secure him a loan: "In fact I should imagine among your intimate friends nothing could be more easy than to arrange a loan on the terms and in the manner that I suggested. Your Brother I do not doubt will or can do nothing. But there is Keats, who certainly can, and Alsager, from whom I should expect much" (*SL*, 1: 550). He goes on to say, however, that Hunt will probably need to rely on Horace Smith, successful as a businessman as well as a poet. This letter suggests that Shelley and Hunt believed that Keats had the means to help a friend, that he simply did not want to, that unlike Shelley, with his princely magnanimity, Keats was too self-concentrated, selfish perhaps.

These tangled financial relations are, I believe, the subtext for Keats's discussion of poetry in his letter to Shelley. Shelley's suggestion that Keats lacked generosity will, of course, meet with disagreement from Keats scholars who have seen him as a model of caring, generous behavior.[14] Whether he was in fact generous or not, there is still the indication that Shelley and Hunt, perhaps mistaken about Keats's financial situation, doubted Keats's willingness to aid his friend; and we do know that Keats did not like being in debt or feeling a sense of obligation. Keats's brother George later asserted, after reading in Hunt's *Lord Byron and Some of His Contemporaries* of Keats's having housed himself with the Hunts and the Brawnes, that "no Man who ever lived was more impatient at being under an obligation than John"; Keats was, he wrote, "more magnanimous in conferring than in receiving a benefit, he felt too impatient of obligations" (*KC*, 1: 314).

Keats may well have felt impatient in the summer of 1820, residing with Hunt, contemplating accepting help from Shelley. George insists upon Keats's sense of independence, and independence of several sorts can be considered the theme of Keats's struggles to find his place in the Hunt circle as he sought to escape the label of Hunt's student or worked to stay aloof from Shelley; but Keats's letter reveals the hollowness of any abstract sense of individuality, and Shelley's ultimate response will reassert the importance of the group to a strong sense of identity.

In the letter to Shelley, Keats wants to declare his poetic independence, but he knows of his financial dependence. Unable to match Shelley's princely financial status, Keats transforms his problems with gold into theorems about poetry's "realms of gold." This attempt to transmute economics into aesthetics is perhaps clearest in his suggestion that Shelley "curb his magnanimity"; Shelley, he says, drawing on Spenser, needs to "be more of an artist, and 'load every rift' of your subject with ore." This passage on Shelley's magnanimity is sometimes taken to refer to Shelley's poetic productivity and sometimes to Shelley's "passion for reforming the world,"[15] but surely it is also a suggestion that Shelley stop loaning his money to Hunt and Godwin, that Shelley be less of the magnanimous prince Hunt admired, perhaps even that Shelley worry more about his poetry than about acting magnanimously towards Keats himself. Moreover, Keats seeks to convert Shelley's financial magnanimity into poetic prodigality, and thus Keats's own perceived stinginess can then be refigured as artistic control and dedication.

Keats's comments on *The Cenci* again rely on economic images: "There is only one part of it I am judge of; the Poetry, and dramatic effect, which by many spirits now a days is considered the mammon. A modern work it is said must have a purpose, which may be the God – *an artist* must serve Mammon – he must have 'self concentration' selfishness perhaps." We need to be alive to the polemical inversion of Jesus' words that Keats offers here. The Gospels record the phrase about God and Mammon in two different places. In Matthew, they occur in the Sermon on the Mount (5:24), where Jesus says that one must lay up spiritual treasures in God's heaven rather than seeking Mammon's rewards on earth; in Luke, they come as a gloss on the parable of the dishonest steward (16:1–13) and again act as a warning to those who would concentrate on gain in this world. Spenser uses Mammon in the episode Keats echoes as a summary figure for the pursuit of worldly goods. Keats wants to contrast poetry's internal formal riches with poetry's interests in the world, but he does so by invoking a biblical opposition between worldly wealth and spiritual interests. Keats's argument that the artist must be of Mammon's party offers an inversion of religious language and conventional morality that Keats might have expected to appeal to the religious skeptic in Shelley, whom Keats had seen engage in religious disputes with Haydon and to whom Hunt had dedicated his sonnets "On the Degrading Notions of Deity," perhaps written, as I suggested earlier, in a contest with Keats's own "Written in Disgust of Vulgar Superstition." Keats would seem to be playing with biblical injunctions against worldly wealth to establish his credentials as a freethinker, speculating apart from convention.

Conventions are not, however, all he would be free of; Keats wants to assert poetry's absolute independence, arguing that art must serve its own internal, presumably formal, ends rather than some extrapoetical purpose or cause. However, this claim for art's self-contained freedom is complicated by the financial imagery Keats invokes. For the Hunt circle, artistic independence was tied to freedom from certain kinds of economic dependence. We may feel that any involvement with the cash nexus is compromising, that disinterestedness gives way to financial interest as soon as one finds oneself in a capitalist economy. The Cockneys – whose organ the *Examiner* had as its motto Pope's claim "Party is the madness of many for the gain of a few" – defined themselves against men such as Wordsworth and Southey who they felt had become dependent on the government for their income. As John Kinnaird has argued, the Hunt circle's attacks on the Lake Poets' "apostasy" are based more on their surrender of economic independence than on a change in political conviction. We can see such charges in Hazlitt's doggerel lines on Wordsworth's appointment as Stamp-Distributor, where Wordsworth, who once "Scorn'd service purchased by rewards" and thus was able to talk "of Milton and of Freedom," is now seated in *"silent* state," having taken the bait from "Favour's golden hook."[16] Byron's dedication to *Don Juan* attacked "Lakers in and out of place" (l. 6); noting that "Wordsworth has his place in the Excise," Byron asks Southey about his status as poet laureate and his political conversion: "You have your salary – was't for that you wrought?" (ll. 46, 45). In "An Exhortation" – which Shelley sent to the Gisbornes and Hunt in the late spring of 1820 and which he called "a kind of excuse for Wordsworth" (8 May 1820, *SL*, II: 195) – Shelley compares chameleons who "feed on light and air" with poets who are nourished by "love and fame": "Where light is, chameleons change: / Where love is not, poets do: / Fame is love disguised: if few / Find either, never think it strange / That poets range." However, he goes on to exclaim, "Yet dare not stain with wealth or power / A poet's free and heavenly mind" (ll. 1–2, 14–20).[17] We may doubt the independence of men of inherited wealth such as Shelley or of those who tried to earn a living through their writings such as Hunt, but at the time the Hunt circle felt there was a significant difference between the source of their money and that of those such as Wordsworth and Southey whom they saw as party poets. The Hunt circle felt they owed no interest to any interest.

Keats's epistolary assertion of poetic independence reads oddly against this context. The Hunt circle sought to avoid compromising economic entanglements so that they would be free to pursue their ideological goals in their poetry. Keats asserts that one must eschew ideology for poetry, but he does so in the name not of Apollo but of Mammon. His goal seems less pure poetry than better sales. Shelley had written to Keats that *Endymion* did not sell because it was too profusely poetic. Keats responds that Shelley's poetry fails because it is not poetic enough, that it is too controversial, ideological. Keats knew from his experience with *Endymion* how politics could influence the reception of poetry, and thus he might wonder whether it was partisan politics rather than profuse poetry that hindered the sales of *Endymion*. Keats's call for a poetry where every textual rift is filled with the imagination's ore strikes me less as a declaration of art's independence than a recognition, coming with debt, that his art had to serve the market, Mammon. As he says to Shelley in closing the letter, he would not have published his 1820 poems "but from a hope of gain." The astonishing feature of the letter is that Keats, recognizing that circumstances forced him to write for money, attempts to construct a powerful theory of poetry that links together aesthetics and profitability: if one gives up prodigal politics for formal riches, one will strike it rich, poetically and financially. When Lamb in the *Examiner* (30 July 1820, pp. 494–95, reprinted from *New Times*, 19 July 1820) praised "prodigal phrases" in the 1820 volume, Keats may have greatly appreciated the compliment.

Keats, ever tough-minded, follows his argument and imagery to their logical conclusion: if Shelleyan magnanimity threatens art, then the artist must be self-concentrated, selfish perhaps. Shelley's willingness to give of himself, to care about and connect with others, to place some purpose above personal gain or reputation or even his art – this is now found to be a flaw in the poetic temperament. Keats writes later in the letter, "And is not this extraordinary talk for the writer of Endymion?" – presumably indicating that he recognizes the lack of artistic discipline in his own earlier work. But it is extraordinary talk in another way, for *Endymion* is a poem which, in one of Keats's favorite passages (see *KL*, 1: 218–19), uses what he calls his "Pleasure Thermometer" to explore "Richer entanglements, enthralments far / More self-destroying, leading, by degrees, / To the chief intensity: the crown of these / Is made of love and friendship" (1: 798–801). Keats had always seemed to identify the poet as one who is not self-concentrated, who in fact has no self, a position he set forth most famously in differentiating himself from the "wordsworthian or egotistical sublime":

As to the poetical Character itself, (I mean that sort of which, if I am any thing, I am a Member; that sort distinguished from the wordsworthian or egotistical sublime; which is a thing per se and stands alone) it is not itself – it has no self – it is every thing and nothing – It has no character – it enjoys light and shade; it lives in gusto, be it foul or fair, high or low, rich or poor, mean or elevated – It has as much delight in conceiving an Iago as an Imogen. What shocks the virtuous philosop[h]er, delights the camelion Poet. (Letter to Wood-house, 27 October 1818, *KL*, 1: 387–88)

If much of Keats's late work can be viewed, in Paul de Man's words, as "an attack on much that had been held sacred in the earlier work"[18] – with "The Fall of Hyperion" offering a subjective reworking of the purportedly objective "Hyperion," with "Lamia" deconstructing the union of truth and beauty found in "The Eve of St. Agnes," or with the 1819 poem to Fanny Brawne unwriting, as de Man suggests, the nightin-gale ode – then Keats's letter to Shelley can be read as a repudiation of the entire line of epistolary speculation that marks Keats's great letters on the poetic character. If Keats is separating himself from Shelley here or from the Hunt circle, he is also separating himself from his own favorite speculations.

Or more precisely, Keats faces here the contradiction in his theory of the poet's selflessness, a contradiction which de Man locates in a failure to confront the self but which I would suggest lies in an inability to commit the self. The character of the "camelion poet" delights in everything because it delights in no one thing greatly. It has no charac-ter, because it has never inscribed itself in the world, never impressed itself on others by making choices, taking stands: it may play roles – whether Imogen or Iago – but never establishes a firm identity. Keats's poet must refuse purpose, for as a "camelion" the poet must have the total psychic mobility celebrated in Keats's "Fancy": "Ever let the Fancy roam, / Pleasure never is at home" (ll. 1–2). Keats had perhaps felt that this psychological independence embraced selflessness, but in the letter to Shelley he admits the self-concentration, selfishness, in this attempt to exist without purpose: what looked like an attempt to exist without a self is revealed as an inability to conceive of an other import-ant enough to stop the fancy's roaming. Keats's "camelion poet" be-comes Shelley's poet as chameleon who "ranges" because he cannot find a binding love. The irony, intentional in Shelley's "Exhortation" and perhaps unconscious in Keats's letter, is that, just as the abstractly independent individual of classic liberal thought finds himself deter-mined by his place in the market, so does the man of self-concentrated independence find that his freedom lies merely in a hoarding of the self's resources that is determined by a financial situation over which he has no final control. Mammon is the appropriate tutelary spirit for Keats's letter, because the individual supposedly free of the God of ideological commitment is still bound by economic need; the idea of "pure" poetry "liberated" from purpose is a marketing strategy driven by "a hope of gain." This very late Keats, ill and increasingly isolated, does construct here an independence from the group that his scholarly defenders have always desired for him, but it is an empty, uncreative autonomy. In response, Shelley would attempt to rediscover the Keats who had created his great poetry out of the communal project of their shared group.

III

Shelley did not read Keats's letter unmoved. Keats was already much on Shelley's mind as he and his Italian circle anticipated Keats's arrival in the autumn of 1820. Claire Clairmont followed Shelley in reading *Endymion* at this time. Percy, Mary, and Claire all read Keats's 1820 volume after it arrived in early October. In the following months, Shelley issued several queries about Keats and apparently tried to contact him after his arrival in Italy.[19] While *Adonais*, begun in April 1821, is the best-known of Shelley's responses to Keats, there were others, such as the unsent letter to Gifford defending Keats's poetry written in November 1820 and the draft dialogue on Keats's poetry written perhaps in October 1820 upon reading Keats's volume or perhaps in late January or early February 1821 as Shelley moved towards writing the *Defence of Poetry*.[20] Keats was clearly present before Shelley as representing one form of modern poetry when the *Defence* was begun during the spring of 1821. Moreover, Shelley first came to read Peacock's *Four Ages of Poetry*, spurring his writing of the *Defence*, at the same time as he was grappling with Keats's letter and the 1820 volume; it is significant that both letters to Peacock about his attack on poetry contain praises of "Hyperion" (*SL*, II: 244, 262). The *Defence of Poetry* is, among other things, part of Shelley's ongoing meditation on Keats.

While it has repeatedly and correctly been said that Shelley would never have written the *Defence* without the stimulus of Peacock's essay, I would suggest that the *Defence* would have been written differently had it not been for the stimulus of Keats's letter; for Shelley's essay is not only a defense of poetry but also an attack on the principle of self-concentration that Keats had apparently embraced. Shelley's most direct response to Keats comes, as Fred L. Milne has noted, at the end of Shelley's discussion of the notion of utility, a placement which suggests Shelley's attempt to return Keats's notion of art to a social and economic context.

Shelley accuses thinkers such as Peacock of having too narrow a notion of utility, "one of banishing the importunity of the wants of our animal nature, the surrounding men with security of life, the dispersing the grosser delusions of superstition, and conciliating such a degree of mutual forbearance among men as may consist with the motives of personal advantage" (pp. 500–501).[21] In other words, Peacock has identified utility with the forward movement of liberal capitalism, with its technological advances, its tolerant, enlightened religious views, and its laissez-faire ideology. The problem Shelley has with this notion of utility is that it does not attend to "first principles," does not care about pleasure in its "highest sense"; it celebrates minor alleviations of humanity's suffering without transforming our state. Sounding not unlike Marx and Engels of the *Communist Manifesto*, Shelley argues in his *Philosophical View of Reform*,[22] one of the precursor texts for the *Defence* from which he draws material, that liberal capitalism has replaced a feudal and superstitious past with the brutal rule of the rich; the "calculating" notion of utility enables those in power to develop technology and expand the economy without being concerned over the effect these transformations have on those who do the work. The theory of utility is merely an ideological mask for the glorification of the cash nexus.

Shelley's account of the economics of selfishness has its roots in his own writing as far back as the note to *Queen Mab*, "And Statesmen Boast of Wealth," where he argues that all "real wealth" arises from labor but that labor is exploited "not for the necessities, not even for the luxuries of the mass of society but for the egotism and ostentation of a few of its members." He could also draw upon a line of communitarian critiques of capitalist ideology that includes Hazlitt's *Essay on the Principles of Human Action* and Robert Owen's *Observations on the Effect of the Manufacturing System*.[23] Hunt's *Examiner* also repeatedly attacked what it saw as the worst aspect of the post-Napoleonic reaction, "The spirit of money-getting," defined by Hunt in 1816 in language parallel to Shelley's in the *Defence*: "The interest of the few is substituted for those of the many; till by degrees the social virtues are displaced by absolute vices; and instead of turning superfluety to its true glory, and doing justice to those who want, the sum total harmony between man and man consists in not irritating those who possess . . . an egotism of the worst species takes the place of the old healthy varieties of character" (19 January 1817, p. 33). While Shelley joins with Hunt and others in their concern with what he calls "this matter of fact and money loving age" (*SL*, II: 242), the phrasing of his argument is finally determined by Keats's letter, which he echoes at the close of the section on utility:

The cultivation of those sciences which have enlarged the limits of the empire of man over the external world, has, for want of the poetical faculty, proportionally circumscribed those of the internal world; and man, having enslaved the elements, remains himself a slave. To what but a cultivation of the mechanical arts in a degree disproportioned to the presence of the creative faculty, which is the basis of all knowledge, is to be attributed the abuse of all invention for abridging and combining labour, to the exasperation of the inequality of mankind? From what other cause has it arisen that the discoveries which should have lightened, have added a weight to the curse imposed on Adam? Poetry, and the principle of Self, of which money is the visible incarnation, are the God and the Mammon of the world. (*Defence*, pp. 502–3)

Following upon Keats's play on biblical language and alluding to Genesis 3:19, Shelley defines Adam's loss of paradise as a fall into labor. The human project is to redeem us from this fall, but the narrow definition of utility pursued under capitalism, while revolutionizing the technical means of production, leads only to greater disparities of wealth, a greater alienation of those who work, and an ironic enslaving of mankind to material things even as the material world is conquered. We have, Shelley claims, the material means to create an earthly paradise, but we lack the moral vision to do so.

Shelley's complex attack – which most clearly targets the oppressors of the people and the utilitarian would-be reformers – is also a covert riposte to Keats. For Shelley, Keats's identification of the imagination with the self plays into the hands of the utilitarians, who wish to reject the imagination. Keats enters the *Defence*, disguised through the unattributed echo, as the poet of the self, as a worshipper of a demonic parody of Christianity in which Mammon, the god of the unholy and ghostly principle of self, is incarnated in its earthly representative, money.[24] Keats had sought to transmute his personal financial problems into empowering poetic maxims, but despite this attempted displacement his financial imagery had revealed that what he offered was an alliance between poetry and the principle of self. He did so to protect his poetry from what he wanted to see as extra-poetic demands (and, perhaps, to protect his poetry in its "monastery," to use his image, from the "self-destroying" "enthrallments" [*Endymion*, ll. 799, 798] of Fanny Brawne). Shelley insists upon the ideological implications of Keats's private and poetic choices; in other words, Shelley insists here, as he does throughout the *Defence*, on the ties among poetry, politics, and material or technological conditions. Behind Shelley's analysis is what we would now call the crisis in representation, a crisis that for Shelley has economic, political, and poetic configurations.

The importance here of the idea of representation to Shelley is revealed in the draft version of his echo of Keats: "Poetry is the representation of the benevolent principle in man, as {gold} {property} is the representation of the selfish principle: they are the God and the Mammon of the world."[25] Shelley's shift from "representation" to "incarnation" strengthened his play on religious terminology but masked a key issue, an issue that is raised again however by his final substitution of "money" for either "gold" or "property."

Shelley alludes here to a lively contemporary debate over a very practical form of representation: the use of paper currency to represent gold specie. Ever since the 1797 Bank Restriction Act – passed to meet a crisis brought on by the need to send money overseas to support forces arrayed against Napoleon and by a run on the country banks – the Bank of England had made payments through paper currency. Everyone assumed that this practice would come to an end with the victory over Napoleon, but in fact the government continued to restrict payment in precious metals until Peel established the return of gold payments in 1823. Shelley had attacked the use of paper currency and the connected enlargement of the national debt in the *Philosophical View of Reform*. In Shelley's view, influenced not only by Hunt's *Examiner* but also, as Kenneth Neill Cameron has shown, by Cobbett's *Paper against Gold and Glory against Prosperity; or, An Account of the Rise, Progress, Extent, and Present State of the Funds and of the Paper-Money of Great Britain* (1815),[26] the public debt is a system for transferring income from the laboring segment of the population to those who (1) opposed liberty in America and France, (2) profited by the huge government expenditures to prosecute "liberticide wars," and (3) will reap even larger profits from the interest due them as lenders to the government (*Philosophical View of Reform*, pp. 249–50). The government has borrowed money from the rich to pay the rich for goods in order to fight liberty, and now it will pay back to the rich interest raised through taxes on everyone.

Connected with this economic shell game, in Shelley's as in Cobbett's view, is the debasing of the currency through the printing of paper currency, and here Shelley makes explicit the issue of representation: "All great transactions of personal property in England are managed by signs, and that is by the authority of the possessor pressed upon paper, thus representing in a compendious form his right to so much gold,

which represents his right to so much labour." Shelley argues here as he
had in *Queen Mab* that labor is the source of all value. Precious metals
would seem to be an easy and accurate way to represent labor, but
Shelley already sees difficulties: "The precious metals have been from
the earliest records of civilization employed as the signs of labour and
the titles to an unequal distribution of its produce." The intervention of
a system of representation already alienated labor (as Shelley writes in
Queen Mab [III: 231–32], a "commerce of sincerest virtue needs / No
mediative signs of selfishness") and made it susceptible to exploitation,
as is most clearly seen, Shelley argues, when the government debases
specie through alloy, thus robbing people of a just payment for their
work. But, as Shelley notes, paper currency is "a far subtler and more
complicated contrivance of misrule." Paper currency is a representation
of a representation, and it is issued to obscure the gap between the sign
and the signified, between the purported value of the paper bill and the
labor it purchases: people work just as hard, but they are paid in a bill
worth a fraction of that labor's value. England's monetary system is
based upon a corrupt and debased form of representation (*Philosophical
View of Reform*, pp. 243–44).[27]

When paper money ceases to represent labor, it comes to represent or
incarnate the "principle of self"; that is, this false sign is overdeter-
mined, operating overtly as a debased representation of labor and
covertly as the incarnation of selfishness and greed. Shelley is drawing
on a protest against paper currency that went well beyond Cobbett or
Hunt. For example, in 1797 Gillray had attacked the suspension of cash
payments in such prints as *Midas, Transmuting All into ~~Gold~~ Paper* (figure 9);
there are poems against paper money, printed in the radical press, such
as Howard Fish's "Epistle to a Friend," which attacks "paper, curst
competitor of gold," and Allen Davenport's "The Topic" (*Sherwin's
Political Register* 2 [1817], 106), which attacks "the Pitt-coined paper."
Shelley also followed William Hone's satiric *Bank Restriction Note* of 1819
(figure 10) in linking paper money to governmental oppression via
prosecutions for counterfeiting.[28]

Hone, like Cobbett and others, sees paper money as the incarnation
of an oppressive system, but his particular focus is on the link between
the rise of paper currency and the imposition of the death penalty. Hone
parodies a Bank of England note, decorating his currency with a picture
of Britannia eating her children, a pound sign made from a noose, and a
series of men and women being hanged. The face of the note proclaims,
"I promise to Perform, During the Issue of Bank Notes, easily imitated,

Fig. 9. James Gillray, *Midas, Transmuting All into ~~Gold~~ Paper*. Print. 9 March 1797.

and until the Resumption of Cash Payments, or the Abolition of the Punishment of Death, For the Gov.ʳ and Comp.ᵃ of the Bank of England. J. Ketch." Hone's *Bank Restriction Barometer* (figure 11), which was issued with the Bank Note, helps to explain his series of references to forgery and hanging. The Barometer tracks the good effects for the nation that would accrue from a return to payments in gold and indicates the horrors that will follow from the "Disappearance of the legal Gold Coin" and the issuing of paper notes by the Bank of England and the country banks; "Paper Accommodation," the Barometer indicates, creates "False Credit, Fictitious Capital, Mischievous Speculation," but more important for Hone, the very ease with which the bills can be counterfeited leads to the "Frequent and useless inflictions of the barbarous Punishment of Death" against those who are tempted into forgery. Hone argues that the Bank Note – as it is involved in only fictional credit and capital – represents the oppressive system that keeps in place the public debt and paper currency, a system upheld through the imposition of the death penalty.

Shelley almost certainly knew of Hone's parody from a description in the *Examiner* on 17 January 1819 (p. 58). Frederick Hackwood indicates that the Note was published on 26 January 1819 (and it was advertised as published that day in the *Times*), which suggests that Hunt saw an early version of the Note, such as the sketch Hackwood offers dated 12 January. Hunt would seem to have known of the Note at the time of its creation, which indicates closer ties between the Hunt circle and Hone (perhaps through Hazlitt) than we might have suspected: Clarke mentions visiting Hone and notes that Mary Novello Clarke placed some material in one of his journals (*Recollections*, p. 47); Lamb wrote a poem to Hone; Keats celebrated his court victory against the government (December 1817, *KL*, 1: 191); and Shelley himself had contributed to Hone's defense fund after his arrest in 1817. In *Oedipus Tyrannus; or, Swellfoot the Tyrant*, Shelley's satire on the Queen Caroline affair, he follows Hone in making the connection between paper money and capital punishment. The interestingly named Mammon, Arch-Priest of Famine, disinherits his son, Chrysaor (= gold ore), for having argued for "public faith / Economy, and unadulterate coin"; he entails his estate upon his daughter "Banknotina / And married her to the gallows" (1.i.201–2, 206–7). Like Hone, Shelley sees money incarnating or representing not labor but the principle of self, the guiding principle behind the existing economic, social, and political system.

Representation also obscures the "first principle" of government and

Fig. 10 William Hone, *Bank Restriction Note*. Engraving by George Cruikshank. 26 January 1819.

THE

BANK RESTRICTION BAROMETER;

OR, SCALE OF EFFECTS ON SOCIETY OF THE

Bank Note System, and Payments in Gold.

BY ABRAHAM FRANKLIN.

*** *To be read from the words* " BANK RESTRICTION," *in the middle, upwards or downwards.*

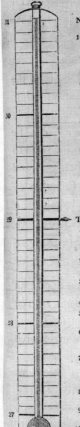

NATIONAL PROSPERITY PROMOTED.

10. The Number of useless Public Executions diminished.

9. The Amelioration of the Criminal Code facilitated.

8. The Forgery of Bank Notes at an end.

7. Manufacturers and Journeymen obtain Necessaries and Comforts for their Wages.

6. The Means of Persons with small Incomes enlarged.

5. A Fall of Rents and Prices.

4. The Circulating Medium diminished.

3. Fictitious Capital and False Credit destroyed.

2. Exchanges equalized, and the Gold Coin preserved, if allowed to be freely exported.

1. The Gold Currency restored.

Consequences, if taken off, will be as above:—viz.

THE BANK RESTRICTION.

Consequences of its Operation are as follows:— viz.

1. Disappearance of the legal Gold Coin.

2. The Issues of Bank of England Notes and Country Bank Notes extended.

3. Paper Accommodation, creating False Credit, Fictitious Capital, Mischievous Speculation.

4. The Circulating Medium enormously enlarged.

5. Rents and Prices of Articles of the first Necessity, doubled and trebled.

6. The Income and Wages of small Annuitants, and Artisans and Labourers, insufficient to purchase Necessaries for their Support.

7. Industry reduced to Indigence, broken-spirited, and in the Workhouse: or, endeavouring to preserve independence, lingering in despair, committing suicide, or dying broken-hearted.

8. The Temptation to forge Bank of England Notes increased and facilitated.

9. New and sanguinary Laws against Forgery ineffectually enacted.

10. Frequent and useless inflictions of the barbarous Punishment of Death.

GENERAL DISTRESS INCREASED.

See next Page.

Fig. 11 William Hone, *The Bank Restriction Barometer.*
Engraving by George Cruikshank. 26 January 1819.

betrays the people to the principle of self. For Shelley, as Michael
Scrivener has argued, the first principle of government is self-govern-
ment, an anarchist's vision of a society that governs itself from below
without the intervention of a system of representation.[29] However,
Shelley as a practical reformer supports a system such as that in the
United States, where there is "no false representation." The problem
with England is that its system of representation is corrupt or rotten. In
Shelley's *Philosophical View of Reform*, governments are to be judged by
how closely they approximate to an ideal in which each individual
would stand for himself or herself, just as the economic system is most
just when labor stands for itself. Once a system of representation is
introduced, the first principle (what Shelley calls "actual" representation) is abandoned, but one can still have a good government ("virtual"
representation) based on reasonable ratios of representation, just as one
can have a sound financial system based upon just ratios between labor
and gold. As paper debases the currency, so have developments in
England – mainly increases in the "unrepresented multitude," which
changed the ratio of those represented to those not represented from 1 : 8
in 1641 to 1 : 20 in 1688 and 1 to "many hundreds" in 1819 – diluted
representation so as to make it "false": "The number therefore of those
who have influence on the government, even if numerically the same as
at the former period, was relatively different. And a sufficiently just
measure is afforded of the degree in which a country is enslaved or free,
by the consideration of the relative number of individuals who are
admitted to the exercise of political rights" (pp. 234, 242). Shelley wants
to go beyond complaints about "rotten boroughs" to make an argument
for universal manhood suffrage; and he makes it clear that the corruption of the system that leads to this demand is not just a matter of
statistics but also of historical shifts in power. When Parliament and the
lords who controlled it stood against royal power in the seventeenth
century, it sided with the people and was thus the "virtual," if not a
"legal and actual," representative of the will of the people. But with the
accession of William III, an alliance was made between the aristocrats
and the throne so as to make "the Crown the mask and pretence of their
own authority. At this period began that despotism of the oligarchy of
party, and under colour of administering the executive power lodged in
the king, represented in truth the interests of the rich" (p. 243). The
system of political representation, like the economic system, has been so
distorted from its first principle that it comes to represent not the people
but only the wealthy and their ideology, the principle of self.

While Shelley draws on Godwin, Cobbett, Hume, and others in such arguments, he writes in the language of Hunt and his circle. Hunt, in his early journal the *Reflector*, had already drawn an analogy between false political representation and paper money. In a piece entitled "On the Public Spirit of the Times, and the State of Parties" (1.2 [1811], 451–66), Hunt has a reformer respond to a question put by a "Parliamentary Jobber" about whether paper represents money: "Yes it does, just as you and your friends represent the people, unlike in every possible respect, and as flimsy, as easy to be seen through, and as superabundant, as the popular strength has been sterling, solid, and wasted away in foreign wars. Like you also, it is of no real value but to the minister" (p. 466). In another piece, "The Reformers; or, Wrongs of Intellect – A Fragment of a Political Dialogue," sent from "Utopia Lodge, March 1810" (1.1 [1811], 17–28), the author (probably Hunt) objects to linking political representation and property and argues that we would do better to represent the arts and sciences; people with creative talent, not money-getters, should be the acknowledged legislators of the world. Shelley's political and economic arguments, particularly as they are included in the *Defence of Poetry*, clearly arise from the vision of the circle.

But what of poetry? In Keats's letter, Shelley would seem to be the poet of representation, serving a God outside of poetry, while Keats embraces the formal first principles of art. That is, Keats might argue that his formalist theory defended poetry against its devaluation within a theory of representation that subordinates art to something prior to art, something art merely re-presents. In surveying the problem of representation, W. J. T. Mitchell has argued that such "formalist or 'abstract' theories of art have provided the most fundamental challenges to representational models in the modern era... Formalism emphasizes the representational means and manner – the materiality and organization of the 'signifier' or representational object."[30] For Keats, Shelley has devalued his art by serving the God of ideological argument when he should be concerned only with formal qualities, with "the Poetry and dramatic effect." Shelley's response in the *Defence* is that art is not an object to be hoarded like Mammon's money, nor is it a static representation of a preexisting signified; rather it is labor, the activity of imagining, creating. Where Keats would emphasize the aesthetic object, Shelley celebrates the act of creation:

the mind in creation is as a fading coal which some invisible influence, like an inconstant wind, awakens to transitory brightness: this power arises from within, like the colour of a flower which fades and changes as it is developed, and the conscious portions of our natures are unprophetic either of its approach or its departure. Could this influence be durable in its original purity and force, it is impossible to predict the greatness of the results: but when composition begins, inspiration is already on the decline, and the most glorious poetry that has ever been communicated to the world is probably a feeble shadow of the original conception of the poet. (Pp. 503–4)

As we have seen, Shelley, in revising the passage echoing Keats, consciously dropped a phrase that would have posited poetry as a representative parallel to money: "Poetry is the representation of the benevolent principle in man." It is important that he kept the notion of money incarnating or representing the self, whereas he altered the status of poetry from being a representative of another power to being itself a "first principle," a God to stand against the Mammon of money and selfhood. Shelley's analysis of representation finally leads him to place poetry – or, more exactly, the imagination of which poetry is a particular instance – prior to representation. Peacock had argued that poetry began as a trade which, "like all other trades, takes its rise in the demand for the commodity, and flourishes in proportion to the extent of the market."[31] Its trade was flattery of the powerful and its commodity a representation of the ideas and accomplishments of those who rule. In its "golden age," poetry had at least represented all of the ruling culture's ideas, but as history, religion, politics, and philosophy separated themselves off from poetry, it was left with the purely ornamental and sentimental task of evoking the glories of past days; the end of poetry's decline might very well be a purely decorative art, bereft of all content, serving only Keats's Mammon of formalism. Throughout the *Defence*, Shelley works to protect the imagination from a series of such reductive formulations that turn it into a representation of something else – a shadow of the truths perceived by reason, a reflection of prophetic insights, a mere ornamental recollection of the past, insignificant next to central cultural forms such as science and law.

Citing Tasso on the parallel between the poet and the creating God, Shelley argues that the imagination – like labor or self-governance – does not re-present but constitutes, creates. For Shelley, what the art object offers does not exist prior to the creative act; he is concerned with neither representation nor expression but creation, the work in art not the work of art. Immediately following the passage on poetry and the Mammon of self, Shelley cites the functions of poetry as "two fold; by one it creates new materials of knowledge, and power and pleasure; by the other it engenders in the mind a desire to reproduce and arrange them according to a certain rhythm and order which may be called the beautiful and the good" (p. 503). Poetry creates and orders. It provides truth, beauty, and the good. Poets "are not only the authors of language and of music, of the dance and architecture and statuary and painting: they are the institutors of laws, and the founders of civil society and the inventors of the arts of life and the teachers, who draw into a certain propinquity with the beautiful and the true that partial apprehension of the agencies of the invisible which is called religion" (p. 482). Poetry does not represent anything, not even benevolence; it is represented by other things – by individual works of art, by philosophy, by religion, by human institutions, by benevolent acts. Peacock would render poetry the representation of an external, prior culture and then a mere echo of such a representation. Keats appears in his letter as a poet who is forced to accept the Peacockian assertion that poetry can no longer represent the world and insists that instead art should merely represent itself, should merely reflect back upon its own means. And, of course, Keats also sounds like Peacock's earliest poet, plying his trade with "a hope of gain." In Shelley's view, Keats has made a false idol out of art, worshipping the image rather than the real activity that lies behind it. Just as paper currency comes to replace gold, so does Keats's self-concentrated aesthetic object replace creativity, betraying poetry to the principle of self. Standing against Peacock and Keats, Shelley argues that poetry is creative of all culture. Like Vico or Marx, Shelley believes that humanity makes its own history; he would add that he does so through imaginative acts. Where Keats may have seen his arguments in his letter to Shelley as poetical – one must concentrate on form rather than message – or personal – one must make money and not be prodigal – Shelley insists that the personal and the poetical are political, that Keats's embracings of self-concentration and of art as self-contained precious object are linked through the principle of self with oppressive economic and social arrangements that arise through a perversion of representation.

IV

Of course, Shelley's more renowned pronouncement on Keats was not such hidden criticism but the elegy *Adonais*. Such a mélange of praise and censure marks Shelley's attitude towards Keats during 1820–21: defending "Hyperion" to Peacock and others, he criticized the rest of the 1820 volume. The most violent representation of this mixed opinion occurs in the draft dialogue about Keats's book, where one speaker praises the epic fragment while the other calls Keats's poetry "a new knot of abortions engendered by vanity upon idleness."[32] Shelley even opens his preface to *Adonais* with a typically divided assessment of Keats, noting his own "known repugnance to the narrow principles of taste" found in "several of his earlier compositions" but finding "the fragment of *Hyperion* as second to nothing that was ever produced by a writer of the same years" (p. 390). Shelley also states his "intention to subjoin to the London edition of this poem, a criticism upon the claims of its lamented object to be classed among the writers of the highest genius who have adorned our age." This prose argument was never made; *Adonais* itself, after interring what is dead in Keats's poetry, works to establish Keats as "among the writers of the highest genius." More than that, however, *Adonais* is an investigation of what is dead and what is alive or creative in modern, that is, post-Wordsworthian poetry. Whatever the claims in *Adonais* about personal immortality, it is clearly concerned with poetry's survival, with the defense of poetry in the age of reaction. As Scrivener has suggested, *Adonais* is part of Shelley's defense of poetry being mounted in 1821 against what he saw as a variety of reductive visions of the role of the poet.[33]

Adonais thus needs to be read in the context of the *Defence* and of Shelley's response to Keats during 1820 and 1821. Stuart Curran has made the vital argument that *Adonais* is a systematic response to Keats's 1820 volume, pointing in particular to Shelley's reworking of the "Ode to a Nightingale" within the elegy and to his use of "Hyperion" to represent what Shelley values in Keats's poetry.[34] We need to remember that when Shelley first read Keats's 1820 volume, Keats's letter had sensitized him to the presence of a poetry of self-concentration. Critics have been puzzled by Shelley's lack of response to the great odes and the narrative poems, but with the letter as preface, the nightingale ode's turn from possible imaginative engagement to the "sole self" or "Isabella"'s portrait of self-involved desire might very well have struck Shelley as representing a false poetry of the self just as the "Ode on a Grecian Urn" or even "To Autumn" might have seemed to him to embrace the formalism of Mammon. In the opening movements of *Adonais*, as Shelley emphasizes Adonais's mortality, we also get several allusions to what Shelley finds mortal in Keats's poetry, his poetry of self; there are references to the nightingale ode (as well as to the ode "To Autumn"), to the inward-turned Isabella, and to the myths of Echo and

Narcissus which Keats had used in "I stood tip-toe upon a little hill" (*Adonais*, ll. 145, 116–17, 47–48, 127–44). The "Hyperion" fragment, however, clearly appeared to Shelley to be an epic of sympathy and creative engagement, a poem with a vision akin to his own *Prometheus Unbound*, to which he links "Hyperion" in his letters (to Peacock [8 November 1820], to Claire Clairmont [18 November 1820], and to Byron [4 May 1821], *SL*, II: 244, 250, 289).

This use of the nightingale ode and "Hyperion" to define Keats's work – as when Shelley links Keats's poetry to the lyric nightingale and the epic eagle (ll. 145–47) or again when he defines the range of Keats's poetry as extending "from the moan / Of thunder, to the song of night's sweet bird" (ll. 371–72) – repeats a pattern found throughout the response to Keats of Shelley's Pisan circle. For example, Gisborne, in a letter to the Reverend Colonel Finch (30 May 1821) lamenting Keats's death, mentions only two poems, commenting on "his inimitable Ode to a Nightingale" and praising "Hyperion" as an "unequalled modern production" that "announces the full maturity of the richest poetic genius" (Gisborne also already seems to believe that Keats was killed by "critical malignity").35 Even more striking is Hunt's *Indicator* review of Keats's volume (2 and 9 August 1820), which uses the same two poems in its second part to define Keats's range: the nightingale ode is quoted in full, and "Hyperion" is praised. Interestingly enough, the review also mentions Milton's "Lycidas," one of Shelley's models for *Adonais*, and discusses Keats's ill health in relation to the harsh reviews he has received. One is tempted to find the seed of *Adonais* in Hunt's review (just as we can find the impetus for *Peter Bell the Third* in Hunt's review of Wordsworth's poem), to find Hunt mediating between the other two poets one more time.

Given Shelley's multilayered reaction to Keats, we are not surprised to find that *Adonais* opens with a double vision of the dead poet: "he is dead" and yet "till the Future dares / Forget the Past, his fate and fame shall be / An echo and a light unto eternity" (ll. 1, 7–9). The opening stanzas restate the dual vision of the dead poet in a number of ways. In the second stanza, Urania is found at the moment of the poet's death "in her Paradise" while an echo "Rekindled all the fading melodies" that were his poems. Stanza three tells us again that he is dead and yet asks "wherefore" do we cry, "For he is gone, where all things wise and fair / Descend." In fact, we are reminded in the next stanza that Milton died, "but his clear Sprite / Yet reigns o'er earth." This image of Milton has a corresponding passage in the *Defence*, where the immortality of Milton's and Dante's poetry is contrasted with the perishable ideological masks they were forced to wear: "The distorted notions of invisible things which Dante and his rival Milton have idealized, are merely the mask and the mantle in which these great poets walk through eternity enveloped and disguised" (p. 498). *Adonais* seeks the eternal Keats beneath the mask and mantle of his mistaken ideology of Mammon.

In a sense, the entire poem – which ends with Adonais in "the abode where the Eternal are" (l. 495) – works out the double fate set forth in this opening section. The *Defence* expresses a similar idea in a passage that evokes Keats's poetry: "no living poet ever arrived at the fulness of his fame; the jury which sits in judgement upon a poet, belonging as he does to all time, must be composed of his peers ... A poet is a nightingale, who sits in darkness and sings to cheer its own solitude with sweet sounds; his auditors are as men entranced by the melody of an unseen musician, who feel that they are moved and softened, yet know not whence or why" (p. 486). The jury of poetic peers that Shelley envisages here is a key to the argument of *Adonais*: from the early evocation of Milton and of those who struggle for "Fame's serene abode" (l. 45) through the convocation of poet-mourners in stanzas 30–35 and the account of "inheritors of unfulfilled renown" such as Chatterton, Sidney, and Lucan (stanza 45) to the image of the abode of the Eternal that closes the poem, Shelley seeks to define the survival of Keats in a community of poets. This community is an idealized version of the real circle of writers of which Keats had been a part and to which Shelley had alluded in the draft of his preface: one version reads, "The offence of this poor victim seems to have consisted solely in his intimacy with Leigh Hunt M.ʳ Hazlitt & some other of the enemies of despotism & superstition"; again, Shelley writes of having met Keats "at my friend Leigh Hunt's."[36] It is community – the group as mediator between isolated author and abstract audience – that will save the poet from the lack of fame that Shelley's "An Exhortation" argues leads to the poet's self-betrayal to power and wealth.

It is isolation – the lack of fame – that threatens Keats and modern poetry. This isolation has two sites: in the corrupt community created by "despotism and superstition," by false systems of government, finance, and thought, by false systems of representation; and in the work of the poets of the "egotistical sublime." In *Adonais*, corrupt society is embodied in the figure of the critic, one of the preface's "literary prostitutes," one who serves power and money and who corrupts language to "insults" and "slander" (l. 391);[37] such critics are "herded wolves, bold only to pursue; / The obscene ravens, clamorous o'er the dead" (ll. 244–45). Interestingly, the critic will be denied fame: "Live thou, whose infamy is not thy fame! / Live! fear no heavier chastisement from me, / Thou noteless blot on a remembered name! / But be thyself, and know thyself to be!" (ll. 325–28). A destroyer of community and its bonds of language and love, the critic is finally left with only himself, with "Remorse and Self-contempt" (l. 331) – these being, along with Hate, Shelley's deadly sins to be counteracted by his cardinal virtues of "Love, Hope, and Self-esteem" ("Hymn to Intellectual Beauty," l. 37).

The corrupt society which speaks through the critic threatens modern poetry, as seen in its attempted destruction of Adonais. The danger, however, is not only that the poet may be silenced but that he may either sell his poetic soul for fame or remain in solitude and quietude, creating the poetry of self-concentration. *Adonais* continues an argument that Shelley had begun as early as his sonnet "To Wordsworth" and had continued in "An Exhortation" and *Peter Bell the Third*. As these three poems suggest, this problem is connected in Shelley's mind with the career of Wordsworth. In *Adonais*, Shelley extends his criticism of Wordsworth to a concern about modern poetry, including his own, by creating a composite Wordsworthian–Keatsian–Shelleyan poet of the self in what has often been regarded as an embarrassing self-portrait of Shelley as poet-mourner but that Ross Woodman has shown to be a parody of a position Shelley seeks to leave behind.[38] The purpose of this "self-portrait" is not self-pity but an analysis of the principle of self in modern poetry.

Stanzas 31 to 34 have been misread as autobiography. Responding to the hostility this passage has generated, recent defenders of the poem have argued for the abstractness of the portrait, finding not Shelley but the nineteenth-century philosophical poet or the archetype of the young poet doomed to death; Stuart Curran has stressed the identity between Shelley with his "partial moan" (l. 290) and Keats in this passage.[39] What these readings suggest is that we have a generalized, composite portrait here, one in marked contrast to the clearly identifiable depictions of Byron, Moore, and Hunt.

The presence of Keats in this supposed self-portrait of Shelley is particularly intense: the "pardlike Spirit" of line 280 echoes the nightingale ode with its "Not charioted by Bacchus and his pards" (l. 32); "A Love in desolation masked;– a Power / Girt round with weakness" (ll. 281–82) seems to invoke both the stanza in the nightingale ode where a reductive vision of life is offered in which we are ruled by "The weariness, the fever, and the fret," "Where Beauty cannot keep her lustrous eyes, / Or new Love pine at them beyond to-morrow" (ll. 23, 29–30) and the world of the fallen Saturn of "Hyperion" who asks, "Who had power / To make me desolate?" (ll. 102–3); the frail form's head is bound in flowers – "pansies overblown, / And faded violets, white, and pied, and blue" (ll. 289–90) – reminiscent of the nightingale ode's "Fast fading violets" (l. 47) as well as of the "Ode to Psyche"'s "cool-rooted flowers, fragrant-eyed, / Blue, silver, white, and budded Tyrian" (ll. 13–14); the references to Bacchus' ivy (ll. 290–91) seem to echo the description in *Endymion* (IV, 193–211) of Bacchus and his "crew" (a word used in line 295 of *Adonais*) where Bacchus carries an "ivy-dart" that is transformed into "a light spear topped with a cypress cone, / Round whose rude shaft dark ivy tresses grew" (ll. 292–93), with the "dart" reappearing as the "hunter's dart" that strikes the "herd-abandoned deer" (l. 297). Internal echoes also support our sense that Keats/ Adonais is present here: the "pardlike Spirit" is described as "a dying lamp, a falling shower, / A breaking billow;– even whilst we speak / Is it not broken? On the withering flower / The killing sun smiles brightly" (ll. 284–87), words which recall an early account of Adonais, who as "the loveliest and the last, / The bloom, whose petals nipt before they blew / Died on the promise of the fruit, is waste; / The broken lily lies – the storm is overpast" (ll. 51–54). Again, while some find autobiography in Shelley's description of the "frail Form" as "companionless" (ll. 271–72), as "neglected and apart" (l. 296), Keats, who confronted illness and death with only Severn by his side, would seem a more likely candidate than Shelley alive among his Italian circle of friends and loved ones.

While the identification between Shelley and Keats in this passage is usually read as a prelude to Shelley's desire to follow Keats at the poem's close, I believe that what is identified here is the weakness in their poetry, in all modern poetry. This point becomes clearer if we also uncover the presence of Wordsworth in this passage, for then it becomes clear that the "frail Form" is a portrait of a false Wordsworthian– Keatsian–Shelleyan poet of the self who is opposed to the Hyperion– Prometheus poet of sympathy and engagement who writes *Adonais*. Evocations of Wordsworth have been noted by several critics, particularly in Shelley's image of the Actaeon-like destruction of the poet: "he, as I guess, / Had gazed on Nature's naked loveliness, / Actaeon-like, and now he fled astray / With feeble steps o'er the world's wilderness, / And his own thoughts, along that rugged way, / Pursued, like raging hounds, their father and their prey" (ll. 274–79). In annotating this passage, Anthony Knerr mentions Shelley's vision of Wordsworth as Peter Bell, who "touched the hem of Nature's shift, / Felt faint – and never dared uplift / The closest, all-concealing tunic" (IV, 53–55).[40] Ross Woodman has suggested the link between this passage and *Alastor*, with its assault on the Wordsworth of *The Excursion*.[41] The Wordsworthian poet of the egotistical sublime – like the Keats in a Shelleyan reading of the nightingale ode and like part of Shelley himself – flees into the self from the truth revealed in nature. As we have seen, *The Excursion* challenged the younger romantic poets by revising Wordsworth's own early embrace of nature as a turn from society and particularly from social change, with Wordsworth claiming that the "unexpected transports of our age" have brought about a "loss of confidence in social man" (*Excursion*, IV, 261–62). In their differing ways, *Alastor* and *The Revolt of Islam*, *Endymion*, and *Childe Harold* III responded to *The Excursion*, attacking the "egotistical sublime" and seeking a renewed hope for the future. Shelley continues to worry whether he and his fellow poets have escaped the Wordsworthian trap or whether, like the "frail Form," they reveal a "branded and ensanguined brow, / Which was like Cain's or Christ's" (ll. 305–6); the question raised is whether the modern poet must either be a martyr to a repressive society or an apostate to poetry, serving the Mammon of power and money like the critic upon whom the poem calls down "the curse of Cain" (l. 151).

The other mourners oppose this problematic figure, with Byron, Hunt, and Moore standing against the Wordsworthian poetry of the self (and draft versions of the preface and of the poet-mourners section would have added Hazlitt and Horace and James Smith, that is, other members of the Hunt circle).[42] Cameron and Knerr have stressed the political allegiances of the mourning Byron, Moore, and Hunt; they are clearly not present because of their attitudes towards Keats, since of the three only Hunt was his supporter.[43] Byron is here, Knerr notes, as "the leading liberal poet of the age" and as the clearest example of the poet who, rather than retreating inward, has turned outward, becoming in *Adonais* the "Pythian of the age" able to destroy his conservative opponents (ll. 248–51). Hunt appears as one of the opponents of "despotism & superstition" in the draft of Shelley's preface and one of the writers – along with Godwin, Hazlitt, and Bentham – who Shelley in the *Philosophical View of Reform* hoped would bring about profound political change through their work.

The political import of *Adonais* was certainly recognized by conservative reviewers, who were quick to brand the poem as another piece of

Cockney nonsense. *Blackwood's* (10 [December 1821], 696–700) labelled
the elegy "Cockney" and found that it was weak flattery forced upon the
public by the *"Pisan* triumvirate" of Shelley, Byron, and Hunt; the
Literary Gazette (8 December 1821, pp. 772–73) assaulted the poem and its
subject, contending that Keats was a "radically presumptuous profligate," "made presumptuous chiefly by the treacherous puffing of his
cockney fellow gossips, and profligate in his poems merely to make them
saleable ... For what is praise of cockneys but disgrace, or what honourable inscription can be placed over the dead by the hands of notorious
libellers, exiled adulterers, and avowed atheists" – the attacks being
levelled at Hunt, Byron, and Shelley. Clearly reviewers saw *Adonais* as
part of the radical work of the Hunt and Pisan circles; Shelley's conservative opponents understood the presence of Hunt and Byron in the
poem. Moore seems the odd figure in this group until we remember
Hunt's imitations of Moore's epistles, Shelley's dedication of *Peter Bell the
Third* to Moore in his incarnation as Thomas Brown, Historian of the
Fudges, or Hazlitt's review of *The Fudge Family in Paris* in the *Yellow Dwarf*
(25 April 1818; reprinted in *Political Essays* [1819], *CWH*, VII: 287–97),
where Moore is praised as "the poet and the Patriot. He is neither a
coxcomb nor a catspaw,– a whiffling turncoat, nor a thorough-paced
tool, a mouthing sycophant, 'a full solempne man,' like Mr. Wordsworth,– a whining monk, like Mr. Southey,– a maudlin Methodistical
lay-preacher, like Mr. Coleridge." Like Hazlitt, Shelley links Moore to
the liberal party of poets standing in opposition to Southey, Coleridge,
and Wordsworth.

Adonais seeks to rescue Keats from a Wordsworthian poetry of self-
concentration and to place him in the Pisan extension of the Hunt circle
to which Shelley had invited him. The poem argues that Keats does not
belong with the Wordsworth who supported the Lowthers and issued
Peter Bell but with Milton, "Who was the Sire of an immortal strain, /
Blind, old, and lonely, when his country's pride, / The priest, the slave,
and the liberticide, / Trampled" (ll. 30–33). Keats does not belong with
the laureate Southey ("A heart grown cold, a head grown grey in vain"
l. 358) but with Chatterton, destroyed by the society that praised the
apostate. Keats's peers are Sidney, who "fought / And as he fell and as
he lived and loved / Sublimely mild" (ll. 401–3), and Lucan, killed by the
tyrant Nero, not Coleridge writing lay sermons to protect the status quo.
Shelley, confronted with Keats's espousal of the Mammon of formalism
and the turn to the self, might have agreed with Jerome McGann that
Keats's 1820 volume was a "great and (politically) reactionary book"

seeking "to dissolve social and political conflicts in the mediations of art and beauty";[44] but in "Hyperion" – the poem that perhaps, as Ruthven has argued, works through Keats's anxieties about money, that perhaps, as Sharp has argued, offers a vision of religious reform, that perhaps, as Watkins has contended, sets forth "republican or libertarian principles"[45] – Shelley saw something else. The poet of the nightingale ode might be tolled back to the sole self of Wordsworthian quietist isolation. But the poet of "Hyperion" was ready to create a poetry of magnanimous and imaginative self-sacrifice, to "die into life," as Adonais does in Shelley's poem, where "He is made one with Nature" (l. 370), where "He is a portion of the loveliness / Which once he made more lovely" (ll. 379–80). In "Hyperion," with its embrace of the Hunt program of paganism and progress, Shelley finds a poetry of hope set against what struck him as Wordsworthian despondency. The poet of "Hyperion" belongs with Byron, Moore, and Hunt, with Hazlitt and Horace Smith, with Shelley. *Adonais* returns Keats to the ideal circle of liberal writers of which the Hunt circle in London and Shelley's Pisa were particular embodiments. They are true poets and patriots and, like Keats, seek "the abode where the Eternal are."

The poet of *Adonais* is also ready to die into life: "What Adonais is, why fear we to become?" (l. 459). The end of *Adonais* offers the poetry that Shelley promises in the *Defence* against the principle of self. Shelley unfurls the wings the Keats of the letter would have bound to create an art of magnanimity, an art that places his rival before himself as a beacon in eternity. The astounding close of Shelley's poem should be read as an embodiment of Shelley's poetry of creativity, a poetry that does not re-present any given of the self or the world but strives to envision anew. The last four stanzas, in the words of the *Defence*, make "us the inhabitants of a world to which the familiar world is a chaos" (p. 505); that is, they imagine a world ordered beyond present understanding, and thus not reducible to present meanings, Platonic, Christian, or otherwise. Shelley the skeptic may find that "Rome's azure sky, / Flowers, ruins, statues, music, words, are weak / The glory they transfuse with fitting truth to speak" (ll. 466–68). But Shelley still believes in the Light, Beauty, Benediction, and Love (ll. 478–85) that will forever remain beyond the reach of poetry. The "deep truth is imageless," but it is the task of the poet to quest through newly minted images into those depths, to offer "mirrors of the gigantic shadows which futurity casts upon the present" (p. 508).

Harold Bloom has called the final lines "this great but suicidal stanza," finding in it "the sepulcher of a humanist and heroic quest":[46]

> The breath whose might I have invoked in song
> Descends on me; my spirit's bark is driven,
> Far from the shore, far from the trembling throng
> Whose sails were never to the tempest given;
> The massy earth and sphered skies are riven!
> I am borne darkly, fearfully, afar:
> Whilst burning through the inmost veil of Heaven,
> The soul of Adonais, like a star,
> Beacons from the abode where the Eternal are.   (Ll. 487–95)

Instead, I believe, we find Shelley committing himself to this quest even
unto death. Beginning with Shelley's friend John Taaffe, critics have
heard Dante's *Paradiso* (canto II.1–9) echoed here, but I think we should
hear another moment in Dante, that of Ulysses' last voyage, where the
questor leaves behind all known shores to challenge the limits placed on
humanity.[47] Shelley offers one last inversion, for the breath that drives
him here is not God's punishing whirlwind as in Dante but the power of
poetry, and where Ulysses and his crew are destroyed approaching
Mount Purgatory, Shelley and his circle are still borne – even if "darkly,
fearfully" – towards the paradise of poets. They will not get there alone:
it is Shelley who has placed Keats/Adonais in the abode of the Eternal,
and it is Keats who will lead Shelley there. Shelley, defending what he
felt was the true wealth of the imagination against false systems of
representation and defending the Keats of "Hyperion" against the
Keats of self-concentration, demanded a different kind of poetry than
Keats's poetry of self-concentration and sought to portray a different
Keats from the one found in his famous letter, a Keats who belonged
with Byron, the "Pythian of the age," and Moore, singer against
Ireland's "saddest wrong," and Hunt, enemy of "despotism & superstition," and Shelley, the magnanimous poet of *Adonais*. Keats finds his
true independence, his identity, his immortality in the group. Shelley's
community of poets – modelled on Hunt's circle – is imagined defeating
the Mammon of the closed self and the closed text to inhabit the city of
poetry on earth.

V

There is certainly something in Shelley's death! (Haydon, *Diary*, 5 August 1822)

Shelley's is one of many attempts, including this one, to keep alive the power of the Hunt circle, a power grounded most specifically in perhaps a year and a half of close contact and in a little more than five years of mutual inspiration and competition. In *Adonais*, Shelley comes not so much to bury Keats as to praise the power of the poetry arising out of the Hunt circle, to keep alive the hope for modern culture. Shelley was not, of course, alone in finding the death of Keats a moment for cultural reflection as a rather large number of tributes in poetry and prose followed upon Keats's death.[48] In the poetic memorials, as always in the elegiac tradition, the death of the poet gives rise to poetry and thus to the promise of poetry's continuing power even in the face of death. For example, John Taylor, Keats's publisher, was spurred to write "Sonnet on the Death of the Poet J. Keats," published in the *London Magazine* (3 [May 1821], 526), as he finds his poetic voice in lamenting the loss of the voice of the poet of the nightingale ode, "Thou very sweetest bird / That ever made a moonlight forest ring": "Shall thy rich notes no more, no more be heard?"

Others joined Shelley in linking Keats to his circle, as when Procter connects him with Byron and Shelley – the "three English poets who had been compelled by circumstances to adopt a foreign country as their own."[49] "P.," the author of "Verses to the Memory of John Keats, the Poet," writes from the appropriately Cockney locale of Islington Green and pits the Cockney Keats of "I stood tip-toe" (which is quoted in the poem) against the laureate Southey with his *Vision of Judgment*.[50] "P." also creates an affiliative pantheon for Keats, linking him to Chatterton, as does Shelley, while a piece in the *Gossip* has Keats join in death both Chatterton and Henry Kirke White.[51] Cowden Clarke, in a letter to the *Morning Chronicle* (27 July 1821), not only returns Keats to his circle of friends and particularly to the company of Hunt but also attacks Gifford and the other conservative reviewers for destroying Keats. While Shelley's account of Adonais' death at the hands of vicious critics has come to be seen as, at best, a sentimentalizing distortion – James A. W. Heffernan calls it "an insult" and a "slander"[52] – Shelley was joined by many in seeing Keats's death as an occasion for the defense of poetry against the assault of conservative reviewers. Nicholas A. Joukovsky has unearthed a satire published in the July 1821 number of the *Newcastle Magazine* which attacks the *Blackwood's* crew for its assault upon Keats – who again has joined other poets in the land of the dead – and which calls upon Byron, as does Shelley, to respond.[53] Procter in his elegy for Keats imagined poets rallying around the dead and maligned Keats, for whom "Too late came love to show the world thy worth / Too late came glory for thy youthful head"; ignored or scorned by critics, Keats – saved from the lack of fame and love that besets the poet in Shelley's "Exhortation" – will be praised by poets and lovers:

> Mourn; poets! mourn;– he's lost! O minstrels, grieve!
> And with your music let his fame be fed!
> True lovers, 'round his verse your sorrows weave
> And maidens! mourn, at last, a poet dead![54]

The *Imperial Magazine*, while attacking the Cockney *Liberal* (4 [1822], 1139–42), printed "STANZAS. To the memory of MR. KEATS, the poet, who died at Rome on this day Twelvemonth," by H.D. (4 [1822], 735) that seem to invoke Shelley's *Adonais* in opposition to works such as Wordsworth's "Thanksgiving Ode": "heard ye not the notes expire, / And melt into a funeral song? / Oh! 'twas a song of grief and woe, / Unlike the odes of reeking slaughter, / It sang of him that's now laid low." Again, the obituary for Keats in the *New Monthly Magazine* (1 May 1821, pp. 256–57) contends that "The base attack made with the hope of crushing the rising genius of young Keats, can never be forgotten," particularly as it came "from the mean motive of a dislike to his political tenets." While the contention that Keats was literally killed by bad reviews deserved the skepticism and scorn of Byron, there were many who recognized that the attacks on Keats were part of a systematic, ideologically driven attempt to control contemporary culture and to destroy what it could not control. Keats's death was a personal loss for the Hunt circle that also reminded them of the struggle for cultural life in which they were engaged.

If Shelley wanted to point not only to the loss in Keats's death but to the hope offered by Keats's poetry, others found the same hope in Shelley's poetry at his death. While Haydon, in the passage above in which he finds "something" in Shelley's death, joined conservative reviewers in finding divine retribution in the destruction of the atheist, most of Shelley's friends greeted his death with panegyric. Hunt wrote to Horace Smith (20 July 1822, *Correspondence*, 1: 194) of the death of Shelley, "my divine-minded friend, your friend, the friend of the universe, he has perished at sea." Smith himself wrote a collaborative piece praising Shelley for the *Paris Monthly Review* (7 [August 1822]) which has been discovered by Stuart Curran; as Curran notes, Smith seems to write in response to Shelley's *Adonais*, and he contrasts the viciousness of the attacks levelled against Shelley with Shelley's benevolence as he "imagined plans for promoting the welfare of the great circle of mankind, while he formed the happiness of the little one in which he moved."[55] It is striking that in both Hunt's and Smith's accounts Shelley's role in his immediate circle is linked to his hopes for transforming the world: as in his own *Adonais*, the Hunt and Pisan circles are invoked as models of a world remade.

A similar point would be made by John Chalk Claris, who did not know Shelley but who was a friend of Hunt's and probably of Horace Smith's and who later met Mary Shelley.[56] Writing under his pseudonym "Arthur Brooke," Claris issued an *Elegy on the Death of Percy Bysshe Shelley* (1822), placing his poem and its subject firmly in the Hunt circle: published by the Olliers, the elegy is "Affectionately Inscribed" to Leigh Hunt; it invokes Byron, "he who once hath breathed / His dirge sublime o'er Ireland's buried pride" in his "Monody on Sheridan"; and it evokes the camaraderie of this group of poets, calling Shelley "the friend, the poet" who will be sung by a "mutual mind," by one of those "whom loftier thoughts in holiest brotherhood bind" (p. 11). Though not part of the Hunt group when Shelley was in England, Claris was at times accused of being a Cockney, and this poem was attacked in the *Weekly Literary Register and Review of the Fine Arts, Sciences, and Belles Lettres* (21 September 1822) and then linked to Shelley's *Adonais* in the next number. Claris's praise of Shelley's work to "Unveil foul superstition's idiot faith" would also call forth a religious response in *Verses on the Death of Percy Bysshe Shelley* (1822), by Bernard Barton, the "Quaker Poet" and friend of Southey. Just as *Adonais* was seen by conservatives as an attempt to "puff" the Cockney Keats, so was Claris's poem seen as an effort to praise the politically and religiously radical Shelley. The Cockney culture wars continued to rage over the death of Shelley as they had over Keats.

In fact, one of the things the reviewers disliked about "Arthur Brooke"'s piece is that it is imitative of Shelley. Claris's elegy attempts to do in a small compass for Shelley what Shelley did for Keats. "Brooke" clearly knows *Adonais* well, he appears to have read the *Prometheus Unbound* volume, and his "Sonnet, to the Author of 'The Revolt of Islam'" (in *Retrospection; With Other Poems*, 1822) demonstrates his enthusiasm for Shelley's earlier attempt to keep revolutionary hope alive. His elegy seeks to follow Shelley by sustaining the inspiration of Shelley's verse.

Shelley, described as "our hope" (p. 9) and "last defence" against tyrants (p. 12), though attacked like Adonais by "human reptiles" (p. 15), is finally seen as "a new Prometheus [who] brought to men / Lost

Hope's abandoned flame" (p. 13). Claris imagines Shelley's poetry accomplishing after his death the vision of a renewed life that Shelley had offered in *Prometheus Unbound*: his soul has "fore-shared" in an era – "no fabulous Age of Gold" – when "Love [will] be Law, and Gentleness be Power" (p. 14). "The spark" scattered from Shelley's unextinguished hearth will "survive in many a heart" to create a community of admirers through the "communicated glow, / Which 'tis the bard's proud privilege to impart" (p. 13).

None of Shelley's colleagues in Hunt's circle struggled more over Shelley's death than Hunt himself. Timothy Webb has offered the best account of Hunt's efforts to find a vehicle for his feelings in either verse or prose[57] as Hunt attempts several poems, as he sketches out an unpublished essay for the *Liberal*, and as he pens various versions of a biography of Shelley, the most important being those in *Lord Byron and Some of His Contemporaries* and Hunt's *Autobiography*; importantly, Webb establishes generosity, even the community of property, as a central value binding Hunt and Shelley – magnanimity is still the key term in their relationship. In the opening to the later "Jaffar, Inscribed to the Memory of Shelley" (1850), Hunt again returned to this master theme of their friendship: "Shelley, take this to thy dear memory;– / To praise the generous is to think of thee."

Hunt tried several times to write a poem about Shelley's death. There are some first rough attempts included in the notebook Hunt began for his journey to Italy; interestingly enough, much of the notebook is given over to the manuscript of Hunt's satire on Gifford, *Ultra-Crepidarius*, so that the volume juxtaposes lament for Shelley with an attack on a conservative opponent, much as *Adonais* links grief for Keats with anger at his critics.[58] These efforts, presumably made close upon Shelley's death, never get beyond a few lines as Hunt moves back and forth between prose and verse:

Sound of the church-bells about me in a strange catholic country, dying away first tremblingly, & then not. When they have done, I seem as if I had to begin life anew, and yet while they are sounding, I think of nothing but the dead & gone.

One has been taken, & the other left.

Instead of the health which I looked for in his society to restore the springs of life, I waste them with the perpetual pull ⟨?⟩ of sorrow.
When I think of it
To make me shriek myself, & madden as I sit.

The statement "One has been taken, & the other left" could, of course, mean that Shelley has been taken and Hunt is left. However, it could also refer to Shelley who has been taken and Keats who left Hunt in England. The two were often linked together in death – as in Thomas Wade's "Shelley and Keats, and Their 'Reviewer'" ("Two heavenly doves" attacked by a "crow" and "his fellow-flock of carrion things"), printed by Hunt in his later *Tatler* (1831), or in William Bell Scott's "To the Memory of P. B. Shelley" and "To the Memory of John Keats" from the early 1830s.[59] Hunt repeatedly links the two poets, most clearly in works such as the *Autobiography* – where Shelley is always praised above Keats – but also in revisions to *The Feast of Poets*, where in the various versions Keats and Shelley are always joined together:

1832:
> And Keats, with young tresses and thoughts, like the god's;
> And Shelley, a sprite from his farthest abodes.

1832:
> And Shelley, besides most magnificent pine,
> Had the plant which thy least touch, Humanity, knows;
> And Keats had forest-tree, ivy [basil in 1844, 1857], and rose.

1860:
> And Keats, the God's own young historian of Gods;
> With Shelley, diviner still, planning abodes
> For earth to enjoy with surpassers of Plato.

Hunt also brings them together in some unpublished lines to Shelley, where Keats appears as "one / Other sweet fervid voice, which late I heard."[60] Here Hunt also wishes to establish his close ties to Shelley: "Beloved Shelley, friend, immortal heart, / Whose name so long has been shut up in mine." Drawing the dead Shelley back into the lived life of the circle, Hunt recalls their time together, "when heretofore / Thou satst beside our hearth, half lifted up / On pinions of seraphic will, and breath'dst / Fires of sweet faith, and beauteous scorn of scorn." This prophetic Shelley inspires Hunt, just as Shelley had taken heart from Adonais; given "breath" by Shelley, "chaunting to thy spirit," Hunt now sees the reformed world that might be created by Shelleyan hope: "What golden hours await this yearning globe, / By hope at last, and honied breath like thine, / Spun like a starry bee." Hunt still turns to Shelley and to Keats for a human faith and beauty to pursue in spite of despondence.

Shelley did not succeed in recreating the Cockney School in Pisa – Horace Smith never made it, Keats died, Shelley drowned. The *Liberal*, after offering several extraordinary issues of collaborative effort, collaps-ed, and Byron left for Greece.[61] The living group did not survive the deaths of its most powerful voices. However, just as Shelley recreated the group in verse, so would Hunt bring them together in his prose memorials to his friends, as would Procter and Clarke and, in his own way, Haydon. We cannot speak of Shelley or Keats without thinking of the other, and for this fact they have again to thank Leigh Hunt, for in his telling of the drowning of Shelley, where he dies with Hunt's own copy of Keats's 1820 poems in his pocket, Hunt created an image of these two poets bound together that we have never quite abandoned.

The man who brought Keats and Shelley together first in 1816 and last in his memorial writings – the man who offered himself as mediator between Keats and Shelley, bringing the book of one into the hands of the other – has not been placed together with them in the pantheon of romantic poets. Hunt – and Horace Smith and John Hamilton Reynolds and Cornelius Webb and many others – have faded from our group portrait of romanticism. But Hunt too was celebrated in verse at his death, by yet another member of the Cockney School, who saw in Hunt's death the passing of the last great member of their group:

> The world grows empty: fadingly and fast
>> The dear ones and the great ones of my life
>> Melt forth, and leave me but the shadows rife
> Of those who blissful made my peopled past;
> Shadows that in their numerousness cast
>> A sense of desolation sharp as knife
>> Upon the soul, perplexing it with strife
> Against the vacancy, the void, the vast
> Unfruitful desert which the earth becomes
>> To one who loses thus the cherished friends
>> Of youth. The loss of each beloved sends
> An aching consciousness of want that dumbs
> The voice to silence,– akin to the dead blank
> All things became, when down the sad heart sank.

Charles Cowden Clarke thus observed the passing of his friend and all the other friends, including Keats and Shelley, who went before him, but in a second linked sonnet he returns to the message of hope that had been the burden of Shelley's *Adonais* and of Hunt's attempted responses to Shelley's death.

> And yet not so would thou thyself have view'd
> Affliction: thy true poet soul knew how

The sorest thwartings patiently to bow
To wisest teachings; that they still renew'd
In thee strong hope, firm trust, or faith imbued
    With cheerful spirit,– constant to avow
    The "good of e'en things evil," and allow
All things to pass with courage unsubdued.
Philosophy like thine turns to pure gold
    Earth's dross; imprisonment assumed a grace,
    A dignity, as borne by thee, in bold
Defence of liberty and right, thy face
Reflected thy heart's sun 'mid sickness, pain,
And grief; nay, loss itself thou mad'st a gain.[62]

Recalling Hunt's imprisonment for liberty's sake, drawing upon Hunt's evocation of cheerfulness in an age of despondency, Clarke evokes the three great values of the Hunt circle, the Cockney School – freedom, community, and hope. As Keats, then Shelley, then Hunt died, the members of the circle found themselves no longer able to engage in the companionable competition that Hunt had organized in their sonnet contests and elsewhere, but they could still – experiencing the destruction of death and the preservation offered by poetry – strive with one other in prayerful verse as they confronted the sore needs of loss. While they found themselves subject, in the words of *Prometheus Unbound*, to "chance, and death, and mutability," they continued to write poems celebrating the "eternal Love" they bore for one another. In the love and camaraderie of the Hunt circle, in the solidarity of the Cockney School, they found the faith to believe – in the face of oppression, imprisonment, death – that men and women might together still imagine and thus make a world of perpetual reform.

Notes

INTRODUCTION: OR, THE VISIONARY COMPANY, INC.

1 See Marjorie Levinson, "The New Historicism: Back to the Future," in *Rethinking Historicism: Critical Readings in Romantic History*, ed. Levinson (Oxford: Basil Blackwell, 1989), pp. 18–63; Jerome Christensen, *Lord Byron's Strength: Romantic Writing and Commercial Society* (Baltimore: Johns Hopkins University Press, 1993); and Alan Liu, "The Power of Formalism: The New Historicism," *English Literary History* 56 (1989), 721–71, and "Wordsworth and Subversion, 1793–1804: Trying Cultural Criticism," *Yale Journal of Criticism* 2 (1989), 55–100. For an attempt to map out the current situation of historicism, see Jeffrey N. Cox and Larry J. Reynolds, "The Historicist Enterprise," in *New Historical Literary Study: Essays on Reproducing Texts, Representing History*, ed. Cox and Reynolds (Princeton University Press, 1993), pp. 3–38.

2 See Larry J. Reynolds, "Re-vision of the American Renaissance," *Quorum* 6 (1990), 209–22.

3 Shelley, *Proposals for an Association of Philanthropists*, in *Shelley's Prose or The Trumpet of a Prophecy*, ed. David Lee Clark (Albuquerque: University of New Mexico Press, 1954), p. 63.

4 Leonidas M. Jones, *The Life of John Hamilton Reynolds* (Hanover, N.H.: University Press of New England, 1984), p. 33. The quoted phrase is Reynolds's.

5 See Stuart Curran, "The View from Versailles: Horace Smith on the Literary Scene of 1822," *Huntington Quarterly* 40 (August 1977), 357–71.

6 See Byron, *The Complete Miscellaneous Prose*, ed. Andrew Nicholson (Oxford: Clarendon Press, 1991), pp. 211–12.

7 Tim Chilcott, *A Publisher and His Circle: The Life and Work of John Taylor, Keats's Publisher* (London: Routledge & Kegan Paul, 1972), pp. 13–14.

8 Among the important work done on the dialogue between Wordsworth and Coleridge are Thomas McFarland, *Romanticism and the Forms of Ruin: Wordsworth, Coleridge, and the Modalities of Fragmentation* (Princeton University Press, 1981); Paul Magnuson, *Coleridge and Wordsworth: A Lyrical Dialogue* (Princeton University Press, 1988); Lucy Newlyn, *Coleridge, Wordsworth, and the Language of Allusion* (Oxford University Press, 1988); and Gene Ruoff,

Wordsworth and Coleridge: The Making of the Major Lyrics, 1802–1804 (New Brunswick, N.J.: Rutgers University Press, 1989). The best book on the Shelley–Byron connection is Charles Robinson, *Shelley and Byron: The Snake and Eagle Wreathed in Fight* (Baltimore: Johns Hopkins University Press, 1976).

9 As in William St. Clair, *The Godwins and the Shelleys: A Biography of a Family* (Baltimore: Johns Hopkins University Press, 1989).

10 Fredric Jameson, *The Political Unconscious: Narrative as a Socially Symbolic Act* (Ithaca: Cornell University Press, 1981), p. 53.

11 Alan Liu, "Local Transcendence: Cultural Criticism, Postmodernism, and the Romanticism of Detail," *Representations* 32 (Fall 1990), 94.

12 Sartre, *Search for a Method*, trans. Hazel E. Barnes (New York: Knopf, 1963), pp. 135–36.

13 See Donald R. Dickson, *The Tessera of Antilia: Utopian Brotherhoods and Secret Societies in the Early Seventeenth Century* (Brill, forthcoming); also Nikolaus Pevsner, *Academies of Art Past and Present*, 2nd ed. (New York: Da Capo, 1973); Martha Ornstein, *The Role of Scientific Societies in the Seventeenth Century* (University of Chicago Press, 1928); and Joan Evans, *A History of the Society of Antiquaries* (Oxford University Press for the Society of Antiquaries, 1956).

14 Ezell, *The Patriarch's Wife: Literary Evidence and the History of the Family* (Chapel Hill: University of North Carolina Press, 1987).

15 Jurgen Habermas, *The Structural Transformation of the Public Sphere: An Inquiry into a Category of Bourgeois Society*, trans. Thomas Burger and Frederick Lawrence (Cambridge: MIT Press, 1989).

16 See John Guillory, *Cultural Capital* (University of Chicago Press, 1993), and Pierre Bourdieu, *Distinction: A Social Critique of the Judgement of Taste*, trans. Richard Nice (London: Routledge & Kegan Paul, 1984).

CHAPTER I. THE COCKNEY SCHOOL ATTACKS: OR, THE
ANTIROMANTIC IDEOLOGY

1 Sidney Colvin, *Keats* (1887, rpt. London: Macmillan, 1961), states that poems by the sonnet's author, Cornelius Webb, make one think of Hunt or of Keats "in his weaker moments" (p. 38).

2 See George L. Marsh, "A Forgotten Cockney Poet – Cornelius Webb," *Philological Quarterly* 21 (July 1942), 323–33; Edmund Blunden, "The Obscure Webb(e)," *TLS*, 18 December 1959, p. 748; and, for a less sympathetic account of Webb and Cockneyism, Donald Reiman, "Introduction," in Webb's *Sonnets* and *Summer* (New York: Garland, 1978), pp. v–xii.

3 Webb's other surviving works are *The Absent Man* (1857), *Lyric Leaves* (1832), *The Man about Town* (1838), and *The Posthumous Papers, Facetious and Fanciful, of a Person Lately about Town* (1828 for 1827). Neither *Heath Flowers* nor *The Reverie*, announced in *New Monthly Magazine* 7 (1 February 1817), 57, and 8 (1 January 1818), 536, has been located.

4 Marsh cites H. Buxton Forman, Keats's *Works*, Glasgow edition (1901), IV:

41–42, on the presentation copy of *Poems* (owned by Dykes Campbell) having an inscription apparently in Webb's handwriting stating that it was given to him by Keats. Marsh also gives (pp. 332–33) Webb's poem published in *Literary Speculum* 2 (1822), 368.

5 Webb is linked to Hunt and Keats in two anonymous letters, "To the Editor of the *Anti-Gallican Monitor*" (8 June, 16 July 1817), reprinted in Schwartz, *KR*, pp. 77–83, where John Wilson (according to Schwartz) says that Keats is "the worst of the whole fry" of poets around Hunt; "His dedication is almost as bad as that of another youth who *patronized* Mr. *Hunt's* school. – (I think I saw a sonnet of his lately in the Anti-Gallican,) and is as perfectly incomprehensible." Schwartz identifies the other member of Hunt's school as Webb, since a sonnet by "C." (for Cornelius perhaps) appeared in the *Anti-Gallican* for 16 March 1817. If Schwartz is correct, then perhaps the so far undiscovered *Heath Flowers*, announced for February 1817, contained as its dedication the poem later used by *Blackwood's* to open the Cockney School attacks. Nicholas Roe, *John Keats and the Culture of Dissent* (Oxford: Clarendon Press, 1997), p. 129n, suggests that *Blackwood's* was quoting from a lost "Epistle to a Friend" sent to Maga by Webb with three sonnets in a letter of September 1817 (National Library of Scotland MS 4002).

6 Clarke, like Keats, was ushered into print by Hunt, with his first publications, "Walks round London" and a verse piece, "On Visiting a Beautiful Little Dell near Margate," appearing in the second volume (for 1820) of the pocket book.

7 Roe, *Keats and the Culture of Dissent*, pp. 274–75, transcribes from National Library of Scotland MS 4009, "Blackwood Papers 1822."

8 See Susan Egenolf's "Varnished Tales: History and Artifice in the Novel, 1789–1830," Ph.D. dissertation, Texas A&M University (1995), p. 145.

9 McGann, "Keats and the Historical Method in Literary Criticism" (1979), *The Beauty of Inflections: Literary Investigations in Historical Method and Theory* (Oxford: Clarendon Press, 1988), pp. 17–65; Levinson, *Keats's Life of Allegory: The Origins of a Style* (Oxford: Basil Blackwell, 1988), pp. 1–38.

10 Lockhart was not even the first to use the Cockney designation; the *Satirist* (13 [1 October 1813], 302–3) called "Mr. Examiner Hunt" the "Bard of Horsemonger Lane" (where Hunt was in prison for seditious libel) and noted that his attempts "to save Hampstead from oblivion" had managed to relieve all "cockney apprehensions on this head." On *Blackwood's*, see Margaret Oliphant, *Annals of a Publishing House: William Blackwood and His Sons, Their Magazine and Friends*, 2 vols. (New York: Scribner, 1987); Alan Lang Strout, "*Maga*, Champion of Shelley," *Studies in Philology* 29 (1932), 95–119; Strout, "Lockhart, Champion of Shelley," *TLS*, 12 August 1955, p. 468; Strout, *A Bibliography of Articles in Blackwood's Magazine, 1817–1825* (Lubbock: Texas Tech, 1959); and Charles E. Robinson, "Percy Bysshe Shelley, Charles Ollier, and William Blackwood: The Contexts of Early Nineteenth-Century Publishing," in *SR*, pp. 183–226. Kim Wheatley, in

"The *Blackwood's* Attacks on Leigh Hunt," *Nineteenth-Century Literature* 47 (June 1992), 1–31, counters readings of Lockhart as making either personal or class-based attacks, arguing for the extemporaneous literary quality of his reviews, as Lockhart creates Hunt and Z. within a self-deconstructing Gothic fiction that ends up writing him as much as he writes the reviews. I would stress that *Blackwood's* launches a political attack upon an ideological enemy.

11 Reprinted in *KR*, pp. 77–80 (p. 78).

12 Hunt also started the polemical battle with his political enemies. As early as his *Feast of Poets* (1811 in the *Reflector*; reprinted in an expanded version in 1814 and again in 1815), he had attacked many of his contemporaries, heaping abuse particularly upon Gifford, editor of the *Quarterly Review*. On the role of the *Feast* in the Cockney controversy, see Barnette Miller, *Leigh Hunt's Relations with Byron, Shelley and Keats* (New York: Columbia University Press, 1910), pp. 121–58.

13 Keats's attack on the French School and particularly Pope would infuriate Byron; members of the group did not always agree. P. M. S. Dawson's interesting "Byron, Shelley, and the 'New School,'" in *SR*, pp. 89–108, discusses Byron's and even Shelley's difficulties with Keats's poetry insofar as it was committed to the "system" of poetry set forth by Hunt, though their target is ultimately not Hunt but Wordsworth.

14 Hunt refers to part of this definition in his *Autobiography*, pp. 493–94: "The Cockney school of poetry is the most illustrious in England; for, to say nothing of Pope and Gray, who were both veritable Cockneys, 'born within the sound of Bow Bell,' Milton was so too; and Chaucer and Spenser were both natives of the city."

15 Geoffrey Bullough, "The Later History of Cockaigne," *Wiener Beiträge zur Englischen Philologie* 75 (1973), 22–35, finds *Blackwood's* establishing the link between the use of "Cockaigne" – originally an imaginary country marked by luxury and idleness – as a nickname for London and "Cockney" as a label for residents of part of London, a link already suggested in Johnson's *Dictionary* (1785 ed.).

16 Levinson, *Keats's Life of Allegory*, pp. 1–25. Hunt also was the target of such attacks; writing of his piece "The Florentine Lovers" published in the *Liberal, Blackwood's* asks, "But is there not something effeminate, Cockneyish, and Sporus-like, in a male writer speaking so of male lips? If Leigh Hunt be indeed an unfortunate woman, disguised in yellow breeches, this slaver about lips may be excusable; but if he really be of the sex assumed, nothing can be more loathsome" (12 [December 1822], 774). Marlon Ross, *The Contours of Masculine Desire* (Oxford University Press, 1989), pp. 170–71, and Rodney Stenning Edgecombe, *Leigh Hunt and the Poetry of Fancy* (London: Associated University Presses, 1994), pp. 25–37, note the connections between the Cockney School attacks and assaults on women writers. Susan Wolfson has done essential work on how Keats was "feminized" by the attacks in "Feminizing Keats," in *Critical Essays on John Keats*, ed. Hermione

de Almeida (Boston: G. K. Hall, 1990), pp. 317–56, and "Keats and the Manhood of the Poet," *European Romantic Review* 6 (Summer 1995), 1–37. Mary Wilson Carpenter has argued that attacks on Hunt's handling of sex might suggest a radical feminist potential in his writings: "The Hair of Medusa: Leigh Hunt, *Tait's Edinburgh Magazine*, and the Criticism of Female Beauty," in *LT*, pp. 17–40.

17   McGann, *Beauty of Inflections*, pp. 29–30.

18   Jones, "The 'Cockney' and the Nation, 1780–1988," in *Metropolis London: Histories and Representations since 1800*, ed. David Feldman and Gareth Stedman Jones (London: Routledge, 1989), pp. 280–81. Jones is primarily interested in the way the twentieth century draws on and manipulates an image of the cockney constructed during the 1890s.

19   McGann, *Beauty of Inflections*, p. 31. See also Christopher Ricks, *Keats and Embarrassment* (Oxford: Clarendon Press, 1974); John Bayley, "Keats and Reality," *Proceedings of the British Academy*, 1962, pp. 91–125; William Keach, "Cockney Couplets: Keats and the Politics of Style," *SiR* 25 (Summer 1986), 182–96; and Nicholas Roe, "Keats's Lisping Sedition," *Essays in Criticism* 52 (January 1992), 36–55. Edgecombe offers an interesting connection between the Cockney style and the rococo in *Hunt and the Poetry of Fancy*, pp. 17–50.

20   Smith, *The Politics of Language 1791–1819* (Oxford: Clarendon Press, 1984), p. 9.

21   As a number of scholars have pointed out, there is a tension between the attempts by *Blackwood's* to link the Hunt circle to a dangerous urban radical tradition and its efforts to dismiss the group as petty and marginal, as "suburban" poets; see Elizabeth Jones, "The Suburban School: Snobbery and Fear in the Attacks on Keats," *TLS*, 27 October 1995, pp. 14–15, and "Keats in the Suburbs," *KSJ* 45 (1996), 23–43; Wheatley, "The *Blackwood's* Attacks"; and Roe, "Keats's Lisping Sedition."

22   Hunt had already criticized the Lake School for parochialism and narrowness in the notes to his *Feast of Poets* (1814), where he speaks of their "affectation of universal superiority" (p. 77), argues that their government offices have robbed them of independence (p. 78), urges society and city life on Wordsworth (p. 107), and praises Byron as the cosmopolitan poet (p. 125); Byron's assault on the Lakers in *Don Juan* would seem to owe quite a bit to Hunt's position.

23   R. H. Horne, in an essay comparing Wordsworth and Hunt, argued that "Cockney" meant "pastoral, minus nature": *A New Spirit of the Age* (London: Smith, Elder, 1844), p. 316.

24   Curran, *Poetic Form and British Romanticism* (Oxford University Press, 1986), p. 114.

25   Reiman, "Introduction," p. viii.

26   J. W. Polidori, M.D., *Ximenes, The Wreath, and Other Poems* (London: Longman, Hurst, Rees, Orme & Bentley, 1819), p. ii.

27   Gilmartin, *Print Politics: The Press and Radical Opposition in Early Nineteenth-*

Century England (Cambridge University Press, 1997), pp. 195–226.

28 Blunden, *Leigh Hunt: A Biography* (1930, rpt. Hamden, Conn.: Shoe String, 1970), p. 47.

29 While Keats's interest in politics has long been questioned, it has recently been demonstrated how closely interwoven his poetry and politics are; see McGann, *Beauty of Inflections*; Levinson, *Keats's Life of Allegory*; Roe, *Keats and the Culture of Dissent*; the volume *Keats and History*; and the special issue of *SiR* (25 [Summer 1986]) edited by Susan Wolfson. On the move to historicize Keats, see Grant Scott, "Tabloid Keats," *European Romantic Review* 6 (Summer 1995), i–xii.

30 There were counterattacks by the group, mainly by Hunt in the *Examiner*, but also by Reynolds in the *Alfred, West of England Journal and General Advertiser* (6 October 1818, rpt. *Examiner*, 11 October 1818), and in a letter, probably by John Scott, to the editor of the *Morning Chronicle* (3 October 1818) which notes that Keats was being attacked because of the "war" being waged by the *Quarterly* against Hunt. Hazlitt penned a "Reply to 'Z.'" after *Blackwood's* (3 [1818], 550–52) issued "Hazlitt Cross-Questioned," but he did not publish it, since he instead brought suit against Blackwood. On the group's response to the attacks, for example, see Herschel Baker, *William Hazlitt* (Cambridge: Harvard University Press, 1962), pp. 370–81; Walter Jackson Bate, *John Keats* (Cambridge: Harvard University Press, 1963), pp. 224–26, 366–68; John O. Haydon, *The Romantic Reviewers* (University of Chicago Press, 1968), pp. 176–215; and Alan Lang Strout, "Hunt, Hazlitt, and *Maga*," *English Language Notes* 4 (June 1937), 151–59.

31 On the project of the *Liberal*, see William Marshall, *Byron, Shelley, Hunt, and the "Liberal"* (Philadelphia: University of Pennsylvania Press, 1960).

32 21 November 1822: Huntington Library MS 6601. See also Keats's letter to Woodhouse (21, 22 September 1819), where he speculates that someone is detaining and opening his mail.

33 Though as late as 1821 in his *Letter to John Murray Esq.*, Byron, while raising questions about the Cockney School, still praises Hunt as a man and a poet, though disagreeing with him on Pope and poetic theory: *The Complete Miscellaneous Prose*, ed. Andrew Nicholson (Oxford: Clarendon Press, 1991), pp. 156–57.

34 See, for example, Lockhart's first Cockney School attack, in *Blackwood's* 2 (October 1817), 38–41, where he exclaims, after noting that Hunt asserted a connection with Byron, "How must the haughty spirit of Lara and Harold contemn the subaltern sneaking of our modern tufthunter"; Lockhart's review of *The Revolt of Islam* in *Blackwood's* 4 (January 1819), 475–82, where he, noting that Shelley "is of the 'COCKNEY SCHOOL,' so far as his opinions are concerned," also states that "Mr Shelly, whatever his errors may have been, is a scholar, a gentleman, and a poet; and he must therefore despise from his soul the only eulogies to which he has hitherto been accustomed – paragraphs from the Examiner, and sonnets from Johnny Keats"; and

Lockhart's review of *Prometheus Unbound* in *Blackwood's* 7 (September 1820), 679–87, where he defends his attack on Keats, saying, "The truth is, we from the beginning saw marks of feeling and power in Mr Keats' verses, which made us think it very likely, he might become a real poet of England, provided he could be persuaded to give up all the tricks of Cockneyism, and forswear for ever the thin potations of Mr Leigh Hunt." Hunt would later write caustically to Clarke, "The other day, there was an Ode in Blackwood in *honour of the memory of Shelley*; and I look for one to Keats. I hope this will give you faith in glimpses of the golden age" (11 February [no year], in *Recollections*, p. 224). Even Cornelius Webb could be partially rescued from the Cockney label in a review of his *Glances of Life* in, of all places, the *Quarterly Review* (57 [September 1836], 223–29).

Blackwood's was particularly at pains to separate Byron from Hunt. In its review of the *Liberal* (12 [December 1822], 700), it called on Byron to "cut the Cockney." When Byron continued to work with Hunt, *Blackwood's* responded with an attack that recalls its most vicious assaults on Keats: Byron is "so enervated by the unworthy Delilahs which have enslaved his imagination, as to be reduced to the foul office of displaying blind buffooneries before the Philistines of Cockaigne ... I feel a moral conviction that his lordship must have taken the Examiner, the Liberal, the Rimini, the Round Table, as his model ... Indeed there are some verses which have all the appearance of having been interpolated by the King of the Cockneys" (14 [July 1823], 88–89). As always, the ultimate target is Hunt.

35 Matthews, "Introduction," in *Keats: The Critical Heritage* (New York: Barnes & Noble, 1971), p. 24. See Willard B. Pope, "Leigh Hunt & His Companions," *KSJ* 8 (1959), 89–91, for Haydon's account of his attack on Hunt and how he almost allowed Lockhart to print it over Lockhart's pseudonym, Z.

CHAPTER 2. THE HUNT ERA

1 On the group's interactions, beyond accounts by the participants (i.e. Hunt, Clarke, Procter, Medwin, Peacock) and the standard biographies (by i.e. Bate, Ward, Gittings, White, Holmes, Blunden, Jones), see Donald Reiman's fine "Keats and Shelley: Personal and Literary Relations," *SC*, v: 399–427; and Barnette Miller, *Leigh Hunt's Relations with Byron, Shelley and Keats* (New York: Columbia University Press, 1910).

2 On Hunt, see, for example, Cosmo Monkhouse, *Life of Leigh Hunt* (London: Walter Scott, 1893); Edmund Blunden, *Leigh Hunt: A Biography* (1930, rpt. Hamden, Conn.: Shoe String, 1970); Louis Landré, *Leigh Hunt (1784–1859): Contribution à l'histoire du Romantisme anglais*, 2 vols. (Paris: Société d'Edition, 1935); James R. Thompson, *Leigh Hunt* (Boston: Twayne, 1977); Ann Blainey, *Immortal Boy: A Portrait of Leigh Hunt* (New York: St. Martin's, 1985); Rodney Stenning Edgecombe, *Leigh Hunt and the Poetry of Fancy* (London: Associated University Presses, 1994); and *LT*.

3 Letter to Clarke, 21 November 1827, enclosed with letter to Isabella Towers, *Letters of William Hazlitt*, ed. Herschel Moreland Sides with Willard Hallam Bonner and Gerald Lahey (New York University Press, 1978), p. 347. On editing Hazlitt's letters, see Charles E. Robinson, "William Hazlitt to His Publishers, Friends, and Creditors: Twenty-Seven New Holograph Letters," *KSR* 2 (1987): 3–4 and the reviews cited on p. 3n.

4 *Literary Recollections of Barry Cornwall*, ed. Richard Willard Armour (Boston: Meador, 1936), pp. 86–87.

5 *Medwin's Conversations of Lord Byron*, ed. Ernest J. Lovell, Jr. (Princeton University Press, 1966), pp. 253–54.

6 Donald H. Reiman, "Leigh Hunt in Literary History: A Response," in *LT*, p. 74.

7 Cameron, "Leigh Hunt," in *Romantic Rebels: Essays on Shelley and His Circle*, ed. Kenneth Neill Cameron (Cambridge: Harvard University Press, 1973), p. 159. Cameron quotes Saintsbury (p. 155) from *The Cambridge History of English Literature*, XII: 245. Archer's comments come from his edition of *Dramatic Essays by Leigh Hunt* (London: Walter Scott, 1894), p. vii. See also Edmund Blunden, *Leigh Hunt's "Examiner" Examined* (London: Cobden-Sanderson, 1928), and the introductions to *Leigh Hunt's Literary Criticism*, ed. L. H. Houtchens and C. W. Houtchens (New York: Columbia University Press, 1956), and *Leigh Hunt's Political and Occasional Essays*, ed. L. H. Houtchens and C. W. Houtchens (New York: Columbia University Press, 1962).

8 Thompson, *The Making of the English Working Class* (1963; rpt. New York: Random House, 1966), p. 675.

9 Reiman, "Hunt in Literary History," pp. 77–78.

10 See Colbert Keaney, "B. R. Haydon and *The Examiner*," *KSJ* 27 (1978), 108–32.

11 See Carl R. Woodring, "Leigh Hunt as Political Essayist," in *Leigh Hunt's Political and Occasional Essays*, p. 35. Southey wrote in "On the State of Public Opinion, and the Political Reformers" (1816, rpt. in *Essays, Moral and Political* [London: John Murray, 1832]), "Marat and Hebert followed in the train of Voltaire and Rousseau; Mr. Examiner Hunt does but blow the trumpet to usher in Mr. Orator Hunt in his tandem, with the tri-color flag before him" (I: 368).

12 Thorton Hunt, *Proserpina*, in Blunden, *Hunt*, p. 359. See also Molly Tatchell, "Elizabeth Kent and *Flora Domestica*," *Keats–Shelley Memorial Bulletin* 27 (1976), 15–18; and Alan Bewell, "Keats's 'Realm of Flora,'" in *New Romanticism: Theory and Critical Practice*, ed. David L. Clark and Donald C. Goellnicht (University of Toronto Press, 1994), pp. 71–100.

13 See Derek Hudson, *Thomas Barnes of the "Times"* (Cambridge University Press, 1944).

14 Woodring, "Leigh Hunt as Political Essayist," p. 41.

15 See Hazlitt's comments on Owen in *Examiner*, 4 April 1816, pp. 493–95; Peter H. Marshall, *William Godwin* (New Haven: Yale University Press,

1984), pp. 310–11.

16 William St. Clair, *The Godwins and the Shelleys: The Biography of a Family* (Baltimore: Johns Hopkins University Press, 1989), p. 425; Marshall, *Godwin*, p. 341.

17 See Kenneth E. Kendall, *Leigh Hunt's "Reflector"* (New York: Humanities Press, 1971).

18 While Moore is not often thought of as part of Hunt's circle, Clarke referred to him as Hunt's friend (*Recollections*, p. 44; see also Howard Mumford Jones, *The Harp That Once – A Chronicle of the Life of Thomas Moore* [New York: Holt, 1937), pp. 142–43, 147). Moore wrote verses in praise of the imprisoned Hunt, Hunt reprinted a number of Moore's poems in the *Examiner* (for example, "Little Man and Little Soul," 18 August 1813; "The New Costume of the Ministers," 1 November 1812; and "The Sale of Tools," 31 January 1813), and he adopted the pseudonym "Harry Brown," a tribute to the "Thomas Brown" of Moore's *Two-Penny Post Bag*. Shelley wrote to his publisher Charles Ollier to ask, "Whenever I publish, send copies of my books to the following people for me. Mr. Hunt Godwin Hogg Peacock Keats Thos. Moore Hor. Smith Lord Byron (at Murrays)" (9 September 1819, *SL* II: 118). This is a pretty good list of the central members of the circle, with Hunt having pride of place, and thus the inclusion of Moore would seem to be significant.

19 In a letter to his sometime mentor John Freeman Milward Dovaston, 19 July 1814, Reynolds indicates that he met Hunt during the period of his imprisonment at Colbath Fields: "And I have the pleasure to say that Hunt, (of the Reflector, to whom I have been introduced and can now boast of as a Friend) thinks very highly of it [the *Inquirer*, a journal modelled on Hunt's *Reflector*]. Of this Gentleman's Genius I entertain very great ideas, and he certainly has the richest fancy (except My Ld Byron & Moore) of any Man living." In *Letters from Lambeth: The Correspondence of the Reynolds Family with John Freeman Milward Dovaston 1808–1815*, ed. Joanna Richardson (Woodbridge, Suffolk: Boydell & Brewer, 1981), p. 118.

20 See, for example, the satire "Don Juan Unread" in *Blackwood's* (6 [November 1819], 194), where Byron is placed with the Cockneys (as is, interestingly, Tom Moore): "There's Godwin's daughter, Shelley's wife, / A writing fearful stories; / There's Hazlitt, who, with Hunt and Keats / Brays forth in Cockney chorus / There's pleasant Thomas Moore, a lad / Who sings of Rose and Fanny; / Why throw away these wits so gay / To take up Don Giovanni." Thorton Hunt also included Byron in his positive description of the circle in *Proserpina*, pp. 363–64.

21 Charles E. Robinson, *Shelley and Byron: The Snake and Eagle Wreathed in Fight* (Baltimore: Johns Hopkins University Press, 1976), pp. 2–3, 4–5. See also John Buxton, *Byron and Shelley: The History of a Friendship* (New York: Harcourt Brace & World, 1968), and William D. Brewer, *The Byron–Shelley Conversation* (Gainesville: University Press of Florida, 1994).

22 See *Examiner*, 23 April 1815, p. 269; 11 June 1815, p. 381; 30 July 1815, p. 491;

21 April 1816, pp. 249–50. Hunt's poem appeared on 28 April 1816, pp. 266–67.

23 On Byron and Hunt, see William H. Marshall, *Byron, Shelley, Hunt, and "The Liberal"* (Philadelphia: University of Pennsylvania Press, 1960), pp. 2–11.

24 See, for example, Marjorie Levinson, *Keats's Life of Allegory: The Origins of a Style* (Oxford: Basil Blackwell, 1988), pp. 15–16, 18–19, 22–23; P. M. S. Dawson, "Byron, Shelley, and the 'New School,'" in *SR*, pp. 89–108. Byron's intellectual disagreements with the Cockneys are clarified in the Pope/Bowles controversy; see his unpublished "Some Observations upon an Article in *Blackwood's Edinburgh Magazine*" (1820) and *Letter to John Murray Esq.* (1821), in *The Complete Miscellaneous Prose*, ed. Andrew Nicholson (Oxford: Clarendon Press, 1991), pp. 88–119, 120–60.

25 See also Beth Lau, *Keats's Reading of Romantic Poets* (Ann Arbor: University of Michigan Press, 1991), pp. 115–46; and Wolf Hirst, "Lord Byron Cuts a Figure," *Byron Journal* 13 (1985), 36–51.

26 See, among others, Asa Briggs, "The Language of 'Class' in Early Nineteenth-Century England," in *The Collected Essays of Asa Briggs*, 2 vols. (Urbana: University of Illinois Press, 1985), I: 3–33; Harold Perkin, *The Origins of Modern English Society 1780–1880* (London: Routledge & Kegan Paul, 1969), pp. 176–217; Raymond Williams, "Class," in *Keywords: A Vocabulary of Culture and Society* (Oxford University Press, 1976), pp. 51–59.

27 See Eleanor M. Gates, "Leigh Hunt, Lord Byron, and Mary Shelley: The Long Goodbye," *KSJ* 35 (1986), 149–67.

28 Klancher, *The Making of English Reading Audiences, 1790–1832* (Madison: University of Wisconsin Press, 1987), p. 8.

29 Fraistat, "Illegitimate Shelley: Radical Piracy and the Textual Edition as Cultural Performance," *PMLA* 109 (May 1994), 409–23.

30 Blunden, *Hunt*, p. 218.

31 Derek Hudson, *History of "The Times"*, vol. I, *"The Thunderer" in the Making, 1785–1841* (New York: Macmillan, 1935), p. 486.

32 The reference to Lamb is to his "Essay on Ears." On the musical evenings, see David R. Cheney (ed.), *Musical Evenings or Selections, Vocal and Instrumental, by Leigh Hunt* (Columbia: University of Missouri Press, 1964). The theaters were important meeting places for the group. Clarke's father, also an admirer of Hunt, met him at a performance of *Timon of Athens* starring Kean (*Recollections*, p. 18). Hunt, of course, had been a theatrical reviewer, as had Hazlitt, and Clarke, Reynolds, and Keats all served as reviewers for the *Examiner* or the *Champion*. Keats imagines a meeting in the theater between Hunt and Reynolds in one of his letters: "I think I see you and Hunt meeting in the Pit" (to J. H. Reynolds, 21 September 1817, *KL*, I: 162).

33 *Literary Recollections of Barry Cornwall*, pp. 84–85.

34 See E. Pereira, "Sonnet Contests and Verse Compliments in the Keats–Hunt Circle," *Unisa English Studies* 25 (May 1987), 13–23; Edmund Blunden, "The Keats–Shelley Poetry Contests," *Notes and Queries* 199 (December 1954), 546.

35 *Journals*, p. 163. This is apparently the same discussion mentioned by Clarke in which Hunt and Coulson debated Shelley and Hazlitt on the merits of the monarchy (*Recollections*, p. 26).

36 Procter, *Autobiographical Fragment and Biographical Notes with Personal Sketches of Contemporaries, Unpublished Lyrics and Letters of Literary Friends*, ed. Coventry Patmore (London: Bell, 1877), p. 125.

37 *The Autobiography and Memoirs of Benjamin Robert Haydon*, ed. from his *Journals* by Tom Taylor (New York: Harcourt Brace, 1926), I: 253.

38 Procter, *Autobiographical Fragment*, p. 197.

39 Thompson, *Making of the English Working Class*, p. 633.

40 See Peter Thorslev, "Post-Waterloo Liberalism: The Second Generation," *SiR* 28 (Fall 1989), 437–61.

41 Edmund Burke, *Reflections on the Revolution in France*, ed. Conor Cruise O'Brien (Harmondsworth: Penguin, 1968), p. 175.

42 "Preface," in *Laon and Cythna*, *The Complete Works of Percy Bysshe Shelley*, ed. Roger Ingpen and Walter E. Peck (1926–30 rpt. New York: Gordian Press, 1965), I: 241–42.

43 Thompson, *Making of the English Working Class*, p. 747.

44 Raymond Williams, *Marxism and Literature* (Oxford University Press, 1977), esp. p. 119.

45 M. H. Abrams, "English Romanticism: The Spirit of the Age," in *Romanticism and Consciousness*, ed. Harold Bloom (New York: Norton, 1970), p. 111.

46 Jerome J. McGann, *The Romantic Ideology: A Critical Investigation* (University of Chicago, 1983), p. 1.

47 Scrivener, *Radical Shelley: The Philosophical Anarchism and Utopian Thought of Percy Bysshe Shelley* (Princeton University Press, 1982), pp. 198–210.

48 See, for example, the *Quarterly Review* 21 (April 1819), 460, on Shelley: "This is one of that industrious knot of authors, the tendency of whose works we have in our late Numbers exposed to the caution of our readers – novel, poem, romance, letters, tours, critique, lecture and essay follow one another, framed to the same measure, and in subjection to the same key-note, *while the sweet undersong of the weekly journal, filling up all pauses, strengthening all weaknesses, smoothing all abruptness, harmonises the whole strain*" (emphasis added).

49 While Keats remembered Shelley "advising me not to publish my first-blights, on Hampstead heath" (16 August 1820, *KL*, II: 286), Keats's publisher recalled Shelley speaking to him "about the printing of a little volume of Keats's first poems"; see John Dix, *Pen and Ink Sketches of Poets, Preachers, and Politicians* (London: David Bogue, 1846), p. 144, and *SC*, V: 408. Charles E. Robinson, "Percy Bysshe Shelley, Charles Ollier, and William Blackwood: The Contexts of Early Nineteenth-Century Publishing," in *SR*, p. 188, suggests that Shelley paid for the advertising for Keats's volume, which was announced in newspapers along with Shelley's *A Proposal for Putting Reform to the Vote*.

50 On Shelley and audience, see Stephen C. Behrendt, *Shelley and His Audiences*

(Lincoln: University of Nebraska Press, 1989). On Keats, see Andrew Bennett, *Keats, Narrative and Audience: The Posthumous Life of Writing* (Cambridge University Press, 1994). For broader treatments, see, for example, A. S. Collins, *The Profession of Letters: A Study of the Relation of Author to Patron, Publisher, and Public, 1780–1832* (London: Routledge, 1928); Jon P. Klancher, *English Reading Audience*; and Clifford Siskin, *The Historicity of Romantic Discourse* (Oxford University Press, 1988), esp. pp. 106f.

51 Arthur F. Marotti, *John Donne, Coterie Poet* (Madison: University of Wisconsin Press, 1986); Harold Love, *Scribal Publication in Seventeenth-Century England* (Oxford: Clarendon Press, 1993); and Margaret J. M. Ezell, *The Patriarch's Wife: Literary Evidence and the History of the Family* (Chapel Hill: University of North Carolina Press, 1987), "The *Gentleman's Journal* and the Commercialization of Restoration Coterie Literary Practices," *Modern Philology* 89 (1992), 323–40, and "Reading Pseudonyms in Seventeenth-Century English Coterie Literature," *Essays in Literature* 21 (Spring 1994), 14–25.

52 Ezell, "'To Be Your Daughter in Your Pen': The Social Functions of Literature in the Writings of Lady Elizabeth Brackley and Lady Jane Cavendish," *Huntington Library Quarterly* 5 (1988), 281–96.

53 Jean-François Lyotard and Jean-Loup Thébaud, *Just Gaming*, trans. Wald Godzich (Minneapolis: University of Minnesota Press, 1985), p. 9, quoted in Bennett, *Keats, Narrative and Audience*, p. 4.

54 Ezell, *Patriarch's Wife*, pp. 65–66.

55 W. M. Rossetti gives the account, which was passed on to him by Browning, who had heard it from Hunt; see Shelley, *Poetical Works*, ed. W. M. Rossetti (1870), II: 602. Hunt also published "A Hate Song. Dialogue between the Poet and a Lady" under his "Harry Brown" pseudonym in the *Examiner* (22 August 1819, p. 537) and again in the *Indicator* (17 January 1821).

56 *Blackwood's* 6 (October 1819), 76; see also the "Cockney School No. V," 5 (April 1819), 97–100, and John Poole, *Two Papers: A Theatrical Critique and an Essay (Being No. 999 of the Pretender) on Sonnet-Writing and Sonnet-Writers in General, Including a Sonnet on Myself; Attributed to the Editor of the Ex-m-n-r* (London: John Miller, 1819).

57 See Stillinger, *Complete Poems*, p. 426, and "Keats's Extempore Effusions and the Question of Intentionality," in *Romantic Revisions*, ed. Robert Brinkley and Keith Hanley (Cambridge University Press, 1992), pp. 309–10. Tom Keats indicated on the original draft that the poem was "Written in 15 minutes," suggesting it was written in a sonnet-writing competition. Hunt's sonnets to Shelley were published in *Foliage* along with the sonnet-contest poems "To the Grasshopper and the Cricket" and "The Nile."

58 *Shelley's Poetry and Prose*, p. 103n. Coldwell, "Charles Cowden Clarke's Commonplace Book and Its Relationship to Keats," *KSJ* 10 (Winter 1961), 90. One wonders if Hunt's "To T. L. H., Six Years Old, During a Sickness" and Lamb's "To T. L. H. a Child," both published in the *Examiner* – though six months apart – and both copied into Mary Shelley's

journal for 1 February 1817, were part of another writing contest.

59 On the crowning incident as a contest, see Walter Jackson Bate, *John Keats* (Cambridge: Harvard University Press, 1963), pp. 137–40, and the note to this poem in Stillinger's edition, p. 427. Woodhouse's note opposite "God of the golden bow" in W² tells the story of the crowning, and lines 1 and 9 of Keats's poem suggest the time limits of a sonnet contest.

60 Hunt and Samuel Adams Lee (eds.), *Book of the Sonnet* (Boston: Roberts Brothers, 1867), I: 276.

61 See the Leigh Browne-Lockyer collection of manuscript volumes, commonplace books, and the like held at the Keats House, Hampstead (marked LBL and KH and hereafter so cited); Clayton E. Hudnall, "John Hamilton Reynolds, James Rice, and Benjamin Bailey in the Leigh Browne-Lockyer Collection," *KSJ* 19 (1970), 11–37; and Leonidas M. Jones, *The Life of John Hamilton Reynolds* (Hanover, N.H.: University Press of New England, 1984), pp. 58–60, 63–64, 76–77.

62 See Hudnall, "Leigh Browne-Lockyer Collection," p. 36; and Paul Kaufman, "The Reynolds–Hood Commonplace Book: A Fresh Appraisal," *KSJ* 10 (Winter 1961), 50.

63 Darnton, "What Is the History of Books?" in *Reading in America: Literature and Social History*, ed. Cathy N. Davidson (Baltimore: Johns Hopkins University Press, 1989), pp. 27–52.

64 Hélène Cixous, "Castration or Decapitation?" trans. Annette Kuhn, *Signs* 7 (1981), 36–55.

65 University of Iowa MS c36n. The poem appeared in the *Examiner* (12 May 1816) and *Foliage* (1818).

66 The copy of Hunt's volume is held at the University of Iowa (828 H94lf 1815 cop. 3); Reynolds's volume of *Poems* is at the Houghton Library, Harvard. On the Shelley insertions, see Ingpen and Peck, *Works*, IV: 407.

67 On this volume, held at the Houghton Library, Harvard, see Jack Stillinger, *The Texts of Keats's Poems* (Cambridge: Harvard University Press, 1974), p. 59. As a letter from Hazlitt to Towers (21 November 1827, *Letters of William Hazlitt*, pp. 345–46) makes clear, she also asked for pieces from others; Hazlitt sent her a version of "On Personal Identity" (*CWH*, XVII: 268–69).

68 Stillinger, "Keats's Extempore Effusions," p. 315. He extends his argument in *Multiple Authorship and the Myth of Solitary Genius* (Oxford University Press, 1991), pp. 25–49. See also Zachary Leader, *Revision and Romantic Authorship* (Oxford: Clarendon Press, 1996), pp. 262–315.

69 The phrase is Peacock's, in his *Memories of Percy Bysshe Shelley*, vol. VIII of *The Works of Thomas Love Peacock* (London: Constable, 1934), p. 141. Certain aspects of Peacock's version have been challenged; see Frederick L. Jones, "The Revision of *Laon and Cythna*," *Journal of English and German Philology* 32 (1933), 366–72. Moore also read the poem, presumably for Longman's; in any event, he sent "a most kind and encouraging letter," as Shelley wrote to Ollier (11 December 1817, *SL*, I: 580).

70 See MS of *Rimini* with Byron's comments, British Library, Ashley 906.

71 There was a vogue for Robin Hood in the group: Hunt wrote a series of Robin Hood poems, his ballads published in the *Indicator* (15, 22 November 1820); and publisher John Taylor wrote three sonnets on Sherwood Forest. Taylor's sonnets are reproduced in Mabel A. E. Steele, "The Authorship of 'The Poet' and Other Sonnets: Selections from a 19th Century Manuscript Anthology," *KSJ* 4 (Winter 1956), 70–80. See also Thomas R. Mitchell, "Keats's 'Outlawry' in 'Robin Hood,'" *Studies in English Literature* 34 (Autumn 1994), 753–69.

72 To Haydon, 22 November 1816, *The Letters of John Hamilton Reynolds*, ed. Leonidas M. Jones (Lincoln: University of Nebraska Press, 1973), p. 7.

73 In the 1 February 1818 *Examiner*, p. 73, we find this: "TO THE EDITOR OF THE EXAMINER. SIR,– The subject which suggested the beautiful Sonnet, in a late number, signed 'Gilrastes' [Shelley's pseudonym in the 11 January *Examiner*], produced also the enclosed from another pen, which, if you deem it worthy insertion, is at your service. H.S." Smith's poem follows, entitled here "Ozymandias" but included in his *Amarynthus* volume under the longer title.

74 To Sarah Leigh, 24 November 1815, transcribed in Hudnall, "Leigh Brown-Lockyer Collection," p. 34.

75 Reynolds to Richard M. Milnes, 22 June 1848, *Letters of Reynolds*, p. 66.

76 Butler, *Peacock Displayed: A Satirist in His Context* (London: Routledge & Kegan Paul, 1979), pp. 66–67, 99.

77 Jones, *Life of Reynolds*, p. 19. See Reynolds to Dovaston, 11 and 14 March 1810 (*Letters from Lambeth*, p. 49): "I have to tell you that I and some friends have opened a work among ourselves after the stile of the spectator now what I want of you is to send me a few Essays and I will insert them in the 'Inspector' (the name of our book) I have written the first essay which is received with *universal applause*."

78 See Huntington Library MS HM 12242, which seems to contain among other things notes for HM 12248 "Memorable Names by Leigh Hunt, An Original Draft of an Unpublished Book"; the Novello commonplace book, Special Collections, University of Iowa; and "Autograph MS of Ultra-Crepidarius in note book with MS notes of day by day sea-journey to Italy from England, 1822–23 and other poems and prose reflections," Beinecke Library, Yale University.

79 Clarke's commonplace book, held in the Novello–Clarke Collection, Brotherton Collection, University of Leeds, has been summarized and excerpted by John Barnard in "Charles Cowden Clarke's 'Cockney' Commonplace Book," in *KH*, pp. 65–87. See also Coldwell, "Clarke's Commonplace Book," pp. 83–95, and Roe, *Keats and the Culture of Dissent*, pp. 93–105.

80 See Edmund Blunden, "Keats's Friend Mathew," *English* 1 (1936), 46–55.

81 "The Literary Diary or, Improved Common-Place-Book," signed "J. H. Reynolds Aug. 1816," Bristol Central Library. Reynolds wrote an essay in

which he discusses his use of commonplace books: "From Living Authors, a Dream" (*Scots Magazine*, August 1820, rpt. in *Selected Prose of John Hamilton Reynolds*, ed. Leonidas M. Jones [Cambridge: Harvard University Press, 1966], pp. 251–58).

82 Kaufman, "Reynolds–Hood Commonplace Book," p. 47.

83 Ibid., p. 46; Stillinger, *Texts of Keats's Poems*, pp. 47–50. Stillinger notes that Woodhouse refers to another volume, "Reynolds's volume of Poetry," that apparently included copies of poems by Keats, Reynolds, and Hunt. See *KC*, I: 63–65, a letter (23 November 1818) to Taylor from Woodhouse, who proposes his own ending to Keats's "In Drear-Nighted December," as we again see a coterie member willing to alter a friend's verse.

84 See Jones, *Life of Reynolds*, pp. 33–36.

85 The Clarke manuscript, from a later period, is held at the University of Iowa (MS c58h). Bailey's essay, which he wanted Taylor to publish in 1818, is part of his scrapbook, held in the Houghton Library, Harvard; see Hyder E. Rollins, "Benjamin Bailey's Scrapbook," *KSJ* 5 (Winter 1956), 15–30.

86 The group had also planted six sweetbriars in commemoration of their friendship, and Bailey wrote inscriptions for various saplings planted at Slade; see Hudnall, "Leigh Browne-Lockyer Collection," p. 17. It is worth noting (as does Hudnall) a parallel incident: Keats and Bailey, while boating near Oxford, found "one particularly nice nest which we have christened 'Reynolds's Cove'" (Keats, letter to Reynolds, 21 September 1817, *KL*, I: 162).

87 On the organization of romantic volumes of verse, including ones by Keats and Shelley, see Neil Fraistat's fine *The Poem and the Book: Interpreting Collections of Romantic Poetry* (Chapel Hill: University of North Carolina Press, 1985).

88 See G. E. Bentley, Jr., "Leigh Hunt's Literary Pocket-Book, 1818–1822: A Romantic Sourcebook," *Victorian Periodicals Newsletter* 8 (December 1975), 125–28.

89 On Taylor, see Edmund Blunden, *Keats's Publisher: A Memoir of John Taylor* (1936, rpt. London: Cape, 1940); and Tim Chilcott, *A Publisher and His Circle: The Life and Work of John Taylor, Keats's Publisher* (London: Routledge & Kegan Paul, 1972). Other publishers brought out several works by members of the circle, the most famous being John Murray, who was, of course, Byron's publisher and who also printed, for example, Hunt's *Story of Rimini*. Again, James Cawthorn and John Martin published Reynolds's *Safie*, Hunt's *Feast of Poets*, and Cam Hobhouse's *Journey through Albania*, and Martin himself had published Charles Wentworth Dilke's continuation of Dodsley's volumes of early plays (1816) and Charles Armitage Brown's opera *Narensky* (1814).

90 Hunt was a particularly important reviewer for the young poets, offering reviews in the *Examiner* of Shelley's *Revolt of Islam* (25 January, 1 and 22 February, 1 March 1818), *Rosalind and Helen* (9 May 1819), and *Prometheus Unbound* (9, 16, and 23 June 1823) and of Keats's *Poems* (1 June, 6 and 13 July

1817); he reviewed Keats's 1820 volume in the *Indicator* (2 and 9 August 1820), where he also treated Shelley's *The Cenci* (25 July 1820). To give additional examples: Hazlitt reviewed Hunt's *Rimini* in the *Edinburgh Review* (June 1816), Lamb reviewed Keats's 1820 volume in the *Examiner* (30 July 1820), Reynolds offered in the *Champion* accounts of Keats's *Poems* (9 March 1817) and Hazlitt's *Characters of Shakespeare's Plays* (20 and 27 July 1817) and defended *Endymion* in the *Alfred* (6 October 1818, rpt. *Examiner*, 11 October 1818), and Shelley wrote a review of Peacock's *Rhododaphne* for the *Examiner*, which, however, never appeared.

CHAPTER 3. JOHN KEATS, COTERIE POET

1 Although see, for example, Martin Aske, *Keats and Hellenism* (Cambridge University Press, 1985), pp. 38–52; John Barnard, *John Keats* (Cambridge University Press, 1987), pp. 15–34; Andrew Bennett, *Keats, Narrative and Audience: The Posthumous Life of Writing* (Cambridge University Press, 1994), pp. 61–72; Morris Dickstein, *Keats and His Poetry: A Study in Development* (University of Chicago Press, 1971), pp. 26–52; Marjorie Levinson, *Keats's Life of Allegory: The Origins of a Style* (Oxford: Basil Blackwell, 1988), pp. 227–54; and Susan J. Wolfson, *The Questioning Presence: Wordsworth, Keats, and the Interrogative Mode in Romantic Poetry* (Ithaca: Cornell University Press, 1986), pp. 206–26.

2 For an account of the early reception history of Keats, see G. M. Matthews, *Keats: The Critical Heritage* (New York: Barnes & Noble, 1971), pp. 1–37, and J. R. MacGillivray, *Keats: A Bibliography and Reference Guide with an Essay on Keats' Reputation* (University of Toronto Press, 1949), pp. xi–lxxxi, 63–75; for an account of early biographies of Keats, see William Henry Marquess, *Lives of the Poet: The First Century of Keats Biography* (University Park: Pennsylvania State University Press, 1985). For an excellent account of the "aesthetization" of Keats, see Nicholas Roe, "Introduction," in *KH*, pp. 1–16. See also Susan Wolfson, "Keats Enters History: Autopsy, *Adonais*, and the Fame of Keats," in *KH*, pp. 17–45; and Donald C. Goellnicht, "The Politics of Reading and Writing," in *New Romanticisms: Theory and Critical Practice*, ed. Goellnicht and David L. Clark (University of Toronto Press, 1994), pp. 101–31.

3 Barnard, *Keats*, p. 15.

4 Bate, *John Keats* (Cambridge: Harvard University Press, 1964), p. 73; de Man, "The Negative Road," in his edition *Selected Poetry of John Keats* (New York: New American Library, 1966), p. 11.

5 Earlier work on Keats and history includes Clarence De Witt Thorpe, "Keats's Interest in Politics and World Affairs," *PMLA* 46 (1931), 1228–45; Carl Woodring, *Politics in English Romantic Poetry* (Cambridge University Press, 1970), pp. 77–83; and June Q. Kock, "Politics in Keats's Poetry," *Journal of English and German Philology* 71 (1972), 491–501.

6 'Contamination" is a term used by both Ralph Cohen, "Generating

Literary Histories," and Edward Said, "Figures, Configurations, Trans-figurations," to describe the entrance of the ideological into the literary, in *New Historical Literary Study: Essays on Reproducing Texts, Representing History*, ed. Jeffrey N. Cox and Larry J. Reynolds (Princeton University Press, 1993), pp. 39–53, 316–30.

7　Levine, "Introduction: Reclaiming the Aesthetic," in *Aesthetics and Ideology*, ed. Levine (New Brunswick, N.J.: Rutgers University Press, 1994), p. 4.

8　Keach, "Cockney Couplets: Keats and the Politics of Style," *SiR* 25 (Summer 1986), 190.

9　See Nicholas Roe, *John Keats and the Culture of Dissent* (Oxford: Clarendon Press, 1997), pp. 27–50, 202–29.

10　See, for example, the *Examiner* for 23, 30 September 1810. One can see why Woodhouse said (probably incorrectly) of the latter poem, "written prob-ably when much in company with Leigh Hunt" (Allot, p. 17). See also Vincent Newey, "Keats, History and the Poets," in *KH*, p. 167.

11　On Keats's examination at Apothecaries' Hall and the date at which he could practice, see Hermione de Almeida, *Romantic Medicine and John Keats* (Oxford University Press, 1991), pp. 22–33; Bate, *John Keats*, pp. 66, 703–94; Donald C. Goellnicht, *The Poet-Physician: Keats and Medical Science* (University of Pittsburgh Press, 1984), pp. 12–47; and William Hale-White, *Keats as Doctor and Patient* (1938, rpt. Folcroft, Pa.: Folcroft Press, 1970), pp. 30–32.

12　See Bate, *Keats*, p. 195, and even Edmund Blunden, *Leigh Hunt: A Biography* (1930, rpt. Hamden, Conn.: Shoe String, 1970), p. 96. It is worth noting that the *Champion* probably got this poem not from Keats but from Reynolds, who had received a copy in a letter from Keats (17 April 1817, *KL*, I: 132) (see Jack Stillinger, *The Texts of Keats's Poems* [Cambridge: Harvard University Press, 1974], p. 71). On Keats's poetry in the *Examiner*, see Terence Allan Hoagwood, "Keats and Social Context: 'Lamia,'" *Studies in English Literature* 29 (1989), 675–97; and John Kandl, "Private Lyrics in the Public Sphere: Leigh Hunt's *Examiner* and the Construction of the Public 'John Keats,'" *KSJ* 44 (1995), 84–101.

13　See Greg Kucich's fine *Keats, Shelley, and Romantic Spenserianism* (University Park: Pennsylvania State University Press, 1991).

14　The only significant difference in organization between Keats's volume and Hunt's is that Hunt closes with a set of translations, including a final long poem by Catullus. This structure, almost a mark of Hunt-circle verse, is also found in Keats's 1820 volume, which opens with three narrative poems, has a section of shorter poems, and closes with the classicizing "Hyperion" fragment in the place of Hunt's translations. Again, Reynolds's *Garden of Florence* volume of 1821 opens with two narrative poems and a long descriptive piece, "Devon," before going on to shorter verses including a number of sonnets and an epistle and closing with another narrative, "The Ladye of Provence."

15　See Stuart M. Sperry, *Richard Woodhouse's Interleaved and Annotated Copy of Keats's "Poems" (1817)*, Literary Monographs 1 (Madison: University of

Wisconsin Press, 1967), p. 150. Stillinger argues that, since the MS of Keats's draft is marked by Clarke, he was probably the third of the "friends" mentioned in the note (*Texts of Keats's Poems*, p. 188).

16 Quoted in Edmund Blunden, *Keats's Publisher: A Memoir of John Taylor* (1936, rpt. London: Cape, 1940), pp. 42–43.

17 See Richard D. Altick, *The Cowden Clarkes* (London: Oxford University Press, 1948), p. 27; Blunden, *Hunt*, p. 76; Peter H. Marshall, *William Godwin* (New Haven: Yale University Press, 1984), p. 312.

18 Allot (p. 65) links this sonnet to Hunt's "Quiet Evenings. To Thomas Barnes, Esq. Written from Hampstead" (first published as "Sonnet to T. B. Esq." in the *Examiner* for 14 February 1813) and "To T. M. Alsager, Esq. with the Author's Miniature, on Leaving Prison" (in *Feast of Poets*, 1815).

19 See *Poems, Transcripts, Letters, &c.: Facsimiles of Richard Woodhouse's Scrapbook Materials in the Pierpont Morgan Library*, ed. Jack Stillinger (New York: Garland, 1985), pp. 231–33, for Woodhouse's account of the occasional nature of this valentine.

20 See Stuart Sperry, "Keats's First Published Poem," *Huntington Library Quarterly* 29 (February 1966), 191–97.

21 Special Collections, University of Iowa, MS H94gra.

22 Jerome McGann, *The Beauty of Inflections: Literary Investigations in Historical Method and Theory* (Oxford: Clarendon Press, 1988), p. 27.

23 As Ernest de Selincourt notes in *The Poems of John Keats*, 5th ed. (London: Methuen, 1926), p. 395, these lines "shew Keats to be already the pupil of the *Examiner*."

24 Woodhouse – who wrote a sonnet entitled "To Apollo – Written after Reading Sleep & Poetry" – also notes (in *Poems, 1817: A Facsimile of Richard Woodhouse's Annotated Copy in the Huntington Library*, ed. Jack Stillinger [New York: Garland, 1985]) at line 354 of "Sleep and Poetry," "The thought of writing this poem arose at the house of Leigh Hunt" (pp. 225, 230).

25 Though see Marjorie Norris, "Phenomenology and Process: Perception in Keats's 'I Stood Tip-toe,'" *KSJ* 25 (1976), 43–54; and the items listed in n. 1 above.

26 Keats may also be recalling Reynolds's "A Recollection," published with *The Eden of the Imagination* (1814), where Reynolds uses the phrase "I stood upon the hill" twice (ll. 1, 16) to organize his poem.

27 See *The Poetical Works of John Keats*, ed. H. W. Garrod, 2nd ed. (Oxford University Press, 1958), pp. lxxxiv–lxxxviii; Stillinger, *Texts of Keats's Poems*, pp. 122–24; and Allot, p. 88.

28 See Robert M. Ryan's fine "The Politics of Greek Religion," in *Critical Essays on John Keats*, ed. Hermione de Almeida (Boston: G. K. Hall, 1990), pp. 261–79.

29 See the review by "G.F.M." in *European Magazine* 71 (May 1817), 434–37, esp. p. 435; and Hunt's review in the *Examiner*, 1 June, 6 and 13 July 1817, esp. p. 429. For Keats and the *Excursion*, see Beth Lau, *Keats's Reading of Romantic Poets* (Ann Arbor: University of Michigan Press, 1991), pp. 48–59.

30 Clayton E. Hudnall, "John Hamilton Reynolds, James Rice, and Benjamin Bailey in the Leigh Browne-Lockyer Collection," *KSJ* (1970), 21.

31 Stephen Gill, *William Wordsworth: A Life* (Oxford: Clarendon Press, 1989), p. 326.

32 Dupuis, *Origin of All Religious Worship* (1798, rpt. New York: Garland, 1984). Toland, *Letters to Serena* (1704, rpt. New York: Garland, 1976), particularly letter III, "The Origin of Idolatry, and Reasons of Heathenism." A useful introduction to this debate is Burton Feldman and Robert D. Richardson's *The Rise of Modern Mythology 1680–1860* (Bloomington: Indiana University Press, 1972).

33 Butler, "Myth and Mythmaking in the Shelley Circle," in *SR*, pp. 1–19, and Gaull, *English Romanticism: The Human Context* (New York: Norton, 1988), pp. 182–88.

34 Gaull, *Romanticism*, p. 186; Ronald Paulson, *Representations of Revolution (1789–1820)* (New Haven: Yale University Press, 1983), p. 22.

35 Marilyn Butler, *Romantics, Rebels, and Reactionaries: English Literature and Its Background, 1760–1830* (Oxford University Press, 1981), p. 131.

36 Bush, *John Keats: His Life and Writings* (1966, rpt. New York: Macmillan [Collier Books], 1967), p. 35.

37 The turn to Milton for a neo-pagan ideology may strike us as bizarre, but Milton was often offered as a precursor for the Hunt circle's radical positions. Seen as the model of the poet-patriot (William Godwin wrote in his *Lives of Edward and John Philips, Nephews and Pupils of Milton, Including Various Particulars of the Literary and Political History of Their Times* [London: Longman, Hurst, Rees, Orme & Brown, 1815], "He is our poet... He is our patriot" [p. v]), Milton was used, for example, by Hunt to defend free love, when in his review (*Examiner*, 1 March 1818, p. 140) of Shelley's *Revolt of Islam* he tweaks moralists with the fact that "Milton, whom they admire, set about ridiculing it [custom], and paying his addresses to another woman in his wife's life-time, till the latter treated him better." Milton's commitment to Christianity was questioned in a letter from Godwin to Hunt (Huntington Library MS HM 11635) dated 7 December 1818: "It was stated to me yesterday by Mrs. James Ogilvie, the Orator ⟨?⟩, that you had informed him, that it was now known from incontestible authority, that Milton died embracing the creed of atheism." Hunt mentions the episode in a letter to Mary Shelley, 9 March 1819, in which he reports that he had never said any such thing but had said "that Milton, latterly, never went to any place of worship, or had any worship in his house" (*Correspondence*, I: 128).

38 *The Palm at the End of the Mind*, ed. Holly Stevens (1967, rpt. New York: Random House, 1972).

39 See Bate, *Keats*, pp. 45–46, 134; E. B. Hinckley, "On First Looking into Swedenborg's Philosophy: A New Keats-Circle Letter," *KSJ* (Winter 1960), 12–25; and Robert M. Ryan, *Keats: The Religious Sense* (Princeton University Press, 1973).

40 Hazlitt, "On Mr. Wordsworth's *Excursion*," *Examiner*, 21 and 28 August 1814; reprinted in *Round Table* (1817), *CWH*, IV: 113, 114.

41 Spenser, *The Faerie Queene*, ed. A. C. Hamilton (New York: Longman, 1977). *The Golden Ass of Apuleius*, trans. William Adlington (1639, rpt. London: David Nutt, 1893).

42 Williams, *Keywords: A Vocabulary of Culture and Society* (Oxford University Press, 1977), p. 243.

CHAPTER 4. STAGING HOPE: GENRE, MYTH, AND IDEOLOGY IN THE DRAMAS OF THE HUNT CIRCLE

1 Relevant translations include Hunt's *Amyntas* (1820) from Tasso, Shelley's version of Euripides' *Cyclops* (1819), and Peacock's adaptation of lines from Guarini's *Il Pastor Fido* (1803?). The most interesting of the group's abandoned projects is Hunt's contemplated *Prometheus Throned*, "in which I intended to have described him as having lately taken possession of Jupiter's seat": letter to Percy Shelley, July 1819, *Correspondence*, I: 132. Texts for the plays cited are *Shelley's Poetry and Prose*; *Proserpine & Midas: Two Unpublished Mythological Dramas by Mary Shelley*, ed. A. Koszul (London: Humphrey Milford, 1922) (although these plays were written in 1820, only *Proserpine* appeared during Shelley's lifetime, in *Winter's Wreath* [1832]); Horace Smith, *Amarynthus, the Nympholept: A Pastoral Drama, in Three Acts, with Other Poems* (London: Longman, Hurst, Rees, Orme & Brown, 1821); Barry Cornwall, *Dramatic Scenes, and Other Poems* (London: C. & J. Ollier, 1819) and *Marcian Colonna, an Italian Tale; with Three Dramatic Scenes, and Other Poems* (London: John Warren/C. & J. Ollier, 1820); Hunt, *The Descent of Liberty: A Mask* (London: Gale, Curtis & Fenner, 1815) (text but not preface in Milford's edition), and *Amyntas, a Tale of the Woods; from the Italian of Torquato Tasso* (London: T. & J. Allman, 1820). One might also want to connect Byron's "mysteries" of *Cain* and *Heaven and Earth* to these efforts as revisions of biblical materials.

2 Reynolds also published as a pamphlet *An Ode* (London: John Martin, 1815), dealing with Napoleon's fall and exile to Elba; see Leonidas M. Jones, *The Life of John Hamilton Reynolds* (Hanover, N.H.: University Press of New England, 1984), pp. 57–58.

3 Reynolds also wrote a letter of praise to Hunt, who thanked him publicly in the *Examiner*, in another coterie exchange; see *Letters from Lambeth: The Correspondence of the Reynolds Family with John Freeman Milward Dovaston 1808– 1815*, ed. Joanna Richardson (Woodbridge, Suffolk: Boydell, 1981), p. 131.

4 On the theater of the day, see, for example, Michael Booth, *English Melodrama* (London: Herbert Jenkins, 1965); Booth, *Prefaces to Nineteenth-Century Theatre* (Manchester University Press, 1980); Jeffrey N. Cox, *Seven Gothic Dramas 1789–1825* (Athens: Ohio University Press, 1992); Joseph Donohue, *Theatre in the Age of Kean* (Totowa, N.J.: Rowman & Littlefield, 1975); R. Leacroft, *The Development of the English Playhouse* (Ithaca: Cornell

University Press, 1973); and Allardyce Nicoll, *Early Nineteenth-Century Drama 1800–1850*, vol. IV of *A History of English Drama 1660–1900* (Cambridge University Press, 1960). Recent work on the romantic drama has been collected in special numbers of *Nineteenth-Century Contexts* 15 (1991) and *Wordsworth Circle* 23 (Spring 1992), both edited by Terence Allan Hoagwood and Daniel P. Watkins, and in an issue of *Texas Studies in Language and Literature* 38 (Fall/Winter 1996) called "Romantic Performances," edited by Theresa Kelley. On the romantic drama, see, for example, Catherine Burroughs, *Closet Stages: Joanna Baillie and the Theater Theory of British Romantic Women Writers* (Philadelphia: University of Pennsylvania Press, 1997); Julie Carlson, *In the Theatre of Romanticism: Coleridge, Nationalism, Women* (Cambridge University Press, 1994); Cox, *In the Shadows of Romance: Romantic Tragic Drama in Germany, England and France* (Athens: Ohio University Press, 1987); Stuart Curran, *Shelley's "The Cenci": Scorpions Ringed with Fire* (Princeton University Press, 1970); Joseph Donohue, *Dramatic Character in the English Romantic Age* (Princeton University Press, 1970); Marjean Purinton, *Romantic Ideology Unmasked: The Mentally Constructed Tyrannies in Dramas of William Wordsworth, Lord Byron, Percy Shelley, and Joanna Baillie* (Newark: University of Delaware Press, 1994); Alan Richardson, *A Mental Theatre* (State College: Pennsylvania State University Press, 1988); and Daniel P. Watkins, *A Materialist Critique of English Romantic Drama* (Gainesville: University Press of Florida, 1993).

5 Hunt: "There is no such thing as modern comedy, tragedy, nor even farce" (*Examiner*, 5 January 1817, p. 7); see also *Defence of Poetry*, p. 491, where Shelley rejects neoclassical tragedy and melodrama.

6 On the production, see John Genest, *Some Account of the English Stage from the Restoration in 1660–1830* (1832, rpt. New York: Burt Franklin, 1965), VIII: 480. *The London Stage 1660–1800*, ed. William Van Lennep, Emmett L. Avery, Arthur H. Scouten, George Winchester Stone, Jr., and Charles Beecher Hogan (Carbondale: Southern Illinois University Press, 1960–79) lists over 440 performances of *Comus* between its revival in 1738 and 1800; it was offered at least once every year during that period except in 1754, 1757, and 1768–70.

7 Allardyce Nicoll, *A History of Early Eighteenth Century Drama*, vol. II of *A History of English Drama 1660–1900* (Cambridge University Press, 1927), pp. 258–62.

8 Frank Sayers, *Poems, Containing Dramatic Sketches of Northern Mythology, etc.*, 4th ed. (Norwich, 1807), also contains two monodramas, a key form used by Goethe and Matthew Lewis among others; a translation of Euripides' *Cyclops*, a precursor of the pastoral drama also adapted by Shelley; and a translation of part of Catullus' "The Epithalamion of Peleus and Thetis," a poem important to Hunt and Keats, as we will see in chapter 5. Performance information is taken from *London Stage*.

9 Terry Castle, *Masquerade and Civilization: The Carnivalesque in Eighteenth-Century English Culture and Fiction* (Stanford University Press, 1986), p. 28.

10　Roe, *John Keats and the Culture of Dissent* (Oxford: Clarendon Press, 1997), p. 74.

11　See Kevin Gilmartin, *Print Politics: The Press and Radical Opposition in Early Nineteenth-Century England* (Cambridge University Press, 1996), pp. 195–206.

12　See Roger Fiske, *English Theatre Music in the Eighteenth Century* (Oxford University Press, 1973), pp. 3–66. Johnson's comment is from his "Life of John Hughes" and is quoted in Fiske, p. 51. See also Lucyle Hook, "Motteux and the Classical Masque," in *British Theatre and the Other Arts, 1660–1800*, ed. Shirley Strum Kenny (Washington, D.C.: Folger Shakespeare Library, 1984), pp. 105–15.

13　Stephen Orgel, *Ben Jonson: The Complete Masques* (New Haven: Yale University Press, 1969), p. 9. See also Orgel's *The Jonsonian Masque* (1965, rpt. New York: Columbia University Press, 1981) and *The Illusion of Power: Political Theater in the English Renaissance* (Berkeley and Los Angeles: University of California Press, 1975); Joseph Lowenstein, *Responsive Readings: Versions of Echo in Pastoral, Epic, and the Jonsonian Masque* (New Haven: Yale University Press, 1984); and Enid Welsford, *The Court Masque* (New York: Russell & Russell, 1962).

14　Paterson, *Pastoral and Ideology: Virgil to Valéry* (Berkeley and Los Angeles: University of California Press, 1987).

15　Curran, *Poetic Form and British Romanticism* (Oxford University Press, 1986), p. 114.

16　Hunt's much later *Jar of Honey from Mount Hybla* (1848) offers an account of the pastoral in general.

17　Letter to Jean-Antoine Galignani, 14 July 1826 ⟨?⟩, in Charles E. Robinson, "William Hazlitt to His Publishers, Friends, and Creditors: Twenty-Seven New Holograph Letters," *KSR* 2 (1987), 32–33. See also Hazlitt's *Lectures Chiefly on the Dramatic Literature of the Age of Elizabeth* (1820).

18　Hunt's passage from Guarini appeared in *Ainsworth's Magazine* (June 1844) and then in *A Jar of Honey from Mount Hybla* (1848). Shelley's translation of Euripides, dated 1819, was first published in *Posthumous Poems* (1824). Both Rapin's theory that *Cyclops* was the origin of pastoral drama and the contention that these plays arose from Theocritus and Bion can be found in the account of Hunt's *Amyntas* in the *Monthly Review* (2nd ser., 93 [September 1820], 211); Genest links *Cyclops* to Jonson's pastoral *The Sad Shepherd* (*English Stage*, VIII: 545). On Shelley's reading, see *SL*, II: 467ff. Peacock's lines from Guarini were apparently dated "February 1, 1803"; they first appeared in Henry Cole's edition of Peacock's *Works* (1875). Horace Smith cites his influences in the preface to *Amarynthus*, p. viii.

19　Jeannette Marks, *English Pastoral Drama from the Restoration to the Date of the Publication of "Lyrical Ballads" (1660–1798)* (London: Methuen, 1908), lists about seventy-five pastoral plays between 1700 and 1798. See also Walter W. Greg, *Pastoral Poetry & Pastoral Drama* (New York: Russell & Russell, 1959).

20　Butler, *Romantics, Rebels and Reactionaries: English Literature and Its Background,*

1760–1830 (Oxford University Press, 1981), pp. 113–37. On the range of erotic themes, see, for example, Nancy Cotton Pearse, *John Fletcher's Chastity Plays: Mirrors of Modesty* (Lewisburg, Pa.: Bucknell University Press, 1973); and Lynn Hunt, "The Many Bodies of Marie Antoinette and the Problem of the Feminine in the French Revolution," in *Eroticism and the Body Politic*, ed. Hunt (Baltimore: Johns Hopkins University Press, 1991), pp. 108–30.

21 Kurt Heinzelman, in his excellent "Roman Georgic in the Georgian Age: A Theory of Romantic Genre," *Texas Studies in Language and Literature* 33 (Summer 1991), 182–214, reminds us not to conflate the georgic and the pastoral, though, as we would expect from Heinzelman's critique of romantic poets (and scholars), Smith may do exactly that.

22 Northrop Frye, *Anatomy of Criticism* (Princeton University Press, 1957), pp. 164–71.

23 Hunt also objected to the treatment of chastity in *The Faithful Shepherdess* as "a conscious and laboured contradiction to Fletcher's ordinary ideas respecting women and chastity. Beaumont and Fletcher both seem to think, that if they make a woman chaste, they make her every thing; which is the mistake of a gross habit of life, and after all not a very sincere one" (p. xxiii).

24 Raymond Williams, *Marxism and Literature* (Oxford University Press, 1977), p. 66.

25 Jerome McGann, *The Romantic Ideology* (University of Chicago Press, 1983), pp. 1–14.

26 That even this apparently spontaneous response is not some piece of Keatsian idiosyncrasy but instead an expression of a larger cultural attitude is also made clear by Haydon's journal, where he claims that his "putting in Voltaire by the side of Newton is naturally making a stir amongst all the Deists in the country"; he notes that "Hunt has received a letter from Norwich complaining of its *injustice*" and goes on to recite his debates with Hunt over Voltaire, all of this occurring just as Keats was joining the Hunt circle (see the entries of 19 and 25 October 1816, *Diary*, II: 54–63). The issue would be raised again in *Annals of the Fine Arts* (5 [1820]) when the picture was exhibited.

27 Alan Richardson, "*Proserpine* and *Midas*: Gender, Genre, and Mythic Revisionism in Mary Shelley's Dramas," in *The Other Mary Shelley: Beyond "Frankenstein"*, ed. Audrey A. Fish, Anne K. Mellor, and Esther H. Schor (Oxford University Press, 1993), pp. 124–37.

28 Associated with these plays is a draft of a Mary Shelley essay, "The Necessity of a Belief in the Heathen Mythology / to a Christian" (included in Koszul's edition, pp. xxiv–xxvi), that continues the work of ideological critique through mythological revisionism that marks the work of the Hunt circle, as in, for example, Hunt's *Indicator* (19 January 1820, pp. 113–16) essay "The Spirit of the Ancient Mythology."

29 Barry Cornwall also took up the myth of Proserpine in a dramatic scene

included in *Marcian Colonna* (1820).

30 Gubar, "Mother, Maiden and the Marriage of Death: Woman Writers and an Ancient Myth," *Women Studies* 6 (1979), 301–15.

31 Cixous, "Castration or Decapitation?" trans. Annette Kuhn, *Signs* 7 (1981), 36–55.

32 See Jeffrey N. Cox, "The French Revolution in the English Theater," in *History and Myth: Essays on English Romantic Literature*, ed. Stephen C. Behrendt (Detroit: Wayne State University Press, 1989), pp. 33–52.

33 I draw upon the description of the pantomime in David Mayer, *Harlequin in His Element: The English Pantomime, 1806–1836* (Cambridge: Harvard University Press, 1969), esp. pp. 23–28. See also R. J. Broadbent, *A History of Pantomime* (1901, rpt. New York: Benjamin Blom, 1964), M. Wilson Disher, *Clowns and Pantomimes* (1925, rpt. New York: Benjamin Blom, 1968), Maurice Sand, *The History of the Harlequinade*, 2 vols. (1915, rpt. New York: Benjamin Blom, 1968), and A. E. Wilson, *King Panto: The Story of Pantomime* (New York: Dutton, 1935).

34 Curran, *Shelley's Annus Mirabilis: The Maturing of an Epic Vision* (San Marino, Calif.: Huntington Library, 1975), pp. 112, 187–91. See also Lisa Vargo's fine "Unmasking Shelley's *Mask of Anarchy*," *English Studies in Canada* 13 (March 1987), 49–64, which makes points about Shelley's use of the masque parallel to mine.

35 *Poems of Thomas Carew*, ed. Arthur Vincent (1899; rpt. Freeport, N.Y.: Books for Libraries Press, 1972).

36 William Godwin, at least, did know Carew's masque. In *Lives of Edward and John Philips, Nephews and Pupils of Milton* (1815), he speaks of Carew's masque and its music (p. 131), written by Henry Lawes, whom he also identifies as the composer of the music for *Comus*. On Shelley's interest in the masque, see Curran, cited above; Richard Cronin, *Shelley's Poetic Thoughts* (New York: St. Martin's, 1981), pp. 51–55; David Norbrook, "The Reformation of the Masque," in *The Court Masque*, ed. David Lindley (Manchester University Press, 1984), pp. 94–110; R. B. Woodings, "Shelley's Sources for 'Charles the First,'" *Modern Language Review* 64 (July 1969), 267–75, and "'A Devil of a Nut to Crack': Shelley's *Charles the First*," *Studia Neophilologica* 40 (1968), 216–37.

37 See Fredric Jameson's discussion of the dialectic between ideology and utopia that draws on the work of Ernst Bloch: Jameson, *The Political Unconscious: Narrative as a Socially Symbolic Act* (Ithaca: Cornell University Press, 1981), pp. 281–99, and *Marxism and Form* (Princeton University Press, 1971), pp. 60–83; also Ernst Bloch, *The Principle of Hope*, trans. Neville Plaice, Stephen Plaice, and Paul Knight (Cambridge: MIT Press, 1986), and *The Utopian Function of Art and Literature: Selected Essays*, trans. Jack Zipes and Frank Mecklenburg (Cambridge: MIT Press, 1989).

CHAPTER 5. COCKNEY CLASSICISM: HISTORY WITH FOOTNOTES

1 Sir William Hamilton, letter to Josiah Wedgwood, July 1786; quoted in

Wolf Mankowitz, *The Portland Vase and the Wedgwood Copies* (London: Andre Deutsch, 1952), p. 29.

2 Horace Walpole, letter to Lady Ossory, 19 August 1785, in *The Yale Edition of Horace Walpole's Correspondence*, ed. W. S. Lewis, vol. XXXIII (New Haven: Yale University Press, 1965), p. 489.

3 Walter Benjamin, "The Work of Art in the Age of Mechanical Reproduction," in *Illuminations*, ed. Hannah Arendt, trans. Harry Zohn (New York: Schocken, 1968), pp. 217–51. On the issues here discussed, see also Terry Eagleton, *The Ideology of the Aesthetic* (Oxford: Basil Blackwell, 1990), and Susan Stewart, *On Longing: Narratives of the Miniature, the Gigantic, the Souvenir, the Collection* (Durham, N.C.: Duke University Press, 1993), pp. 151–69. For a different reading of some similar issues, see Elizabeth Jones, "Writing for the Market: Keats's Odes as Commodities," *SiR* 34 (Fall 1995), 343–64.

4 See *The Autobiography and Memoirs of Benjamin Robert Haydon*, ed. Tom Taylor (New York: Harcourt Brace, 1926), I: 321. See also Edward Miller, *That Noble Cabinet: A History of the British Museum* (Athens: Ohio University Press, 1974), and Ian Jenkins, *Archaeologists and Aesthetes in the Sculpture Galleries of the British Museum 1800–1939* (London: British Museum Press, 1992).

5 See Aileen Dawson, *Masterpieces of Wedgwood in the British Museum* (Bloomington: Indiana University Press, 1984); D. E. L. Haynes, *The Portland Vase* (London: Trustees of the British Museum, 1964); Allison Kelly, *The Story of Wedgwood* (New York: Viking, 1975); Carol Macht, *Classical Wedgwood Designs* (New York: M. Barrows, 1957); Mankowitz, *The Portland Vase*; Guy Manners, *The Wedgwood Portland Vase* (London: Josiah Wedgwood & Sons, 1974); Josiah Wedgwood, *Description of the Portland Vase* (1790); Neil McKendrick, John Brewer, and J. H. Plumb, *The Birth of a Consumer Society: The Commercialization of Eighteenth-Century England* (Bloomington: Indiana University Press, 1982), esp. pp. 99–144; and the catalog *The Genius of Wedgwood*, ed. Hilary Young (London: Victoria & Albert Museum, 1995), for the excellent exhibition at the Victoria and Albert Museum, 9 June – 17 September 1995. Erasmus Darwin, *The Botanic Garden*, part I (1791, rpt. New York: Garland, 1978), pp. 88–89. On Sir William Hamilton, see B. Fothergill, *Sir William Hamilton: Envoy Extraordinary* (New York: Harcourt Brace & World, 1969), and the catalog, *Vases & Volcanoes: Sir William Hamilton and His Collection*, by Ian Jenkins and Kim Sloan (London: British Museum Press, 1996).

6 Susan Sontag, *The Volcano Lover: A Romance* (New York: Farrar Straus & Giroux, 1992), pp. 137–38.

7 *Times*, 7 and 12 February 1845; *Gentleman's Magazine*, N.S. 23 (1845), 300; and Haynes, *The Portland Vase*, pp. 11–12.

8 Jerome McGann, *The Beauty of Inflections* (Oxford University Press, 1985), p. 44. The dismissal of a prototype for the urn ranges from Sidney Colvin's *John Keats: His Life and Poetry, His Friends, Critics, and After-Fame* (New York: Scribner, 1917), pp. 415–16, to Cleanth Brooks's *The Well Wrought Urn* (New York: Harcourt Brace, 1947), p. 153 (where we are told that knowing more

about what Keats saw or knew does not help us understand the poem), to Bruce E. Miller's "Form and Substance in 'Grecian Urn,'" *KSJ* 20 (1971), 65 ("the urn of this poem is no real vase at all").

9 McGann follows Ian Jack's account of the *Annals* in Jack's *Keats and the Mirror of Art* (Oxford: Clarendon Press, 1967), pp. 46–57. Theresa M. Kelley, in her fine "Keats, Ekphrasis, and History," in *KH*, pp. 212–37, suggests possible disagreements between Keats, Haydon, and the *Annals* over romantic classicism. See also Grant F. Scott, "Beautiful Ruins: The Elgin Marbles Sonnet in Its Historical and Generic Contexts," *KSJ* 39 (1990), 123–50.

10 On the links between commerce and the arts during the period, see Elie Halévy, *England in 1815*, vol. 1 of *A History of the English People in the Nineteenth Century*, trans. E. I. Watkin and D. A. Barker (1924; 2nd rev. ed. London: Ernest Benn, 1949), pp. 486–98; and Colin Campbell, *The Romantic Ethic and the Spirit of Modern Consumerism* (Oxford: Basil Blackwell, 1987). On reproductions in various media, see Richard D. Altick, *The Shows of London* (Cambridge: Harvard University Press, 1978), pp. 390–403. On Keats's acquaintance with books reproducing images of classical works of art, see Jack, *Keats and the Mirror of Art*, pp. 216–18.

11 See Keats, letter to Fanny Keats, 13 March 1819, *KL*, II: 45–46; Hunt's piece "Casts from Sculpture and Gems" in *Indicator*, 17 November 1819; Shelley, letter to Peacock, 21 March 1821, *SL*, II: 276–77; and Jack, *Keats and the Mirror of Art*, pp. 100–105.

12 Benjamin, "The Work of Art in the Age of Mechanical Reproduction," pp. 220–21.

13 Josiah Wedgwood, letter to Sir William Hamilton, 24 June 1786, Wedgwood Museum MS E 18976, excerpted in *The Selected Letters of Josiah Wedgwood*, ed. Ann Finer and George Savage (London: Cory, Adams & Mackay, 1965). On an engraving Hamilton had made which places the vase back in what was supposed to be the site where it was discovered, see *Vases & Volcanoes*, pp. 190–91.

14 Ian Jack, *Keats and the Mirror of Art*, p. 217, considers the Portland but dismisses it in favor of neo-Attic urns. Neil G. Grill, "Keats's Odes and Two *New Monthly Magazine* Sonnets to an Antique Grecian Vase," *Keats–Shelley Memorial Bulletin* 26 (1975), 11–14, suggests that Keats may have drawn on a poem published in the *New Monthly Magazine* (12 [1819], 64) entitled "Sonnet on an Antique Grecian Vase, When the Same Subject as That of the Portland Vase Is Sculptured in Basalt." Dwight E. Robinson, "Ode on a 'New Etrurian' Urn: A Reflection of Wedgwood Ware in the Poetic Imagery of John Keats," *KSJ* 12 (1963), 11–36, argues for the impact on Keats of Wedgwood's adaptation of the Borghese Vase.

15 *Autobiography of Haydon*, I: 321; Jack, *Keats and the Mirror of Art*, p. 217. For an example of contemporary discussions of the Portland, see James Dalloway, *Of Statuary and Sculpture among the Ancients with Some Account of Specimens Preserved in England* (London: Murray, 1816), pp. 302–3.

16 Letter to Josiah Wedgwood, July 1786, quoted in Mankowitz, *The Portland Vase*, p. 29.

17 Randall L. Skalsky, "Visual Trope and the Portland Vase Frieze: A New Reading and Exegesis," *Arion* 19 (Winter 1992), 42–71. The British Museum now links the Portland Vase to Catullus 64. See also W. Watkiss Lloyd in *Classical Museum* 6 (1849), 253–78; J. Milligen in *Transactions of the Royal Society of Literature* 1 (1829), 99–105; J. J. Winckelmann, *Geschichte der Kunst des Altertums* (Vienna, 1776), part 2, pp. 861f. Winckelmann was well known in England at the time through translations such as that by Fuseli (whom Hunt knew), *Reflections on the Painting and the Sculpture of the Greeks* (1765). On interpretations of the Portland Vase prior to 1950, see Haynes, *Portland Vase*, pp. 27–31.

18 Keats may refer to Catullus' poem in "Sleep and Poetry" (ll. 331–38), where he is looking at a picture of Bacchus and Ariadne, and in "Isabella" (ll. 95–96), where he mentions Theseus' abandonment of Ariadne. Woodhouse cites a Catullan reference (65, l. 3) for the tenth line of "Woman! When I behold thee flippant, vain": *Woodhouse's Annotated "Poems"*, ed. Jack Stillinger (New York: Garland, 1985), p. 99.

19 George Lamb's *Poems of Caius Valerius Catullus, Translated with a Preface and Notes* (London: Murray, 1821) was reviewed in *Blackwood's*, where, typically, Hunt as "the King of the Cockneys" is attacked for his translation of the Atys, which "has certainly nothing of Catullus, whatever it may have of Cockaigne" (*Blackwood's* 9 [August 1821], 513). Reynolds also wrote a piece on Lamb's translation for the *London Magazine* 4 (July 1821). Hunt published translations of Catullus in the *Examiner*, the *Poetical Register*, *The Feast of Poets* (1814), and *Foliage* (1818). Byron refers to Moore and Catullus in *English Bards and Scotch Reviewers* (1809), l. 227; his unpublished poem to Moore is entitled "To Thomas Moore, Written the Evening before His Visit to Mr. Leigh Hunt in Horsemonger Lane Gaol, May 19, 1813." Byron's adaptations of Catullus are found in *Hours of Idleness* (1807), and he refers to the poet in *Don Juan*, *The Age of Bronze*, and elsewhere. There is a translation from Catullus in the collection Byron's friend Cam Hobhouse edited, *Imitations and Translations from the Ancient and Modern Classics Together with Original Poems Never Before Published* (London: Longworth, 1809). Coleridge published "Catullan Hendecasyllables" of 1799 in 1834; John Hookham Frere translated Catullus 10 (18??), among other poems; Reynolds offered "A Paraphrase of Catullus's Address to His Vessel" in *The Inquirer, or Literary Miscellany* 1 (May 1814), 17; and Landor – who wrote an essay on Catullus – offered several translations in *Poems and Epigrams* (1842). For Shelley, compare *Queen Mab*, VIII.23–24 and Catullus 64, ll. 270ff. Karl Pomeroy Harrington, in *Catullus and His Influence* (New York: Cooper Square, 1963), pp. 196–206, details various romantic translations and borrowings; writing of Frere's satire based on Catullus 45, Pomeroy states, "That political satire could adopt this form is sufficient indication how thoroughly familiar educated English circles at the end of the eighteenth

century were with Catullus" (p. 205).
20 On the neoterics, see Charles Martin, *Catullus* (New Haven: Yale University Press, 1992), pp. 15–18.
21 Julia Haig Gaisser, *Catullus and His Renaissance Readers* (Oxford: Clarendon Press, 1993), p. 274.
22 In vol. VII of *The Works of Thomas Love Peacock*, ed. H. F. B. Brett-Smith and C. E. Jones (London: Constable, 1931).
23 See Elizabeth Story Donno, "The Epyllion," in *English Poetry and Prose 1540–1674*, ed. Christopher Ricks (New York: Peter Bedrick, 1987), pp. 57–72; *Elizabethan Minor Epics*, ed. Elizabeth Story Donno (Cambridge University Press, 1963); and William Keach, *Elizabethan Erotic Narratives* (New Brunswick, N.J.: Rutgers University Press, 1977).
24 See, for example, Joan Grundy, "Keats and the Elizabethans," in *John Keats: A Reassessment*, ed. Kenneth Muir (University of Liverpool Press, 1958), pp. 1–19.
25 Lipking, *Abandoned Women and Poetic Tradition* (University of Chicago Press, 1988), p. 30.
26 The often noted links between Catullus' poem and Virgil's epic are made by Lamb in his notes to his translation (I: 117). Clarke, in *Recollections*, tells us that Keats intimately knew the *Aeneid*, "with which epic, indeed, he was so fascinated that before leaving school he had voluntarily translated in writing a considerable portion," a task he completed during his apprenticeship (pp. 124–25).
27 Published in *An Autobiographical Fragment and Biographical Notes, with Personal Sketches of Contemporaries, Unpublished Lyrics, and Letters of Literary Friends*, ed. Coventry Patmore (London: George Bell & Sons, 1877), p. 237.
28 Published in *Fitz-Gwarine: A Ballad of the Welsh Border, in Three Cantos. With Other Poems Legendary, Incidental, and Humorous* (London: Longman, Hurst, Rees, Orme, & Brown, 1816).
29 See Rodney Stenning Edgecombe, *Leigh Hunt and the Poetry of Fancy* (London: Associated University Presses, 1994), pp. 95–114, on Hunt's use of Ovid and Musaeus.
30 E. B. Hungerford, *Shores of Darkness* (New York: Columbia University Press, 1941).
31 Jack, *Keats and the Mirror of Art*, p. 283 n. 13. William Empson, *The Structure of Complex Words* (New York: New Directions, 1951), pp. 368–74. Paul Hamilton, "Keats and Critique," in Marjorie Levinson, Marilyn Butler, Jerome McGann, and Paul Hamilton, *Rethinking Historicism: Critical Readings in Romantic History* (Oxford: Basil Blackwell, 1989), p. 112. Kenneth Burke also notes the "brede"/"breed" pun in "Symbolic Action in a Poem by Keats," *Accent* 4 (Autumn 1943), 30–43. See also Stuart Peterfreund, "The Truth about 'Beauty' and 'Truth': Keats's 'Ode on a Grecian Urn,'" Milton, Shakespeare, and the Uses of Paradox," *KSJ* 35 (1986), 62–82; and Philip Fisher, "A Museum with One Work Inside: Keats and the Finality of Art," *KSJ* 33 (1984), 85–102.

32 Marjorie Levinson, *Keats's Life of Allegory: The Origin of a Style* (Oxford: Basil Blackwell, 1988). Andrew Bennett also writes of Keats's poetry as being "so disturbing and so seductive" because of "its uncertain but irreducible and scandalous instabilities": *Keats, Narrative and Audience: The Posthumous Life of Writing* (Cambridge University Press, 1994), p. 1.

33 Walter Jackson Bate, *John Keats* (Cambridge: Harvard University Press, 1964), p. 403. Allot, p. 435n. Levinson, *Keats's Life of Allegory*, pp. 206–11, usefully discusses what she calls "the stylistic vulgarity of Book 3."

34 Nicholas Roe, *Keats and the Culture of Dissent* (Oxford: Clarendon Press, 1997), p. 86. Rajan, *Dark Interpreter: The Discourse of Romanticism* (Ithaca: Cornell University Press, 1980), pp. 133–36. Watkins, *Keats's Poetry and the Politics of the Imagination* (London: Associated University Presses, 1989), pp. 104–20.

35 For example, Cleanth Brooks finds the world of the urn "deathless because it is lifeless," and it is lifeless because it escapes the "ironic fact that all human passion *does* leave one cloyed; hence the superiority of art": *The Well Wrought Urn*, p. 159. Helen Vendler finds the paradoxical portrayal of an unfading love alongside the sense of passion as cloying to arise from "the generating motive of the poem – the necessary self-exhaustion and self-perpetuation of sexual appetite": *The Odes of John Keats* (Cambridge: Harvard University Press, 1983), p. 141.

36 Fredric Jameson, *The Political Unconscious: Narrative as a Socially Symbolic Act* (Ithaca: Cornell University Press, 1981), p. 102.

37 Anne K. Mellor also makes this connection in *English Romantic Irony* (Cambridge: Harvard University Press, 1980), p. 84 & n. In "Ode on a 'New Etrurian' Urn," Robinson mentions the possible link between Keats's poem and Emma Hamilton (pp. 28–30).

38 On Emma Hamilton and Nelson, see, for example, *Memoirs of Emma, Lady Hamilton with Anecdotes of Her Friends and Contemporaries*, ed. W. H. Long (1815; rev. ed. London: W. W. Gibbings, 1891); Jack Russell, *Nelson and the Hamiltons* (New York: Simon & Schuster, 1969); Edward Gill, *Nelson and the Hamiltons on Tour* (Monmouth: Alan Sutton and Nelson Museum, 1987); David Howarth and Stephen Howarth, *Lord Nelson* (New York: Penguin, 1988); Norah Lofts, *Emma Hamilton* (New York: Coward, McCann & Geoghegan, 1978); and Flora Fraser, *Emma, Lady Hamilton* (New York: Knopf, 1987).

39 Quoted in Altick, *The Shows of London*, p. 82. See also Eric Jameson, *The Natural History of Quackery* (Springfield, Ill.: Charles C. Thomas, 1961), pp. 112–32.

40 Peter Pindar, "Postscript (Sub Rosa)" to "A Lyric Epistle to Sir William Hamilton" (1794), in *The Works of Peter Pindar* (London: J. Walter, J. Robinson, Longman, Hurst, Rees, Orme & Brown, 1812), III: 189–90; Walpole, *Correspondence*, vol. XI (New Haven: Yale University Press, 1944), p. 349. *Blackwood's* imagined a similar fate for Hunt after he travelled to Italy to join Shelley and Byron: "The pictures and statues will drive him

clean out of his wits. He'll fall in love with some of them" (11 [March 1822], 364).

41 Goethe, *The Italian Journey*, trans. W. H. Auden and Elizabeth Mayer (New York: Pantheon, 1962), pp. 199–200.

42 *Indicator* 31 (10 May 1820). Tennyson's comment is quoted in A. Dwight Culler, "Monodrama and the Dramatic Monologue," *PMLA* 90 (1975), 369. On attitudes, painting, and monodrama, see *Lady Hamilton in Relation to the Art of Her Time: An Exhibition Organized by the Arts Council of Great Britain* (London: Arts Council, 1972); and Kirsten Gram Holstrom, *Monodrama, Attitudes, Tableaux Vivants* (Stockholm, 1967).

43 *Memoirs of Lady Hamilton*, p. 49. Keats never mentions Emma Hamilton, but he was interested in Nelson; see Dorothy Hewlet, *Adonais: A Life of John Keats* (Indianapolis: Bobbs-Merrill, 1938), p. 116.

44 See Altick, *The Shows of London*, pp. 342–49.

45 Quoted in Russell, *Nelson and the Hamiltons*, p. 161.

46 *The Letters of Mary Nisbet of Dirleton, Countess of Elgin*, ed. Lt.-Col. Nisbet Hamilton Grant (New York: Appleton, 1928), p. 22.

47 See Paulson, *Rowlandson: A New Interpretation* (Oxford University Press, 1972), pp. 84, 91, and *Representations of Revolution (1789–1820)* (New Haven: Yale University Press, 1983), pp. 206–9.

48 Paulson, *Representations of Revolution*, p. 160.

49 There is a much stranger inversion of the Pygmalion story, one which brings death to female desire as a young girl dies lusting for a statue, in Henry Hart Milman's Oxford prizewinning poem "The Belvidere Apollo" (1812, rpt. in *Oxford Prize Poems* [Oxford: J. Parker, 1819]).

50 James Joyce, *Portrait of the Artist as a Young Man* (New York: Viking, 1964), p. 205.

51 Haydon speaks in similar terms about his Christ's entry into Jerusalem: "My Picture today struck me when I was in Town as the most enchanting of all sights . . . It came over [me] like a lovely dream. I sat & dwelt on it like a young girl on a lover (when she is unobserved). I adored the Art that could give such sensations, such sweet sensations. I felt its beauty, its superiority, to all temporary dispute and petty passion" (25 October 1816, *Diary*, II: 62).

52 See also Roe, *Keats and the Culture of Dissent*, pp. 60–71.

53 Levinson, *Keats's Life of Allegory*; Susan Wolfson, "Feminizing Keats," in *Critical Essays on John Keats*, ed. H. de Almeida (Boston: G. K. Hall, 1990), pp. 317–57.

CHAPTER 6. FINAL RECKONINGS: KEATS AND SHELLEY ON THE
WEALTH OF THE IMAGINATION

1 Reiman, "Keats and Shelley: Personal and Literary Relations," in *SC*, V: 413. For accounts of Keats's life during this period, see Walter Jackson Bate, *John Keats* (Cambridge: Harvard University Press, 1964), pp. 644–53;

Robert Gittings, *John Keats* (London: Heinemann, 1968), pp. 394–405; and Aileen Ward, *John Keats: The Making of a Poet* (New York: Viking, 1963), pp. 357–73.

2   See *Maria Gisborne & Edward E. Williams, Shelley's Friends: Their Journals and Letters*, ed. Frederick L. Jones (Norman: University of Oklahoma Press, 1951), pp. 35–37, 40, 44–45. John Gisborne's letter to Shelley concerning Keats's health is not extant. The Gisbornes' arrival in Italy and delivery of the volume and letter to Claire Clairmont can be reconstructed from Shelley's letters to the Gisbornes, 11 October 1820, to Marianne Hunt, 29 October 1820, and to Claire Clairmont, 29 October 1820 (*SL*, II: 55, 239–40, 241–44). Richard Holmes places the delivery on 11 October: *Shelley: The Pursuit* (New York: Dutton, 1975), p. 613.

3   Shelley appears to have written two other letters to Keats after the latter arrived in Italy. See William Sharp, *The Life and Letters of Joseph Severn* (London: Sampson Low, Marston & Company, 1892), for Severn's information that Keats in Naples "received a letter from Shelley, then in Pisa, urging him to come northward, and be the guest of him and his wife; a most generous letter, and the second he had received from that fine poet and noble man" (p. 63). See also the cancelled beginning of a letter to Keats in Shelley's letter to Claire Clairmont of 18 February 1821 (*SL*, II: 610), which Jones speculates did not reach Severn in Rome until after Keats's death.

4   Huntington Library MS 24059.

5   Letter of Mary Novello to Hunt, 30 November 1823, Huntington Library MS 12282.

6   Ward, *Keats*, p. 367; Peter Quennell, *Byron in Italy* (London: Collins, 1941), p. 250; Douglas Bush, *Keats: His Life and Writings* (New York: Macmillan, 1966), p. 191.

7   Charles Armitage Brown indicates that Keats wished to keep his relationship with Fanny Brawne a secret. Keats may have told Hunt during the summer of 1820, however, as Hunt's reminiscence about visiting with Keats the house in which his brother had died suggests: "The house was in Well Walk. You know the grove of elms there. It was in that grove, on the bench next the heath, that he suddenly turned upon me, his eyes swimming with tears, and told me he was 'dying of a broken heart.' He must have been wonderfully excited to make such a confession; for his was a spirit lofty to a degree of pride. Some private circumstances pressed on him at the time; and to these he added the melancholy consciousness, that his feeble state of health made him sensible of some public annoyances, which no man would sooner otherwise have despised... My weaker eyes are obliged to break off. He lies under the wall of Rome, not far from the remains of one, who so soon and so abruptly joined him. Finer hearts, or more astonishing faculties, never were broken up than in those two. To praise any man's heart by the side of Shelley's is alone an extraordinary panegyric": *Wishing Cap Papers* (Boston: Lee & Shephard, 1873), pp. 238–

39. This passage, which of course links Keats to Shelley once again, covers all the difficulties besetting Keats – his health, his love for Fanny Brawne, his problems with reviewers, and perhaps even his financial woes (the "private circumstances" that "pressed on him at the time").

8   Gittings, *KL*, transcribes the incomplete word as "metap^cs" for "metaphysics"; Ruthven offers "metaphor" in "Keats and *Dea Moneta*," *SiR* 15 (Summer 1975), 453 n. 10.

9   See Kurt Heinzelman, "Self-Interest and the Politics of Composition in Keats's *Isabella*," *English Literary History* 55 (Spring 1988), 159–93; Marjorie Levinson, *Keats's Life of Allegory: The Origins of a Style* (Oxford: Basil Blackwell, 1988), pp. 255–99; and K. K. Ruthven, "Keats and *Dea Moneta*," pp. 445–59.

10 Jack Stillinger, "The Brown–Dilke Controversy," *KSJ* 11 (1962), 39–45.

11 See the letter by Brown, the harshest critic of George's actions, to C. W. Dilke, 6 September 1824, *The Letters of Charles Armitage Brown*, ed. Jack Stillinger (Cambridge: Harvard University Press, 1966), pp. 182–85, where he quotes Keats as saying that his "brother did not act rightly in leaving him so." Fanny Brawne wrote to Fanny Keats that Keats had told her, "George ought not to have done this": *Letters of Fanny Brawne to Fanny Keats, 1820–1824*, ed. Fred Edgcumbe (Oxford University Press, 1939), p. 34. Taylor and Hessey wrote to George Keats on 17 February 1821 concerning Keats's lack of money, saying, "Before he left this country he had no money left in his possession as you know" (*KC*, I: 102).

12 Taylor, letter to Michael Drury, 19 February 1821, *KC*, I: 217–20. See also Edmund Blunden, *Keats's Publisher: A Memoir of John Taylor* (1936, rpt. London: Cape, 1940), pp. 81–86.

13 See Clarke's recollection of Trelawny speaking of Shelley as "a being absolutely without selfishness"; "the poorest cottagers knew and benefitted by his thoroughly *practical* and unselfish nature during his residence at Marlowe, when he would visit them" (*Recollections*, p. 151). Trelawny wrote of Shelley as being "totally devoid of selfishness"; see H. J. Massingham, *The Friend of Shelley: A Memoir of John Trelawny* (London: Cobden-Sanderson, 1930), p. 172. In *Records of Shelley, Byron, and the Author* (1878, rpt. New York: Benjamin Blom, 1968), Trelawny again praised Shelley's generosity and criticized Godwin and Hunt, who borrowed heavily from him (pp. xii–xiv). Hunt himself often wrote of Shelley's generosity, as in his unpublished essay for the *Liberal* on Shelley (British Library MS Ashley 915, transcribed by Timothy Webb, "Percy Bysshe Shelley 1792–1822," *KSR* 7 [Autumn 1992], 43–61), where he speaks of Shelley's "extreme want of selfishness" (p. 43). Horace Smith portrays Shelley as a generous Samaritan, unappreciated by the interestingly named "nation of Mammonites"; quoted in Arthur H. Beavan, *James and Horace Smith* (London: Hurst & Blackett, 1899), pp. 169–70. Byron also accounted Shelley "the *least* selfish" man he knew (*L&J*, IX: 119).

14 See, for example, Ronald A. Sharp in "Keats and the Spiritual Economies

of Gift Exchange," *KSJ* 38 (1989), 66–81. Sharp quotes Woodhouse, for example, who wrote to Taylor, "I wish [Keats] could be cured of the vice of lending – for in a poor man, it is a vice" (*KL*, II: 151). Of course, Shelley makes two different assumptions: first, that Keats is not poor, and second, that he does not like to lend. Sharp is finally interested in a kind of spiritual generosity, in which Keats's works are seen as a gift to posterity. However, the instances of economic language from Keats's poetry that he cites – such as "And can I e'er repay the friendly debt" (from the verse epistle to Charles Cowden Clarke, l. 77) or "repay her scorn for scorn" (from "On Fame," l. 13) – strike me as being more concerned with debt and repayment than with gift-giving. There seems little doubt that Keats disliked being in debt; it is less clear whether he entered into the spirit of gift exchange. Perhaps we can resolve this tension through Cixous's analysis of the Realm of the Proper and the Realm of the Gift. Keats's "self-concentration," his concern about having his "own unfettered scope," his worries about repayment all suggest his entanglement in the Realm of the Proper, where property is important, where self-identity is sought; see Hélène Cixous, "Castration or Decapitation?" trans. Annette Kuhn, *Signs* 7 (1981), 50. For a similar mixture of money and aesthetics in Keats's difficulties with Haydon, see Theresa M. Kelley, "Keats, Ekphrasis, and History," in *KH*, pp. 221–23. Problems arising from borrowing and lending are something of a recurring theme in the circle as we think, for example, of Hazlitt's turn to Procter and Haydon for funds, Haydon's and then Keats's involvement with the Cripps matter, or Godwin's borrowings, particularly from Shelley.

15 See Kenneth Muir, "Shelley's Magnanimity," in *Essays on Shelley*, ed. Miriam Allot (Totowa, N.J.: Barnes & Noble, 1982), pp. 125–43.

16 John Kinnaird, *William Hazlitt: Critic of Power* (New York: Columbia University Press, 1978), pp. 102–3.

17 *Complete Works of Percy Bysshe Shelley*, ed. Roger Ingpen and Walter E. Peck (1926–30, rpt. New York: Gordian Press, 1965), II: pp. 293–94.

18 Paul de Man, "The Negative Road," in *Selected Poetry of John Keats* (New York: New American Library, 1966), p. xxvii.

19 See *The Journals of Claire Clairmont, 1814–1827*, ed. Marion Kingston Stocking (Cambridge: Harvard University Press, 1968): on 26 and 27 September 1820 (pp. 178–79) she is reading Keats's *Endymion*; by 15 October, she is reading "Isabella," on 8 November she is reading "Lamia," and on 10 November she reads "Hyperion" (pp. 184–85). Mary Shelley's *Journals* (pp. 335–36) tells us that on 17 October 1820 "Shelley goes to Leghorn, and returns very late." Presumably on that trip he retrieves Keats's volume and letter from Claire; on 18 October, he reads Keats's "Hyperion" aloud, and on 19 October, Mary Shelley reads Keats's poems. Shelley writes to Marianne Hunt on 29 October 1820 concerning his opinions of Keats's volume and also requests information about him (*SL*, II: 239–40; see also note 3 above); he praises "Hyperion" in a letter to Peacock on 8 November

1820 (*SL*, II: 244). Shelley may have returned the volume to Claire Clairmont when he accompanied her to Florence on 20 October 1820 (*Journals*, p. 336); he knows by 15 November 1820 that she has enjoyed both "Hyperion" (which she read on the tenth) and *Prometheus Unbound* (*SL*, II: 596).

20   For the unsent letter to Gifford, see *SL*, II: 251–53. The dialogue on Keats is in Bodleian MS Shelley adds. e. 8, transcribed in Neville Rogers, *Shelley at Work* (Oxford: Clarendon Press, 1956), p. 257; in Fred L. Milne, "Shelley on Keats: A Notebook Dialogue," *English Language Notes* 13 (June 1976), 278–84; and in *Shelley's Pisan Winter Notebook (1820–1821): A Facsimile of Bodleian MS. Shelley adds. e. 8*, ed. Carlene A. Adamson (New York: Garland, 1992), pp. 230–33. Milne dates the dialogue with Shelley's reading of Keats in October 1820, but Rogers (p. 257) argues that it was written in late January or early February 1821 as Shelley was preparing to write the *Defence*. On Shelley's divided attitude towards Keats, see Christine Gallant, *Shelley's Ambivalence* (New York: St. Martin's, 1989), pp. 147–48.

21   On the *Defence* and particularly on its links to *Adonais*, see John W. Wright, *Shelley's Myth of Metaphor* (Athens: University of Georgia Press, 1970); P. M. S. Dawson, *The Unacknowledged Legislator: Shelley and Politics* (Oxford: Clarendon Press, 1980), pp. 210–58; Paul Fry, "Shelley's *Defence of Poetry* in Our Time," in *Percy Bysshe Shelley: Modern Critical Views*, ed. Harold Bloom (New York: Chelsea House, 1985), pp. 159–85; and Bruce Hely, "Shelley, Peacock, and the Reading of History," *SiR* 29 (Fall 1990), 439–61.

22   *A Philosophical View of Reform (1819–1820)*, in *Shelley's Prose: or The Trumpet of a Prophecy*, ed. David Lee Clark (Albuquerque: University of New Mexico Press, 1954). See Terence Allan Hoagwood's useful *Skepticism and Ideology: Shelley's Political Prose and Its Philosophical Context from Bacon to Marx* (Iowa City: University of Iowa Press, 1988).

23   Shelley's note to *Queen Mab* is to v: 93–94, in *The Poems of Shelley*, vol. i, ed. Geoffrey Matthews and Kelvin Everest (New York: Longman, 1989), pp. 364–65. Hazlitt, *An Essay on the Principles of Human Action* (1805) appears in *CWH*, i; Heinzelman has called the essay "a response to the heuristic construct that came to be called 'economic man,'" in "Self-Interest and the Politics," p. 162. Owen's *Observations on the Effect of the Manufacturing System* (1815), in *A New View of Society and Other Writings* (New York: Dent, 1927), argues that the commercial classes have come to define the national character and that "the governing principle of trade, manufactures, and commerce is immediate pecuniary gain, to which on the great scale every other is made to give way. All are sedulously trained to buy cheap and to sell dear; and to succeed in this art, the parties must be taught to acquire strong powers of deception; and thus a spirit is generated through every class of traders, destructive of that open, honest sincerity, without which man cannot make others happy, nor enjoy happiness himself" (p. 122).

24   While I believe Shelley is responding directly to Keats, his language resonates with the political and poetic discourse of the day. See, for example, Howard Fish's *The Wrongs of Man* (London: Sherwood, Neely &

Jones, 1819), where greed and selfishness have undermined all values –
"Honour,– religion,– equity, and shame, / Are now, alas! but symbols, but
a name" (p. 12) – and where, as in the *Defence*, Mammon comes to represent
this rise of money-getting: "On all let EXECRATION fix her seal, / Who
meanly at the shrine of MAMMON kneel" (p. 10). Again, we find the contrast
between God and Mammon apropos of literature in *The Déjeuné; or,
Companion for the Breakfast Table* 1 (12 December 1820), 357: "But we cannot
serve God and Mammon; we cannot be an author and any thing else."
Hunt in *Indicator* 31 (10 May 1820) contrasts the worship of love and the
worship of Mammon in the same issue where he printed Keats's "La Belle
Dame." Horace Smith includes in his *Amarynthus* volume "To Mammon,"
which opposes the pursuit of money with a life of love and poetry; Hunt's
review of the volume in the *Examiner* contrasts Smith's attitude towards life
with that of "Money-getters" (7 January 1821).

25 Fanny Delisle, *A Study of Shelley's "A Defence of Poetry": A Textual and Critical
Evaluation* (Salzburg: Institut für Englische Sprache und Literatur, 1974), 1:
138. The cancelled language is found in Bodleian MS Shelley d. 1, fol. 34v
rev. top.

26 Cameron, "Shelley, Cobbett, and the National Debt," *Journal of English and
German Philology* 42 (1943), 197–209; see also Cameron, *Shelley: The Golden
Years* (Cambridge: Harvard University Press, 1974), pp. 137–42. While
Cameron downplays Hunt's influence, the *Examiner* frequently addressed
the debt, the sinking fund, taxes, and currency, particularly during the
period when Shelley was coming to know Hunt; see, for example, 12
January and 23 February 1817. In his *Autobiography*, Hunt recounts an
episode at Hampstead when Shelley came to him "with a deep, though not
melancholy, interest in his face"; "I thought he was going to speak of some
family matter, either his or my own, when he asked me, at the close of an
intensity of pause, what was 'the amount of the national debt'" (p. 325).

27 Walter Benn Michaels has addressed paper money, the gold standard, and
representation in *The Gold Standard and the Logic of Naturalism* (Berkeley and
Los Angeles: University of California Press, 1987), esp. pp. 139–80. See also
Georg Simmel, *The Philosophy of Money*, trans. Tom Bottomore and David
Frisby (London: Routledge & Kegan Paul, 1978). Peacock would write
Paper Money Lyrics following the financial crisis of 1825 (published 1837),
which, with references to Southey, Wordsworth, and Coleridge and
others, is another site for contemplating the relations between representa-
tions in fictions and through currency.

28 On Gillray's prints, see M. Dorothy George, *English Political Caricature
1793–1832* (Oxford: Clarendon Press, 1959) II: pp. 28–29. Howard Fish,
Amatory and Other Verses (London: Sherwood, Neely & Jones, 1817), p. 8. For
Davenport's poem, see Michael Scrivener, *Poetry and Reform: Periodical Verse
from the English Democratic Press 1792–1824* (Detroit: Wayne State University
Press, 1992), p. 205. Hone's satiric Note, engraved by Cruikshank, was
issued under the pseudonym "Abraham Franklin" together with a *Bank*

Restriction Barometer; or, Scale of Effects on Society of the Banknote System, and Payments in Gold (London, 1819). The Note but not the Barometer is reproduced in Frederick William Hackwood, *William Hone: His Life and Times* (1912, rpt. New York: Burt Franklin, n.d.), between pp. 200 and 201. For an argument that Keats wrote a poetic commentary on Hone, see Aileen Ward, "Keats's Sonnet 'Nebuchadnezzar's Dream,'" *Philological Quarterly* 34 (1955), 177–88.

29 Scrivener, *Radical Shelley: The Philosophical Anarchism and Utopian Thought of Percy Bysshe Shelley* (Princeton University Press, 1982), pp. 210–18, 3–76.

30 Mitchell, "Representation," in *Critical Terms for Literary Study*, ed. Frank Lentricchia and Thomas McLaughlin (University of Chicago Press, 1990), p. 76.

31 Peacock, *The Four Ages of Poetry*, in vol. VIII of *The Works of Thomas Love Peacock*, ed. H. F. B. Brett-Smith and C. E. Jones (London: Constable, 1934), p. 4.

32 Milne, "Shelley on Keats," pp. 278–79.

33 Scrivener, *Radical Shelley*, pp. 250–56. See also William A. Ulmer, "*Adonais* and the Death of Poetry," *SiR* 32 (Fall 1993), 425–51.

34 Stuart Curran, "*Adonais* in Context," in *SR*, pp. 165–82. See also Margaret de G. Verrall, "Allusion in *Adonais* to the Poems of Keats," *Modern Language Review* 6 (1922), 354–59; L. Abbey, *Destroyer and Preserver: Shelley's Poetic Skepticism* (Lincoln: University of Nebraska Press, 1979), pp. 105–21.

35 John Gisborne, letter to Finch, 30 May 1821, in Elizabeth Nitchie, *The Reverend Colonel Finch* (New York: Columbia University Press, 1940), pp. 86–87. The nightingale ode is often associated with Keats's supposed acknowledgment of his approaching demise and even with a certain weakness that contributed to his death; see the obituary in *New Monthly Magazine* 3 (1 May 1821), 256–57, and the poem by John Taylor in *London Magazine* 3 (May 1821), 526.

36 Bodleian MS Shelley e. 20, fols. 9r and 10r, transcribed in Anthony D. Knerr, *Shelley's "Adonais": A Critical Edition* (New York: Columbia University Press, 1984), pp. 191–93.

37 There is insistent economic imagery surrounding the description of the critic. In a draft of the preface, Shelley wrote that the critic "pr(os)tituted his soul for twenty pounds per sheet" and that reviewers "with some rare exceptions are in general a most stupid & malignant race; and as a bankrupt thief turns thief taker in despair, so an unsuccessful author turns critic": Bodleian MS Shelley e. 20, fols. 1r and 5r, transcribed in Knerr, *Shelley's "Adonais"*, pp. 184–88. See also his unsent letter to Gifford defending Keats, where he writes that the critic who attacked Shelley himself "has doubtless the additional reward of a consciousness of his motives, besides the 30 guineas a sheet or whatever it is that you pay him" (November 1820, *SL*, II: 251).

38 Ross Woodman, "Shelley's Urania," *SiR* 17 (1978), 61–75.

39 Curran, "*Adonais* in Context," pp. 174–75. For attacks on the passage as

self-indulgent autobiography, see, for example, Edward E. Bostetter, *The Romantic Ventriloquists* (Seattle: University of Washington Press, 1963), pp. 213–14; and Milton Wilson, *Shelley's Later Poetry: A Study of His Prophetic Imagination* (New York: Columbia University Press, 1959), pp. 2–5. For arguments that the passage offers a generalized portrait of the poet, see, for example, Carlos Baker, *Shelley's Major Poetry: The Fabric of a Vision* (Princeton University Press, 1963), pp. 243–45; Roswith Riese-von Freydorf, "Die Gestalt des letzten Hirten – Ein Selbstportrait Shelleys? (*Adonais* XXXI–XXXIV)," in *Versdichtung der englischen Romantik*, ed. Teut Andreas Riese and Dieter Riesner (Berlin: Schmidt, 1968), pp. 294–316; Timothy Clark, *Embodying Revolution: The Figure of the Poet in Shelley* (Oxford: Clarendon Press, 1989), pp. 214–23; and Stephen C. Behrendt, *Shelley and His Audiences* (Lincoln: University of Nebraska Press, 1989), pp. 252–55.

40 Knerr, *Shelley's "Adonais"*, p. 84.

41 Woodman, *The Apocalyptic Vision in the Poetry of Shelley* (University of Toronto Press, 1964), pp. 159–78.

42 I have noted the link to Hazlitt in the draft preface. Those mimickers of rejected addresses, Horace and James Smith, appear in Bodleian MS Shelley e. 9, p. 15, transcribed in Knerr, *Shelley's "Adonais"*, p. 156: "And two brothers followed him / And [mimicked] in a quaint & solemn song."

43 Cameron, *The Golden Years*, p. 436; Knerr, *Shelley's "Adonais"*, pp. 83, 87–88.

44 Jerome J. McGann, *The Beauty of Inflections* (Oxford: Clarendon Press, 1988), p. 53.

45 Ruthven, "Keats and *Dea Moneta*," p. 456; Ronald Sharp, *Keats, Skepticism, and the Religion of Beauty* (Athens: University of Georgia Press, 1979), pp. 131–48; Daniel Watkins, *Keats's Poetry and the Politics of the Imagination* (London: Associated University Presses, 1989), p. 88.

46 Harold Bloom, *Visionary Company*, rev. ed. (Ithaca: Cornell University Press, 1971), p. 350.

47 See Richard Hart Fogle, "John Taaffe's Annotated Copy of *Adonais*," *KSJ* 17 (1968), 31–52. There are some sympathetic comments about Dante's Ulysses in Hunt's *Indicator* 9 (8 December 1819), which Hunt's later notes ascribed to Keats; see John Barnard, "Leigh Hunt's Later Notes to *The Indicator*," *KSR* 6 (1991), 61. See also Alan M. Weinberg, *Shelley's Italian Experience* (New York: St. Martin's, 1991), pp. 173–201.

48 Schwartz (*KR*, pp. 296–346) includes most of the major memorials and obituaries. See also Jeffrey C. Robinson, "'My Ended Poet': Poetic Tributes to Keats, 1821–1994," *SiR* 34 (Fall 1995), 441–69.

49 "Death of Mr. John Keats," *London Magazine* 3 (April 1821), 426–27. The author, "L," is identified as Procter by G. M. Matthews in *Keats: The Critical Heritage*, p. 241; see also Bertram Dobell, *Sidelights on Charles Lamb* (New York: Scribner, 1903), p. 192, where Procter is suggested over Lamb as the author.

50 *Literary Chronicle and Weekly Review* (31 March 1821, p. 206), in *KR*, pp. 313–14.

51 "Posthumous Epistle," *Gossip*, 14 April 1821, p. 54. Kirke White appeared in a draft of *Adonais*; see Walter Peck, *Shelley: His Life and Work* (1927, rpt. New York: Burt Franklin, 1969), II: 218.

52 Heffernan, "*Adonais*: Shelley's Consumption of Keats," *SiR* 23 (1984), 285–315. For an excellent account of Shelley's construction of Keats and his critical reception in *Adonais*, see Susan J. Wolfson, "Keats Enters History: Autopsy, *Adonais*, and the Fame of Keats," in *KH*, pp. 17–45.

53 Joukovsky, "New Verse on Keats and the Reviewers," *Keats–Shelley Memorial Bulletin* 29 (1978), 32–39; the anonymous author tells us he plans a second piece (not published) on the death of John Scott, which, as Joukovsky points out, could also be attributed to the Cockney School attacks.

54 Keats House MS KH 441.

55 In Stuart Curran, "Horace Smith's Obituary Panegyric on Shelley," *KSJ* 37 (1988), 33.

56 See Donald H. Reiman, "Introduction," John Chalk Claris, *Thoughts and Feelings and Retrospection and Elegy on the Death of Shelley* (New York: Garland, 1977), pp. viii–ix.

57 Webb, "Religion of the Heart: Leigh Hunt's Unpublished Tribute to Shelley," *KSR* 7 (Autumn 1992), 1–61.

58 "Autograph MS of Ultra-Crepidarius in [blue-morocco 71-page] Note Book with MS Notes of Day by Day Sea-Journey to Italy from England, 1822–23 and Other Poems and Prose Reflections," Beinecke Rare Book and Manuscript Library, Yale University.

59 *Poems by William Bell Scott: Ballads, Studies from Nature, Sonnets, Etc.* (1875, rpt. New York: AMS Press, 1971).

60 Special Collections, University of Iowa, MS H94tos; in Milford's edition, pp. 719–20.

61 Hunt would try again with Hazlitt. In 1825 in Florence, they considered starting "Molini's English Magazine" "to supply English people in Italy, whether travellers or residents, with the best portions of the current literature of their own country," literature which was to include Hunt, Hazlitt, and Lamb. The journal failed because the censors worried about Hunt's religious and political views. See Blunden, *Leigh Hunt: A Biography* (1930, rpt. Hamden, Conn.: Shoe String, 1970), pp. 218–19.

62 Two sonnets entitled "On Hearing of Leigh Hunt's Death," *Recollections*, pp. 271–72.

Index

CAMBRIDGE STUDIES IN ROMANTICISM

GENERAL EDITORS
MARILYN BUTLER, *University of Oxford*
JAMES CHANDLER, *University of Chicago*